Strategic Behavior and Policy Choice
on the U.S. Supreme Court

D1372793

Strategic Behavior and Policy Choice on the U.S. Supreme Court

THOMAS H. HAMMOND, CHRIS W. BONNEAU, AND REGINALD S. SHEEHAN

Stanford University Press
Stanford, California

2005

Stanford University Press
Stanford, California

Printed in the United States of America
on acid-free, archival-quality paper

Library of Congress Cataloging-in-Publication Data

Hammond, Thomas H.
    Strategic behavior and policy choice on the U.S. Supreme Court / Thomas
H. Hammond, Chris W. Bonneau, and Reginald S. Sheehan.
        p.   cm.
    Includes bibliographical references and index.
    ISBN 0-8047-5145-5 (cloth : alk. paper)
    ISBN 0-8047-5146-3 (pbk. : alk. paper)
        1. United States. Supreme Court—Decision making.   2. Judicial process—
United States.   I. Bonneau, Chris W.   II. Sheehan, Reginald S., 1959–
III. Title.
KF8742.H36 2005
347.73'262—DC22

                                                            2005002881

Original Printing 2005

Last figure below indicates year of this printing:
14   13   12   11   10   09   08   07   06   05

To my wife, Christine Hammond: with deep appreciation for her love, support, understanding, and patience throughout the course of this long project.

—*Thomas H. Hammond*

To Larry Baas and Richard Balkema, my professors of political science at Valparaiso University: with deep appreciation and gratitude for stimulating my interest in political science.

—*Chris W. Bonneau*

For my parents, Stokes and Carolyn Sheehan: for always being there and supporting all my endeavors.

—*Reginald S. Sheehan*

Contents

List of Figures and Tables   xi
Preface   xv
Acknowledgments   xix

PART I: THEORIES OF SUPREME COURT DECISION-MAKING

1   Introduction   1
    Plan of the Book   6

2   Seven Distinctions in the Literature   8
    Distinction 1: A Psychological Metaphor vs.
      a Rational-Choice Metaphor   8
    Distinction 2: Theories of Attitude Activation vs.
      Theories of Rational Choice   11
    Distinction 3: Theories of Choice vs. Theories of
      Measurement   14
    Distinction 4: Explaining Final Votes vs. Explaining
      What Final Opinion Is Adopted   15
    Distinction 5: Explaining Just the Final Vote vs. Explaining
      All Five Stages of Decision-Making   17
    Distinction 6: Theories of "Sincere" Rational Choice vs.
      Theories of "Strategic" Rational Choice   19
    Distinction 7: A "Status Quo" Policy vs.
      No "Status Quo" Policy   23
    Conclusion   24

3   Assessing Previous Theories of Supreme Court
   Decision-Making   26

The Pioneers: Pritchett, Schubert, and Murphy   26
Schubert's Attitude-Activation Model   29
The Attitudinal Model   39
Conceptual Problems with the Attitudinal Model   41
Other Issues Involving the Attitudinal Model   52
The Literature on Strategically Rational Justices   55
Conclusion   60

PART II: A FORMAL MODEL OF SUPREME COURT DECISION-MAKING

4 Why Formal Models?   65
The Role of Theories and Models in
    Empirical Research   66
Potential Benefits from Formal Modeling   68
Potential Costs and Other Criticisms of Formal
    Modeling   73
How Can We Be Sure that the Potential Benefits
    Exceed the Potential Costs?   76
Conclusion   78

5 Definitions and Assumptions   79
Lines, Points, and Utility Functions   80
The Status Quo Policy   83
Preferred-to Sets and Win Sets   85
The Number of Justices   89
An Informational Assumption   90
"Sincere" and "Strategic" Behavior   91
The Independence of Cases   92
Joining, Concurring, and Dissenting   92
Costless Opinion Writing   94
Conclusion   94

6 Coalition Formation and the Final Vote   95
When Can the Status Quo Policy Be Upset?   97
What Are the Constraints on the Set of Policies
    that Could Be Adopted?   99
What Policies Do Different Majority Coalitions
    Prefer to SQ?   102
How Do Justices Behave When They Dislike
    the Majority Opinion?   108

The Agenda-Control Version   110
The Open-Bidding Version   125
The Median-Holdout Version   129
Comparison of the Agenda-Control, Open-Bidding,
    and Median-Holdout Versions   134
Is Agenda-Control Behavior Unstable?   137
Summary of Major Results   138

7 Opinion Assignment   139
Self-Assignment as an Opinion-Assignment Strategy   140
Alternative Opinion-Assignment Strategies   142
Opinion Assignment by a Justice Outside $W_{Jmed}(SQ)$ 143
Opinion Assignment by a Justice Inside $W_{Jmed}(SQ)$ 147
Opinion Assignment by a Minority-Side Justice   156
Would an Opinion Assigner Prefer Larger Coalitions?   158
How Much Does Opinion Assignment Matter?   161
Summary of Major Results   162

8 The Conference Vote   163
Different Kinds of Strategic Behavior from Different
    Kinds of Justices   166
Strategic Behavior by the Chief Justice   168
Strategic Behavior by an Associate Justice Who Could
    Become the Opinion Assigner   173
Strategic Behavior by a Low-Seniority Justice Who
    Cannot Become the Opinion Assigner   192
What If Everyone Behaves Strategically?   195
When Does the Chief Justice Self-Assign?   207
Will the Chief Justice Trust What Other Justices Say
    on the Conference Vote?   209
Summary of Major Results   212

9 Certiorari   215
Sincere Behavior on Certiorari Decisions   216
Strategic Behavior on Certiorari Decisions   220
"Aggressive Granting" and "Defensive Denial" When
    Justices Are Strategic   226
Summary of Major Results   227

PART III: FUTURE DIRECTIONS FOR THEORIES OF SUPREME COURT
DECISION-MAKING

10 Empirical Implications   231
       Understanding the Five Stages of Supreme Court
          Decision-Making   233
       "Nonstrategic" or "Sincere" Behavior on the
          Supreme Court   241
       Vote Switching between the Original and Final Votes   243
       Problems of Empirical Measurement   246
       Conclusion   248

11 Future Research   249
       Do the Justices Have Perfect Information about Each Other's
          Preferences?   250
       Do the Justices Always Have Clear and Fixed
          Preferences?   253
       Are Supreme Court Cases Independent from
          Each Other?   254
       Regular and Special Concurrences   259
       How Many Issue Dimensions Are There?   262
       Costly Opinion Writing   268
       Extensions of the Model   269
       Exogenous Preferences and the Impact of The Law   271
       Broader Applications   272
       Conclusion   273

Notes   277
References   289
Index   295

Figures and Tables

FIGURES

3.1   Justices and Case Stimuli in a Unidimensional Space   34

3.2   Justice 1's "Ideal Point" and Case Stimuli in a Unidimensional
       Issue Space, with a "Response Function" Based on Schubert's
       Proximity Model   35

3.3   Three Justices and Case Stimuli in a Unidimensional Issue
       Space, with "Response Functions" Based on Schubert's
       Ordinal Model   36

5.1   An Ideal Point and a Single-Peaked Utility Function   81

5.2   Symmetric and Asymmetric Utility Functions   83

5.3   Preferred-to Sets and Win Sets for Five Justices   86

6.1   Illustration of Proposition 6.1: SQ Cannot Be Changed   98

6.2   Illustration of Proposition 6.2: SQ Can Be Changed   99

6.3   Draft Opinion Outside $W_{Jmed}(SQ)$ Cannot Gain
       Majority Support   101

6.4   Politically Feasible Policies When SQ Is between J_3 and J_4 103

6.5   Politically Feasible Policies When SQ Is between J_4 and J_5 104

6.6   Politically Feasible Policies When SQ Is to the Right of J_5 105

6.7   Outcomes from the Agenda-Control and Open-Bidding Models   110

6.8   Coalition Sizes with SQ to the Right of J_5 112

6.9   Coalition Sizes with SQ between J_4 and J_5 114

6.10   Coalition Sizes with SQ between J_3 and J_4 116

6.11   Multiple Ways of Producing a 7–2 Coalition   124

7.1   What Majority Opinion Would Each Justice Write?   141

7.2   Only the Opinion Assigner Lies Outside $W_{Jmed}(SQ)$ 144

7.3   The Opinion Assigner and Just One Other Justice Lie
       Outside $W_{Jmed}(SQ)$ 145

7.4   The Opinion Assigner and at Least Two Other Justices Lie
       Outside $W_{Jmed}(SQ)$ 147

7.5   The Opinion Assigner Has an Ideal Point Just Inside the
       Outside Boundary of $W_{Jmed}(SQ)$, and All Other Justices Have
       Ideal Points Closer to SQ or on the Minority Side   149

7.6   The Opinion Assigner Has an Ideal Point Just Inside SQ that Is
       Closest to the Outside Boundary of $W_{Jmed}(SQ)$, At Least One
       Justice Lies Outside $W_{Jmed}(SQ)$, and At Least One Justice Lies
       Closer to SQ   150

7.7   The Opinion Assigner Has an Ideal Point in $W_{Jmed}(SQ)$, and At
       Least Two Other Justices (At Least One on Each Side of the
       Assigner) Have Ideal Points in $W_{Jmed}(SQ)$ 151

7.8   The Opinion Assigner's Ideal Point Is Adjacent to SQ and All
       Other Ideal Points Lie to the Outside   152

7.9   The Opinion Assigner Is Adjacent to SQ, At Least One Other
       Justice Lies Inside SQ But Farther from SQ Than the Assigner,
       and At Least One Justice Lies on the Minority Side   154

7.10   Choosing an Opinion Assignment When the Resulting Coalition
       Sizes May Differ   159

8.1   Strategic Behavior by a Chief Justice with a Minority-Side
       Ideal Point   170

8.2   Strategic Behavior by a Senior Associate Justice with a
       Majority-Side Ideal Point Lying to the Right of the
       Chief Justice   178

8.3   Strategic Behavior by a Senior Associate Justice with a
       Majority-Side Ideal Point Lying to the Left of the
       Chief Justice   181

8.4   Strategic Behavior by a Senior Associate Justice with a
       Minority-Side Ideal Point   185

8.5   Strategic Behavior by a Minority-Side Senior Associate Justice,
       with a Minority-Side Chief Justice   190

8.6   The All-Strategic Convergence Condition   198

8.7   The All-Strategic Nonconvergence Condition (a)   203

8.8   The All-Strategic Nonconvergence Condition (b): The Chief
       Justice Has a Majority-Side Ideal Point Outside $W_{Jmed}(SQ)$ 204

8.9   The All-Strategic Nonconvergence Condition (b): The Chief
       Justice Has a Minority-Side Ideal Point   205

9.1   Granting Certiorari by Sincere Justices   218

9.2   Denying Certiorari by Sincere Justices   219

9.3   Voting on Certiorari by Strategic Justices   224

TABLES

8.1   Strategic Behavior by the Chief Justice   173

8.2   Strategic Behavior by the Senior Associate Justice   193

8.3   Strategic Behavior by a Low-Seniority Associate Justice   194

A central question in the study of judicial politics in the United States involves why the Supreme Court adopts the policies that it does. There is surprisingly little consensus on an answer. One major school of thought, advanced over the past decades by Professor Harold Spaeth of Michigan State University and generally known as the "attitudinal model," is that what motivates the justices is their personal attitudes and policy preferences. A substantial body of empirical research does show that the behavior of the justices exhibits some regularities, and these regularities do appear explainable in terms of the justices' personal attitudes and policy preferences.

We argue in this book, however, that this theory of political behavior on the Court has not been developed well enough to allow a comprehensive and systematic empirical test. There are at least three significant problems with the theory as developed thus far.

The first problem is that the foundations of this theory remain unclear. Are the justices to be seen from a psychological perspective, in which a justice's behavior is the expression of preexisting attitudes that have been activated by particular aspects of a particular case? Or are the justices to be seen from a rational-choice perspective, in which a justice's behavior is the outcome of strategic calculations conducted in the pursuit of particular policies? One can find evidence of both perspectives in the literature on the attitudinal model, particularly Segal and Spaeth's *The Supreme Court and the Attitudinal Model* (1993) and *The Supreme Court and the Attitudinal Model Revisited* (2002). In our view, these are very different kinds of perspectives that imply very different kinds of approaches to the study of judicial behavior and that call for very different kinds of empirical evidence. Yet both perspectives have been combined—rather uneasily, in our view—under the rubric of "the attitudinal model."

The second problem is that the attitudinal model has been focused largely on the last stage of Supreme Court decision-making, involving how the justices vote on the final majority opinion. For the most part, the effects of the earlier stages of Court decision-making on the final outcome—these are the stages involving certiorari, the conference vote, opinion assignment, and opinion writing and coalition formation—have been neglected theoretically. One can find fragments of the needed theory at various places in the literature, and these fragments have formed the basis of a considerable amount of useful empirical research. But there has been no rigorous and systematic development of the logic of the attitudinal model (whether from the psychological perspective or the rational-choice perspective) throughout all the stages of the Court's decision-making process.

The third problem is related to the second: although the attitudinal model has been focused largely on how the justices vote on the final majority opinions, as just noted, and although substantial empirical research has attempted to account for these final votes, there is almost no theorizing or empirical research that seeks to account for the content of the final majority opinion on which the justices are voting. This is odd because what is presumably of greatest interest is not why the justices vote as they do (although that is certainly of great interest), but why the Supreme Court adopts some final opinions and not others. It is not adequate merely to say that the Court adopts those final opinions that maximize achievement of the personal policy preferences of the members of a Court majority. The difficulty is that there are many possible Court majorities, which means that one question has simply been replaced by another: which majority should we expect to prevail, and in support of which policy?

The purpose of this book is to lay a foundation for solving these three problems. Our approach involves the development of a formal model of multistage Supreme Court decision-making by strategically rational justices. The model addresses these three problems in the following way. First, the formal model is explicitly a rational-choice model. There is certainly room for—and perhaps even a need for—the development of various kinds of psychological models of judicial decision-making (not only attitude-based models but perhaps also models from learning theory and cognitive psychology). However, one cannot know the capacity of any particular kind of perspective without comprehensively, rigorously, and systematically developing it and exploring its full implications. This is what we seek to accomplish with regard to the rational-choice perspective.

Second, our model explicitly incorporates all stages of Supreme Court decision-making—from the certiorari decision at the outset to opinion writing, coalition formation, and the final vote at the end—in a single integrated model. It shows what implications the choices from the early stages have for the content of the final majority opinion and for how the justices will vote on this opinion. It turns out that some of what the judicial politics literature considers to be rational behavior by the justices would not, in fact, be rational; some of the conventional wisdom, in other words, is incorrect. It also turns out that other parts of the conventional wisdom are incomplete or else rest on implicit (and often unrecognized) assumptions that may be problematic on explicit examination.

Third, our model not only explains how the justices will vote on the final majority opinion, but, even more importantly, the model also explains what this final majority opinion will be. This final majority opinion turns out to be a function not only of the justices' policy preferences on the case, as posited by the attitudinal model, but also of the Court's decision-making procedures and of the current policy status quo on the case. All three kinds of variables interact to produce the final opinion, and none of these variables can be omitted from an analysis.

We think it is no exaggeration to say that our book provides the first comprehensive, rigorous, and systematic model of Supreme Court decision-making. In so doing, it also provides what we consider to be an essential theoretical foundation for the conduct of empirical research on Supreme Court decision-making from the perspective of a rational-choice version of the attitudinal model. For reasons of time and space, we do not attempt any empirical work ourselves. Yet we do expect that the propositions we derive from our model will provide the basis for several years of empirical work by many different scholars. Comprehensive empirical studies such as Maltzman, Spriggs, and Wahlbeck's *Crafting Law on the Supreme Court: The Collegial Game* (2000) are an excellent start on what needs to be done empirically, but as our book makes clear, much more remains to be done.

We emphasize that our book should be seen as a sustained "if . . . then" exercise; that is, *if* the justices are motivated primarily by their personal policy preferences on a case, as Spaeth and many other scholars have argued, *then* the justices should be expected to behave in particular ways at each stage of the Court's decision-making process. If empirical research suggests that the justices do behave in accordance with the expectations of our model, we could claim to have constructed a solid foundation for this general perspective on Supreme Court decision-making. But if this empirical research suggests that the justices do not behave in accordance with our model's expectations, then something is wrong with the general theory or with our translation of the theory into a specific model. It may be that the model must be modified, for example, but if these modifications do not resolve the empirical problems, it might be that the general theory itself has to be modified or even, at the end, abandoned. Nonetheless, as we make clear in our last chapter, there are a great many modifications of our model (all compatible with the basic rational-choice perspective) that may need to be developed and empirically tested before a fundamental assessment can be made of the overall power of the rational-choice version of the attitudinal model.

Our book's most immediate contribution involves the development of a comprehensive and integrated model of Supreme Court decision-making. However, there are long-term contributions that we think are equally important. One long-term contribution is that our model should actually be seen as the beginning, not the end, of the process of building models of Supreme Court decision-making. Our last chapter details some of what these more advanced models might involve. Another long-term contribution is that our model makes possible a more definitive empirical test than has yet been possible of the theory that Supreme Court justices are strategically rational actors who are motivated primarily by their personal policy preferences.

Acknowledgments

The development and writing of this book were nurtured by two streams of intellectual thought for which the Department of Political Science at Michigan State University has long provided a most hospitable home.

First, the Department of Political Science at Michigan State has, for many decades, hired faculty members and supported and trained students interested in the application of formal rational-choice models to political institutions. Although a number of faculty members working in the rational-choice tradition have come and gone, over the past three decades, Dave Rohde provided the intellectual and institutional leadership that made it possible to attract and hire particular faculty members (such as Tom Hammond) who develop or test rational-choice models in a variety of institutional contexts.

Second, under the intellectual leadership of Harold Spaeth over the past four decades, the Department of Political Science became a leading academic center for the study of judicial politics. (It is interesting to recall that Glendon Schubert was on the Michigan State faculty for several years in the late 1950s and early 1960s and played a role in attracting Harold to Michigan State.) Harold's insistence on the scientific study of judicial politics, his development of the attitudinal model (with colleagues such as Dave Rohde and former students such as Jeffrey Segal), and his skeptical attitude toward alternative explanations of Supreme Court voting behavior have all had an immense impact on the study of judicial politics in the United States. Without his intellectual leadership, the department could not have attracted particular faculty members (such as Reggie Sheehan) to teach and conduct research on judicial politics at Michigan State. Throughout the course of this particular project, Harold was immensely helpful in answering questions about Supreme Court history, procedure, and practice, and about the history of the literature in the field of judicial politics.

This book, which applies rational-choice theory to judicial politics, thus represents the confluence of two different streams of departmental history.

Had it not been for Dave, Harold, and the Political Science Department at Michigan State, it is unlikely that we would ever have written this book.

We also gratefully acknowledge the contributions of a variety of other scholars, both at Michigan State and around the country, to the preparation and completion of the book. While working on our original conference paper for this project, written for the 1999 American Political Science Association meetings in Atlanta (see Hammond, Bonneau, and Sheehan 1999), Hammond benefited from several conversations with Bob Lowry. Over the length of the entire project, he also benefited from countless conversations with Professor Melinda Gann Hall and Kirk Randazzo. Bill Jacoby provided essential criticism of an early draft of Chapter 3, as did Larry Baum. We could not be more appreciative of this assistance. Of course, we remain responsible for any and all remaining errors.

All three of us are also grateful for the gracious and supportive comments on the 1999 conference paper by Virginia Hettinger, our discussant at the American Political Science Association meetings that year, and for the very useful comments that Larry Baum, Saul Brenner, and Forrest Maltzman sent to us after the conference.

Don Hammond once again produced a series of elegantly drawn figures for one of Tom Hammond's projects. Everyone should have such a talented and helpful brother!

Finally, material assistance for the project was provided by the Department of Political Science and by the Department's Program for Law and Judicial Politics.

Tom Hammond expresses his gratitude to his wonderful wife, Christine, for her constant encouragement and support throughout the project, and to our great children, Emily and Stuart, for putting up with endless dinner-table conversations about how the never-ending project happened to be going that particular day. Emily was in high school when the project was started; she will have graduated from college when the book finally appears in print. Stuart was in kindergarten when the project was started; he will be starting middle school when the book appears in print.

Chris Bonneau expresses his appreciation to the Department of Political Science at Michigan State University for graciously providing financial support throughout his doctoral program at Michigan State, and to Melinda Gann Hall for being everything a mentor is supposed to be and so much more. He also thanks Paul Brace, Darren Davis, Mark Hurwitz, Matt Kleiman, Kerry Monaco, Dave Rohde, and Becky Tothero for their advice and support throughout the project. And thanks also go to the Department of Political Science at the University of Pittsburgh for the financial support and research time that were provided to him over the past three years.

Reggie Sheehan expresses his appreciation to his wife, Tracie, and his children, Kelsey and Brennan, for constantly reminding him of what is really important in life and insisting that he maintain the right priorities. He also expresses his gratitude to Donald Songer and Harold Spaeth for being supportive mentors and for extending him their friendship throughout his career.

PART ONE

Theories of Supreme Court Decision-Making

[S]cholarship on judicial behavior has given limited emphasis to theory development. Much of the empirical research in the field focuses on particular aspects of judicial behavior without putting them in a broader theoretical context. And students of judicial behavior have made relatively limited use of theoretical developments in other fields and other disciplines. The result is to slow the pace with which scholars build a general understanding of judicial behavior. (Baum 1997, 126)

The chapters in Part I of this book are intended to serve two purposes. The first is to introduce the rationale for the book. This will be done in Chapter 1. The second purpose, to be pursued in Chapters 2 and 3, is to present our thoughts on the judicial politics literature on Supreme Court decision-making. Our motivation for writing these two chapters is nicely summarized by the observation from Baum (1997) quoted above: we agree with Baum that the field of judicial politics has devoted far too little attention to fundamental theoretical issues. Chapter 2 highlights several key conceptual and theoretical issues regarding the judicial politics literature on Supreme Court decision-making. Although this chapter also briefly critiques several major theories of Supreme Court decision-making, the supporting evidence for these arguments is provided primarily in Chapter 3, which conducts a detailed review and examination of these theories.

CHAPTER 1

Introduction

Despite a half century of research on decision-making by the United States Supreme Court, the answer to one of the most central questions—What explains the justices' choices and decisions?—remains a matter of controversy. The answer provided by many students of public law has long been that legal criteria are the primary guide for the justices' choices and decisions. These criteria include such matters as respect for precedent (stare decisis), for the plain meaning of words in the Constitution and statutes, for the original intentions of the Framers of the Constitution, and for the legislative history of the statutes.

In contrast, the answer provided by many students of judicial politics is that, although the justices' discourse in a case invariably involves reference to legal criteria such as these, the justices' actual decisions stem primarily from their personal attitudes toward the legal issues and objects involved in the case or from their personal preferences over the legal policies under consideration. Although the Legal Realists writing in the 1920s and 1930s helped provide an intellectual foundation for this general argument (see Clayton 1999, 16–22), the argument can be traced most directly to C. Herman Pritchett's 1948 book, *The Roosevelt Court: A Study in Judicial Politics and Values, 1937–1947*. This book was the first to systematically examine by quantitative methods the extent to which a justice's "liberalism" or "conservatism" could explain his or her choices and decisions.

A large body of literature was stimulated by Pritchett's work, all driven by his arguments about the centrality of the justices' personal views on various legal issues. Indeed, over the next few decades, several rather different kinds of theories of Supreme Court decision-making were developed within this intellectual context.

In our judgment, however, most of the major theories exhibit significant deficiencies. For example, some theories are based on assumptions that are either unclear or that do not appear consistent with each other. This means that it is difficult to determine just what is driving these theories. Of course, when it cannot be determined what is driving a theory, it is difficult to agree on what expectations—about an individual justice's behavior, or about the Court decisions—are implied by the theory. Hence, it is unclear what hypotheses can serve as tests of the theory. And if the assumptions of a theory are left unclear, or if the basic logic is not precisely specified, it will also be unclear as to what the most appropriate statistical tests might be. Thus, it will be difficult to conduct unambiguous tests of the theory.

Note also that decision-making by the Supreme Court involves several stages:

(1)   The justices must first decide whether they want to hear some case; that is, the justices must decide whether to grant a writ of certiorari.[1]

(2)   If a writ of certiorari is granted, and after hearing oral arguments in the case, the justices meet in conference and make a preliminary decision—the "conference vote," as we will call it—on how they think the case should be decided.

(3)   The Chief Justice, or the most senior associate justice in the majority if the Chief Justice is not in the majority on the conference vote, must then assign the writing of the majority opinion to a justice who voted with this majority.

(4)   The author of the majority opinion must then try to write an opinion that gains the support of a Court majority.

(5)   When the opinion is completed, each justice must then decide whether to join the majority opinion, concur (in various ways), or dissent.

However, few of the theories in the literature systematically analyze all five of these stages of the Court's decision-making process. If some theory is not developed for all five stages of the Court's decision-making process, it is difficult to determine how powerful the theory is; a theory that only explains one stage well is obviously less powerful than a theory that explains all five stages well. Because most of the theories have not been developed for all five stages, it remains difficult to determine whether any of the theories is more powerful than any of its competitors.

Finally, we would observe that nothing in the literature presents any kind of explicit and rigorous formal theory of the Court's multistage decision-making process. This is important because in multimember bodies with multistage decision-making processes (as with the Supreme Court), decisions made at the later stages may be affected by the decisions made at earlier stages. For such institutions, an informal and purely verbal logic is often an unclear guide—and sometimes even a misleading one—for determining what behavior to expect. Some kind of formalization may thus be necessary to clarify precisely what any theory implies should be expected to happen at each stage.

These kinds of problems with the major theories of Supreme Court decision-making give rise to three critical questions:

(1) By what standards should the adequacy of theories about Supreme Court decision-making be evaluated?

(2) Given these standards, how adequate are the major theories?

(3) Given any deficiencies these theories may have, how can improved theories be constructed?

For Question 1, our answer is that theories in Pritchett's tradition of judicial politics should meet the following kinds of standards:

The fundamental assumptions of the theory—about the nature of individual Supreme Court justices and about the character of the justices' interactions with each other—should be selected so that they are consistent with each other (that is, the set of assumptions should be intellectually coherent).

Each of these fundamental assumptions should be made clear and explicit.

The general logic of the theory—that is, how the fundamental assumptions interact with each other to produce decisions by the Court—should be clearly and explicitly described.

The theory should be operationalized in a model that specifies precisely what is assumed about the nature of the justices and that details exactly how justices interact with each other, at each stage of the Court's multistage decision-making process, to produce a final outcome.

The empirically testable implications that the model may have—that is, what choices and decisions any particular set of justices should be expected to make at any particular stage of the Court's decision-making process—should be logically derived from the basic rules and operations of the model.

These general kinds of standards should be uncontroversial, which is not to say that the standards have always been followed.

For Question 2, we have already outlined our answer: each of the major theories in Pritchett's tradition fails, in some significant manner, to meet the full set of standards. Insufficient effort, it appears, has gone into making these theories clear and specific, and little effort has gone into deriving from them any detailed working models of the Supreme Court's multistage decision-making process. Instead, the literature stemming from Pritchett seems to have focused disproportionately on the empirical and methodological issues involved in testing the major theories. Despite the passage of several decades, then, it appears to us that the conceptual and theoretical aspects of Pritch-ett's legacy have remained surprisingly undeveloped.

For Question 3, involving how to construct improved theories of Supreme Court decision-making, we believe that a necessary first step in-volves the development of a better understanding of the conceptual defi-ciencies of the current generation of theories. Indeed, it appears to us that the full extent of these conceptual deficiencies in the major theories of Supreme Court decision-making is insufficiently recognized. Once these problems are identified, then development of an improved generation of theories and models can proceed.

Our answers to this trio of questions thus lead us to the major purposes of this book:

To identify the conceptual problems of the current generation of theories of Supreme Court decision-making.

To formulate a rational-choice theory of Supreme Court decision-making that is built on a clear, consistent, and coherent set of assumptions involv-ing the justices' personal preferences over legal policies.

To construct from this general theory a formal rational-choice model of the Supreme Court's multistage decision-making process.

To derive the logical implications of the formal model in a full range of situ-ations and contexts.

The formal model we develop is a direct descendent of two of the major theories of Supreme Court decision-making: the "attitudinal" theory (see, for example, Segal and Spaeth 1993, 2002) and the "strategic" theory (see Murphy 1964; Epstein and Knight 1998; Maltzman, Spriggs, and Wahlbeck 2000). Both theories presume that the decisions of Supreme Court justices are motivated by the justices' personal views on legal issues and policies. However, the strategic theory further presumes that each justice is strategi-cally rational, in the sense that each justice's decisions throughout a case, from beginning to end, are affected by how the justice expects the other jus-tices to respond.

Because our formal model of multistage decision-making on the Supreme Court assumes that the justices pursue their own personal policy preferences in a strategically rational fashion, our model can thus be seen as formalizing a body of theory that is already central to the judicial politics lit-erature. Indeed, we see ourselves as making relatively few fundamental as-sumptions that have not already been present in the literature, in one way or another, for quite some time. In fact, we think that our formal model could have been developed—and should have been developed—over 20 years ago: the basic theoretical ideas had already been advanced, and the modeling technology was already available. But for reasons we do not understand, no one took up this challenge: judicial politics scholars apparently considered formal theories to be of little use or relevance to them, and formal theorists were apparently not interested in the Supreme Court's internal decision-making practices.[2]

We use our model to derive a series of propositions about how strategically rational justices should be expected to behave at each stage of the Court's decision-making process. Many of our propositions also serve as hypotheses that could be empirically tested. However, developing our formal model turns out to be a lengthy and complex enterprise. And because the model turns out to have a wide range of testable implications for Supreme Court behavior, a full empirical assessment of the model's implications would require several additional years of work, and the results would require many additional pages to describe. For these reasons, we have chosen to retain a narrow focus for the book: we develop our theory, construct our model, and derive the model's empirical implications, but we do not attempt to conduct an empirical assessment of any hypotheses based on our model's propositions.

Despite the lack of an empirical test here, we do argue that the development of a formal model such as ours is an integral element of the "if . . . then" exercises that are critical to scientific progress. That is, *if* the basic premises of our model are assumed to be true, *then* certain kinds of behavior should be expected from the Court. If the justices' empirically observed behavior is as expected, this would lend support to our model. If the expected behavior is not empirically observed, this would suggest that something may be wrong with the test (which would mean that it has to be improved) or that something may be wrong with our model (which would mean that it has to be revised). It is when a model is formalized, and its basic assumptions and logic thereby made clear and explicit, that the scholarly community is best able to diagnose what may have gone wrong. In fact, we believe that scientific progress can often be hastened by initiating an ongoing series of cycles of these kinds of "if . . . then" exercises, with each cycle involving the development, refinement, or redevelopment of the formal model and then its empirical test. Because our model does highlight several ways in which important pieces of the conventional wisdom about Supreme Court decision-making are at odds with how strategically rational justices should be expected to behave (at least according to our model), this suggests that empirical testing of our model is likely to generate interesting results, no matter what the results turn out to be.

We emphasize that we do not necessarily see ourselves as proponents of the theory, model, and propositions that we develop. In fact, each of us harbors his own doubts and hesitations about the empirical validity of various results we develop. Instead, we prefer that our study be seen as providing a service to the field of judicial politics: by developing the full implications of one important class of theories that has been a significant part of the judicial politics literature for several decades now, we hope to enable scholars in this field to make a more thorough and systematic empirical assessment than has yet been possible.

We also emphasize that our rational-choice model is probably the simplest possible model of rational justices who strategically pursue their policy preferences in the Supreme Court's multistage decision-making process. Although more complex models of judicial decision-making could be developed, only an initial effort like ours, one that uses basic assumptions and technology, will indicate the extent to which further theoretical developments are necessary. Thus, whatever the ultimate outcome of these cycles of theoretical and empirical research that we are trying to initiate here, we are confident our formal analysis will turn out to have been a useful and necessary first step.

Plan of the Book

Our book has three parts. In addition to this chapter, Part I contains two other chapters. Chapter 2 discusses seven pairs of assumptions, prominent in the literature in varying degrees, about the nature of Supreme Court justices and about the characteristics of Supreme Court decision-making. Understanding these seven distinctions helps situate our own model within the larger literature on the Court. Chapter 3 illustrates the importance of these seven distinctions by showing how these various assumptions have structured several major studies of Supreme Court decision-making.

Part II contains six chapters where we present our formal model. Chapter 4 discusses why developing formal models may help solve some of the problems we have identified in the judicial politics literature on Supreme Court decision-making. Although the development of formal models has some costs, we believe that at this time in the field of judicial politics, the benefits of developing the formal models far outweigh the costs. Chapter 5 then provides definitions of our key terms and describes the assumptions on which our model is based.

Chapter 6 focuses on Stages 4 and 5 of the decision-making process: coalition formation and the final vote. We start at the end of the decision-making process because, to model strategic behavior, it is necessary to work backward from the final policy decision (in which the actors are primarily interested) so as to figure out what would be the rational decisions for them to make at the successively earlier stages of the decision-making process. Chapter 7 then models opinion assignment (Stage 3), Chapter 8 models the conference vote (Stage 2), and Chapter 9 models the original decision to grant certiorari (Stage 1).

Chapters 6 through 9 all have the same structure. Each opens with a description of the rules and procedures that the Court uses at that particular stage or stages of the decision-making process. The general setup of our model for that stage or stages is then presented and the model is developed. Next we describe the propositions that can be drawn from the model. We have made our presentations as accessible as possible: readers untrained in formal theory should be able to follow the model's logic without great difficulty. Some effort is required, but absolutely no training in higher-level mathematics is needed. We end each chapter with a summary of that chapter's major results.

Part III concludes the book. Chapter 10 presents an overview of what we have learned from our model and highlights several aspects of the empirical literature that our model suggests may be problematic. Chapter 11 describes some of our model's limitations and discusses various kinds of improvements that might be made in our model in future research.

CHAPTER 2

Seven Distinctions in the Literature

Construction of a theory must always begin with some assumptions. The reason, of course, is that something has to be taken as given, as a starting point on which further analysis can be based. But even just within the tradition established by Pritchett, the judicial politics literature on Supreme Court decision-making has made a wide range of assumptions about how to characterize justices as individual decision-makers and about the extent to which these justices interact with each other to produce a decision for the Court.

In this chapter we identify seven key pairs of assumptions in the literature on Supreme Court decision-making, and we show how these different assumptions have led to several different views about decision-making on the Court. Although additional distinctions could be drawn among the assumptions found in the literature on the Court (see Baum 1997 for an analysis), the seven distinctions we emphasize—the seven pairs of assumptions—are critical to the arguments we make in Part II of this book. Identifying and examining these assumptions will help establish the rationale for our own work.

Distinction 1: A Psychological Metaphor vs. a Rational-Choice Metaphor

One fundamental choice that students of Supreme Court decision-making have made involves what basic kind of metaphor to use in guiding their research. A metaphor involves some perspective or way of thinking that is developed in one field of knowledge but that is used to interpret or understand some other field of knowledge. It involves thinking by analogy; that is, one kind of process is seen as an instance of, or is said to work like, some other kind of process. Indeed, as Brown (2003, 14) put it in describing scientific activities in general, "metaphorical reasoning is at the very core of what scientists do when they design experiments, make discoveries, formulate theories and models, and describe their results to others—in short, when they do science and communicate about it."

However, the use of any metaphor is a two-edged sword. In writing about the use and misuse of metaphors in political science, for example, Martin Landau (1972, 78) once observed that "We speak and we write in metaphors, and we could scarcely get along without them. But the consequence may be more than felicity of phrase, for though figurative language can provide powerful analytic tools, it can also be the source of distortion and misrepresentation." In examining the judicial politics literature on the Supreme Court, we find good reason for the caution that Landau advises regarding the use of metaphors.

Two very different kinds of metaphors have been adopted in the literature on the Court. One kind of metaphor involves viewing the judicial decision-making process as if it were some kind of psychological process. Psychological theories of decision-making generally represent the decision-making process as being rather rich and complex in nature. For example, individuals may be motivated by a complex mix of personal concerns, or how they make decisions may be influenced by some fundamental features of the human mind. A psychological theory of individual actors in some institution thus involves a specification of how the actors should be expected to behave if their decisions were driven primarily by these personal concerns, for example, or by these fundamental features of the human mind.

Because many different kinds of psychological theories are available, a variety of applications to judicial decision-making can be made. For example, some prominent psychological theories of Supreme Court decision-making have involved the impact of the justices' political, social, or economic attitudes toward legal objects and legal situations on the justices' decision-making behavior (e.g., Segal and Spaeth 1993, 2002). Other judicial theories have been more social-psychological in nature, involving whether the justices follow various kinds of norms or roles that are expected to guide their decision-making behavior and their interactions with each other (e.g., Gibson 1981). Sometimes this social-psychological analysis focuses on whether a justice's desire to be liked or admired by other justices will influence his own decision-making behavior; a common concern here is whether a justice conforms to what other justices are thought to want. Whatever the particular application, the basic premise of the psychological metaphor here is that Supreme Court decision-making can be fruitfully studied as if it were an instance of a psychological process.[1]

The other kind of metaphor involves viewing judicial decision-making as if it were fundamentally a process of rational choice (e.g., Epstein and Knight 1998). Rational-choice theories were originally developed in economics but are increasingly applied throughout the social sciences, especially in political science. These rational-choice theories in political science generally involve a representation of individual decision-making as driven by utility maximization, for example, by some kind of goal maximization. The development of a rational-choice model of individual actors in some institution thus involves a specification of how the actors should be expected to behave if their primary motivation were to maximize utility, for example, by the achievement of their respective personal policy goals.[2]

Whether a study of Supreme Court decision-making uses a psychological theory or a rational-choice theory, we can view its approach to the Supreme Court as metaphorical in nature because neither kind of theory originated in studies of decision-making by Supreme Court justices. That is, neither the psychological theorists nor the rational-choice theorists had Supreme Court justices in mind when developing their theories. Many of these studies in judicial politics thus involve theories that are being transferred into judicial politics from other fields. Ironically, we would note that it is only the legal theories advanced by the students of public law—for example, theories about the influence of stare decisis, plain meaning, original intent, and so forth, on Supreme Court decision-making—that are derived directly from studies of the behavior of Supreme Court justices and (especially) of the opinions they write.[3]

There are costs and benefits to using either the psychological metaphor or the rational-choice metaphor to structure our studies in judicial politics. The psychological theories might be praised for their greater descriptive "realism." However, the greater richness and complexity associated with this realism may lead to greater vagueness and ambiguity about how the theories work and what behavioral expectations can be derived from them. In contrast, although the rational-choice theories are sometimes criticized for their lesser realism, their greater clarity and specificity does allow logical expectations and hypotheses to be more easily and explicitly derived, and thus more rigorously tested.

Of course, whatever kind of metaphor is chosen, it is essential that the metaphor be consistently followed throughout construction of the resulting theory. If the metaphor is changed midstream, or if another metaphor is adopted without the first one being abandoned, one might legitimately complain about "mixed metaphors" as a result of the difficulty of determining just what the general nature of the resulting theory actually is. For example, one major study of Supreme Court decision-making—Segal and Spaeth (1993, see also 2002)—refers rather explicitly to both the psychological and the rational-choice metaphors as basic elements of its own theory. This apparent reliance on what we think are two quite different metaphors has led to substantial uncertainty as to what is actually thought to be driving the justices' behavior; we will discuss this matter later in this chapter and in Chapter 3 as well.

The basic metaphor we have chosen to guide the development of our theory and models in this book is the rational-choice metaphor: each justice will be seen as a rational individual who seeks to maximize achievement of his or her own policy goals. This perspective will be consistently maintained throughout our book.

Distinction 2: Theories of Attitude Activation vs. Theories of Rational Choice

These two different kinds of metaphors in the judicial politics literature—the psychological metaphor and the rational-choice metaphor—have led to two rather different ways of describing what motivates the justices and how they make their decisions. In the most prominent versions of the psychological metaphor, justices are usually described as having preexisting attitudes toward particular legal objects and legal situations. In any one legal case, the presence of some kind of legal object in some kind of legal situation is seen as activating in each justice some kind of preexisting attitude, which then leads the justice to vote in a particular way on the case. We will refer to these as theories of attitude activation. Several major studies published after Pritchett's book (e.g., Schubert 1965) have used these kinds of theories.

With the rational-choice metaphor, justices are usually described as having preexisting preferences over particular legal policies. In a legal case each justice is seen as pursuing his or her most preferred policy by making particular kinds of choices. Several studies published after Pritchett's book have also taken this approach (e.g., Murphy 1964), although few of them have used the approach in an explicit and systematic manner.

We have six different reasons for considering the theories of attitude activation to be problematic representations of Supreme Court decision-making.

The first problem with theories of attitude activation is that they downplay the notion of individual choice to a remarkable degree. In fact, as we will note in Chapter 3, this kind of theory was explicitly described by one of its original creators—Schubert (1965)—as closely related to classical stimulus-response models in psychology: when particular stimuli are presented to a justice, some preexisting attitude of the justice is "activated" (this is the term that is widely used in this literature), and some kind of attitude-driven behavioral response is the result. The term *activated* clearly implies that once the stimuli are present, the expression of the attitude and the justices' behavior that results are automatic.[4] However, we are reluctant to describe intelligent and well-informed justices, whose professional lives have involved making complex judicial choices over many years on the Court, as exhibiting behavior that can be readily captured by a stimulus-response model and that can be described as automatic in nature. In general, it does not seem easy to describe behavior that is driven by attitude activation as deliberately chosen in any meaningful sense.

The second problem with the theories of attitude activation is that, given a justice's attitudes, such a theory should be able to tell us what decisions the justice should be expected to make. However, it is not clear how the attitude-activation theories actually convert a justice's attitudes into a decision. For example, it seems likely that each justice will have many different attitudes, both positive and negative, toward many different legal objects and situations in any one case, but the attitude-activation theories in the literature are silent on how these multiple attitudes are combined or integrated in a way that generates a decision by the justice in the case. Although greater descriptive realism of the individual's decision-making process is often said to be a virtue of the psychological theories, it is ironic that the attitude-activation theories used in the Supreme Court literature actually seem to place the process whereby a justice's attitudes are converted into decisions in a "black box."

The third problem with the attitude-activation theories in the literature is that it is unclear whether they could generate a specific prediction of what legal policy an individual justice would select, even if he or she were the sole justice comprising the Court. The difficulty is that behavior stemming from attitude activation is not necessarily related to the pursuit of any particular policy goal: activating an attitude is clearly not the same as pursuing a policy goal. For example, harboring a negative attitude toward some class of plaintiffs is not the same as believing that this class of plaintiffs should be denied various constitutional protections. Indeed, a justice might think that constitutional protections are especially important for individuals (such as criminals, the poor, and racial minorities) about whom the public and public officials are likely to have negative attitudes. In general, a theory based on attitudes may tell us relatively little about what policies a justice will find it desirable or necessary to support.

The fourth problem with the attitude-activation theories involves an ongoing debate in the literature as to whether Supreme Court justices are strategically rational; a strategically rational justice would base her own choices, at each stage of the Court's decision-making process, on how she expects these choices—and the responses of the other justices—to affect the extent to which she can achieve her own policy goals. However, it is not clear whether a justice who makes her decisions on the basis of attitude activation can also act in a strategically rational fashion. If the judicial behavior that results when an attitude is activated is automatic (as we have argued it must be under the theory of attitude activation), how could this behavior be strategically calculated as well? Indeed, if it can be demonstrated (logically, empirically, or both) that justices have strong incentives to be strategically rational in the decision-making process, or that justices demonstrably do act in a strategically rational fashion, then this raises questions about the adequacy of the attitude-activation theories as explanations of Supreme Court decision-making.

The fifth problem is that the attitude-activation theories in the judicial politics literature focus solely on explaining the justices' final votes and say nothing about what the content of the opinions will be. In fact, these theories seem unable to tell us much about anything beyond the final vote. But if we are most interested in the content of the Supreme Court's opinions, then this is an important weakness of the attitude-activation theories.

The sixth problem is that because the Court is a multimember body, an attitude-activation theory (like any other kind of theory) should also tell us what decisions the Court as a whole would adopt, given the attitude-activated behavior of the individual justices. However, the attitude-activation theories are only theories of how individual justices might respond to particular features of a case; they are not theories of how nine justices collectively produce a final decision. In fact, these theories tell us virtually nothing about how the justices will interact, or even whether they will interact, as they make a final decision for the Court as a whole. Indeed, there are even some suggestions in the attitude-activation literature that justices do not even take each other's views into account at all, at least when they are deciding how to cast their final votes. But if it can be demonstrated that justices have strong incentives to interact in significant ways when making their final decisions, or that justices demonstrably do interact when making their final decisions (which is what Maltzman, Spriggs, and Wahlbeck 2000 demonstrate), this would again raise some questions about the adequacy of the attitude-activation theories as explanations of Supreme Court decision-making.

For these six reasons, then, we view these attitude-activation theories as problematic representations of decision-making by Supreme Court justices. In contrast, the rational-choice model we develop includes a fully specified logic of how an individual justice will go about making a policy choice, how the justices will interact with each other to produce a policy choice for the Court as a whole, and what that policy choice will be.

Distinction 3: Theories of Choice vs. Theories of Measurement

The next major distinction we want to highlight in the literature involves *theories of choice* versus *theories of measurement*. Theories of choice are intended to characterize the general logic of how a particular individual, or the members of a group, make their choices. These theories thus provide a means for deducing what choices an individual justice, or a group of justices, should be expected to make under specified conditions. For example, we can use a theory of choice to predict that a justice with some particular policy goal will make some particular choice when facing some particular situation.

In contrast, theories of measurement are aimed at describing, characterizing, and measuring the choices that some individuals have already made. For example, given the choices already made by a group of justices, theories of measurement are intended to help us find whatever patterns these choices may exhibit.

It thus seems obvious that in the overall research enterprise, a theory of choice is conceptually prior to a theory of measurement. Research on Supreme Court decision-making should thus begin with the construction of a theory of choice by the justices, and only when an adequate theory of choice has been developed should a theory of measurement be selected or developed for use in testing the theory.

Indeed, we would go further and assert that, to the greatest extent possible, the theory of measurement that is selected should be logically derived from the theory of choice that is being used to explain how and why the choices are made in the first place; in this way we can be most assured that the theory of measurement is the most appropriate one possible. This is especially important when strategically rational actors are playing a complex political game with each other. Some of the most obvious measurement techniques will likely miss some of the crucial (but subtle) implications that such a game has for the behavior that should actually be observed.[5]

In fact, we would even argue that unless an adequate theory of choice is in hand, it will be difficult to identify the most appropriate theory of measurement. If our theory involves claims about what choices individual justices would make but this theory is inadequately developed (perhaps in the sense that its predictions about individual behavior are unclear), then it will also be unclear what expectations we should derive about the individual's behavior. Hence, it will be unclear what it is about the individual's behavior that should be measured, and it will also be unclear what significance we should give to the measurements of that behavior.

Unfortunately, the literature on Supreme Court decision-making seems to have paid far more attention to problems of pattern-finding and measurement than to developing and specifying the theories and models of individual and collective choice on which the pattern-finding and measurement techniques should be based. For example, one seminal study in the judicial politics literature on Supreme Court decision-making—Schubert (1965)—placed an overwhelming emphasis on developing and applying various theories and models of measurement; as we will demonstrate in Chapter 3, relatively little attention was paid to describing and justifying the underlying theory of choice.

In contrast, the theory and model we develop here are clearly based on a logic of rational choice. And we expect that the clarity and specificity of our model will ultimately help methodologists develop the most appropriate tests of the model.

Distinction 4: Explaining Final Votes vs. Explaining What Final Opinion Is Adopted

Three additional distinctions structure the judicial politics literature on Supreme Court decision-making in critically important ways. Although these distinctions are intertwined in complex ways, we will discuss each separately to simplify exposition.

The first of these distinctions involves a choice of what the dependent variable should be in studies of Supreme Court decision-making: should these studies primarily try to explain the justices' final votes on the final opinions, or should these studies primarily try to explain the content of the final opinions on which the justices are voting?

Interestingly, only the public law literature has focused much attention on the content of the Supreme Court's final opinions. In this literature, efforts are often made to explain (in a qualitative sense) why some particular justice will write any particular opinion, or will react to some opinion in a particular way. This has necessarily involved extensive qualitative analysis of Supreme Court opinions. However, to the best of our knowledge, the public law literature contains no explicit theories, much less operational models, of how and why a justice will write one opinion rather than another, nor does the public law literature contain any explicit models of how justices interact to generate the content of any particular majority opinion.

In contrast, the judicial politics literature on Supreme Court decision-making has generally focused on explaining the justices' votes on the final opinions rather than on explaining the content of the opinions. One major reason why judicial politics scholars have chosen this dependent variable seems to have been their belief that rigorous evaluation of hypotheses about the justices' decision-making behavior is best conducted by using quantitative measures of the justices' behavior rather than by using various kinds of qualitative evidence. Because quantitative data have long been available on the justices' final votes, whereas quantitative data remain unavailable on the content of the justices' opinions, it thus seems natural for judicial politics scholars to have focused on explaining the justices' votes on the final opinions rather than on trying to explain the content of the final opinions.

However, we suspect there is another reason for this focus on explaining the final votes rather than the content of the final opinions. The reason involves a distinction between treating a Supreme Court opinion as primarily serving to affirm or reverse some lower-court ruling versus treating the opinion as primarily establishing some general legal policy. It seems to us that scholars who use attitude-activation theories have been led by their theories (such as in Schubert 1965) to an implicit assumption that the Court's primary task is to affirm or reverse a lower-court ruling. We advance this explanation because the attitudinal models seem to be capable of producing only binary "acceptable-vs.-unacceptable" judgments about cases with particular sets of legal stimuli, and this capability leads rather naturally to a focus on the binary "affirm-vs.-reverse" aspects of Supreme Court decisions. From this perspective, then, the Court's decision-making agenda must be seen as limited to a consideration of what the lower court has already provided (for example, the evidence, the arguments, and the final ruling). Once the Court has agreed to accept a case, the Court's available options—to affirm or to reverse the lower-court ruling—can thus be treated as exogenously determined by what the lower court did. And if the Court's agenda contains just these two exogenously determined options, then the primary focus of research should obviously be on explaining the justices' votes over these two options; after all, which one of these two options happens to gain a majority of the justices' votes will automatically become the Court's decision.[6] In other words, we are suggesting that the nature of the explanatory theories that have been adopted—in particular, the attitude-activation theories—may have induced these judicial politics scholars to focus their efforts on explaining just the final votes.

However, if the Court's primary concern is in establishing some general legal policy (by using a particular case as its vehicle), then the Court's decision-making agenda should be seen as endogenously determined, at least to some degree. That is, the Court should be seen as determining for itself what the available set of options will be on the final vote. The reason for this is clear: when establishing some general legal policy, the justices will not want to constrain themselves to just the ruling of the lower court and the associated evidence and arguments from that case; instead, the justices will feel free to consider a wide variety of previous cases, rulings, and arguments. From this perspective, then, if the Court's agenda on the final vote is endogenously determined by the justices themselves, it follows that there are likely to be far more than just two options—to affirm or to reverse—available for them on the final vote. Indeed, every option ranging from the most preferred policy of the most "conservative" justice to the most preferred policy of the most "liberal" justice might be considered as possible opinions. So if the Court's agenda is endogenously determined by the justices themselves (as evidence from McGuire and Palmer 1995, for example, clearly suggests), and because this means that there are many potential options on the Court's agenda rather than just the two options (to affirm or to reverse) generated by the lower court's ruling, this would suggest that research on Supreme Court decision-making should include a strong emphasis on explaining why one particular policy became the final majority opinion, given the many other policies that were also available. For this broader purpose, the attitude-activation theories would seem inappropriate.

There is also an obvious but nonetheless compelling reason why the judicial politics literature should follow the lead of the public law literature and focus more directly on the content of the Court's final opinions: what is most important about Supreme Court decisions is their broad policy content. After all, the rationale for studying the Supreme Court in the first place is because the Court establishes legal policies that govern broad and significant aspects of our country's political, social, and economic life. Of course, the legal fates of particular plaintiffs and defendants are obviously important to the plaintiffs and defendants themselves, which means that whether the lower-court ruling is affirmed or reversed will be critical to them. However, judicial politics scholars do not usually study the Court or its cases because they are especially interested in the legal fates of particular plaintiffs and defendants. Instead, they study the Court because they are interested in the broad policy rules that emerge from these cases.

In our view, then, an adequate theory of Supreme Court decision-making should lead to predictions about the content of the opinions on which the justices are voting, and about which policy (if any) will gain majority support; if this theory also leads to predictions of how the individual justices will vote on the final opinions, so much the better. The model we develop in this book predicts the content of the majority opinion that the justices will produce, and it also predicts the votes of the individual justices on this opinion as well as their behavior at the earlier stages of decision-making as they seek to influence the content of this opinion.

Distinction 5: Explaining Just the Final Vote vs. Explaining All Five Stages of Decision-Making

This debate over what should be the dependent variable—the final vote or the content of the final opinion?—is closely related to a debate over what stages of the Court's decision-making process should be included in the research. As we have noted, the early generations of judicial politics scholars focused primarily on the justices' final votes, but a variety of other scholars—originally Murphy (1964) and more recently Epstein and Knight (1998) and Maltzman, Spriggs, and Wahlbeck (2000)—have argued that what happens at the earlier stages of the decision-making process can have a substantial impact on what final opinion is adopted. Indeed, given our discussion of endogenous agenda-setting by the justices in Distinction 4, we would suggest that the agenda-setting occurs primarily at the stages preceding the final vote: it undoubtedly occurs at the first stage (involving whether certiorari is granted) but it would also seem to occur at the second stage involving the conference vote (where justices reveal their initial views on a case), at the third stage (where the opinion assigner is selected), and at the fourth stage (where the opinion writer is appointed and prepares the final opinion).

If the decisions that the justices make at these earlier stages influence the content of what they are voting on at the final stage, a question can thus be raised as to how the justices' final votes should be interpreted. Some scholars have explicitly argued—see especially Segal and Spaeth (1993, 2002)—that the justices' final votes are unadulterated manifestations of their true policy attitudes or preferences. The implication is that studies that explain the justices' final votes will not be biased in any significant manner as a result of any problems with the dependent variable, which in this case is the justices' final votes.

However, if the agenda-setting at the earlier stages affects what particular arguments and policies become enshrined as the majority opinion at the final stage, this suggests that whether a justice supports or opposes this final opinion will be influenced by the prior agenda-setting process. If so, this means that the statistical results based on these final votes might be biased as a result of this prior agenda-setting process.

To illustrate, consider the following pair of examples. First, assume that the prior agenda-setting process produces final opinions that routinely gain the support of seven of the nine justices. These seven justices would thus appear to have policy preferences rather similar to each other and different from the remaining two justices. Second, assume that the nine justices' preferences do not change but that the prior agenda-setting process does change, so that the final opinions that are produced can gain the support of only five of the nine justices. These five justices would thus appear to have policy preferences rather similar to each other, although the two other original coalition members (from the seven-member coalition in the first example) would now appear to have preferences similar to the remaining two justices. Thus, the prior agenda-setting process could produce results that classify two of the justices in rather different ways, even though these jus-tices' most preferred policies have not changed; in effect, it is the expression of the justices' preferences that would be changed by the agenda-setting pro-cess, not the preferences themselves. But because it is the expression of the preferences, via the justices' final votes, that is captured by standard statistical analyses, it follows that the prior agenda-setting process can influence the conclusions that are drawn about the extent to which a justice's preferences are similar to, or different from, the other justices' preferences.[7]

For these reasons, we think it is essential that a theory of Supreme Court decision-making, and any models derived from this theory, should explain the justices' behavior at all five stages of the Court's decision-making pro-cess. Only in this way can an unbiased assessment be made of the meaning of each justice's final votes. To the best of our knowledge, our model is the first in judicial politics to incorporate all five of the decision-making stages.

Distinction 6: Theories of "Sincere" Rational Choice vs. Theories of "Strategic" Rational Choice

The two distinctions just made—explaining the justices' final votes vs. explaining the content of the opinions on which the final votes are cast, and explaining only the justices' final votes vs. explaining the justices' behavior at all five stages of the Court's decision-making process—are closely related to yet another debate in the literature, this one regarding the general nature of the justices' rationality.

As we have previously suggested, a "rational" justice is seen as trying to make choices that result in a final Supreme Court policy that is as close as possible to the policy he or she most desires. However, there is a debate in the literature over just how to characterize the nature of the justices' ration-ality. Some scholars—especially Segal and Spaeth (1993, 2002)—have argued that at the final stage of Supreme Court decision-making, where votes are being cast on the final opinion (or opinions), justices are not acting "strate-gically" in any fashion because they do not have to: each justice can maxi-mize the chances of getting his or her most preferred outcome simply by endorsing the opinion he or she most prefers. In the formal modeling liter-ature, this kind of "nonstrategic" rationality is sometimes referred to as "sin-cere" rationality.

In contrast, other scholars—especially Epstein and Knight (1998)—have argued that justices should be seen not merely as rational but as strategically rational. Indeed, Epstein and Knight have defined "rationality" as including "strategic rationality" (xi, footnote a), and they argue that justices act in a strategically rational manner throughout all stages of the Court's decision-making process, including the final vote. Their rationale for this argument is that, because the justices' decisions at each stage are interdependent, a justice must consider the possible reactions of the other justices before he or she makes a decision at any stage. From this perspective, then, a strategically rational justice—that is, one who takes the other justices' reactions into account when making his or her own decisions—will get the best possible policy outcome, within the constraint of needing the support of at least some other justices, whereas a justice who fails to anticipate the reactions of the other justices, even on the final vote, may see the Court adopt a less desirable policy as a result.

To understand this debate, it is helpful to distinguish between strategic rationality at the earlier stages of decision-making and strategic rationality on the final vote. As we will demonstrate in Chapter 3, the two sides of this debate seem to have converged, at least to some degree, on an agreement that justices are strategically rational at the earlier stages of the Court's decision-making process. Thus, at these earlier stages, when a strategically rational justice anticipates the possible reactions of other justices, the justice might thereby choose to vote against his or her most preferred policy because this behavior, which may look "self-denying" (and thus irrational), actually leads to a better outcome for the justice when the Court's final opinion is adopted. In contrast, a justice who is rational but nonstrategic would presumably not engage in any of this "self-denying" behavior at any stage of the decision-making process; in effect, this justice would behave as if he or she were the sole decision-maker at every stage of the Court's decision-making process.

However, the question of whether justices act strategically on the final vote is a more complex issue, and it is one on which disagreement persists. As we have noted, theorists such as Segal and Spaeth (1993, 2002) have explicitly argued that justices are not strategic on the final vote because they do not have to be strategic. Theorists such as Epstein and Knight (1998) consider justices to be strategic actors throughout the Court's decision-making process, including the final stage, because they have strong incentives to be strategic.

In our view, whether a justice is seen as having an incentive to behave strategically on the final vote critically depends on what the Court is assumed to be doing on the final vote. As we posed the question under Distinction 4 above, is the Court seen as primarily affirming or reversing some ruling by a lower court, or is the Court seen as primarily choosing a general policy whose characteristics are not entirely constrained by some lower-court ruling and the associated evidence and arguments? If one assumes that the Court is primarily just affirming or reversing a lower-court ruling, then there are obviously just two options from which a justice might choose: to affirm or to reverse. And if there are just two options, strategic rationality and sincere (nonstrategic) rationality dictate precisely the same behavior: a rational justice will simply support the opinion—to affirm or to reverse—that leads to the final outcome that he or she wants more. In other words, when there are only two options, how the other justices may vote is indeed irrelevant.[8]

In contrast, if one assumes that the Court is choosing a general policy whose content is not entirely constrained by some lower-court ruling, then there are likely to be more than two possible options. And if there are more than two possible options, then there is good reason to think that a strategically rational justice's behavior will sometimes differ from a sincerely rational justice's behavior.

For example, assume there are three possible choices that a justice might make on the final vote in a case: write an opinion on behalf of the policy she most prefers, endorse one alternative opinion, or endorse a second alternative opinion. For simplicity, assume that the other eight justices have already voted, yielding four votes for the first alternative opinion and four votes for the second alternative opinion. If our justice writes her own opinion, she would thereby ensure that no opinion gains a majority: there would be a 1–4–4 split. But if she endorses either the first alternative opinion or the second alternative opinion, this would ensure that whatever opinion she endorses would gain a 5–4 Court majority. It is important to note that if she endorses one of the alternative opinions, that opinion would become the new Court policy, whereas if she writes her own opinion, the legal status quo on this issue would remain in effect because there would be only a plurality opinion and not a majority opinion on the case.

Now assume that she prefers the policy in the first alternative opinion to the policy in the second alternative opinion, and that she prefers the legal status quo least of all. By writing an opinion supporting her most preferred policy—this might plausibly be characterized as nonstrategic behavior—she would thus end up with the status quo, which is her least preferred outcome. But if she votes for the first alternative opinion, she would end up with the policy in that opinion, and recall that she prefers this policy to the legal status quo. Because she gets a better outcome here from voting for something other than her most preferred policy, she clearly benefits from strategic behavior on this final vote.

We should also emphasize here that formal mathematical studies have shown that all voting rules—which necessarily include the Supreme Court's voting practices on the final vote—are vulnerable to manipulation via strategic voting whenever there are more than two options.[9] The illustration provided above is thus just one example of a very general rule.

Hence, we think the issue of what the Court is seen as doing—is it merely affirming or reversing lower-court rulings, or is it setting broad national policies?—turns out to be critical to the debate over whether Supreme Court justices are acting strategically on the final vote. If the Court is merely affirming or reversing a lower-court ruling, then it has only two options, which means that the debate over strategic behavior on the final vote is moot because strategic and nonstrategic rationality would predict the same behavior. But if the Court has more than two options available, then it follows that justices will sometimes benefit from behaving strategically on the final vote. And we would note here that a justice almost always has at least the following three options: to write her own opinion (for example, a special occurrence), to join opinion X (a majority opinion), or to join opinion Y (a dissenting opinion). In general, then, a claim that final-stage voting in the Supreme Court provides no incentives for strategic behavior is completely unwarranted.

Note that if justices do behave strategically on the final vote, this again calls into question the assumption that the justices' final votes are unadulterated indicators of their true policy attitudes or preferences. In the illustration just presented, for example, the justice is not voting for her most preferred policy but in standard quantitative analyses in the judicial politics literature, her vote would be treated as if she were voting for her most preferred policy. For this reason, then, the justices' final votes might again be considered to be biased indicators of their true attitudes or preferences. Hence, failing to take strategic behavior into account in a statistical analysis might again bias the results.

We might remark that we initially sought to develop two classes of rational-choice models, one built on an assumption that justices are sincerely (nonstrategically) rational throughout the entire decision-making process, and the other built on an assumption that justices are strategically rational throughout the entire decision-making process. Our thinking was that by specifying each kind of model, it would then be possible to conduct empirical tests to see which version gains the most support. However, as we attempted to develop the logic of each model, we came to the conclusion that it is sometimes unclear how nonstrategic justices would behave at the earlier stages of the decision-making process. We discuss these problems at various places in Parts II and III of this book.[10]

In fact, it was not even clear what nonstrategic behavior would look like on the final vote. After all, one might plausibly expect a completely nonstrategic justice to write his or her own unique opinion on every case; only with his or her own unique opinion could a justice ensure that his or her own views on a case would be most accurately represented. This would seem to be the purest possible nonstrategic behavior. Of course, if every justice behaved this way, the result would be that every case would produce nine different opinions. But because this pattern of seriatim opinions was characteristic of Supreme Court decisions for only the first decade of its existence (that is, before the appointment of Chief Justice Marshall), it suggests yet again that justices are almost always at least somewhat strategic when casting their final votes.

For these reasons, then, the model we have developed for this book is only a model of justices who are strategically rational throughout all five stages of the Supreme Court's decision-making process.

Distinction 7: A "Status Quo" Policy vs. No "Status Quo" Policy

Our last distinction involves the question of whether a theory of Supreme Court decision-making includes an explicit notion of a status quo policy. That is, does the theory assume that there exists some kind of ongoing legal policy that currently governs the issue area before the Court even considers granting certiorari to a case? The presence of a status quo policy is directly and intimately related to critical aspects of almost every kind of theory of Supreme Court decision-making. Yet the role that this status quo policy necessarily plays in a theory of Supreme Court decision-making seems to have been seldom recognized, at least in any explicit sense, in the judicial politics literature.

Theories of attitude activation have certainly ignored any role for the status quo policy. For example, studies of attitude activation by legal stimuli (see, e.g., Schubert 1965) make no mention of any kind of role for a status quo policy. As we have noted, in these attitude-activation theories, some legal stimuli lead to the activation of an attitude by a justice, and this activated attitude leads automatically to some kind of behavior by the justice on the case (for example, affirming a lower-court ruling or reversing it). But whether this behavior, such as affirming or reversing the lower-court ruling, results in a policy that is better for the justice than what was previously in effect (that is, the status quo policy) seems not to have been considered.

In fact, most of the rational-choice theories in the judicial politics literature (see, e.g., Epstein and Knight 1998) also seem to have overlooked the role of the status quo policy as well. We find this surprising, but we suspect the reason is that the rational-choice theorizing here has remained informal and has tended to focus on how any one individual justice will make decisions; the precise character of the interactions among the justices could thus have been inadvertently overlooked. But once several justices are explicitly assumed to be interacting with each other, each justice trying to get the others to support a policy as close as possible to what he or she most prefers, the role of the status quo policy simply cannot be ignored. The reason is that some justices may find that the status quo policy is relatively close to what they most prefer anyway. These justices will thus want policy not to be changed very much (and if it is changed, they will want it to be changed only in the direction of what they most prefer). Because other justices whose most preferred policies lie farther from the status quo will want to change the status quo policy to a much greater extent, the justices whose most preferred policies are close to the status quo will object and refuse to support any great change. If the justices whose most preferred policies are close to the status quo comprise a majority of the Court, this means in effect that they will constrain how much the other justices can get the Court to change its policies.

There is nothing at all remarkable about these observations about the status quo: it is commonplace in political science to observe that some political actors want to protect the status quo more than other actors. Yet the judicial politics literature seems to have neglected the role of this critical variable. The only part of the literature on Supreme Court decision-making where the status quo policy seems to have played a role involves studies of certiorari: these studies have been quite explicit in suggesting that justices with particular policy preferences may oppose granting certiorari on a case if they think the final opinion that would result would make policy worse for them, not better (see, e.g., Boucher and Segal 1995; Brenner and Krol 1989). However, theories involving the final vote seem not to have given the status quo policy any equivalent level of consideration.

Our own model of decision-making by strategically rational justices will demonstrate that the location of the status quo policy has a major impact on what final policy is chosen and on the sizes of the coalitions supporting and opposing this final policy.

Conclusion

These seven pairs of distinctions have played a significant role in structuring the current literature on Supreme Court decision-making. Different studies have adopted different assumptions, and these different assumptions have had far-reaching—although not always recognized—consequences for the nature of the theories that have been developed.

Our identification and examination of these seven distinctions in this chapter thus provide the rationale for our own modeling efforts in Part II of the book. However, some of the arguments we have advanced in this chapter may be controversial, and they may be persuasive only if substantially more justification is provided. That justification is provided in Chapter 3, where we show how these seven pairs of assumptions have played a major role in structuring and shaping several major works on the Supreme Court. In addition, by probing into the details of what our predecessors have done, we can provide an even deeper understanding of the intellectual tradition from which our own work is derived.

CHAPTER 3

Assessing Previous Theories of Supreme Court Decision-Making

In Chapter 2, when we examined seven key distinctions in the literature on Supreme Court decision-making, we advanced some strong arguments about the adequacy of previous theories. However, to make a concise presentation, we did not delve into all the details and evidence for these arguments. In this chapter we now develop the reasons for our arguments in greater depth by assessing several key studies of Supreme Court decision-making. We begin with the early scholars: Pritchett, Schubert, and Murphy. We then examine the attitudinal model of Harold Spaeth and associates. We close with a discussion of the recent literature on strategically rational justices.

The Pioneers: Pritchett, Schubert, and Murphy

As noted in Chapter 1, C. Herman Pritchett's book, *The Roosevelt Court: A Study in Judicial Politics and Values, 1937–1947* (1948), was the first effort to systematically evaluate whether Supreme Court justices pursued their policy preferences via their formal decisions. Although Pritchett described himself as a "political scientist interested in the social and psychological origins of judicial attitudes and the influence of individual predilections on the development of law" (1948, xi), he chose not to base his study on any specific sociological or psychological theories. Instead, he primarily sought to describe the policy views of the justices in order to examine what consequences they had for the decisions made by the Court.

Pritchett's research strategy was to examine all nonunanimous decisions of the Court from 1937 to 1947, arguing that "the fact of disagreement demonstrates that the members of the Court are operating on different assumptions, that their inarticulate major premises are dissimilar, that their value systems are differently constructed and weighted, that their political, economic, and social views contrast in important respects" (1948, xii). Pritchett contrasted his emphasis on the importance of the justices' political, economic, and social views with earlier portraits of the Supreme Court as an apolitical institution populated by justices motivated solely by legal concerns. For example, Pritchett noted that "Every Court before the Roosevelt Court had enjoyed the protection of perhaps the most potent myth in American political life—the myth that the Court is a nonpolitical body, a sacred institution on which politics must not lay its profane hands" (1948, 14). Pritchett considered this "myth" to be a misinterpretation of the reasons for the justices' decisions: "According to the myth, interpretation of the Constitution was not a task allowing of individual interpretation or judicial discretion, and it was precisely because of this assumption that it was believed safe to grant the Court such extraordinary powers. The justices did not make law; they simply discovered the law and applied it in the circumstances of individual cases" (1948, 15). Such an explanation left no room for an individual justice's own policy preferences to play a role.

Pritchett also saw quantitative empirical techniques as providing insights into Court behavior that were not available by other means. For example, in the first sentence of his preface (1948, xi), he cited a quotation from Lord Kelvin that was inscribed on his own Social Science Research Building at the University of Chicago: "When you cannot measure, your knowledge is meager and unsatisfactory."[1] Later in his preface, Pritchett acknowledged, "I am fully aware of the limitations of statistical methods in dealing with materials of the kind involved here. The greater precision and certainty which such methods appear to yield may, under the circumstances, be in part illusory. Nevertheless, I am convinced that the counting and the charting have a positive contribution to make to an understanding of the motivations of the present Court" (1948, xv). By using a simple quantitative technique to determine how often individual justices voted with each other, Pritchett identified some patterns of behavior that he interpreted as evidence that the personal policy preferences of the Roosevelt Court justices had indeed influenced their decisions.

Despite the provocative nature of Pritchett's 1948 study, his general approach and specific line of argument gained few adherents over the next decade. A few quantitatively oriented studies were published in the 1950s (see, e.g., Thurstone and Degan 1951; Kort 1957; Horn 1957; Schmidhauser and Gold 1958; Ulmer 1958), but the next major work that used Pritchett's general approach to the Supreme Court appeared only in 1959 with the publication of Glendon Schubert's *Quantitative Analysis of Judicial Behavior*.[2]

Schubert specified that the foundations for his study were similar to those of Pritchett's. For example, he noted that "One of our basic assumptions, which we think has become sufficiently well accepted to be considered a part of the orthodoxy of contemporary public law, is that the decision-making of Supreme Court justices is 'political' in the sense that the primary role of the Court is to make public policy" (1959, 10). He went on to say that "Our primary concern is with the *motivations* which lead individual members of this small group to choose, in their conjoint voting behavior, to select certain alternatives (i.e., preferred outcomes) rather than others" (1959, 11, emphasis in original). Schubert then described his own study as borrowing techniques from several other social science disciplines, such as sociology (his chapter 3 used bloc analysis), economics (his chapter 4 used game theory), and psychology and psychometrics (his chapter 5 used scalogram analysis). Even so, the chapters had a common theme, which was that the primary motivation for the justices' voting decisions was their personal policy preferences.

Because one of Schubert's major concerns involved the development of quantitative methods for analyzing judicial behavior, his book focused on Supreme Court activities for which numerical data could be gathered. For this reason, his book primarily involved an analysis of quantifiable matters, such as how many cases the Court had accepted for decision and who had voted with whom on the final votes. The Court's internal decision-making activities remained hidden from view (data about the justices' conference votes, for example, were not yet available) and so were largely ignored.

Schubert was even willing to describe the justices as rational actors, as he did in his chapter 4 when he used game theory to analyze coalition behavior on the final votes. Indeed, as far as we are aware, his chapter on game theory is the first study in judicial politics to make explicit reference to the rationality of justices who are pursuing their policy objectives (see especially 1959, 174–77); as Schubert described the matter,

The theory of games offers highly suggestive possibilities for the study of judicial behavior. The models of game theory are highly formalized. Designed to assist in the analysis of interest conflicts, they incorporate basic concepts borrowed from psychology and economics. These are the concepts of *rationality* and *utility*. A game theoretic model, accordingly, describes how a player *who wishes to behave rationally* can best *maximize his share of the utility* which is assumed to be the object of play. (1959, 174–75, emphasis in original)

However, because Schubert's effort to rely on quantitative data narrowed his primary focus to the justices' final votes (although he did examine some case-selection issues), this had the side effect (presumably unintended, given his comments on game theory) of deemphasizing the role that strategically rational behavior by the justices might play in the Supreme Court's decision-making process.[3]

The next major study that used this rational-choice approach—Walter

Murphy's *Elements of Judicial Strategy*—was published in 1964. Murphy described the central purpose of his book as addressing the question, "How can a Justice of the Supreme Court most efficiently utilize his resources, official and personal, to achieve a particular set of policy objectives?" (1964, 3–4). Although intellectually compatible with Schubert's work, Murphy's book did diverge from Schubert's 1959 study in two ways. First, because *Elements* considered qualitative as well as quantitative evidence, it could evaluate the Court's decision-making processes that occurred after the certiorari vote but before the final vote. As Murphy noted, to understand the Court, "we must have information beyond voting and opinion analyses" (1964, 200). Second, because *Elements* included the decision-making processes preceding the final vote, it was necessary to consider the impact that strategic behavior by the justices at the earlier stages might have on the final outcomes.

For these reasons, Murphy's book took a different path than Schubert's, both theoretically and empirically. As a theoretical exercise, his book sought to deduce (albeit informally) how the justices' policy preferences might affect their decisions throughout the Court's decision-making processes. Here Murphy pushed the focus on rationality further than had Schubert, suggesting that "the policy-oriented Justice in this model acts much like the rational man of economic theory. He has only a limited supply of such resources as time, energy, staff, prestige, reputation, and good will, and he must compute in terms of costs and revenues whether a particular choice is worth the price which is required to attain it" (1964, 35–36). And as an empirical enterprise, Murphy's book sought to demonstrate that the justices' decisions resulted from their strategically rational pursuit of policy goals. Murphy relied on an array of anecdotes and illustrations—all qualitative evidence—that were drawn from biographies, court records, and the justices' personal papers. This evidence supported Murphy's thesis that the justices were taking each other's expected behavior into account when making decisions and were strategically evaluating current choices in terms of future consequences.

Schubert's Attitude-Activation Model

Despite its broader approach, Murphy's book did not have the immediate and sustained impact one might have expected. Indeed, before the 1990s, his presumptions about strategic behavior by Supreme Court justices were adopted by only a handful of studies in the judicial politics literature. His book's lack of impact may have stemmed from the fact that its publication in 1964 was immediately followed, in 1965, by the appearance of Glendon Schubert's next major study of Supreme Court politics, *The Judicial Mind: The Attitudes and Ideologies of Supreme Court Justices, 1946–1963*. Schubert's quantitative approach in *Quantitative Analysis* and then *The Judicial Mind*, it appears, was rapidly becoming the preferred approach for judicial politics

scholars, perhaps because it was seen as a better example of how to participate in "the behavioral revolution" then underway in political science at
large. Murphy's qualitative approach, although focusing on what was unde-
niably judicial "behavior," may not have seemed to embody what "the
behavioral revolution," with its emphasis on the analysis of quantitative data,
was all about.

Even so, Schubert's new book did share with Murphy's a focus, as Schubert put it (1965, 5), on "the political ideologies and attitudes of Supreme
Court justices, as manifested in their decision-making behavior." In fact,
Schubert described his new book as following the tradition that Pritchett
had established in *The Roosevelt Court*:

> Pritchett's major contribution in that book is implied by the subtitle: "A Study in
> Judicial *Politics* and *Values*." From a theoretical point of view, the significance of his
> work lies in his interpretation of the Court's policies in terms of a single major atti-
> tudinal dimension: liberalism and conservatism. By "values," he meant essentially the
> same thing as I shall discuss when I talk about "attitudes"; and by "politics," he
> meant the observable differences in the decisional behaviors of the justices, which
> he attributed to conflict in values among them, and which I shall discuss under the
> alternative concept of their attitudinal differences. As he remarked in his preface,
> what he was attempting to do was "to examine into the *personal* foundations of judi-
> cial decisions" by which he meant "that the present justices are motivated by their
> own preferences"—no more so, he presumed, than had been their predecessors, but
> certainly no less so, either. This book of mine has the same objective. (1965, 6–7,
> emphasis in original)

Schubert described his approach in *The Judicial Mind*, more than he did in
Quantitative Analysis and just as much as Murphy did in *Elements*, as motivated by the aspects of psychology in which rationality plays a key component:

> This kind of psychology emphasizes the rational aspects of human thinking and
> choice-making; and although it seems probable that both rational and irrational
> processes are operative in the decision-making of Supreme Court justices, I am pre-
> pared to make the basic assumption that the former are the more important influ-
> ences for men in their position. The reason for this is that the roles of Supreme
> Court justices are defined in such a way as to give maximal emphasis to the impor-
> tance of rational factors. (1965, 13)

Schubert listed here a variety of factors that heightened the importance of
rationality, such as the legal training of the justices, the institutional tradi-
tions of the Court, and the fact that the Court's decisions must be supported by reasons that are exposed to the criticisms of dissenting justices and of
other critics outside the Court. Thus, his own enterprise, Schubert continued, involved the "psychology of rationality" because it seemed "to provide
a better fit for the work of Supreme Court justices" than did alternative psychological approaches (1965, 13).

Schubert's phrase, "the psychology of rationality," thus seemed to combine both of the major metaphors that were subsequently so prominent in the field (see the discussion of Distinction 1 in Chapter 2). But although some elements of *The Judicial Mind* did invoke the language of the rational pursuit of personal policy preferences, by far the major emphasis was on a psychology focused on attitudes.

Schubert clearly had an ambitious agenda. For example, early in *The Judicial Mind*, in referring to "a theoretical model that I have constructed," he asserted that "The theory is about how and why the justices arrive at the particular decisions that we can observe them to have made. The model of Supreme Court decision-making that I shall present is a logical consequence of the theory of motivation that I shall discuss, and the model has a demonstrable capacity to serve as the basis for making predictions about the future behavior of the justices" (1965, 5). However, there are two significant problems with what Schubert referred to as his "model of Supreme Court decision-making."

First, recalling Distinction 3 from Chapter 2, we note that Schubert focused most of his efforts on developing a theory and model of measurement. In fact, Schubert devoted very little space—literally just three paragraphs, on pages 26, 27, and 28, in his 288-page book—to developing and justifying any specific model of choice. Moreover, the model of choice that Schubert did adopt here was actually crafted by one of the methodologists on whose work Schubert was relying, and Schubert appears to have adopted this model of choice primarily because it allowed him to use the methodologist's model of measurement, involving multidimensional scaling. Indeed, when Schubert referred to a "model of Supreme Court decision-making," it is not clear whether he was referring to the model of measurement he intended to use—the multidimensional-scaling methodology—or to the model of choice that the justices were presumed to be using when they generated the voting data that the scaling methodology was intended to process.

Second, we argue that the model of choice that Schubert did briefly discuss is limited in its utility. In particular, although this model of choice may be able to help us characterize some aspects of how a justice might make an affirm-vs.-reverse decision, the model seems limited in the extent to which it can help us understand the choice of a policy by any one justice or by the Court as a whole. Here we will see the importance of Distinction 4 from Chapter 2, involving the difference between explaining the justices' final votes and explaining the content of the final opinions on which the justices are casting their final votes.

Let us consider in greater detail these two problems with Schubert's work.

AN EMPHASIS ON A MODEL OF MEASUREMENT

One key piece of evidence about Schubert's major concerns comes from his own reflections on the intellectual origins of his work:

There are three principal sources that have functioned as the well-springs for my own work, both theoretical and methodological, in this book. These persons upon whose earlier theoretical work I have relied are all social psychologists who have made major contributions to the field of attitude measurement: Louis L. Thurstone, who pioneered in the development of multiple factor analysis; Clyde H. Coombs, whose work in the theory of data and nonmetric factor analysis was critical to my own thinking about the possibility of combining multiple factor analysis and multidimensional cumulative scaling in a composite model; and Louis Guttman, whose work in the theory of linear cumulative scaling and in the principal and elementary components of cumulative scales is of fundamental importance to both the theory underlying my model, and its empirical validation. (1965, 22)

Thus, the origins of Schubert's model of measurement lie in the work of social psychologists whose major theoretical contributions were, as Schubert himself put it, in "the field of attitude measurement." That is, these scholars were primarily interested in developing techniques for analyzing data on choices that had already been made. Notice that Schubert was not citing as influential the work of any psychologists, or other social scientists, whose major theoretical contributions were to the theory of how individuals or groups make choices in the first place.

An additional piece of evidence that Schubert was not emphasizing the development and testing of any particular theory of choice comes from his own comments on the uses of his model of measurement. For example, he stated that in his book, "I shall attempt to provide a substantive interpretation of the major trends in the Court's policy-making during the past seventeen terms, on the basis of measurements of aggregate data relating primarily to the manifest voting behavior and inferred political attitudes of the justices" (1965, 10). This passage, along with the overall composition of his book, clearly suggest that Schubert's enterprise was fundamentally an inductive one aimed at description: his model of measurement was to be used for finding patterns in the justices' voting behavior, and the patterns he found were intended to help him describe the attitudes of the justices who were voting. We stress again that Schubert put very little emphasis on constructing and justifying a model of individual or group decision-making and then testing it systematically, or even showing how it could be tested.[4]

THE LIMITED USEFULNESS OF THE ATTITUDE-ACTIVATION MODEL

Nonetheless, Schubert's inferences were not taking place in a theoretical vacuum about how actors such as Supreme Court justices make decisions;

as he put it, "I wish to make clear that the kind of psychology that I shall employ is . . . associated with the use of psychometrics in relation to stimulus-response, cognitive and learning theory" (1965, 13). Schubert was thus able to describe his key assumption in the following way: "My view of decisions is that these are the products of sets of judicial attitudes that have been activated by particular stimuli" (1965, 10). Notice that even though Schubert had earlier talked about the "psychology of rationality," his language here is far from any conception of "rational choice" that a justice might make: a justice's decision stems simply from attitudes that have been "activated"—Schubert consistently used this term—by the presence of particular kinds of legal stimuli in a case.

To understand Schubert's model of attitude activation by legal stimuli, it is necessary to understand how this model was constructed and how it worked. We will examine Schubert's model in some detail because, as it turns out, it is the only explicit model of attitude activation that we can find in the judicial politics literature on Supreme Court decision-making. Unfortunately, Schubert's presentation is difficult to understand, in part because of its brevity, but the following is our best effort at developing an understanding. Our central argument is that Schubert's model has very limited usefulness for clarifying the nature of Supreme Court decision-making.

For our purposes, the most critical part of Schubert's analysis presents ideas that he attributed to Coombs (1964). In Schubert's interpretation (1965, 27), how a justice responds to some level of a legal stimulus in a case depends on the location of the justice's "ideal point." One definition of a justice's ideal point that Schubert used is that it is "the position with which he identifies himself—where he perceives himself to be located" on the issue dimensions that have been identified (1965, 27). Schubert then noted that the justice's ideal point and the case's level of legal stimulus can both be measured on a common space; as he put it, "Defining the subscript i as the generic category for an individual's ideal point, and j as the corresponding category for stimulus-points, Coombs then defines a *joint* genotypic space as one which includes sets of both i- and j-points."

What this approach then implies is that an "attitude" is a function of the relationship between the location of the ideal point and the location of the stimulus on the common dimension. However, the specific nature of an "attitude" depends on what particular model of choice a justice is assumed to be using, and Schubert discussed two different variations of a model of choice; both are from Coombs (1964). One variant, to which Schubert devoted very little attention, is referred to as the "proximity model"; the other model is referred to as the "ordinal model." To use Schubert's own descriptions here:

FIGURE 3.1

Justices and Case Stimuli in a Unidimensional Space

According to the proximity model, the individual accepts (responds positively to) all stimuli whose *j*-points he perceives as being located within a critical distance from his own *i*-point (*i.e.,* the position with which he identifies himself—where he perceives himself to be located in the space); and he rejects (responds negatively to) all other stimuli that he perceives to be located elsewhere in the same space. According to the ordinal model, however, both the *i*-point and the *j*-point are compared in relation to the directionality of the dimensions which define the space: the individual responds positively if his own position equals or exceeds that of the stimulus, and otherwise he responds negatively. (Schubert 1965, 27–28)

To illustrate these two variants of Schubert's model of choice, let us begin with the proximity model. Consider a line representing a measure of how much of some stimulus is present in a legal case; see Figure 3.1.[5] Each legal case exhibits, or is characterized by, some amount of this stimulus, and for any particular category of cases (such as civil rights or civil liberties), the possible cases in this category can be ordered from left to right on the basis of how much of the stimulus is present. In the diagram here, cases toward the left have less of the stimulus than do cases to their right. The different points on the line, with the differing levels of the stimulus, are the "*j*-points"; thus, the case at point j_1 has less of the stimulus than the case at point j_2.

A diagram of the proximity model can now be presented; see Figure 3.2. Each point on the horizontal axis represents a stimulus level on the issue dimension, as in Figure 3.1, while the vertical axis represents the justice's responses to cases with varying stimulus levels. We also draw what we will call a "response function" that graphically summarizes what Schubert said about how a justice would respond to the varying levels of the stimulus. In the diagram in Figure 3.2, the "ideal point" of Justice 1 is at i_1. Hence, in this diagram, for a case with a stimulus level such as j_1 or j_3, the justice will treat it as falling in the negative (and thus "unacceptable") region, but for a case with a stimulus level such as j_2, Justice 1 will treat it as falling in the positive (and thus "acceptable") region.

However, Schubert only briefly discussed this proximity model. His major reason seems to have been that it is incompatible with the kind of multidimensional scaling methods that he wanted to apply to Supreme

FIGURE 3.2

Justice 1's "Ideal Point" and Case Stimuli in a Unidimensional Issue Space,
with a "Response Function" Based on Schubert's Proximity Model

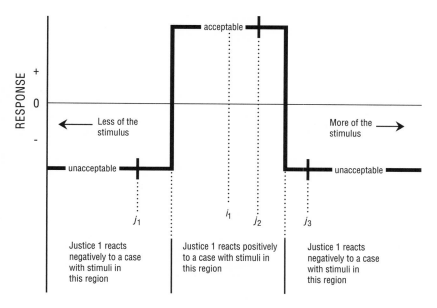

Court voting data; as he put it, it is the ordinal model "that is pertinent to measurement relationships in factor analysis and in cumulative scaling" (1965, 28). In other words, this appears to be an instance in which a scholar selected a theory of choice for reasons stemming from his preferred theory of measurement; it does not seem that Schubert was selecting a theory of measurement for reasons stemming from the characteristics of some preferred theory of choice. (Recall our discussion of these matters in Distinction 3 in Chapter 2.)[6]

Next consider Schubert's ordinal model, as depicted in Figure 3.3. The horizontal and vertical axes are as in Figure 3.2, but the response functions that we draw to summarize what Schubert said about the justices' behavior now have a different shape. For example, Justice 1, who has an ideal point at i_1, would respond negatively to (and thus find "unacceptable") any case with less of the stimulus than at i_1, but would respond positively to (and thus find "acceptable") any case with a stimulus level greater than i_1. Thus, Justice 1 would not uphold a case with the stimulus level at j_1 but would uphold cases with stimulus levels at j_2, j_3, or j_4. Justice 2, with an ideal point at i_2, would respond negatively to (and thus find "unacceptable") any case with

FIGURE 3.3

Three Justices and Case Stimuli in a Unidimensional Issue Space, with "Response Functions" Based on Schubert's Ordinal Model

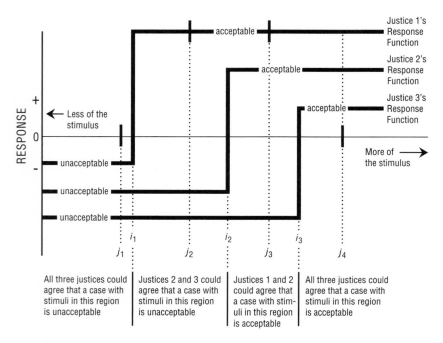

All three justices could agree that a case with stimuli in this region is unacceptable	Justices 2 and 3 could agree that a case with stimuli in this region is unacceptable	Justices 1 and 2 could agree that a case with stimuli in this region is acceptable	All three justices could agree that a case with stimuli in this region is acceptable

less of the stimulus than at i_2, but would respond positively to (and thus find "acceptable") any case with a stimulus level greater than i_2. Thus, Justice 2 would not uphold cases with stimulus levels at j_1 or j_2 but would uphold cases with stimulus levels at j_3 or j_4. Finally, Justice 3, with an ideal point at i_3, would respond negatively to (and thus find "unacceptable") any case with less of the stimulus than at i_3, but would respond positively to (and thus find "acceptable") any case with a stimulus level greater than i_3. Thus, Justice 3 would not uphold cases with stimulus levels at $j_1, j_2,$ or j_3 but would uphold cases with the stimulus level at j_4.

Now the key question is: does this depiction of individual decision-making constitute an adequate model of how a Supreme Court justice might make a decision on a case? We argue that Schubert's ordinal model, which provides the foundation for much of the multidimensional scaling in his book, has at best only a limited range of usefulness for the study of Supreme Court decision-making. We have four reasons for making this judgment.

What Determines a Case's Stimulus Level?

For our first reason, we begin by noting that although we have used phrases such as "respond positively to (and thus find 'acceptable') any case with a stimulus level of i_1 or more," just what it is about a case that exhibits the indicated amount of the stimulus is not clear. Schubert did say that "The cases on the Court's dockets are conceptualized as complex stimuli, which (in effect) ask questions about issues to which the justices are asked to respond" (1965, 37). But just what aspects of a case are the justices being asked about? After all, a "case" for the Supreme Court always has two sides—a plaintiff's arguments and a defendant's arguments—plus there will be a ruling by some lower court, and perhaps some amicus briefs as well. So which of these represents the case's "stimulus level" here? Or is the case's "stimulus level" some kind of aggregate of all of these? Schubert's book does not provide a clear answer.

Can Schubert's Model Predict the Content of the Final Opinion?

Our second reason for thinking that Schubert's model has a limited usefulness involves what we consider to be the clearest and most plausible way of identifying a stimulus level for a case. In this interpretation, a case's stimulus level stems from the lower court's ruling, which endorsed some level of the stimulus as legally acceptable. Given a lower-court ruling that endorsed some level of the stimulus as legally acceptable, a Supreme Court justice might then respond by considering this level of the stimulus to be either acceptable or unacceptable; if the level is acceptable, the justice would vote to affirm the lower-court ruling, whereas if the level is unacceptable, the justice would vote to reverse the ruling. This interpretation might provide a coherent way of integrating lower-court rulings, positive and negative responses to different stimulus levels, acceptable-vs.-unacceptable judgments, and affirm-vs.-reverse decisions on lower-court rulings within the context of Schubert's ordinal model.

However, even this interpretation of Schubert's model has only a limited usefulness because the model does not appear capable of explaining the choice of the *content* of the final opinion (see our discussion of Distinction 4 in Chapter 2). Of course, there is one simple sense in which Schubert's model could be seen as explaining the choice of the content of the final opinion: by affirming some lower-court ruling, the Supreme Court could be interpreted as adopting that ruling as its own general policy. However, this interpretation is not entirely satisfactory. The reason is that the Court does not generally just endorse or reject the lower-court's ruling on a case; instead, the justices are voting on a policy proposal crafted by one of their own fellow justices, and this proposal is not necessarily limited just to affirming or reversing some lower-court ruling. Unfortunately, it does not appear that Schubert's ordinal model of choice can explain how justices might behave in this less-constrained choice situation.

To illustrate this problem, consider Figure 3.3 again. Assume that some lower-court ruling states that a stimulus level at j_3 or above should be legally acceptable. Because a policy at j_3 or above is acceptable to Justices 1 and 2 but unacceptable to Justice 3, we might expect that a majority opinion endorsing the lower-court ruling would be adopted; the Court majority would thus be adopting a policy that says that a stimulus level at j_3 or above is legally acceptable. However, note that there are stimulus levels lying between i_2 and j_3 that would also be acceptable to Justices 1 and 2. That is, these two justices could, in principle, endorse a policy that stated that stimulus levels above i_2 are legally permissible; this alternative policy would include (but not be restricted to) the lower court's ruling that any stimulus level at j_3 or above is acceptable. In fact, because a policy lying anywhere between i_2 and j_3 is closer to both the i_1 and i_2 ideal points, there may be some reason to think that Justices J_1 and J_2 would prefer such an alternative policy to the policy at j_3. However, Schubert's ordinal model does not provide any mechanism by which these stimulus levels between i_2 and j_3 could somehow be included in the final ruling: given the justices' ideal points, his model seems to be driven entirely by the stimulus level—for example, at j_3—of the case under consideration. Hence, it is not clear that Schubert's model would accurately predict what policies real-world justices would actually select in this case.

We conclude that although Schubert's ordinal model may be able to generate an affirm-vs.-reverse response to the lower-court ruling, it does not seem able to identify any alternative policy some of the justices might plausibly wish to adopt. Nor does his model provide any mechanism by which such an alternative policy could be selected by the Court.[7]

Is the Status Quo Policy Irrelevant?

Our third reason for judging Schubert's ordinal model to be inadequate involves what the justices would do regarding a level of stimulus in a lower-court ruling that would normally lead the justices to reverse the ruling as "unacceptable." Consider the possibility that this lower-court ruling, although in principle "unacceptable" to a majority of the justices, might nonetheless be considered a better policy by a majority of the justices than some status quo policy that the lower-court ruling is overturning. Unfortunately, Schubert's model appears to treat the stimulus levels in a case merely as "acceptable" or "unacceptable" and does not allow a justice to make judgments like, "This lower-court ruling is far from ideal, but it is nonetheless an improvement over the policy that was previously in place."

That is, his model of choice does not allow for the possibility that some justices might want to adopt some new policy (as represented by the lower-court ruling in the case) simply because this new policy is better than the status quo policy. In fact, the status quo policy, although presumably critical to any kind of policy-oriented decision-making, plays no role at all in Schubert's model.

Do the Justices Not Interact with Each Other?

Our fourth reason for judging Schubert's ordinal model to be inadequate is that there is nothing in the model that says anything whatsoever about how the justices might interact with each other in order to produce a final opinion. In fact, the implicit assumption is apparently that what one justice chooses to do, at any stage of the decision-making process (certainly including the stages involving coalition formation and the final vote), has no relevance at all for what the other justices do, or what the Court collectively does. In effect, "Supreme Court" decisions are simply the aggregate of what the individual justices independently choose to do; there are no interactions among the justices. If there is good reason to think that the justices do, in fact, interact with each other, including at the final stages involving coalition formation and the final vote, then Schubert's model is fundamentally incomplete.

SUMMARY

For these reasons, then, we conclude that Schubert's ordinal model of choice is not an adequate model of the logic by which an individual justice makes a policy-related choice (whether just on affirm-vs.-reverse decisions or on the content of the final opinion). And his model certainly does not adequately characterize policy choice by the Supreme Court as a collective body.

The Attitudinal Model

Many of these themes from the early literature were combined into what has become known as "the attitudinal model," as developed by Harold Spaeth and his associates over the past three decades (see, e.g., Rohde and Spaeth 1976; Spaeth 1979; and especially Segal and Spaeth 1993, 2002). The attitudinal model has become the most widely recognized and influential representation of decision-making on the Supreme Court, and little can be published without citing at least some of the arguments by Spaeth and associates. In this section, we will describe the attitudinal model. Then, in the following two sections, we will examine its conceptual foundations.

The central argument of the attitudinal model is that the personal views of the justices—that is, their attitudes or policy preferences—have a dominant impact on the justices' decisions and choices. As Segal and Spaeth (2002, 86) described this argument: "This model holds that the Supreme Court decides disputes in light of the facts of the case vis-à-vis the ideological attitudes and values of the justices. Simply put, Rehnquist votes the way he does because he is extremely conservative; Marshall voted the way he did because he was extremely liberal."

This argument has been used for descriptive, explanatory, and predictive purposes involving Supreme Court decision-making. For descriptive purposes, the attitudinal model is a set of statistical procedures, primarily involving a variety of multidimensional scaling techniques, used for telling us how many issue dimensions characterize Supreme Court decision-making. One result (see, e.g., Rohde and Spaeth 1976, chap. 6) is that several dozen different scales have been distinguished; they organize Court decision-making into a large number of narrow and issue-specific dimensions. Efforts have also been made to determine whether these numerous but narrow issue-specific scales actually represent some smaller number of broader and more fundamental issue dimensions. The major argument here (see, e.g., Rohde and Spaeth 1976, 138) has been that most cases involve one of three major values: one called "Freedom," one called "Equality," and one sometimes called "New Dealism" (which is a set of values involving the public regulation of private economic activities). On each of these scales, "liberal" justices could be distinguished from "moderate" and "conservative" justices. The fact that the scales and dimensions could be reliably generated from the justices' numerous votes on the Supreme Court is taken as an indication that the justices' liberal-vs.-conservative values organize many of these issue areas.

For explanatory purposes, these clustering and scaling techniques have also been used to tell us how well the issue dimensions that are found actually account for the Court's final decisions. In Rohde and Spaeth (1976, 137–38), for example, it was reported that the three major dimensions—Freedom, Equality, and New Dealism—collectively "explain more than 85 percent of the Court's decisions during both the Warren and Burger Court periods." A similar figure was reported in Spaeth (1979, 132). In addition, various statistical procedures have been used to generate scale scores for individual justices on the various dimensions (see, e.g., Segal and Spaeth 1993, tables 6.6–6.8). These scale scores have then been used in empirical studies as indicators of each justice's liberalism or conservatism. The results often appeared to show that each justice's liberalism or conservatism has a substantial impact on his or her behavior on the Court.

Finally, for predictive purposes there have been two different kinds of activities. One is that the scale scores for the individual justices—how liberal or conservative they are—have been used to "postdict" (our term) how the individual justices voted on some past case; the other is that the scale scores have been used to predict how the justices will vote on some upcoming case. The postdiction exercise began with the empirical observation that some lineup of justices had already occurred on a particular case—9–0, 8–1, 7–2, 6–3, or 5–4. The goal was to predict who voted with whom, given the lineup that had already occurred (see, e.g., Segal and Spaeth 1993, 222–23). For example, given the empirical observation of a 6-to-3 lineup in a particular case, the desire was to predict who the six justices in the majority were and who the other three justices in the minority were. These predictions came directly from scores previously derived for the justices on the relevant issue-specific scale: if the six-person majority was on the "conservative" side of an issue, the prediction of who voted with the majority was made by counting (from the "right," as it were) the six justices with the most conservative scale scores, whereas the remaining three justices (on the "left") were predicted to be those who voted with the minority.

The other enterprise involved predicting not only who would be in the affirm and reverse blocs but also the sizes of these affirm and reverse blocs. The procedures involved were described at length in Rohde and Spaeth (1976, 145–55) and Spaeth (1979, chap. 6); they are too complex to be described here. In effect, though, the individual justices' scale scores were combined with the basic facts of each case in a way that generated a prediction of whether each justice would vote to affirm or reverse the lower court's ruling.

Conceptual Problems with the Attitudinal Model

Despite the attitudinal model's central place in the literature on Supreme Court decision-making, it is not immune to criticism. In particular, we will identify what we consider to be some fundamental conceptual problems with the attitudinal model, especially with the description advanced by Jeffrey Segal and Harold Spaeth.

It is important to recognize that two editions of Segal and Spaeth's key work have now been published: *The Supreme Court and the Attitudinal Model* (1993) and *The Supreme Court and the Attitudinal Model Revisited* (2002). The 1993 edition has the more thorough presentation of the attitude-activation version of the attitudinal model. The 2002 edition has the more thorough presentation of the rational-choice version of the attitudinal model, and the attitude-activation version gets less attention than it did previously. However, it is also important to understand that the decreased emphasis on the attitude-activation version of the attitudinal model in the 2002 edition is not accompanied by any criticism of that version. For this reason, we believe it

is legitimate to closely analyze the 1993 edition's presentation of the attitude-activation version of the attitudinal model.

We might also note that although the 2002 edition gives much greater
emphasis to the rational-choice version of the attitudinal model, most of this
emphasis is placed on the rational-choice models involving the Supreme
Court's external relationships with Congress and the president (see, e.g.,
Marks 1988; Gely and Spiller 1990). In contrast, this second edition gives little emphasis to rational-choice models of the Court's internal decision-making processes, which is our focus in this book. Segal and Spaeth's rationale is
that these internal models (unlike the separation-of-powers models) have
not been empirically tested as much; see Segal and Spaeth (2002, 102–3).

With this background, we now turn to our analysis of the attitudinal
model. We identify four significant conceptual problems with the model.

HOW CONSISTENT ARE THE ATTITUDINAL MODEL'S ASSUMPTIONS?

The first conceptual problem with the attitudinal model stems from our
argument in Chapter 2 that the fundamental assumptions of a theory should
be coherent and consistent. That is, they must plausibly be seen as belong-
ing together (for example, they all have their origins in the same metaphor);
they should involve concepts that are related to each other in some identi-
fiable fashion; they should fit together in a sensible way; the style of thinking in the theory—that is, the kind of "logic" that it utilizes—should be
used consistently throughout all parts of the theory; and the grounds on
which the theory's claims and arguments are justified should not shift from
one part of the theory to another. Given this general perspective, it is important to note that Segal and Spaeth (1993, 33) claimed that their attitudinal
model "rests on a common set of assumptions."

Nonetheless, our discussion of Distinction 1 in Chapter 2 leads us to a
critical question: is the attitudinal model based on a psychological metaphor
involving justices' attitudes whose expression is activated by the stimuli of legal objects and legal situations, or is the attitudinal model based on a rational-choice metaphor involving justices who make choices that are intended to maximize the achievement of their personal policy goals?
According to Segal and Spaeth (1993), the answer seems to be that the attitudinal model is somehow based on both metaphors.

The key pages in Segal and Spaeth (1993) are pages 67–69; they contain
Segal and Spaeth's own literature review regarding the behavioral tradition
in judicial politics, primarily beginning with Pritchett but then considering
Schubert's work in some detail. Segal and Spaeth presented a diagram (see
their figure 2.1 on page 68) characterizing in graphical terms some key as-

pects of Schubert's model, and here they advanced (68) a minor criticism of Schubert's ordinal model, arguing that its "ideal points" (the *i*-points) could more accurately be referred to as "indifference points." Their criticisms of Schubert's model, however, extended no further than this terminological issue. In fact, once Segal and Spaeth made their observation about "indifference points," they immediately proceeded to say, in the next paragraph, that "David Rohde and Harold Spaeth provided an alternative approach to Schubert's attitudinal model" (1993, 68), thereby leaving it unclear whether Rohde and Spaeth (1976), and, later, Segal and Spaeth (1993), were accepting, rejecting, or simply modifying Schubert's model as a foundation for their own work.

What Segal and Spaeth described as "an alternative approach" incorporated material from Rohde and Spaeth (1976). Segal and Spaeth quoted from that earlier book: "the primary goals of Supreme Court justices in the decision-making process are *policy goals*. Each member of the Court has preferences concerning the policy questions faced by the Court, and when the justices make decisions they want the outcomes to approximate as nearly as possible those policy preferences" (Segal and Spaeth 1993, 68–69; originally from Rohde and Spaeth 1976, 72, emphasis in original). This passage appears to be a straightforward introduction to the rational-choice approach and so would seem to be unrelated to attitude-activation theories. But then Segal and Spaeth immediately followed with this next passage (1993, 69):

Central to the Rohde and Spaeth model is the construct of attitudes. Quoting psychologist Milton Rokeach, they define an attitude as a (1) relatively enduring, (2) organization of interrelated beliefs that describe, evaluate and advocate action with respect to an object or situation, (3) with each belief having cognitive, affective, and behavioral components. (4) Each one of these beliefs is a predisposition that, when suitably activated, results in some preference response for the attitude object or situation, or toward the maintenance or preservation of the attitude itself. (5) Since an attitude object must always be encountered within some situation about which we also have an attitude, a minimum condition for social behavior is the activation of at least two interacting attitudes, one concerning the attitude object and the other concerning the situation.

The problem, in our view, is that these two passages—one from Rohde and Spaeth (1976) and the other from Rokeach (1968)—represent fundamentally different metaphors. The metaphor in the first Rohde-Spaeth passage explicitly treats a justice's decisions as involving the pursuit of policy goals. In this conception, each justice has a policy goal, and the justice makes those decisions that would maximize achievement of this goal. Clearly, this metaphor is one of rational, calculated choice aimed at getting some particular policy adopted. In contrast, the psychological metaphor, as represented by the second passage, from Rokeach (1968), treats a justice's decisions as representing attitudes that are activated by particular kinds of stimuli. (Notice that Rokeach, like Schubert, explicitly refers to attitudes that are "activated.") That is, if particular kinds of stimuli are presented to the justice, the stimuli will activate a particular attitude in the justice, and although the passage is not entirely clear on this, it appears that some kind of predictable behavior by the justice will be the automatic result.

However, consider two aspects of this psychological conceptualization of a justice's decision. First, nothing in the passage from Rokeach posits what we would normally refer to as the justice's "policy goal"; for example, what is it that the justice is trying to "achieve" or to "gain"? The answer is not clear: the justice's "social behavior" here (this is Rokeach's term from the passage quoted above) looks more like the expression of an attitude—a "preference response for the attitude object," as Rokeach put it—rather than any kind of choice. Second, there seems to be no element of calculation in the justices' selection of behavior, and there is certainly nothing that looks remotely like strategizing by the justice (as in, "If I do this, and the other justices do that, and then I do this in response, then what would the final outcome be?"). Instead, it seems that the behavior (such as voting in a particular way) simply follows automatically when a particular attitude is triggered by some stimulus.[8]

Adding to our difficulty in understanding this psychological conceptualization of a justice's decision is the fact that Segal and Spaeth clearly suggest that they have two different attitudinal theories in mind. In particular, they ended their literature review with the following passage:

Against the legal model we present the attitudinal model, which holds that justices make decisions by considering the facts of the case in light of their ideological attitudes and values. The attitudinal model emanated from the criticisms of the classical legal model made by the legal realists in the 1920s. The behavioral school of political science that began to flower in the 1950s and continues to bloom today brought it to fruition. We presented two variants of the attitudinal model—one by Glendon Schubert, who based his work on the spatial theories of Clyde Coombs, and the other by David Rohde and Harold Spaeth, who based their work on the psychological theories of Milton Rokeach. (1993, 73)

This passage leaves us quite uncertain as to what is thought to be driving the justices' behavior in the attitudinal model, and nowhere else in Segal and Spaeth (1993) are these conceptual matters discussed any further. So is Supreme Court decision-making characterized by the rational calculation of which option maximizes the achievement of personal policy goals? This is what seems to be implied by the basic approach in Rohde and Spaeth (1976). Or is Supreme Court decision-making characterized by the psychological t a content.

activation and expression of attitudes? And if it is the latter, which of the "two variants of the attitudinal model"—one based on Schubert, the other on Rokeach—forms the core of the attitudinal model? Because Segal and Spaeth provided no answers to these questions, and because we are unable to answer these questions ourselves, we are reluctant to agree with Segal and Spaeth's claim (1993, 33) that their attitudinal model of Supreme Court decision-making "rests on a common set of assumptions."

As already noted, Segal and Spaeth gave much less emphasis to these attitude-activation arguments in the 2002 edition of their book. Nonetheless, they still made explicit reference (2002, 89–91) to the attitude-activation theories of Schubert and Rokeach. Indeed, Segal and Spaeth (2002, 86) specifically stated that "The attitudinal model represents a melding together of key concepts from legal realism, political science, psychology, and economics." Unfortunately, however, the characteristics of this "melding together" remain largely unspecified.

Furthermore, in the 2002 edition, Segal and Spaeth even classified these various approaches in ways we have difficulty understanding. For example, their chapter 3, titled "Models of Decision Making: The Attitudinal and Rational Choice Models," included separate sections on "The Attitudinal Model" and "The Rational Choice Model." But inside the section on "The Attitudinal Model" was a subsection that Segal and Spaeth (2002, 92) labeled "The Economics Influence," and they illustrated this influence by reference to Rohde and Spaeth (1976), whose overall organizing approach, as Segal and Spaeth themselves clearly stated, is based on rational-choice theory. The puzzle is why this subsection on "The Economics Influence" did not appear instead in the subsequent section titled "The Rational Choice Model" (2002, 97–110); after all, what is central to the economic style of thinking, and to the influence of economics on the other social sciences, is the rational-choice approach.

In sum, it appears to us that the basic conceptual problems with "the attitudinal model"—is it based on a rational-choice theory or some kind of attitude-activation theory?—have not been resolved in the 2002 edition.

Nonetheless, we are not asserting that rational-choice and various kinds of psychological perspectives on decision-making are inherently incompatible with each other. On the contrary, in the past two decades, there has been considerable research on psychologically sophisticated theories of rational choice, although much controversy continues about the most appropriate perspectives (see, e.g., Hogarth and Reder 1987 and Dawes 1998). But this blending of psychology and rational choice must be done with care, and as far as we can determine, the psychological metaphor and the rational-choice metaphor simply sit side by side in various pieces of the attitudinalist Supreme Court literature without the reader being shown how the two metaphors can be integrated or reconciled and thereby turned into a single coherent theory.[9]

The second conceptual problem with the attitudinal model involves what it does and does not do. Recall from Chapter 2 our Distinction 4 between a justice's final vote and the content of the final opinion. Interestingly, this is a distinction on which Segal and Spaeth (1993, 261) themselves placed considerable emphasis:

> The decision on the merits merely indicates whether the ruling of the court whose decision the Supreme Court reviewed is affirmed or reversed and, consequently, which party has won and which has lost. The opinion of the Court, by comparison, constitutes the core of the Court's policy-making process. It specifies the constitutional and legal principles on which the majority rests its decision, it guides the lower courts in deciding future cases, and it establishes precedents for the Court's own subsequent rulings—even if such decisions and their supporting opinions can be overturned by future Supreme Courts.

Thus, it is the content of the opinion, as Segal and Spaeth asserted here, that "constitutes the core of the Court's policy-making process." Moreover, they had earlier emphasized that the justices are free to write almost any opinion they want: because of the lack of institutional constraints on the Court, Segal and Spaeth suggested, "the justices . . . may freely implement their personal policy preferences as the attitudinal model specifies" (1993, 73).

However, except insofar as a Supreme Court decision affirms some lower-court ruling and thereby endorses something about that ruling's content, to our knowledge the attitudinal model has never been used to predict the content of "the opinion of the Court" on which the justices are casting their final votes. Through the use of multidimensional scaling procedures, scale scores have been generated for use in testing hypotheses about how the individual justices will vote on some final opinion. But in general, the attitudinal model seems to be only a way of explaining the justices' votes on that final opinion; it has not been used to explain the content of the final opinion itself.

We conclude, then, that the attitudinal literature has not been entirely consistent about what the purposes of the attitudinal model are said to be on the one hand, and what its features and capabilities actually are on the other. As we just noted, Segal and Spaeth emphasized the importance of the content of the final opinion, and they also emphasized that the justices are free to write almost any opinion they want. But one of the theories that was then adopted—the attitude-activation theory—is ill-suited to the general features of Supreme Court decision-making, involving endogenous agenda-setting by the justices and great freedom of choice on their part, whose importance Segal and Spaeth themselves have highlighted.

In contrast, the rational-choice version of the attitudinal model provides a far better fit to the general context and setting that Segal and Spaeth have highlighted because it easily accommodates the kinds of freedoms that Segal and Spaeth said the justices enjoy. Unfortunately, however, Segal and Spaeth left the rational-choice model, as an explanation of the Court's internal decision-making processes, rather undeveloped. In Part II of our book, we will show how the rational-choice model can be used to predict not only how the individual justices will vote on the final opinion but also what the content of the final opinion will be.

EXPLAINING THE FINAL VOTES VS. EXPLAINING
BEHAVIOR AT EARLIER STAGES

The third conceptual problem with the attitudinal model is that, in focusing primarily on the final vote, it fails to incorporate, in any clear fashion, the earlier stages of the Court's decision-making process. Although it is true that the final vote determines which of the many possible opinions will be selected as the Court's majority opinion in a case, the menu of opinions under consideration on the final vote is shaped by decisions made at the earlier stages of the decision-making process. Thus, an account that examines only the final vote leaves the reader with an incomplete understanding of the Court's full decision-making process.

This criticism raises a question as to whether the attitudinal model is in fact relevant only to the final vote or whether it applies equally well to the earlier stages of the Court's decision-making process. Some literature has argued that the attitudinal model is relevant only to the final vote. For example, Epstein and Knight commented that the attitudinal model, "at least according to its most important contemporary advocates (Jeffrey A. Segal and Harold J. Spaeth), *is designed to explain only voting behavior*" (1998, xii, footnote b, emphasis in original). In fact, Epstein and Knight even remarked that "according to . . . correspondence from Segal," the attitudinal model "does not attempt to explain choices other than the vote on the merits of cases" (1998, 57, footnote a).

It is clear that the attitudinal model was initially created as an effort at explaining the justices' final votes. And certainly much of the research by Spaeth and associates has, over the years, retained a focus on explaining these final votes. On the other hand, Segal and Spaeth (1993) did evaluate the literatures on certiorari, the conference vote, opinion assignment, and coalition formation (see their chapters 5, 6, and 7) in order to demonstrate that the attitudinal model could help explain the justices' behavior at these earlier stages as well. Moreover, Segal and Spaeth also subsequently emphasized that although "the attitudinal model is a complete and adequate *model of the Supreme Court's decisions on the merits*" (that is, the final votes), they went on to say that "We do believe that the attitudinal model has *implications* for cert votes, for opinion assignment, and for the behavior of lower court judges" (1994, 11, emphasis in original). The 2002 edition also explicitly provided attitudinal (in our view, rational-choice) interpretations of these earlier stages of Supreme Court decision-making (see, e.g., Segal and Spaeth 2002, chap. 6–9).

This debate over the intended scope of application for the attitudinal model thus seems to hinge on what one has in mind when the term "the attitudinal model" is used. Epstein and Knight appear to have had a narrow definition in mind, and on this basis criticize Segal and Spaeth's work as too limited. In contrast, Segal and Spaeth themselves appear to have had a broader definition in mind in their 1994 remarks, and on this basis see a broad potential scope of application for their work (as their 1993 and 2002 editions both illustrate).

However, even though Segal and Spaeth identified the attitudinal model's potential scope of application as including the earlier stages of decision-making, they did not fully work out the logic of how the justices' policy preferences should be expected to affect the justices' choices at these earlier stages. Indeed, we might point out that even if the attitude-activation version of the attitudinal model were considered an adequate representation of decision-making on the final vote, it is completely unclear how the justices' decisions that must be made at the earlier stages of the decision-making process could be derived from the process of attitude activation by legal stimuli.

Moreover, as we argued in our discussion of Distinction 5 in Chapter 2 (on the final vote versus explanations of earlier stages of decision-making), if decision-making at the earlier stages affects the content of the draft majority opinion that is available for consideration on the final vote, this implies that how a justice casts his vote at the final stage will be influenced by the prior agenda-setting process. For this reason, we would argue that it is not sufficient for Segal and Spaeth to have said merely that the attitudinal model "has implications for" the justices' behavior at the earlier stages (1994, 11). Instead, because the final votes the justices cast clearly depend on what options are available, we would argue that an adequate model of the voting process at the final stage requires a fully worked-out model of the decision-making process at the earlier stages.

Hence, we must conclude that the attitudinal model is fundamentally incomplete: it cannot be considered a satisfactory explanation of the justices' final votes because it does not take into account what has happened at the earlier stages. In fact, because the final votes depend so critically on what options the earlier stages provided for the final vote, it may be that the final votes that are empirically observed may actually be misleading indicators of the justices' true preferences, as we remarked in our discussion of Distinction 5 in Chapter 2.

DOES THE ATTITUDINAL MODEL IMPLY STRATEGIC BEHAVIOR?

The fourth conceptual problem with the attitudinal model involves whether it adequately allows for the possibility that the justices are behaving in a strategic manner. In particular, there has been a debate, as noted in our discussion of Distinction 6 in Chapter 2, as to whether strategic considerations need to be taken into account in explaining the justices' final votes.

There is unambiguous textual evidence in Segal and Spaeth (1993) that the authors thought that strategic considerations would not enter into the justices' final decisions. In fact, Segal and Spaeth (1993, 73) explicitly argued that there are several significant reasons why justices need not behave strategically in their final votes: "Because legal rules governing decision making (e.g., precedent, plain meaning) in the type of cases that come to Court do not limit discretion; because the justices need not respond to public opinion, Congress, or the President; and because the Supreme Court is the court of last resort, the justices, unlike their lower court colleagues, may freely implement their personal policy preferences as the attitudinal model specifies." We would also add that if a justice is seen as facing a choice on the final vote between just two basic options (to affirm the lower-court ruling or to reverse this ruling), the justice will have no strategic calculation to make; instead, the justice should simply endorse the option—to affirm or to reverse—that he or she prefers. In this case, as we emphasized in our discussion of Distinction 6 in Chapter 2, strategic and nonstrategic rationality would both predict the same behavior by the justices on their final votes.

That Segal and Spaeth indeed saw strategic factors as irrelevant to the justices' final votes gains further support from assessments by Baum (1997) and Epstein and Knight (1998). In Baum's view, Segal and Spaeth's attitudinal model presumes that "justices act only on their interest in the content of legal policy, they seek to achieve good policy rather than good law, and their votes on case outcomes are direct expressions of their preferences rather than deviating from those preferences for strategic reasons" (1997, 25). And Epstein and Knight (1998) have likewise described what they perceived to be Segal and Spaeth's view that strategic considerations play no role in the attitudinal model. For example, they remarked that "The 'attitudinal model'— and not theories grounded in assumptions of strategic rationality—dominates the study of judicial politics" (1998, xii). They also reported that according to correspondence from Segal, the attitudinal model "does not contemplate strategic interaction over votes" (1998, 57, footnote a).

However, there are several reasons why strategic considerations should be expected to affect the justices' final votes. The first reason is that, as we noted in our discussion of Distinction 6 in Chapter 2, it has been mathematically demonstrated that as long as three or more options are on the menu, every voting rule is subject to strategic manipulation by the voters. We illustrated this point in Chapter 2 with an example in which a justice would benefit by strategic behavior on the final vote. The key to the illustration is that there were three options, and we argued that on every final vote in the Supreme Court, a justice who is not writing the majority opinion will always be able to choose from among at least three basic options: to write his or her own opinion (for example, a special concurrence), to join the majority opinion, and to write (or join) a dissenting opinion. Hence, there should be no doubt that these mathematical results are entirely relevant to the justices' final votes: there always exist conditions under which at least one justice will benefit from voting for something other than his or her most-preferred option.

The second reason is that, as we have already mentioned, strategic considerations should be expected to affect the menu of options that the justices are considering on the final vote. What a justice's final vote involves, of course, is a vote on an opinion—a majority opinion, a special concurrence, a dissenting opinion—written by one or more of the justices. But there is every reason to think that the authors of these opinions have strategically crafted their contents so as to attract the votes of other justices (see, e.g., Epstein and Knight 1998; and Maltzman, Spriggs, and Wahlbeck 2000 for substantial empirical evidence on this). That is, the menu of choices that the justices have available for their final votes is itself the product of strategic calculations in the coalition-formation process. And because different menus of choices might lead to different votes by the justices, it seems difficult to avoid the conclusion (as previously suggested) that the justices' final votes may not be accurate indicators of their true preferences.

The third reason is that, as Murphy remarked in *Elements of Judicial Strategy* about the Supreme Court's relationship with the lower courts, "the Justices rarely make either the first or last decision in a case" (1964, 24). That is, a Supreme Court ruling is always going to be applied and implemented by the lower courts, and whether the lower courts will correctly and faithfully implement the Supreme Court's ruling is a matter about which the Court may be justifiably concerned. In other words, the final ruling is presumably a means to an end (at least in part), and not just the end in itself. Thus, the justices may try to develop some forecasts of how the implementing court will behave, and (strategically) adjust their final votes accordingly.

The fourth reason is that a rational justice may decide to join the majority opinion in one case that is unimportant to him in the hopes that this seemingly "collegial" behavior will be reciprocated in a later case that is more important to him and on which he is the majority opinion writer. More generally, a rational justice might try to maintain a particular kind of reputation (for example, for "reasonableness") so that he will be given an opportunity to influence outcomes in future cases (for example, by being assigned the majority opinion on a case that greatly interests him), even if developing such a reputation means compromising his views on the present case. Thus his vote on the current case may not represent his true policy preferences on that case.

The fifth reason is that, when contemplating the final vote, a justice might be influenced by the fact that if a particular decision is made on a case, then an additional series of cases may be generated which the Court will have to consider in the future and on which decisions may also have to be rendered. If so, then the "final vote" on the present case is obviously not the final vote on the larger issues involved in the case, which means that strategic considerations may come into play on the final vote on the present case. Thus, the strategically rational justice will form some expectations as to what the final decisions will be on those potential future cases, and then cast a vote on the present case in light of the desirability of the results expected on the full sequence of future cases. This means that a justice would not necessarily vote so as to gain her most preferred outcome on the present case if she thinks it might set an undesirable precedent for future cases.

The sixth reason is that Segal and Spaeth (1993, 329–30), their own arguments about nonstrategic voting to the contrary, argued that if the Court is in a potentially threatening situation, as when the president, Congress, and public are likely to be united in opposition to an upcoming Court decision, "the justices tend to arrive at a decision greater than minimum winning in size" (1993, 329); Rohde (1972a) and Rohde and Spaeth (1976, chap. 9) discussed this kind of strategic behavior at greater length. Thus, Segal and Spaeth did acknowledge that, at least on occasion, the justices will behave strategically on the final vote, for external political reasons.

Our conclusion here is that Segal and Spaeth cannot sustain their claim that justices are not strategic on the final vote. There are simply too many reasons to think otherwise.

SUMMARY

We have now completed our analysis of four major conceptual problems with the attitudinal model. Given these conceptual problems, we are inclined to disagree with the assertion that "the attitudinal model is a complete and adequate *model of the Supreme Court's* decisions on the *merits*" (Segal and Spaeth 1994, 11, emphasis in original). At the very least, it is certainly not a complete model because it ignores the justices' strategic concerns on the final vote and because it does not even try to explain the content of the final opinions.

Other Issues Involving the Attitudinal Model

Three additional issues must be clarified in order to gain a satisfactory understanding of the attitudinal model and the debates surrounding it. One issue involves whether justices behave strategically in the earlier stages of Supreme Court decision-making. The second issue involves whether "the attitudinal model" is actually a "model" at all. The third involves whether empirical research by attitudinalist scholars can be considered to be valid, given all the conceptual problems we have identified with their theory.

STRATEGIC BEHAVIOR AT THE EARLIER STAGES OF DECISION-MAKING

Unlike the question of whether justices behave strategically on the final vote, there should be little debate over the question of whether the justices behave strategically at the earlier stages of Supreme Court decision-making. Although some critics have claimed that the attitudinal model does not allow the kind of strategic behavior clearly found in the earlier stages of Court decision-making, there is substantial evidence that Segal and Spaeth (1993) did in fact see strategic factors as playing a role in the earlier stages of a case.

For example, their discussions of the evidence for the attitudinal model in the certiorari decision, in the conference vote, in opinion assignment, and in coalition formation (again, see chapters 5–7 in the 1993 edition, and chapters 6–9 in the 2002 edition) all clearly involve strategic calculations by policy-minded justices. Indeed, as Segal and Spaeth (1994, 11) noted, "Certainly justices engage in strategic behavior in certiorari voting, and just as certainly opinion assigners pay careful attention to ideological proclivities when handing out assignments." And they also went on to say that, "nothing in the attitudinal model, which was developed explicitly to explain the decision on the merits, requires these [attitudinal] factors to be sole explanations of the justices' behavior at other stages."

In sum, it is our view that the debate as to whether the justices' earlier behavior is influenced by strategic considerations should come to an end: both Segal and Spaeth and their critics seem to agree that justices are strategic at the earlier stages of decision-making. Nonetheless, Segal and Spaeth did not provide any kind of carefully specified model of precisely what to expect from the attitudinal model at these earlier stages.

IS "THE ATTITUDINAL MODEL" A MODEL OR A THEORY?

The next issue that must be discussed involves how the attitudinal model should be characterized in the most general of terms: is it actually a model, or is it simply a general theory?

We begin by reiterating the standard scientific distinctions among the terms *theory, model*, and *hypothesis*, which we briefly mentioned in Chapter 1. In general usage, a *theory* is a broad claim about how the world (or, in this case the Supreme Court) works and why it works the way it does; that is, some general kinds of variables are asserted to lead, in predictable sorts of ways, to particular kinds of decisions or outcomes. A *model* is a specific operationalization of a theory; that is, a model takes the variables highlighted by the theory and constructs a series of specific "if . . . then" statements (as implied by the theory) that show that if particular initial conditions hold (that is, if particular values or states of the variables hold), then particular decisions or outcomes are the logical consequence. Finally, a *hypothesis* is a prediction, drawn from one of the "if . . . then" statements in a model, stating that if the initial conditions (as specified by the "if" in the "if . . . then" statement) are empirically observed to hold, then the particular decisions or outcomes (as specified by the "then" in the "if . . . then" statement) should be empirically observed as well; it is this hypothesis that can be empirically tested.

The question we raise is this: is "the attitudinal model" a model in the sense just defined, or is it primarily a theory that has not yet been clearly specified and operationalized in a model? Our own answer to this question is clear and unequivocal: the attitudinal model should not be considered a model at all; instead, it is far more accurate to refer to it as a general theory of decision-making by Supreme Court justices which, aside from Schubert (1965), has never been operationalized in a specific model.

The reason we say this is that neither of the two broad kinds of theories that are said to comprise the attitudinal model—that is, the attitude-activation theories and the rational-choice theory—has been converted, in the judicial politics literature on the Supreme Court, into anything approximating a series of logically constructed and clearly specified "if . . . then" statements about the most important aspects of Supreme Court decision-making. That is, there is little in the attitudinal literature that spells out how, under particular specified conditions (that is, who the justices are and what their views are on a particular case), a particular specified result or set of results (that is, who writes the majority and minority opinions, what the opinions consist of, and who joins or dissents from these opinions) can be logically derived.[10]

We do want to acknowledge that in the early years of the development of the attitudinal model, from the 1950s into the early 1970s, the theories and statistical tools that were available to judicial politics scholars were primarily created by sociologists, psychologists, and psychometricians from the 1930s to the early 1960s; these theories and tools were imported into political science during the heyday of the "behavioral revolution" in the 1950s and 1960s. In contrast, political science did not have a well-developed conceptual technology for constructing rational-choice models of decision-making: the necessary concepts and tools were only being developed in economics in the 1940s (in the work of Black 1948a,b; see his 1958 volume, which incorporates his earlier work) and in the 1950s (in the work of Arrow 1951 and Downs 1957). This kind of work from economics did not even begin to filter into political science until the 1960s (via Riker 1962, for example), and it certainly did not establish a significant presence until the 1970s at the earliest. However, because an extensive set of tools for constructing rational-choice models is now available, students of Supreme Court decision-making should now be able to construct complete and consistent models of choice by strategically rational justices; for one example, see Part II of our book.

RATIONAL-CHOICE RESEARCH BY ATTITUDINALIST SCHOLARS

Despite our conceptual criticisms of the attitudinal model, we suspect that many of the empirical conclusions about Supreme Court behavior by attitudinalist scholars will turn out to be correct. Our reason for this conjecture is that although the attitudinalist scholars have frequently made reference, as we have seen, to attitude-activation theories as a foundation for their own work, what they nonetheless seem to have had in mind when conducting much of their empirical work, especially in recent years, has actually been the rational-choice approach. That is, although these scholars have advanced a variety of arguments that we consider conflicting and confusing regarding what the justices were doing theoretically (for example, the mixing of two incompatible metaphors), what the scholars seem to have done in much of their empirical research was to develop and test a theory derived primarily from just the metaphor involving the rational pursuit of personal policy goals

If this observation is accurate, then it is likely that this empirical work by the attitudinalist scholars can withstand scrutiny from the viewpoint we develop in this book. Indeed, at least some of the propositions derived from our models appear to be rather similar to some of the hypotheses informally developed in a number of empirical studies by attitudinalists. Hence, we think that at least some of the attitudinalists' empirical evidence will turn out to be consistent with our argument that the justices' choices and decisions are motivated by their personal preferences over the legal policies under consideration in a case.

The Literature on Strategically Rational Justices

Although Schubert used game theory in his 1959 book to analyze the relative power of different blocs on the Court, and although Murphy adopted theories of goal-maximizing behavior as the basic metaphor for his 1964 book, it was not until the early 1970s, in the work of David Rohde on coalition formation (Rohde 1972a) and opinion assignment (Rohde 1972b), that the next developments in the rational-choice approach to Supreme Court decision-making were made. In fact, Rohde's work in these two papers can be seen as the first quantitative studies that were based on the premise that justices were strategically rational.

In the first paper, Rohde explicitly assumed (1972a, 209) that "the justices of the Supreme Court are rational decision makers," and here he made reference (1972a, 209, footnote 4) to Luce and Raiffa's *Games and Decisions* (1957), the classic early text on game theory. Rohde also noted explicitly that "we assume that the justices are motivated in their decisions by their own personal preferences about the policy issues that come before the Court for decision. That is, each justice wants to have the policy output of the Court approximate as closely as possible his own position on the issue in question" (1972a, 210). Rohde then used scaling techniques previously developed in the judicial politics literature (he cites Schubert 1959 and Spaeth and Peterson 1971) to develop a list of 25 different issue areas involving civil liberties cases in the Warren Court (1953–1968 terms). Within each of these issue areas he tested several hypotheses about coalition formation, hypothesizing that minimum winning coalitions—that is, 5-to-4 votes when all nine justices are voting—would form as long as the Court was facing no external threats. Rohde's version of minimum-winning coalition theory was taken from Axelrod (1970), although Rohde noted of course that the original minimum-winning coalition theory was formulated by Riker (1962).

Although Rohde did not theoretically explore at any length the issue of strategic rationality by justices, one purpose of his article was to determine whether the justices changed their coalition-formation behavior for strategic reasons stemming from the external political situation faced by the Court. Under conditions of potential external threat, Rohde hypothesized, the justices would tend to form coalitions that are larger than minimum-winning because the justices' solidarity might provide the Court with some measure of protection. His empirical results did appear to suggest that these kinds of strategic considerations were indeed important to the justices in their final votes.

Although there are several reasons to be cautious about how these empirical results are interpreted (see our discussion in Chapter 10), one reason should be mentioned here. Rohde's use of the logic of rational choice led

him to the conclusion that the justices should be expected to form minimum-winning coalitions under nonthreatening conditions. However, his
analysis makes no reference to any role for the status quo policy (recall our
discussion of Distinction 7 in Chapter 2), and we will demonstrate in Chapter 6 that, given some status quo policy in a case's general issue area, there is
no necessary reason why rational justices would form minimum-winning
coalitions. Instead, how large the final coalitions will be depends simply on
how many justices consider the majority opinion writer's final opinion to be
better the status quo. Indeed, it could easily happen that all of the justices would want to replace this status quo policy with some other policy;
that is, a unanimous coalition could be the outcome of decision-making by
rational, policy-maximizing justices. A winning coalition will necessarily be
minimal in size only if just five justices consider the final opinion to be better than the status quo.

In the Rohde (1972b) study of opinion assignments, the same basic rational-choice assumptions were made as in his previous paper. The justices
were again described as "rational actors" (1972b, 652) who were pursuing
their most-preferred policies (1972b, 662). Moreover, Rohde also explicitly
viewed the justices making the majority opinion assignments as strategic decision-makers seeking to maximize achievement of their policy goals. The
opinion assigners were then hypothesized to assign opinions either to themselves (on the cases most salient to them) or to the other justices whose
views were most similar to their own (on the remaining cases) in order to
achieve their own policy goals.

However, despite Rohde's initial use of the language of rational choice,
he resorted to a different kind of language, far more reminiscent of Schubert's attitude-activation model, for describing the cumulative scaling techniques that he used to generate the issue dimensions on which his tests of
hypotheses about opinion assignment were based. As Rohde remarked here,

> The theory of cumulative scaling, as it applies to judicial decision making, holds that
> the cases that come to the Court for decision form various "stimulus-classes" con-
> taining stimuli to which the justices respond in reaching a decision. Differing
> extremes of stimuli produce varying degrees of division in the Court within an
> issue area. Some justices may respond favorably to a very weak stimulus, while oth-
> ers may respond favorably only to a strong stimulus. (For example, some justices may
> decide against any type of censorship of reading matter, while others may find only
> the most severe or outlandish censorship unacceptable.) (1972b, 664)

This use of Schubert's attitudinal language appeared when Rohde was
describing the construction of his issue scales, but not at all when he discussed his basic theoretical arguments or the implications of his empirical
results. (Rohde's first article also used Schubert's scaling techniques—see

Rohde (1972a, 211, footnote 11)—but Rohde did not discuss the psychological foundations of these techniques to the extent that he did in his second article.)

Thus, Rohde's articles also appear to rest on two different metaphors: the issue dimensions were said to be generated by the justices via a psychological stimulus-response process, but decisions within each dimension were said to be made via a process of strategically rational choice. However, there was no discussion of why these two different—but obviously important—aspects of the Court's decision-making process should be characterized in such different ways, nor how they might be related or combined in one integrated model of judicial decision-making.

RECENT STUDIES OF STRATEGICALLY RATIONAL JUSTICES

Rohde's (and Murphy's) assumption that justices were strategically rational was only occasionally adopted in empirical studies over the next 25 years. A few other scholars (see, e.g., Rathjen 1974; Brenner 1982; Brenner and Krol 1989; Krol and Brenner 1990) also conducted empirical research on Supreme Court decision-making that assumed strategic behavior by the justices at various stages of decision-making before the final vote. However, it was only in the mid-1990s that the assumption that justices were strategically rational actors became a major theme in the judicial politics literature on the Supreme Court (see, e.g., Boucher and Segal 1995; Maltzman and Wahlbeck 1996a,b; Wahlbeck, Spriggs, and Maltzman 1998). Moreover, these new studies were no longer accompanied by references to any kind of attitude-activation theory.

Two recent and important books provide very substantial theoretical and empirical support for the argument that Supreme Court justices are strategic actors. The first book, Epstein and Knight's *The Choices Justices Make* (1998), can be seen as the successor to Murphy's 1964 book, *Elements of Judicial Strategy*, in that it presented a thorough and wide-ranging analysis of the arguments about why Supreme Court justices should be considered strategic actors. The book also provided compelling evidence—via a combination of both qualitative and quantitative data—that the justices behave strategically in all stages of the Court's decision-making process, from certiorari through the final vote.

Epstein and Knight argued that there are four ways in which justices must act strategically in pursuit of their policy goals (see the discussion in their chapter 3). First, rational justices will have to bargain with each other over granting or denying certiorari at the outset and joining an opinion coalition at the final stage, for example. Second, rational justices will have to engage in "forward thinking"; that is, they will have to base their own actions on the expected actions of other justices at each stage and at later stages. Third, rational justices will have to try to manipulate the agenda: that is, they will have to decide the issues on which the case will be decided, ignoring some that were raised by the parties, and raising others that were not. Finally, rational justices will have to engage in sophisticated opinion writing: all opinions of the Court will be the result of strategic calculations by both the author and the justices who join the opinions. In sum, Epstein and Knight claimed that justices have to be strategically rational in all aspects of the Court's decision-making process if they are going to pursue their most-preferred policies.

The primary limitation of Epstein and Knight's book is one that its authors explicitly acknowledged: they advanced their arguments about strategic behavior without showing how to conduct a rigorous and fully strategic analysis of the range of possible cases. For this, a formal model of strategic behavior in the Court's multistage decision-making process is needed. But as Epstein and Knight remarked,

We realize that many may be surprised that a book on strategic analysis of the Supreme Court contains no game-theoretic, or formal, models. But that reaction would reflect a misunderstanding of the nature of our enterprise. Our goal has been to develop a picture of judicial choice, a conception of the mechanisms of strategic behavior that characterize decision making on the Court. As such our task has been to analyze the basic logic of strategic action, identify the ways it manifests itself in the choices of justices, and provide a framework for understanding its implications for research on the Court. If we have provided a basis for incorporating strategic choice into various approaches to studying the Supreme Court, we have accomplished our goal. (1998, 185)

They went on to emphasize that "strategic analysis is not synonymous with formalization; various forms of strategic behavior can be fruitfully analyzed without a formal model" (1998, 185–86).

Even so, they did not wish to downgrade the importance of formal analysis; its benefits, they suggest, "should not be underestimated" (Epstein and Knight 1998, 186). Indeed, they went on to say that "if scholars want to explain a particular line of decisions or a substantive body of law as the *equilibrium* outcome of the interdependent choices of the justices and other actors, they must demonstrate why the choices are in equilibrium, and a formal model is an essential part of such a demonstration." Nonetheless, they emphasized that "strategic behavior is a broader and more extensive phenomenon than what can be captured by formal equilibrium analysis" (1998, 186).

In sum, Epstein and Knight's book clearly presents a theory, because it lays out a broad description of the general assumptions and rationale for strategic behavior by justices on the Supreme Court. However, as Epstein and

Knight explicitly acknowledged, their work does not present any kind of model of strategic behavior on the Court that shows us how to conduct a systematic analysis, based on strategically rational calculations, that tells us what particular Supreme Court decisions should be expected under what particular conditions. Our own work can thus be seen as starting where Epstein and Knight's book ended.

The second recent book—Maltzman, Spriggs, and Wahlbeck's *Crafting Law on the Supreme Court: The Collegial Game* (2000)—is a counterpart to Epstein and Knight's book. Building on the earlier attitudinalist and policy-preferences literatures, and then on the arguments of Epstein and Knight about strategic behavior, Maltzman et al. crafted a variety of hypotheses about strategic behavior and then tested these hypotheses with an extensive body of empirical data on the behavior of justices as they interact to produce the Court's opinions. Thus, where Epstein and Knight provided a detailed rationale for why it is important to study the Supreme Court from the viewpoint of strategic behavior, Maltzman et al. provided thorough empirical tests of a wide range of hypotheses about strategic behavior. Their empirical findings upheld many of their hypotheses.

But like Epstein and Knight (1998), however, Maltzman et al. did not develop an explicit and rigorous formal model of strategic behavior from which their hypotheses are derived: their logic remained purely verbal and informal. Although their hypotheses usually seem reasonable, it is not always clear that the hypotheses actually represent the behavior that should be expected from strategically rational actors.

For example, one of their hypotheses that appears to be intuitively plausible is this:

Opinion Distance Hypothesis: The chief justice is more likely to assign cases to associates who are ideologically proximate to himself. (Maltzman, Spriggs, and Wahlbeck 2000, 36)

(Rohde 1972b also advanced this hypothesis.) However, this "closest associate" assignment strategy is not, in fact, always the most beneficial behavior for a strategic opinion assigner. Instead, we show in Chapter 7 that there are conditions under which a strategic opinion assigner will benefit from assigning the opinion to someone whose most-preferred policy is not closest to his but whose most-preferred policy is actually more extreme than his (that is, the assignee's most-preferred policy is farther from the status quo policy than is the assigner's most-preferred policy). Without formal analysis, it is unlikely that this error in logic would have been discovered.[11]

We would also note that during our model-building process we were forced to develop three different versions of strategic behavior involving coalition formation and the final vote. Again, informal analysis—by both

Epstein and Knight (1998) and Maltzman, Spriggs, and Wahlbeck (2000), indeed by most of the judicial politics literature on Supreme Court decision-making—seems to have overlooked these kinds of complications. Nonetheless, the kind of rigorous and sophisticated empirical testing in which Maltzman et al. engaged may prove crucial in determining which of these three versions of strategic behavior constitutes the best explanation, especially because it is not clear a priori which version might best account for the justices' behavior on the Court.[12]

In a sense, then, this trio of books—Epstein and Knight (1998), Maltzman, Spriggs, and Wahlbeck (2000), and our own book here—comprise a set of complementary studies of Supreme Court decision-making. Epstein and Knight (1998) provide a rationale for why strategic behavior should be observed within the Court. Maltzman et al. (2000) present a series of empirical tests of hypotheses informally derived from assumptions about strategic behavior. And our book begins the process of developing the formal model of strategic behavior that is necessary for the derivation of logically sound hypotheses.

Conclusion

Our contribution to the study of Supreme Court decision-making will involve the development of a formal model of strategically rational Supreme Court justices involved in a multistage decision-making process. In Chapter 2, and in this chapter as well, we have provided our reasons for the development of the rational-choice approach, but we have only briefly mentioned why we adopt the methodology of formal modeling. Although we address this question in the next chapter (which begins Part II), we do want to suggest here that the inadequate conceptual development of "the attitudinal model" as a theory may stem in part from a characteristic of most judicial politics research to date: judicial politics scholars have been content to employ informal, verbal techniques to develop their theories and to derive the empirical implications from the theories. Their theories have thus been developed without the use of any kind of rigorous formal techniques.

Of course, the lack of a rigorous formal approach to rational-choice modeling of Supreme Court decision-making was understandable in the early years of judicial politics research on the Court; as we have already suggested, the necessary analytical techniques were unavailable. But in our view, continued insistence on this informal approach will increasingly constrain the field's theoretical (and thus empirical) development. The reason is that whenever multiple actors—such as the nine Supreme Court justices—are interacting with each other so as to make a policy choice, an informal verbal approach will have difficulty in accurately characterizing the complex strategic logic of the situation the justices face. Moreover, for multistage decision processes—as with the Court's decision-making procedures involving case selection, then opinion assignment, then opinion writing, then coalition formation, and then the final vote—we think the informal verbal approach will be completely inadequate for working through the logic of this even more complex problem. Our solution to these problems is to develop a formal model of strategically rational decision-making throughout the full range of the Supreme Court's procedures.

We end this chapter by noting that our formal model forges a linkage—indeed, forces a linkage—between the judicial politics scholarship that has focused, usually in a quantitative fashion, on policy preferences and voting (as with the research involving the attitudinal model) and the scholarship, currently falling more in the public law tradition, which has focused, in a largely qualitative fashion, on the content of the legal policies and doctrines embodied in the majority, concurring, and dissenting opinions. Heretofore these bodies of scholarship have been quite unrelated to each other. Indeed, as we have already suggested, the quantitative research on the attitudinal model has largely ignored the content of the Supreme Court's decisions, even though it is this content that is presumably motivating the policy-minded justices. Our formal model shows how the contents of the opinions are inextricably linked to the questions involving who votes how, and on what, at the various stages of the Supreme Court's decision-making process.

PART TWO

A Formal Model of Supreme Court Decision-Making

In Part I, we discussed the reasons why a new generation of theories and models of Supreme Court decision-making must be developed. The last body of literature discussed in Part I involved the theory of strategic rationality. The purpose of Part II is to convert the theory of strategic rationality into a formal model of multistage Supreme Court decision-making by strategically rational justices. Chapter 4 discusses some reasons why formal modeling is a useful enterprise for the study of Supreme Court decision-making. Chapter 5 presents the basic assumptions of our formal model. Chapters 6, 7, 8, and 9 then present our model. Chapter 6 covers coalition formation and the final vote. Chapter 7 covers opinion assignment. Chapter 8 covers the conference vote. Chapter 9 covers certiorari.

CHAPTER 4

Why Formal Models?

The field of judicial politics has flourished over the past half century without resort to formal modeling. Surely, then, judicial politics scholars who study Supreme Court decision-making should be allowed to continue what they have been doing so successfully for so many years! Our own view, as Chapters 2 and 3 make clear, is that despite the apparent health and robustness of the field, the foundations of the field—the fundamental theories of Supreme Court decision-making—leave much to be desired. Hence, in those two chapters, we mentioned some ways in which formal modeling might help improve the quality of theorizing about the Supreme Court. In this chapter, we give more extensive consideration to the benefits (and costs) of formal modeling in the conduct of research on Supreme Court decision-making.

Our general perspective begins with an assertion that science is the systematic correction of error. Science involves the correction of error in the sense that it is intended to help us correct our errors regarding what we believe about how the world works. Thus science progresses if what we believe about how the world works is subject to a reduced burden of error. And science also involves the systematic correction of error in the sense that the conduct of science involves a variety of procedures and practices, involving both collective and individual behavior, which have demonstrated their usefulness over time in identifying and correcting error. The collective behavior involves (among other things) the institutionalization of methods of intellectual exchange, such as refereed journals and conferences in which research papers are presented, whereby errors can be identified and made public. This process of error identification is helped if the support for scholars (for example, positions, salaries, research funds) is politically, economically, and socially decentralized, so that no one theoretical viewpoint can become dominant just because of political, economic, or social power.

However, what most interests us here is behavior closer to the individual level involving the identification and correction of error on particular research questions by individuals or small groups of scholars within some field of inquiry. In this chapter, we will examine the role that the development of theories and models, and especially formal models, can play in helping scholars identify, correct, and avoid errors in research in their chosen field.

The Role of Theories and Models in Empirical Research

There should be little controversy about the essential role of theory in the conduct of empirical research.[1] After all, one cannot even compose a meaningful description of how a political institution behaves without guidance from some kind of theory about the institution. The reason is that although there are an infinite number of "facts" that we could collect about an institution, humans have only a finite amount of time to collect this infinite number of facts, only a finite capacity for storing these facts, and only a finite capability for making sense of them. Hence, describing an institution requires that decisions be made about the particular handful of facts to which we should pay attention and the multitude we can safely ignore. Only through reference to some kind of theory can we even begin to decide which facts are potentially relevant to an adequate description of the institutional behavior and which are not. Indeed, even determining what should be identified as a fact in the first place is likely to be influenced by one's general theoretical perspective.

Of course, it is an empirical matter whether some particular facts are actually relevant to the institutional behavior in which we are most interested, and thus worth including in one's description. If our empirical research tells us that these particular facts are not relevant (that is, their presence is not correlated with other variables of clearer importance), then we must reformulate our theory so as to construct a more adequate description. So even the simple act of description is not, in fact, quite so simple after all. Instead, even an adequate description is the product of a complex cycle of interactions between theory formulation and empirical test.

If a good theory is essential for the simple act of description, it will certainly be essential for explanation and prediction. But although it may be generally agreed that a good theory is essential for any kind of description, explanation, or prediction, there might be less agreement that the development of some kind of model, based on the theory, is equally essential. It is a common practice, just for example, for judicial politics scholars to derive a set of hypotheses directly from their theory, without developing any kind of explicit operational model for use as the foundation for the hypotheses. We would argue, however, that the derivation of a model from the theory is an essential part of the research enterprise. One reason is that almost every general theory in the field of judicial politics has several possible interpretations. For instance, consider our discussion of the attitudinal theory of Supreme Court decision-making in Chapter 3: is this theory a psychological theory of attitude activation, or is it a theory of strategically rational calculation? Developing a model, or perhaps an entire family of models, sensitizes us to the different interpretations that are possible for the theory; that is, model development helps us understand what our theory might mean. By developing different models attuned to the different interpretations of the theory, we can then test each model to see which works best empirically. In this way, we can determine which of the possible interpretations of the theory is most likely to be the best.

In contrast, if we proceed directly from the development of a theory to the development of a set of hypotheses, thereby skipping the development of any kind of model, we might unwittingly treat the hypotheses we derive from the theory as the only hypotheses that can be derived. If we then reject these hypotheses on empirical grounds, we may end up concluding that the theory is false, even though what may be false is merely that particular interpretation of the theory. That is, some version of the theory may in fact be true, but we would be rejecting all versions of the theory because of our focus on the wrong interpretation. Hence, the development of a model—or, preferably, a family of models—may help us avoid rejecting what may be a true theory. Or we might accept these particular hypotheses on empirical grounds without realizing that there is an alternative interpretation of the theory, and thus an alternative set of hypotheses, that might gain even stronger empirical support. Either way, then, a research strategy that includes model development is likely to have better error-correction and error-avoidance capabilities than a strategy that neglects model development.

As essential as model development is, however, it does not completely solve the problem of how to interpret a theory. The reason is that model development that takes place only via informal verbal methods may prove to be an inadequate way of making the theory operational. For example, the essentials of the theory may be correct, but the use of informal verbal methods to derive a model from the theory may yield erroneous interpretations of the theory. One way of coping with these difficulties is to develop a formal model rather than just an informal verbal model.

What distinguishes a formal model from an informal verbal model? One difference is the formal model's extra degree of explicitness in its assumptions and logic. Although this is indeed a difference from an informal verbal model, it is a difference more in degree than in kind. After all, it is the rare verbal model whose assumptions and logic are entirely implicit. Thus, one can think of a continuum involving the extent to which a theory's assumptions and logic are made clear and explicit. From this viewpoint, formal models differ from informal verbal theories only in that they lie somewhat further along the continuum.

A second difference is that in a formal model the assumptions, logic, and derivations are expressed in abstract, symbolic terms. However, although important, this difference between formal models and informal verbal theories should not be exaggerated. The reason is that even an informal verbal model is itself abstract and symbolic. As something that occurs within the human mind, it could not be otherwise. Words are symbols no less than mathematical notations.

There is a third difference, though, that we do think is critical for distinguishing a formal model from an informal verbal model: the symbols used in a formal model are selected and defined in such a way that they can be manipulated via the rules of mathematics. Even if the basic premises of an informal verbal model are made clear and explicit, their consequences and implications cannot be as rigorously derived informally via words as they can be derived formally via mathematics. Indeed, the reason that humans developed mathematics in the first place was because words alone were inadequate for some important purposes involving computation and logical deduction.

Thus, our general argument is that formal modeling can help us better understand, explore, and test the theories and models that we already have in mind about Supreme Court decision-making. Indeed, our view is that the enterprise of formal modeling yields such benefits that it should be considered an essential part of research on Supreme Court decision-making. Let us consider in somewhat greater detail the nature of these benefits.

Potential Benefits from Formal Modeling

Formal modeling can help us better understand, explore, and test our theories in several different ways. To be sure, none of these benefits follows necessarily from the formal modeling; this is why we will use phrases such as "*can* have this benefit" or "*may* have this benefit" rather than "*will* have this benefit." Yet in our view, the use of formal modeling makes it considerably more likely that these benefits will be realized.

INCREASED EXPLICITNESS

As we have already noted, formalization forces us to be as explicit as possible about the basic premises and assumptions of our theory. For example, formalization makes us specify exactly which actors we are including. It makes us say precisely what goals these actors have. It makes us detail exactly what kinds of institutional rules are being examined. It makes us specify the precise nature of the relationships among the actors. In sum, making all these assumptions explicit establishes a clear starting point for the rest of the analysis.

In fact, the initial process of making these assumptions explicit may be enlightening just by itself because it often forces us to clarify aspects of our own ideas that we had not previously understood. For example, formalization may force us to recognize the role of critical variables or significant relationships that are intimately involved in what we are studying but that we had inadvertently overlooked in our informal verbal theorizing.

It is interesting to note that a formal model often seems to be more complex than the theory or informal verbal model it is meant to represent. In fact, formal models are sometimes criticized for being overly complex, at least compared to the informal theories from which they are derived. This apparent increase in complexity often stems from the fact that our intuitive understanding of a problem, as embodied in some initial theory, may be built on assumptions that we did not even recognize we were making. In other words, the formal model's greater complexity often stems from the effort to make explicit what we already believe and from the fact that what we already believe usually turns out to be considerably more complicated than we had initially realized.

RIGOROUSLY DERIVED IMPLICATIONS

With our initial assumptions made explicit and expressed in some kind of symbolic notation, we then need to know what the implications of these assumptions are. It is here that the rules of mathematics—such as geometry, calculus, or probability theory—can be used to rigorously derive the implications of the assumptions. The mathematics helps us avoid mistakes in deriving these results, and it renders any mistakes we do commit more visible to others and thus more amenable to correction. In effect, the mathematics is a way of ensuring that our logical derivations are, in fact, logical.

Indeed, for studies of especially complex problems, such as how the multimember Supreme Court makes its decisions via its multistage procedures, the formal logic of mathematics may be the only practicable means of deducing any of the logical implications of the assumptions. That is, only a formal representation may be able to capture the complexity of the procedures yet still allow the theory's implications to be rigorously derived and thereby made amenable to empirical test.[2]

ENFORCED PARSIMONY

Formal modeling almost always forces theoretical parsimony on the modeler. The reason is that the mathematics in formal models can quickly become intractable as a result of the complexities introduced by adding too many variables. If the model is too complex, no results may be derivable at all or the results that can be derived may be almost impossible to interpret.

This risk of intractability means that a formal modeler must usually keep the model relatively simple by including only what are suspected to be the most fundamental variables. If empirical tests of this model do not yield satisfactory results, an equally parsimonious alternative model may have to be developed by throwing out some old variables and including some new ones. In this way, then, formal modeling enforces the philosophical predisposition toward explanatory parsimony embodied in Occam's Razor.

We would also note that a simple model can serve as a kind of baseline for judging how adequate some theory is. If most of the variance in some empirical data is explained by the simple model, then greater theoretical complexity may not be needed.

INCREASED SURPRISE VALUE

Because a formal model uses mathematics to derive the implications of the initial assumptions, results will sometimes be produced that were not expected from the original theory or informal verbal model. Formal models with substantial "surprise value" are often highly regarded, at least if these nonobvious or counterintuitive results are later empirically verified.

We would point out, for example, that our model of opinion assignment (see Chapter 7), contrary to virtually all previous theorizing, predicts that there are conditions in which an opinion assigner gets a better outcome, given his or her own policy goals, by assigning the opinion to another justice whose policy goals are not the closest to the assigner's policy goals. This is certainly a counterintuitive prediction, given the intuitive plausibility of the conventional wisdom. If the prediction is empirically supported, it would be a telling example of the surprise value of our formal theory.

ENHANCED ORGANIZING CAPABILITY

So potent is the vision of the surprise value of results generated by formal models that formal models are sometimes judged primarily on the basis of whether they yield novel, unexpected, or counterintuitive results. In our view, however, this great emphasis on surprise value is unfortunate because formal models can sometimes produce another kind of insight that may be at least as important. This underrecognized virtue of formal models is their capacity to organize, systematize, and make general sense of what we already know. That is, we may have many well-substantiated facts at our disposal but no way of determining whether they collectively exhibit any kind of meaningful pattern or relationship.

For example, consider the fundamental role that Mendeleev's periodic table of the elements played in organizing and making sense of the large amount of chemical knowledge that had accumulated by 1869, when Mendeleev first published his schema in a chemistry journal. Or consider the equally fundamental role that Darwin's theory of evolution by natural selection played in organizing and making sense of the large amount of knowledge about living organisms that taxonomists and natural historians had compiled by 1859, when Darwin published *The Origin of Species*. Although both of these theories certainly had great surprise value (Mendeleev's table, for example, enabled him to predict—accurately, as it turned out—the existence and characteristics of elements that had not yet been discovered), the theories also played an enormously important role in organizing, systematizing, and making sense of the chemical and biological information that was already in scientists' hands.

Thus, when empirical researchers generate seemingly uninteresting observations such as "Sometimes Y_1 occurs, but sometimes Y_2 occurs instead," the classification scheme generated by the formal model may show why Y_1 could occur only under some conditions and Y_2 could occur only under the remaining conditions. Such a classification scheme can thereby turn an unorganized collection of empirical observations, which, taken individually, seem of no great significance, into a far more interesting and enlightening overall picture. In fact, we are inclined to think that because of its emphasis on logical completeness (that is, the need to work out the implications of all possible values of the explanatory variables), formal modeling is especially well suited for creating classification systems for organizing and systematizing empirical evidence already in hand.[3]

IMPROVED EMPIRICAL TESTING

Formalization of a theory can also be expected to improve the quality of our empirical tests. This is another underrecognized virtue of formal modeling. Formalization can improve the quality of empirical tests in two different ways.

One kind of improvement involves the number, variety, and specificity of the empirical tests. Just by itself, an informal verbal model may allow us to deduce some general statements like, "If variable X increases, then variable Y should be expected to increase as well." This statement can be taken as a hypothesis to be empirically tested. However, formalization of the theory may suggest several additional tests or some more refined tests. For example, formalization may lead to a derivation of the functional form of the relationship between X and Y: is it linear or nonlinear, for instance, or does their relationship not even turn out to be monotonic? Formalization may also specify whether other variables should be expected to mediate the relationship between X and Y; that is, there may be some kind of interaction effect that must be taken into account in a statistical specification. If formalization can thereby increase the number, variety, and specificity of the testable hypotheses that can be derived from a theory, and if these additional hypotheses are subsequently supported by the empirical data, we thereby gain increased confidence that our model, and by implication the theory from which it is derived, is on the right track.

A second kind of improvement involves the statistical specifications used for an empirical test. If the statistical specifications are not derived from a formal model of these relationships or do not otherwise correspond to the implications of the underlying theory in some critical manner, then it is more likely that the specifications will misrepresent the relationships under examination and thereby produce misleading results and inferences. For example, if the formal model demonstrates that the relationship between two variables is nonmonotonic but the statistical specification that is adopted presumes monotonicity (as do many of the most commonly used techniques, such as linear regression), then the statistical results should not be trusted.[4] Thus, whenever possible, the statistical specification used in the test of a theory should be derived directly from a formal model of the relationships under examination.

IMPROVED THEORIES

Finally, we would argue that the greater capacity for formal models to be empirically falsified, because of their greater explicitness and transparency, should make theoretical improvements more possible. The reason is that if the empirical results do not support the model, then the clarity and explicitness stemming from the formalization may be able to aid a diagnosis of what went wrong. That is, because we know precisely what we have done and why, we can more easily determine if the problem was in the assumptions, in the central logic of the model, in the derivations of testable hypotheses from that logic, or somewhere in the empirical test itself. In other words, error correction is likely to be improved if we have a clearer idea of what we might have to correct.

We should acknowledge that there is nothing about the formal model that by itself will tell us where the problem lies. Accurate diagnosis of the source of error will always be a complex and difficult task, and it may take many iterations through the cycle of theory formulation, model development, formal modeling, hypothesis testing, and theory reformulation before we are able to produce a powerful and well-verified theory. Nevertheless, the clarity and explicitness enforced by formal modeling may help ease this process.

Potential Costs and Other Criticisms of Formal Modeling

Every research strategy has costs as well as benefits, and the development of formal models is no exception. In this section, we will identify and discuss some of these costs along with a number of common criticisms of formal theory and formal modeling.

First, one undeniable cost of formal modeling is that it requires the researcher to invest in the development of substantial technical skills. For example, it may require learning particular kinds of mathematics or, in the case of theories represented by computer simulation, one or more computer languages. There is an opportunity cost here: time and energy invested in learning these techniques are time and energy that cannot be spent on other fruitful research activities. Indeed, the mathematics required for certain kinds of problems will undoubtedly exceed the training and capabilities of most of us. For this reason, formal modeling often requires collaboration among scholars with different kinds of skills. Of course, this is increasingly the case in the social sciences anyway, where to conduct high-quality research, one scholar's substantive knowledge must often be joined to another scholar's methodological skills.

Second, precisely because of the demanding technical requirements for understanding a formal model, the audience for its results is sometimes small. We certainly agree that a small audience is a cost, but whether formal models necessarily have a small audience depends in part on other factors. At least some of this problem of accessibility probably stems not so much from anything intrinsic to the formal models themselves but from formal modelers who lack interest in making their results accessible to a broad audience. A burden that formal modelers share with sophisticated methodologists is that it is often difficult, although rarely completely impossible, to make their results accessible to a larger audience.

We would also note that this problem of accessibility is something that judicial politics faced a decade or two ago, when sophisticated statistical tools began to be used in the field. The response of some scholars was to condemn the use of the tools, but another response—clearly more productive for the field in the long run—was simply to learn to use the tools themselves (or at least to insist that their graduate students learn them).

Third, an alleged cost of formal models is that they often "oversimplify reality." We would respond by pointing out that the development of formal models, like that of informal verbal theories, is a cumulative process. The earliest models of many institutions were indeed quite simple, and might be regarded as overly so. However, as the characteristics of these simple initial models came to be understood, refinements were gradually added so as to better approximate various features of real-world institutions and processes.

As a result, the formal models of the 1980s and 1990s are substantially more attuned to the complexities and nuances of real-world institutions than were the formal models of the 1960s and 1970s.[5]

Nonetheless, we would emphasize that every useful model—formal or informal—must remain a simplification of reality. That is, to be useful for scientific purposes, every model must leave things out. Indeed, every study of some political process has to make radical simplifications in the representation of what is being studied. In this regard, formal modeling differs not at all from less formal approaches to answering important questions: all approaches will inevitably and unavoidably simplify. In fact, a model that is as complex as reality itself could not be used for any scientific purpose at all: it would be impossible to test any such model, for example, because its complexity would make it impossible to derive testable hypotheses from it. In other words, a model that tries to include everything will end up explaining nothing.

Thus the central issue is not, "Does this model simplify?" (Answer: "Of course it does!") Instead, the central issue involves questions like these: Do we know precisely what the simplifications have been? Do we know what the consequences of the simplifications are? Can we determine whether these simplifications are the best ones, given our scholarly purposes?

Of course, the criticism of formal modeling here may not involve simplification but oversimplification: some of the most important things, it is argued, are often left out. We would respond that although reliable judgments can sometimes be made, on the basis of prior knowledge or experience, as to what should be included in a model and what can be left out, one primary test of whether a model leaves out important things is a pragmatic empirical one: how adequately does the model explain or predict key aspects of the real world, or otherwise account for actual events? If a simple model fails its encounter with the real world, it is of little consequence (although it may well serve as a useful stepping stone to a better model). But if a simple model works well empirically, even though it leaves out supposedly important things, this may indicate that these other things are not, in fact, quite so important.

Fourth, another alleged cost of formal modeling (closely related to the third) is that formal models have little connection to real-world institutions and processes. We would acknowledge that some formal modelers may be more interested in refining their mathematical models than in increasing their models' relevance to the real world; in effect, the technique and the model may become the objects of fascination, not the real-world applications.

However, lack of interest in the real world is by no means an inevitable or even widespread trait of formal modelers. Indeed, most formal modelers would probably agree that formal modeling cannot—and certainly should not—take place in an empirical vacuum. One reason among many is that formal modelers would have little idea as to what institutions or processes are worth modeling in the first place if empiricists did not give them at least some clues as to what seems to be significant, and what does not, in the real world. As we remarked at the beginning of Chapter 2, construction of a theory must begin with some assumptions, and it is often the work of empiricists (even ostensibly atheoretical journalists and historians) who give the formal theorists some clues as to where their modeling might start.

Why, then, has formal modeling in political science sometimes lacked the empirical grounding that students of political institutions might wish? One major reason stems from the fact that its intellectual roots lie not in political science but in the discipline of economics. Some of these roots in economics involve research on committee decision-making by majority rule (see especially Black 1948a, 1948b, 1958). Unfortunately, most other economists ignored this research for many years, and most political scientists remained completely unaware of its existence until the 1970s. Other roots of formal modeling involve some highly abstract problems and paradoxes (such as the impossibility theorem of Arrow 1951) discovered by welfare economists in the 1930s, 1940s, and 1950s, but as with Black's work, most political scientists remained unaware of the significance of these findings until long after their publication. Almost by necessity, then, the training of the early generations of formal modelers in political science involved the study of procedures, problems, and paradoxes seemingly far removed from political science and the everyday world of politics.

In addition, from the 1950s through the 1970s, there was only a handful of formal modelers in political science. As a result, it took many years for this small cadre to develop a sense of what kinds of formal models could be developed, what analytical techniques were helpful, and what uses their models might have in explaining real-world politics. Had there been more modelers, progress in real-world applications might have been faster.

We would also point out that much of the early research in formal modeling involved efforts to understand the basic properties of decision-making procedures, especially majority rule, which are fundamental to democratic institutions. Although the focus here was not on any particular real-world institution, formal modelers would assert that real-world institutions cannot be fully understood unless the implications of the procedures that they utilize are also fully understood. This abstract research on decision-making procedures can thus be considered to have laid an essential foundation for later, more empirically grounded studies of many different kinds of majoritarian institutions, such as Congress or the Supreme Court.

Fifth, yet another criticism of formal models is that they are rarely tested empirically.[6] This may have been a legitimate criticism in the past, but its causes were not entirely the fault of the modelers. One cause stemmed simply from specialization and the division of academic labor: in general, the technical skills required by formal modeling are quite different from those required by empirical testing. Thus, the scholars who were competent at developing formal models were not necessarily competent at testing them (although many early formal modelers were in fact quite well-trained methodologically), and many of the scholars who were competent methodologists seem to have lacked any interest in testing the formal models. Increasingly, however, the graduate students now being trained in formal modeling are also receiving extensive training in methodology as well, so this problem is steadily resolving itself. Indeed, there is now an excellent book—Rebecca Morton's *Methods and Models: A Guide to the Empirical Analysis of Formal Models in Political Science* (1999)—that is primarily devoted to the question of how to empirically evaluate formal models in political science.

A final criticism is that formal theorists are arguing that formal theorizing should completely replace every other kind of theorizing in political science. We would make three responses to this concern. First, we would concede that although some formal theorists may harbor this view (and sometimes even be so rash as to express it in public), there is no evidence that very many formal theorists actually share this view.

Second, we would observe that many formal models—perhaps even most—actually have their origins in various kinds of informal verbal theories or models. Hence, reducing the production of informal verbal theories and models would ultimately serve only to reduce the number, variety, and empirical relevance of the formal models. In general, there is an intimate and mutually beneficial relationship between formal modeling on the one hand, and informal verbal theorizing and modeling on the other hand: each kind of theorizing is likely to be improved by the other, and neglecting either of them for the other would leave both impoverished.

Third, we would acknowledge that the simplicity, explicitness, and deductive rigor of formal models may be ill suited to problems whose understanding requires great sensitivity to nuance and historical context. There may always be important research questions that do not seem amenable to formalization but for which insightful verbal theories can be developed. It would be a shame if some kind of understanding of these kinds of questions is not pursued merely because we do not (yet!) know how to formalize our theories about them.

How Can We Be Sure that the Potential Benefits Exceed the Potential Costs?

For any research practice that is advocated—such as formal theorizing—the expected benefits, involving the identification and correction of error, should exceed the expected costs. For any particular research project, at least some of the costs will be unavoidable (for example, the investment in the development of technical skills) and will have to be paid up front, before any possible benefits could possibly be accrued. Moreover, it might be argued that by adding a new stage to the research cycle, there is some probability that new errors will be committed. This might be especially worrisome for formal modeling because it is such a complex activity that it might be thought to increase the overall likelihood that serious errors will be committed in the research cycle.

We certainly acknowledge that formal modeling entails some costs and that errors can be committed—and will be committed—in the development of formal models. But of course, this is true for the tasks entailed by the other stages of the research cycle as well: everything scholars do will be costly and error prone. Thus, the relevant question is not whether costs will be incurred and errors will be committed in the development of formal models—of course they will. Instead, the question is whether the benefits that may flow from the construction of formal models are sufficient to override these costs. This is a legitimate concern, and we would respond to it in the following ways.

First, in our view some of the characteristics of formal theorizing—especially the emphasis on the explicitness and clarity of the assumptions, and the logical rigor of the deductions—are so critical to high-quality theorizing that, under most circumstances, formal theorizing needs little further justification. Because formal theory is a way of making one's theorizing clearer and more rigorous, then the burden of proof that this is overly costly or even inappropriate falls on those who are arguing, in effect, for less clarity and for less rigor.

Beyond these virtues of clarity and rigor, however, we would suggest that the assessment of formal modeling (like the assessment of other research practices) must ultimately be a pragmatic one: does the process of formal modeling, and do the formal models that are thereby produced, yield results that are worth the costs?

For this particular project on the Supreme Court, we would assert that the conceptual distinctions that we identified in Chapter 2, and the criticisms of earlier theoretical works that we raised in Chapters 2 and 3, stemmed in good part from a sensitivity to conceptual and theoretical issues gained from our prior experience with formal modeling. Identification of these conceptual and theoretical issues certainly did not require a formal perspective (strictly speaking, few of the points we raised in those two chapters were mathematical in nature), but we would claim that this formal perspective certainly helped us identify and understand these issues.

We would also assert that informal verbal theorizing regarding the

Supreme Court's multistage decision-making process can lead—and, we would assert, has already led—to logical errors in the formulation of a variety of well-known hypotheses about the justices' behavior. We discovered that these logical errors had been made only through the development of our formal model. In Part II and in our discussions in Chapters 10 and 11, for example, we will describe some pieces of the conventional wisdom in the judicial politics literature on Supreme Court decision-making that cannot easily be derived from the assumption that justices attempt to maximize achievement of their personal policy goals (at least in the most straightforward sense). Either something must be wrong with the assumption or something must be wrong with the conventional wisdom. Moreover, we also discovered that at least two different pieces of the conventional wisdom are difficult to reconcile with each other, given the assumption that justices are maximizing their personal policy goals: if one of these pieces of the conventional wisdom is in fact true, then the other cannot be, and vice versa.

Conclusion

Not too long ago, most students of judicial politics found it unnecessary to devote much time to the study of statistical methods. Now, however, most students of judicial politics consider advanced statistical methods to be an essential tool for the study of Supreme Court decision-making. We are advancing a similar argument about formal modeling: it should be considered an equally essential tool for the study of Supreme Court decision-making. By itself, of course, formal modeling is not sufficient for developing an adequate understanding of Supreme Court decision-making: as we argued earlier in this chapter, the interplay between formal modeling and the other stages of the research cycle is critical to the advancement of knowledge. But we do think that the results and observations in our book can be taken as evidence that formal modeling is a useful component of the full research cycle on Supreme Court decision-making and thus can assist in the systematic correction of error that is the essence of science.

CHAPTER 5

Definitions and Assumptions

In Chapters 2 and 3, we traced the history of the rational-choice metaphor as used in the literature on the Supreme Court. In Chapter 4, we then presented a series of arguments as to why formal modeling should be considered an essential part of any research strategy for studying decision-making on the Supreme Court. Those three chapters establish our rationale for why a formal model of multistage Supreme Court decision-making by strategically rational justices should be developed. In this chapter, we present the definitions and assumptions for such a model.

Our model is built on four fundamental assumptions:

ASSUMPTION 5.1. Each justice has preferences over the legal policies that might be considered by the Supreme Court on each case.

ASSUMPTION 5.2. Each justice has a most-preferred policy among the legal policies that the Supreme Court might consider on each case.

ASSUMPTION 5.3. Each justice's sole objective is to have the Supreme Court adopt a policy as close as possible to his or her most-preferred policy on each case.

ASSUMPTION 5.4. Each justice pursues his or her most-preferred policy on each case in a strategically rational manner.

Given these four assumptions, it should be apparent that our model is a direct descendant of the rational-choice theory of Supreme Court decision-making developed by Murphy (1964), Rohde (1972a,b), and Epstein and Knight (1998). The model is also related to the rational-choice theory (but not to the psychological or attitudinal theories) developed or discussed by Schubert (1959), Rohde and Spaeth (1976), and Segal and Spaeth (1993, 2002). However, turning the rational-choice theory advanced by these scholars into a formal model requires additional definitions and assumptions, which we describe in this chapter.

We should emphasize that the model we construct says nothing about the origins of the justices' policy preferences. We take the justices' policy preferences as given; we seek only to determine the impact of these preferences on each justice's choice at each stage of the Court's decision-making process.

Lines, Points, and Utility Functions

We next make an assumption about the issue space within which Supreme Court decision-making takes place. Various strands of the attitudinalist and rational-choice literatures represent policy-making as taking place on a liberal-vs.-conservative issue dimension: policies toward the left on this dimension represent more liberal policies, and policies toward the right represent more conservative policies. We will follow the lead of these literatures and make the following assumption:

ASSUMPTION 5.5. Supreme Court policy-making on each case takes place in a one-dimensional issue space.

With this assumption, the set of all possible Supreme Court policies involved in some case can be represented by a line, and any particular policy can be represented by a point on the line. A formal model in which policy-making takes place along a line like this is commonly called a *spatial model*.[1]

Assumption 5.5 can be interpreted in three different ways. One interpretation is that every case before the Supreme Court reflects a common liberal-vs.-conservative issue dimension. Although the facts and arguments may differ from case to case, the justices will all interpret these facts and arguments in the framework of a single liberal-vs.-conservative dimension.[2] A second interpretation is that each case is characterized by its own unique liberal-vs.-conservative issue dimension. That is, because the facts and arguments in each case are unique, it might be that the single issue dimension in each case is unrelated to the issue dimensions that underlie other cases. A third interpretation is that various groups of cases share a common issue dimension, though the nature of this dimension differs from group to group. But whatever the interpretation, all that matters for our formal model is that, for each case under consideration, the issue space is unidimensional.

Because each justice is assumed to have a policy that he or she most desires (Assumption 5.2), this means that there is a point on this line that the justice prefers over any other point on the line. The term that is normally used to describe this justice's most-preferred point is that it is his or her *ideal point*:

DEFINITION 5.1. A justice's ideal point is his or her most-preferred policy on the line representing the issue dimension.

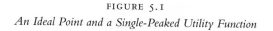

FIGURE 5.1

An Ideal Point and a Single-Peaked Utility Function

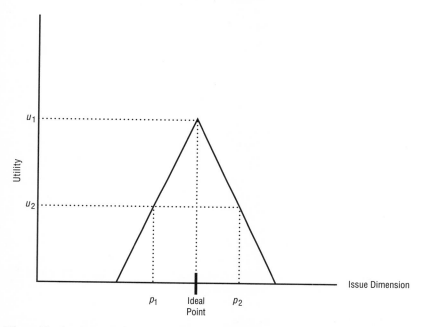

Thus, if a justice could unilaterally select the policy that the Court adopts in some case, the justice would choose the policy at his or her own ideal point.

Each individual is assumed to have a utility function that generates utilities that decrease monotonically as policies diverge in either direction from the justice's ideal point. This relationship between policies and how much a justice values the policies can be summarized as follows:

ASSUMPTION 5.6. Each justice has a utility function that is single peaked on the issue dimension.

That is, each justice considers policies that are farther and farther leftward from his or her ideal point, or farther and farther rightward, to be less and less desirable. See Figure 5.1 for a diagram of an ideal point and a single-peaked utility function in one dimension.

One aspect of a utility function involves the rate of decline in a justice's utility as policies diverge in either direction from the justice's ideal point. The rate of decline might be the same in either direction or it might be different. In Figure 5.1, for example, note that the justice's ideal point yields utility of u_1, and a policy at a given distance leftward from the justice's ideal point, such as at p_1, yields the same level of utility for the justice, u_2, as the policy that is an equivalent distance rightward from the justice's ideal point, at p_2. This can be summarized as follows:

DEFINITION 5.2A. A justice's utility function is symmetric if policies an equal distance to the left and right of the justice's ideal point yield equal levels of utility for the justice.

However, a justice's utility function could be asymmetric instead:

DEFINITION 5.2B. A justice's utility function is asymmetric if policies an equal distance to the left and right of the justice's ideal point yield unequal levels of utility for the justice.

See Figure 5.2 for a comparison of symmetric and asymmetric utility functions. With the asymmetric utility function shown here, the decline in utility yielded by policies to the left of the ideal point is more rapid than the decline in utility yielded by policies to the right of the ideal point.

In general, the results from our formal model will not depend on whether a justice's utility function is symmetric or asymmetric. However, our diagrams will always assume that the utility functions are symmetric; this makes the diagrams easier for the reader to interpret.

We will refer to justice 1 as "justice J_1," to justice 2 as "justice J_2," and so forth. The ideal points of the justices will be labeled J_1 for justice 1, J_2 for justice 2, and so forth.

We will use the convention that the Chief Justice is male (as with Chief Justices Warren Burger and William Rehnquist). Another justice who turns out to be critically important is the median justice; this person will be labeled J_{med}. We will use the convention that the median justice is female (as with Associate Justice Sandra Day O'Connor).

For simplicity in constructing and making sense of our diagrams, we will usually consider a Supreme Court with just five justices, although we sometimes use seven justices, and occasionally nine justices, when our argument requires it. Our arguments can usually be nicely illustrated with diagrams with just five or seven justices; diagrams with nine justices often become overly complex, with no gain in understanding thereby generated. Needless to say, though, all our arguments could be illustrated with nine-person examples.

Unless otherwise specified, our formal results hold for a Supreme Court consisting of an odd number of justices. However, we do present some results in which there is an even number of justices, as when there is a vacancy on the Court or a justice recuses himself or herself from a case.

FIGURE 5.2

Symmetric and Asymmetric Utility Functions

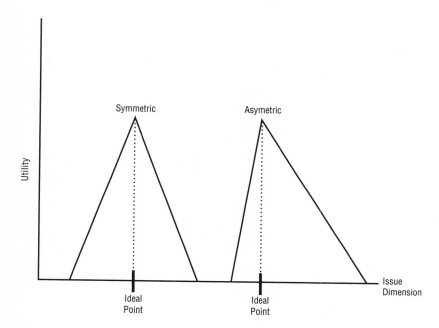

The Status Quo Policy

Among the policies on the single issue dimension is a policy that is the *status quo policy*, labeled SQ. We define this policy as follows:

DEFINITION 5.3. The status quo policy is the current legal state of affairs in the country on the case under consideration.

We make the following assumption about this status quo policy:

ASSUMPTION 5.7. For each legal case there exists a status quo policy.

In our view, the status quo policy plays a critical role in judicial policy-making (recall our discussion under Distinction 7 in Chapter 2). The reason is that for any lawsuit filed on some issue, there will always be some current legal state of affairs in the country on this issue. This current legal state of affairs could have been previously established in a wide variety of ways. For example, the current legal state of affairs could be as follows:

Whatever was defined as legal by previous U.S. Supreme Court rulings.

Whatever was defined as legal by federal laws, in the absence of previous U.S. Supreme Court rulings to the contrary.

Whatever was defined as legal by lower court rulings (for cases originating within the federal court system), in the absence of previous U.S. Supreme Court rulings or federal laws to the contrary.

Whatever was defined as legal by previous state supreme court rulings (for cases arising within any one state), in the absence of previous U.S. Supreme Court rulings or federal laws to the contrary.

Whatever was defined as legal by state laws (for cases arising within any one state), in the absence of previous U.S. Supreme Court rulings, federal laws, or state supreme court rulings to the contrary.

No matter what the origins of this current legal state of affairs, our basic point is that there is one or more constitutional provisions (whether federal or state), or one or more laws (whether federal or state), that have previously been interpreted as governing some public or private activity within the country. For our purpose in this book, the cases in which we are interested involve an interpretation of this constitutional provision (or provisions), or of this law (or laws), which is challenged in a lawsuit filed in the federal courts. Put most simply, one of the parties in the case will be defending this interpretation of the current legal state of affairs while the other party in the case will be challenging this interpretation of the same legal state of affairs. (In other words, we are not interested in cases that do not involve challenges to the legal—constitutional or statutory—status quo.)

It may be that for some public or private activity there is no statute or constitutional provision that clearly governs the activity. When this holds, the general presumption (in the United States) is that the activity is permissible. A new legal case involving this activity might then focus on whether there is any legal rationale for restricting the activity in some way.

Once a federal court issues a ruling, whether the current legal state of affairs changes depends on the content of the ruling. For example, assume that a federal appeals court has issued a ruling that denies a plaintiff's request to modify the current legal state of affairs. In this case, the current legal state of affairs will continue to hold, and the plaintiff's appeal to the Supreme Court (if one is filed) will again involve a request that this current legal state of affairs be modified. It follows that if the Supreme Court accepts the case, the status quo policy for the justices will simply be the current legal state of affairs.

In contrast, assume instead that the appeals court has issued a ruling that modifies the current legal state of affairs. In this case, the legal state of affairs for the country (and thus for the Supreme Court justices) will now exhibit a mixed pattern: (a) a new legal state of affairs will now hold in the circuit of the appeals court that issued the new ruling, and (b) the old (that is, unchanged) legal state of affairs will continue to hold in the rest of the country.[3]

If the Supreme Court refuses an appeal to hear this case, this mixed pattern would then persist as the legal state of affairs in the country. But if the Supreme Court does agree to hear the case, this mixed pattern—the new policy in one circuit, the old policy in the remaining circuits—will comprise the current status quo "policy" for the justices in the Court's decision-making process. If the Court then adopts some new policy in place of this status quo policy (that is, in place of this mixed pattern), this new policy would become the current legal state of affairs for the whole country (that is, not just for one circuit).[4]

Every legal case of interest to us here will thus involve some status quo policy that is being challenged, and the Supreme Court can either uphold this status quo policy or replace it with some alternative policy. It follows that if the status quo policy is a justice's most-preferred policy, the justice's objective will be to maintain this policy. But if the status quo policy is not the justice's most-preferred policy, the justice's objective will be to replace the status quo policy with a policy that is closer to his or her most-preferred policy. If a justice cannot induce the other justices to replace a nonideal status quo policy with something better, the justice will at least try to prevent the status quo policy from being replaced by a new policy that he or she considers to be even worse.

In sum, the current state of legal affairs in the country—the status quo policy—structures every justice's decisions regarding what case to accept, to whom the opinion should be assigned, what opinion to write, and what opinion to endorse or reject. In fact, we would argue that if the justices do not know, or for some reason cannot consider, the location of the status quo policy, they will have great difficulty in determining whether they should support a draft majority opinion: what criteria could each justice then use to determine whether the draft majority opinion is "good enough" to gain his or her support? If a justice does not know the location of the status quo at every stage of the decision-making process, he or she could scarcely make any rational decision at all—that is, a decision that will lead to an outcome that he or she thinks is better than what is already available in the current state of legal affairs.

Preferred-to Sets and Win Sets

We will often need to refer to the set of policies that a justice prefers to the status quo policy. The following terminology will be used:

DEFINITION 5.4. A justice's preferred-to set of the status quo is the set of policies that the justice prefers to the status quo.

We will also need to refer to the set of policies that a majority of justices all prefer to the status quo policy. We will use the following terminology:

FIGURE 5.3

Preferred-to Sets and Win Sets for Five Justices

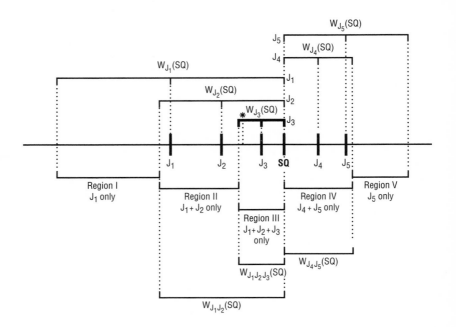

DEFINITION 5.5. The win set of the status quo is the set of policies that a majority of justices prefer to the status quo.

The notation we use for describing preferred-to sets and win sets diverges slightly from the norm in the formal modeling literature. Because an individual justice has only a preferred-to set and only a majority group of justices can have a win set, it is conventional for the notation to mirror this difference in terminology; for example, justice J_1's preferred-to set of SQ would be something like $P_{J1}(SQ)$ and the win set of SQ for justices J_1, J_2, and J_3 on a five-member Court would be $W_{J1J2J3}(SQ)$. However, we find it more convenient to standardize on the win-set notation—$W_{...}(SQ)$—for both individuals and groups, distinguishing the two just by the subscripts on the W. So if we are referring to a set of points that justice J_1 prefers to SQ, we refer to this justice's preferred-to set with the following notation: $W_{J1}(SQ)$. Similarly, if there is a set of points that justices J_1 and J_2 both prefer to SQ, we use the following notation: $W_{J1J2}(SQ)$. With this notation, then, it is simply the number of justices in the subscript that tells us whether they comprise a Court majority.

Note that a preferred-to set or a win set is always constructed with some particular policy as its point of reference. This point of reference will usually be the status quo policy, SQ. Hence, when referring to these preferred-to sets or win sets involving SQ, we should always say "the preferred-to set of SQ" or "the win set of SQ." However, because we rarely use any reference point other than SQ, we will often drop the " . . . of SQ" phrase; when it is omitted, the " . . . of SQ" should always be understood. On occasion, however, the point of reference for a preferred-to set or a win set will be some policy other than SQ; in this case, the reference point will always be explicitly identified. For example, if we are referring to the set of points that justice J_3 prefers to a policy at justice J_5's ideal point, the notation would be $W_{J3}(J_5)$.

In our diagrams we will depict each justice's preferred-to set by what looks like a horizontal, downward-facing bracket. In Figure 5.3, for example, we show the preferred-to set of SQ for each of five justices, J_1 through J_5. One bracket shows the set of points that justice J_1 prefers to SQ, or $W_{J1}(SQ)$, a second bracket shows the set of points that justice J_2 prefers to SQ, or $W_{J2}(SQ)$, and so forth.

In Figure 5.3, each justice's preferred-to set of SQ has three components. Assuming that SQ lies to the right of a justice's ideal point, as with J_3, there is first a segment of the preferred-to set that lies between the ideal point and SQ. The right-hand end of the preferred-to set here—$W_{J3}(SQ)$—is anchored by SQ. Second, there is a point in the preferred-to set that is the justice's ideal point, as with J_3 itself here. Third, there is a segment of the preferred-to set that lies on the other side of the justice's ideal point away from SQ (and thus to the left of the J_3 ideal point here). The left-hand boundary of this preferred-to set indicates the policy that, for the justice, produces an amount of utility equivalent to that produced by SQ: justice J_3 here would thus be indifferent between SQ and a policy at this left-hand boundary of $W_{J3}(SQ)$. Similarly, if SQ lies to the left of the justice's ideal point, as with J_4 in Figure 5.3, the left-hand end of justice J_4's preferred-to set is anchored by SQ itself, so the right-hand boundary of justice J_4's preferred-to set indicates the policy that, for justice J_4, produces utility equivalent to that produced by SQ.[5]

In Figure 5.3, in the region or regions where these brackets overlap each other (one above the other), the number of brackets that overlap tells us how many justices prefer the set of points in the overlapping region to SQ. For example, what we have labeled Region I indicates the set of points that only justice J_1 prefers to SQ. Region II indicates the set of points that only justices J_1 and J_2 prefer to SQ. Region III indicates the set of points that only justices J_1, J_2, and J_3 prefer to SQ. Region IV indicates the set of points that only justices J_4 and J_5 prefer to SQ. And Region V indicates the set of points that only justice J_5 prefers to SQ. This simple diagrammatic device—how many of these bracket lines overlap each other for any given portion of the line?—will be used throughout Chapters 6 through 9 to help distinguish various important regions from each other.

In Figure 5.3, the set of points that justices J_1 and J_2 both prefer to SQ is $W_{J_1J_2}(SQ)$. This set of points is identical to $W_{J_2}(SQ)$, the preferred-to set of the justice whose ideal point is farther from SQ. The set of points that justices J_1, J_2, and J_3 all prefer to SQ is $W_{J_1J_2J_3}(SQ)$, and this set of points is identical to $W_{J_3}(SQ)$, the preferred-to set of the justice whose ideal point is farthest from SQ. The set of points that justices J_4 and J_5 both prefer to SQ is $W_{J_4J_5}(SQ)$, and this set of points is identical to $W_{J_4}(SQ)$, the preferred-to set of the justice whose ideal point is farther from SQ. Thus, preferred-to sets for nonidentical ideal points will always be nested, with the preferred-to set of SQ for one ideal point containing the preferred-to set of SQ of an ideal point that is closer to SQ (assuming the two ideal points are on the same side of SQ).

We will occasionally need to refer to policies that are farther from the status quo policy than some win set or preferred-to set. We will use the word *outside* to refer to these particular policies:

DEFINITION 5.6. The policies that lie outside a win set or a preferred-to set are the policies (a) that do not lie inside the indicated win set or preferred-to set, *and* (b) that are on the side of win set or preferred-to set away from SQ.

Thus, in Figure 5.3, it is the policies to the left of $W_{J_1}(SQ)$—that is, to the left of Region I—that will be said to lie outside $W_{J_1}(SQ)$.

In the following chapters, we will often refer to a policy that is "just inside the outside boundary of $W_{J\ldots}(SQ)$." For example, in Figure 5.3 the point labeled "*" on the bracket indicating the $W_{J_3}(SQ)$ preferred-to set will be described as lying "just inside the outside boundary of $W_{J_3}(SQ)$." What we mean by this is that the indicated justice—in this case, it is justice J_3—can perceive the difference between the policy at * and the left-hand end of the $W_{J_3}(SQ)$ preferred-to set. However, this justice cannot perceive the difference between (a) the policy defining the left-hand end of the $W_{J_3}(SQ)$ preferred-to set, and (b) a policy that is closer than * to the left-hand end of the $W_{J_3}(SQ)$ preferred-to set. Thus, justice J_3 here would clearly prefer the policy at * to the policy defining the left-hand end of the $W_{J_3}(SQ)$ preferred-to set; however, this justice would be indifferent between (a) the policy defining the left-hand end of the $W_{J_3}(SQ)$ preferred-to set, and (b) any policy closer than * to the policy defining the left-hand end of the $W_{J_3}(SQ)$ preferred-to set.[6]

We also need to define another term, *minority side*:

DEFINITION 5.7. A minority-side justice has an ideal point that lies on the side of SQ that contains only a minority of the justices' ideal points; a minority-side policy is a policy that lies on the side of SQ that contains only a minority of the justices' ideal points.

Thus, in Figure 5.3, justices J_4 and J_5 are the minority-side justices, and the minority-side policies are those that lie to the right of SQ. (In our diagrams, the ideal points of the minority-side justices will always lie to the right of SQ.) As with the policies that are outside a majority-side preferred-to set or win set, the minority-side policies to the right of $W_{J5}(SQ)$—that is, to the right of Region V—will be said to lie outside $W_{J5}(SQ)$.

When there are no points that some justice prefers to SQ, this means that his or her preferred-to set is empty. A justice has an empty preferred-to set of SQ only when his or her ideal point is identical to SQ. Similarly, when several justices have no points that they all collectively prefer to SQ, this means that their win set of SQ is empty; this will happen only when SQ lies at or between the ideal points of two or more of these justices. In either case, we use the Ø symbol to refer to an empty preferred-to set or win set. For example, if there exist no points that justice J_1 prefers to SQ (that is, SQ is at justice J_1's ideal point), the notation for this would be $W_{J1}(SQ) = \emptyset$. If there exist no points that justices J_1 and J_2 both prefer to SQ, the notation would be $W_{J1J2}(SQ) = \emptyset$.

When there exist some points that a justice does prefer to SQ, this means that his or her preferred-to set is not empty. For example, when there exist some points that justice J_1 prefers to SQ, as in Figure 5.3, the notation indicating that this set of preferred points is not empty is $W_{J1}(SQ) \neq \emptyset$. Similarly, when there exist some points that several justices collectively prefer to SQ, this means that their win set of SQ is not empty. For example, when there exist some points that justices J_1 and J_2 both prefer to SQ, the notation indicating that this set of mutually preferred points is not empty is $W_{J1J2}(SQ) \neq \emptyset$.

The Number of Justices

We will usually presume that there is an odd number of justices (as with the U.S. Supreme Court). The following two definitions will thus be important:

DEFINITION 5.8. The total number of justices is denoted by J.
DEFINITION 5.9. A bare majority of the J justices is denoted by *maj*.

When there is an odd number of justices, *maj* can be computed from a simple formula: $maj = (J + 1)/2$. A number that is important for granting certiorari is $maj - 1$, which is one less than a bare majority.

For example, when there are nine justices, a bare majority, or *maj*, is five justices: $(9 + 1)/2 = 5$. Thus, the votes of at least five justices are needed for a majority decision on this nine-person Court. For granting certiorari, *maj* − 1 votes are needed; with a bare majority being five justices, the votes of 5 − 1 = 4 justices will be needed. This is, of course, the "rule of four" on the Court.

When there are seven justices, as in some of our diagrams, *maj* is four justices: (7 + 1)/2 = 4. Thus, the votes of at least four justices are needed for a majority decision on this seven-person Court. For granting certiorari, *maj* − 1 votes are needed; hence, the votes of 4 − 1 = 3 justices are needed.

When there are just five justices, as in most of our diagrams, *maj* is three justices: (5 + 1)/2 = 3. Thus, the votes of at least three justices are needed for a majority decision on this five-person Court. For granting certiorari, the votes of 3 − 1 = 2 justices are thus needed.

When there is an even number of justices, *maj* can be computed from an alternative formula: *maj* = (J/2) + 1. For example, when there are eight justices, *maj* is five justices: (8/2) + 1 = 5. Thus, the votes of at least five justices are needed for a majority decision on this eight-person Court. For granting certiorari, *maj* − 1 votes are needed; with a bare majority being five justices, the votes of 5 − 1 = 4 justices are needed. Similarly, when there are six justices, *maj* = 4, and so *maj* − 1 = 3 votes are needed for certiorari, and when there are just four justices, *maj* = 3, and so *maj* − 1 = 2 votes are needed for certiorari.

An Informational Assumption

We will be constructing what the formal modeling literature generally calls a "perfect information" model. For such a model, the following assumption holds:

ASSUMPTION 5.8. Each justice knows the ideal point of every other justice, and all justices know and understand what the Supreme Court's decision-making procedures are.

Our rationale for this assumption is that justices will come to know and understand each other rather well through close working relationships, which may extend over many years. So it should be possible for the justices to form relatively accurate predictions of the locations of each other's ideal points on the issue dimension for any one case. The justices' understanding of the Court's decision-making procedures would then allow them to make accurate predictions of the consequences of any particular choice that they might make at each stage of the decision-making process. Of all our national decision-making institutions, it may be within the Supreme Court that these perfect-information conditions are most closely approximated.[7]

"Sincere" and "Strategic" Behavior

Some of the literature reviewed in Chapters 2 and 3 involved whether Supreme Court justices should be considered "strategically rational." By our definition of rationality, a rational justice attempts to maximize achievement of his or her most preferred policy. Because the Court's decision-making process has multiple stages, we can define *rationality* as follows:

DEFINITION 5.10. A rational justice will make those choices at each stage of the Supreme Court's decision-making process that ensure that a policy that is as close as possible to the justice's ideal point will be approved by a majority of the justices on the final vote.

Our general view is that if a justice is rational, this implies that the justice will be strategically rational as well. This is precisely the Epstein and Knight (1998) argument about strategically rational justices. (Note that in the rational-choice literature, "strategic" behavior is sometimes also referred to as "sophisticated" behavior.)

For a justice to behave in a strategically rational manner at the earlier stages of decision-making, she must consider what final choice by the Court she would most prefer, and then work backward from this most-preferred final choice to determine what choice she should make, at each of the earlier stages of the decision-making process, to ensure that the Court's final choice is as close as possible to what she most prefers. On occasion, this logic will force her to make decisions at the earlier stages that go against what she would do if she were the sole decision-maker for the Court.

For example, consider an appeals court ruling that is more conservative than current Court policy. A liberal justice would thus want to overturn this conservative ruling and restore the previous legal state of affairs. However, if this liberal justice expected that the Court as a whole would uphold the conservative appeals court ruling, thereby enshrining it as official policy for the entire country (rather than just in the single circuit of the appeals court that made the ruling), she would rationally vote not to grant certiorari on the case. Strategically rational behavior will thus sometimes require the justice to reject options she would otherwise support if she were the sole judicial decision maker, and it will sometimes require that she endorse options she would otherwise prefer to reject.

For this reason, understanding the Court's decision-making process—involving first certiorari, then the conference vote, then opinion assignment, then coalition formation, and then the final vote—requires that we begin our analysis with an examination of what should be expected to happen on the final vote. Because the final vote is so intertwined with the process of coalition formation, we will combine them in our analysis in Chapter 6. We will then work our way backward through opinion assignment in Chapter 7, the conference vote in Chapter 8, and certiorari in Chapter 9. We will thus end our formal analysis with what is chronologically the first stage in the Court's decision-making process.

How would a justice behave if she were not strategically rational? That is, how would she behave if she does not consider how her own behavior at the earlier stages of the decision-making process will ultimately affect the policy that is adopted at the final stage? This kind of behavior is sometimes referred to as "sincere" behavior. Unfortunately, as we have already mentioned (see our discussion of Distinction 6 in Chapter 2), it is not always clear how a sincere justice will behave in the presence of other justices. In some cases, two or more interpretations of what comprises sincere behavior may be possible, but in other cases, no interpretation seems especially plausible. For these reasons, we will not attempt to develop a full model of sincere behavior, although we will make occasional remarks on the subject at relevant places in Chapters 6 through 9.[8]

The Independence of Cases

Next, we make an assumption about what each justice assumes to be the final vote in a case:

ASSUMPTION 5.9. Each justice considers policies that might be adopted in any future case to have no relevance to his or her choice of a policy on the current case.

A different way of saying this is that the justices in our model completely discount the future: any future effects of the Court's decision beyond the current case are considered by the justice to be completely unimportant, or are not considered at all. This means, in effect, that each case is a one-period game for each justice; the justices' strategizing extends only as far as the final vote on the current case and not beyond.

Joining, Concurring, and Dissenting

Justices on the Supreme Court have several different ways of expressing their views on the final vote; for example, they can write a majority opinion, they can join (sign) someone else's majority opinion, they can write at least two different kinds of concurring opinions (a regular concurrence and a special concurrence), they can join someone else's concurring opinion, they can write a dissenting opinion, and they can join someone else's dissenting opinion. For our model, however, we impose the following restrictions:

ASSUMPTION 5.10. A majority-side justice who prefers the draft majority opinion to SQ can only join the opinion; it is not possible to write a separate concurrence.

ASSUMPTION 5.11. A majority-side justice who prefers SQ to the draft majority opinion will be described only as not joining the opinion.

ASSUMPTION 5.12. A minority-side justice, who by definition prefers SQ to whatever the draft majority opinion might be, will behave in a way that minimizes how far to the majority side any new policy is located.

The reason for Assumption 5.10 is that we do not have a good understanding, within the context of our model, of whether a majority-side justice who prefers the draft majority opinion to SQ will just join the draft majority opinion or will also write a regular concurrence. Because the draft majority opinion is better than SQ for this majority-side justice, and because writing a regular concurrence does not change the content of the majority opinion (which the justice has also joined), it seems reasonable to simplify our model by assuming that the justice merely joins the draft opinion and does nothing else.

The reason for Assumption 5.11 is that we do not have a good understanding of how a majority-side justice who prefers SQ to the draft majority opinion should be expected to behave. One possibility is that this majority-side justice would dissent because the draft majority opinion is worse than SQ for her. Or instead of dissenting, this majority-side justice might write a special concurrence because she agrees that policy should be moved in the direction of the majority but thinks that the draft majority opinion goes too far. Because it is not clear what this majority-side justice should be expected to do, we will describe this justice simply as "not joining" the draft majority opinion, which allows both for dissenting and for writing a special concurrence.

The reasons for Assumption 5.12 are more complex. If a draft majority opinion is worse than SQ for a minority-side justice, this justice will normally not be able to influence the location of the final majority-side opinion. In this case, we would expect the justice to dissent or join some other justice's dissent; our model does not specify which.

However, there will be circumstances in which a minority-side justice will join, or even write, a majority-side opinion, even though such an opinion would be worse for him than SQ. For example, a minority-side Chief Justice might deliberately vote on the majority side on the conference vote, thereby becoming the majority opinion assigner; he would then assign himself the opinion and proceed to write a majority-side opinion that is very close to SQ. Although policy would still be moving in the majority's direction and away from the Chief Justice's own ideal point, by joining the majority he may be able to keep the final policy change as minimal as possible. The key point is that if he did not adopt this set of tactics (that is, if he simply voted on the minority side on the conference vote), he could end up with an even worse final outcome, as we will demonstrate in Chapters 7 and 8.

Costless Opinion Writing

Our final assumption involves the time and energy it takes for the majority opinion writer to write the majority opinion on a case. We shall make the following assumption:

ASSUMPTION 5.13. Writing the majority opinion is costless for the opinion writer.

This implies that a justice will always want to write the majority opinion on a case whenever possible, and that the only benefits and costs that the justice derives from the case involve the value of the final majority opinion. (One could argue that this assumption is implied by Assumption 5.3, which states that a justice's sole goal is to get a final opinion as close as possible to his or her ideal point.)

Conclusion

This is a very simple library of concepts, assumptions, and notational and diagrammatic tools. Nonetheless, we will demonstrate in the next four chapters that this simple technology can be used to generate a wide range of predictions about the behavior of Supreme Court justices who pursue their policy goals in a strategically rational fashion.

CHAPTER 6

Coalition Formation and the Final Vote

In Chapter 1, we distinguished among five separate stages in which the Supreme Court justices make various kinds of choices and decisions. These five stages are:

STAGE 1. *Certiorari:* the justices make decisions on whether to grant a writ of certiorari, and certiorari is granted if it is supported by at least four justices.

STAGE 2. *Conference vote:* after oral argument, the justices conduct the conference vote.[1]

STAGE 3. *Opinion assignment:* if the Chief Justice is in the majority on the conference vote, he or she has the authority to assign the writing of the majority opinion; if the Chief Justice is in the minority on the conference vote, the most senior Associate Justice in the majority has the authority to assign the writing of the majority opinion.

STAGE 4. *Coalition formation:* the majority opinion writer attempts to write an opinion that will attract a majority of the justices' votes; other justices may write concurring or dissenting opinions for which they may also seek support.

STAGE 5. *Final vote:* the justices decide to join one or more of the draft opinions.

In this chapter, we model stages 4 and 5 of this decision-making process, involving coalition formation and the final vote. We combine our analysis of these last two stages because their activities are so intertwined that it would be difficult to discuss them separately.

At the final vote, the justices indicate their support for one or more of the opinions that have been written. One of the opinions, of course, is the majority opinion. The majority opinion is almost always written by the justice who is given this assignment in stage 3 (opinion assignment). However, an opinion written for the majority can become the majority opinion only if a majority of the justices actually support it. Hence, a justice writing the majority opinion will normally attempt to write an opinion so that it gains the support of a majority; when majority support is successfully gained, the supporters usually (although not always) include the members of the original majority from stage 2 (the conference vote).

If any majority that existed in stage 2 does fall apart, a new majority opinion could be written by some other justice, perhaps even one originally in the stage 2 minority. Occasionally, however, there may not be enough support for any opinion to become the majority opinion; in this case, there will be just a plurality opinion.

A second kind of opinion involves a concurrence—a regular concurrence or a special concurrence—written by a justice who agrees to some extent with the majority opinion but not entirely. Several different concurring opinions can be written, although two or more justices may join together on one concurring opinion.

A third kind of opinion involves a dissent written by a justice who disagrees with any majority opinion. There can be several dissenting opinions, although two or more justices may join together on one dissenting opinion.

Our model of the Supreme Court's decision-making process shows how the policy goal of the majority opinion writer and the policy goals of the other justices will interact with the status quo policy, SQ, to influence coalition formation and the final vote. We conduct our analysis in this chapter by addressing several questions about these final two stages of decision-making:

1. Under what conditions can SQ be upset?

2. What are the constraints on the set of policies that could be adopted?

3. What policies would different majority coalitions prefer to SQ?

4. What opinions and what coalitions should be expected from what we will call the "agenda-control" version of our model?

5. What opinions and what coalitions should be expected from what we will call the "open-bidding" version of our model?

6. What opinions and what coalitions should be expected from what we will call the "median-holdout" version of our model?

7. How different are the results expected from these three different versions of our model?

Our answers to these questions characterize the Court's decision-making processes involving coalition formation and the final vote.

However, this chapter focuses only on the processes by which a majority opinion and a dissenting opinion are selected. We will not consider why a justice might choose to write a concurring opinion. Instead, we simply assume—see Assumption 5.10—that if some final majority opinion is better for a majority-side justice than the status quo policy, SQ, and better than any other available opinion, the justice will support this opinion. If the final majority opinion is better than SQ for a majority of the justices, it becomes the majority opinion. Similarly, we assume that a majority-side justice for whom the draft majority opinion is worse than SQ will not support the opinion; see Assumption 5.11. Finally, we show that under most conditions (for example, when the Chief Justice's ideal point is on the majority side), if some final majority opinion is worse than SQ for a minority-side justice, the justice will not support the opinion but will dissent instead. However, we also show—see Assumption 5.12 and the associated discussion in Chapter 5— that under some conditions (for example, when the Chief Justice has a minority-side ideal point), a minority-side justice will have an incentive to support a majority opinion that he or she considers worse than SQ, in order to avoid an even worse policy.

When Can the Status Quo Policy Be Upset?

The relationship between the location of SQ and the location of the ideal point of the median justice, J_{med}, has a critical impact on what majority opinion will be written and on what the final vote will be on this opinion. Our first four propositions begin the process of characterizing this relationship.[2]

If SQ is located at J_{med}, SQ cannot be replaced by any other policy. The reason is that upsetting SQ requires at least *maj* votes—that is, the votes of at least a bare majority of the Court—from justices who would agree to replace SQ with some other policy. But if SQ is at J_{med}, there will be at most $maj - 1$ justices to the left of SQ who want to replace SQ with some policy to its left, and at most $maj - 1$ justices to the right of SQ who want to replace SQ with some policy to its right. Hence, we can state the following:

PROPOSITION 6.1. If SQ is located at J_{med}, there exists no policy that a majority of justices prefer to SQ.

To illustrate, consider the five-member Court in Figure 6.1, in which SQ is located at J_{med}. Assume that Opinion 1 has been proposed: while Opinion 1 lies inside the preferred-to sets of two justices, J_1 and J_2, three votes are needed for it to replace SQ. Similarly, if someone has proposed Opinion 2, three votes are needed for it to replace SQ, but it lies inside the preferred-to sets of only two justices, J_4 and J_5. In either case, then, SQ will be unchanged.[3]

In contrast, if SQ is not located at J_{med}, SQ can be upset:

PROPOSITION 6.2. If SQ is not located at J_{med}, there exists some policy that a majority of justices prefer to SQ.

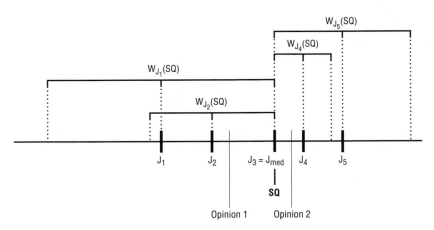

FIGURE 6.1

Illustration of Proposition 6.1: SQ Cannot Be Changed

To illustrate, consider Figure 6.2, in which SQ is not located at J_{med}. First consider Opinion 1: because it lies inside the preferred-to sets of three justices—J_1, J_2, and J_3—it could gain the three votes necessary to replace SQ. In contrast, consider Opinion 2, which lies on the minority side: because it lies inside the preferred-to sets of only two justices, J_4 and J_5, it could not gain the necessary three votes to upset SQ. In this case, then, SQ could be upset by Opinion 1 but not by Opinion 2.

This example in Figure 6.2 highlights a simple pattern that is worth noting:

PROPOSITION 6.3. If J_{med} is located to the left of SQ, SQ is vulnerable to upset by a proposal to its left but not by a proposal to its right; if J_{med} is located to the right of SQ, SQ is vulnerable to upset by a proposal to its right but not by a proposal to its left.

In effect, the decision-making process on the Supreme Court should always be expected to move policy away from SQ and in the direction of the median justice. Whether policy is moved all the way to the Court median, or even beyond, is a key issue that we discuss throughout this chapter.

We also note the following:

PROPOSITION 6.4. If SQ is not at J_{med}, a majority of justices will prefer a policy at J_{med} to SQ.

Again, Figure 6.2 provides an illustration: a policy at J_{med} falls inside the preferred-to sets of J_1, J_2, and J_3, who comprise a majority of the Court.

We should note that Propositions 6.1, 6.2, 6.3, and 6.4 are direct implications of the median-voter theorem, which has been understood for major-

FIGURE 6.2

Illustration of Proposition 6.2: SQ Can Be Changed

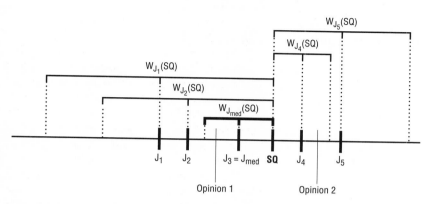

ity-rule institutions in unidimensional issue spaces at least since Black (1948a,b, 1958) and Downs (1957).

What Are the Constraints on the Set of Policies that Could Be Adopted?

Our next several results—Propositions 6.5 through 6.10—involve the policies that the Court might conceivably adopt to replace SQ. These propositions help characterize what majority opinion will be written and what the final vote will be on this opinion.

We begin with the following definition:

DEFINITION 6.1. The set of politically feasible policies contains every policy that could gain the support of a majority of justices in a comparison with SQ.

Given this definition, we can state:

PROPOSITION 6.5. For some SQ not at J_{med}, the set of politically feasible policies is $W_{Jmed}(SQ)$.

To prove this proposition, we will demonstrate that no point outside $W_{Jmed}(SQ)$ is politically feasible. Consider the seven-member Court in Figure 6.3. In this figure, justice J_4 is J_{med}, and note that any proposal lying outside $W_{Jmed}(SQ)$ is worse for J_{med} than SQ; hence, any such proposal will lack J_{med}'s support in a comparison with SQ. For example, consider some proposal, such as Opinion 1, which lies to the left of $W_{Jmed}(SQ)$. By the definition of a median justice, there will be $maj - 1$ justices with ideal points to the left of J_{med} (such as J_1, J_2, and J_3 here), and some or all of these justices may prefer Opinion 1 to SQ (in this case, J_1, J_2, and J_3 all prefer Opinion 1 to SQ because Opinion 1 falls within their respective preferred-to sets). However, because there can be at most only *maj* − 1 justices (such as J_1, J_2, and J_3) who might want to move Court policy from SQ leftward to a location such as Opinion 1 outside $W_{Jmed}(SQ)$, Opinion 1 would be defeated by a majority of justices: J_{med} will prefer SQ to Opinion 1, and any justices with ideal points to the right of J_{med} (such as justices J_5, J_6, and J_7) will prefer SQ as well (because Opinion 1 lies outside all their preferred-to sets). Next, again by the definition of a median justice, there will also be *maj* − 1 justices with ideal points to the right of J_{med}. If all of these *maj* − 1 justices lie between J_{med} and SQ (in the vicinity of J_5, for example), Opinion 1 will lie outside their preferred-to sets of SQ, hence like J_{med} they will prefer SQ to Opinion 1. If any of the *maj* − 1 justices who lie to the right of J_{med} also have ideal points to the right of SQ (see the locations of J_6 and J_7 in Figure 6.3, for example), these justices will also prefer SQ to Opinion 1 because SQ will be closer to them than Opinion 1. Now consider Opinion 2, which lies to the right of $W_{Jmed}(SQ)$. The *maj* − 1 justices whose ideal points lie to the left of J_{med} (for example, J_1, J_2, and J_3) will all prefer SQ to Opinion 2 because SQ is closer to their ideal points than Opinion 2. There are also *maj* − 1 justices to the right of J_{med}. If any of their ideal points lie between J_{med} and SQ (such as J_5), they too would prefer SQ to Opinion 2 because SQ is closer to them than Opinion 2. And even if the ideal points of all of these *maj* − 1 justices lie to the right of SQ and are closer to Opinion 2 than to SQ (such as J_6 and J_7), which means they would all prefer Opinion 2 to SQ, there can be at most *maj* − 1 of these votes for Opinion 2 over SQ.

In general, then, we can conclude that every proposal lying to the left or to the right of $W_{Jmed}(SQ)$ will be rejected by a majority that prefers SQ; only those policies that lie inside $W_{Jmed}(SQ)$ can gain majority support against SQ. We can thus see that $W_{Jmed}(SQ)$, the preferred-to set of the median justice, acts as a fundamental constraint on what proposals would gain majority support over SQ. This can be formulated as a slight elaboration on Proposition 6.5:

PROPOSITION 6.6. For some SQ not at J_{med}, the right-hand and left-hand boundaries of $W_{Jmed}(SQ)$ are the boundaries of the set of politically feasible policies.

Note of course that the boundaries of $W_{Jmed}(SQ)$ are not included in the set of politically feasible policies.

These arguments have a further implication:

PROPOSITION 6.7. J_{med} is a necessary member of any majority that replaces SQ by some other policy.

FIGURE 6.3

Draft Opinion Outside W$_{Jmed}$(SQ) Cannot Gain Majority Support

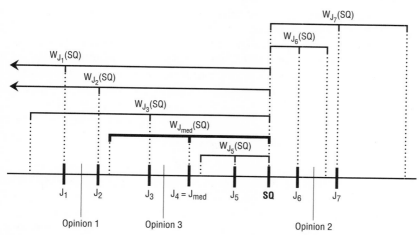

To prove this, consider what would happen if J$_{med}$ were not a member of some coalition that seeks to replace SQ with some other policy. For a proposal to the left of W$_{Jmed}$(SQ), such as Opinion 1 in Figure 6.3, there can be at most *maj* − 1 justices who prefer the proposal over SQ. Similarly, for a proposal to the right of W$_{Jmed}$(SQ), such as Opinion 2 in Figure 6.3, there can be at most *maj* − 1 justices who prefer the proposal over SQ. Hence, this coalition that seeks to replace SQ with some other policy but without the support of J$_{med}$ cannot be a majority coalition because it can contain at most *maj* − 1 justices. We can thus conclude that J$_{med}$ is a necessary member of any majority coalition that seeks to replace SQ by some other policy. In fact, J$_{med}$ is the only justice whose vote is always essential for replacing SQ by some other policy.

Moreover, the following three results hold as well:

PROPOSITION 6.8. If J$_{med}$ prefers some proposal to SQ, this means that there will also be a majority of justices (that is, there will be at least *maj* − 1 other justices) who prefer this proposal to SQ.

PROPOSITION 6.9. The preferred-to set of SQ for a justice will be contained by the preferred-to set of SQ for each justice whose ideal point lies outside the ideal point of the first justice.

PROPOSITION 6.10. W$_{Jmed}$(SQ) will be contained by the preferred-to set of each justice whose ideal point lies to the outside of J$_{med}$.

To illustrate these propositions, see Figure 6.3. Justice J$_{med}$ (who is justice J$_4$

here) prefers Opinion 3 to SQ, because Opinion 3 lies inside $W_{Jmed}(SQ)$. But justices J_1, J_2, and J_3 all lie to the left of J_{med}, and note that their preferred-to sets of SQ all necessarily contain $W_{Jmed}(SQ)$. Because Opinion 3 lies inside $W_{Jmed}(SQ)$, Opinion 3 must lie inside $W_{J1}(SQ)$, $W_{J2}(SQ)$, and $W_{J3}(SQ)$ as well. Therefore, all four justices—J_1 through J_4—prefer Opinion 3 to SQ, which means that this opinion could be adopted by a Court majority.

Propositions 6.5 through 6.10 further highlight the primacy of the median justice in the Supreme Court's decision-making process. Proposals to upset SQ in favor of some new policy will always fail if they cannot gain the support of the median justice.

What Policies Do Different Majority Coalitions Prefer to SQ?

What do these first ten propositions mean for coalition formation and the final vote? Our purpose now is to determine the set of policies that various justices prefer to SQ. The methods we develop in this section provide a useful way of identifying what policy would be selected on the final vote.

Figures 6.4, 6.5, and 6.6 show for a five-member Court the set of points that each justice prefers to SQ, given three different locations for SQ: between J_3 and J_4 in Figure 6.4, between J_4 and J_5 in Figure 6.5, and to the right of J_5 in Figure 6.6. We will demonstrate that these possible locations for SQ will influence what proposals can defeat SQ and who would support each such proposal. Note that for this five-member Court, justice J_3 will be J_{med} in all three figures, and in each figure the preferred-to set of J_3, which is $W_{J3}(SQ)$, defines the set of policies that can upset SQ.

First consider Figure 6.4, in which SQ lies between J_3 and J_4. Because J_1 and J_2 lie to the left of J_3, justices J_1 and J_2 also prefer the points in $W_{J3}(SQ)$ to SQ itself: the reason (see Proposition 6.10) is that $W_{J3}(SQ)$ falls inside both $W_{J2}(SQ)$ and $W_{J1}(SQ)$. We label the points in $W_{J3}(SQ)$ as Region III, and note that justices J_1, J_2, and J_3 would all prefer a proposal in Region III to SQ. However, the policies in Region III all fall outside the preferred-to sets of J_4 and J_5, so these two justices would prefer SQ to any policy to the left of SQ (such as a policy in Region III). Hence, for any proposal in Region III the coalitions on the final vote would be $\{J_1 J_2 J_3\}$ against $\{J_4 J_5\}$.[4]

Region II in Figure 6.4 is the set of points that J_2 prefers to SQ but that J_3 does not prefer to SQ; in effect, Region II contains the set of points in $W_{J2}(SQ)$ minus the set of points in $W_{J3}(SQ)$. Hence, a policy in Region II would be preferred to SQ by justices J_1 and J_2 but not by justice J_3: an outcome in Region II would be worse than SQ for justice J_3. By Proposition 6.7, if justice J_3 (who is J_{med}) fails to support a proposal to replace SQ by some policy in Region II, the proposal will fail. The reason here is that jus-

FIGURE 6.4

Politically Feasible Policies When SQ Is between J_3 and J_4

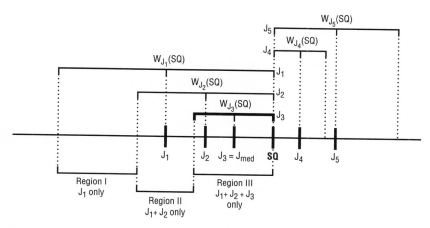

tice J_3 would join with justices J_4 and J_5 to protect SQ against those proposed movements to the left of SQ that justice J_3 considers too extreme
(such as an opinion in Region II). For a proposal in Region II, then, the
coalitions would be $\{J_1J_2\}$ against $\{J_3J_4J_5\}$, hence SQ would remain unchanged. (Notice that because justice J_3 wants to move policy leftward from
SQ but justices J_4 and J_5 want to move policy rightward from SQ, these
members of what seems to be a majority coalition—$\{J_3J_4J_5\}$—could not
agree on a common policy of their own to replace SQ; all they could agree
on is to retain SQ when faced with any other proposal.)

Next, Region I in Figure 6.4 is the set of points that justice J_1 prefers to
SQ but that justices J_2 and J_3 do not prefer to SQ; in effect, Region I contains the set of points in $W_{J_1}(SQ)$ minus the points in $W_{J_2}(SQ)$.[5] A policy in
Region I would thus be preferred to SQ by justice J_1 but not by justices J_2
or J_3. Hence, it follows that justices J_2 and J_3 would join with justices J_4 and
J_5 to protect SQ against a proposal to move policy to Region I; this proposal
would be too extreme a leftward movement in SQ for justices J_2 and J_3, and
justices J_4 and J_5 prefer SQ to any leftward policy change. For a proposal in
Region I, then, the coalitions would be $\{J_1\}$ against $\{J_2J_3J_4J_5\}$, hence SQ
would remain unchanged. (Again, because justices J_2 and J_3 would want to
move policy leftward from SQ but justices J_4 and J_5 would want to move
policy rightward from SQ, these members of what seems to be a majority
coalition—$\{J_2J_3J_4J_5\}$—could not agree on a common policy of their own
to replace SQ; all they could agree on is to retain SQ when faced with any
other proposal.)

FIGURE 6.5

Politically Feasible Policies When SQ Is between J_4 and J_5

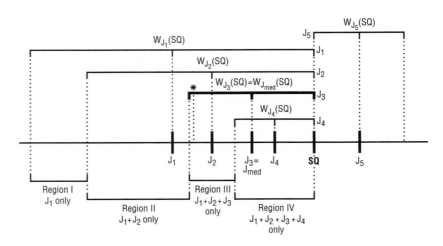

In sum, when J_{med} is adjacent to SQ, as in Figure 6.4, only those propos-als that lie in Region III, which in this case is defined by $W_{Jmed}(SQ)$, are po-litically feasible; all other proposals—that is, those in Regions I and II—will be rejected in favor of SQ by a majority of justices.

In Figure 6.5, SQ lies between J_4 and J_5, which means that justice J_3, who is still J_{med}, is no longer the justice adjacent to SQ. As a result, there are now two distinct regions, not just one, with politically feasible policies. First, con-sider the set of points that justice J_4 prefers to SQ, that is, $W_{J4}(SQ)$. Note that $W_{J4}(SQ)$ falls inside $W_{J3}(SQ)$, $W_{J2}(SQ)$, and $W_{J1}(SQ)$. This means that the points that justice J_4 prefers to SQ are also preferred to SQ by everyone to the left of J_4, that is, by justices J_1, J_2, and J_3. Call this Region IV.

Next, consider the set of points that justice J_3 prefers to SQ but that jus-tice J_4 does not prefer to SQ. This is Region III. It contains the set of points preferred to SQ by justices J_1, J_2, and J_3 but not by justice J_4.

Now consider the set of points that justice J_2 prefers to SQ but that jus-tices J_4 and J_3 do not prefer to SQ. This is Region II. It contains the set of points preferred to SQ by justices J_1 and J_2 but not by justices J_3 or J_4.

Finally, consider the set of points that justice J_1 prefers to SQ but that jus-tices J_2, J_3, and J_4 do not prefer to SQ. Call this Region I. It contains the set of points preferred to SQ by justice J_1 but not by justices J_2, J_3, or J_4.

If the proposal under consideration in Figure 6.5 is in Region IV, all four of the majority-side justices—J_1, J_2, J_3, and J_4—would support any such policy over SQ: such a policy will lie inside all their preferred-to sets. Hence, the coalitions

FIGURE 6.6

Politically Feasible Policies When SQ Is to the Right of J₅

A.

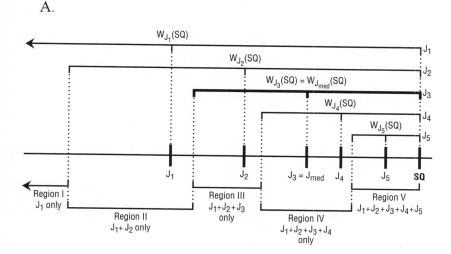

B.

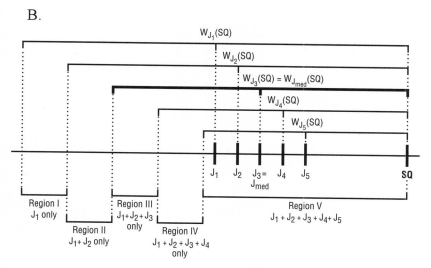

on the final vote here would be $\{J_1J_2J_3J_4\}$ against $\{J_5\}$. If the proposal under consideration is in Region III, the first three justices—J_1, J_2, and J_3—would support any such policy over SQ, but any such policy would be worse than SQ for justice J_4 (as well as for justice J_5). Hence, the coalition would be $\{J_1J_2J_3\}$ against $\{J_4J_5\}$. This policy in Region III would defeat SQ on a 3–2 vote, but it would do so without the support of majority-side justice J_4.

If the proposal under consideration is in Region II, then both justices J_3 and J_4 would defect to the other side: the coalitions on the final vote here would become $\{J_1J_2\}$ against $\{J_3J_4J_5\}$, and SQ would be maintained by a 2−3 vote; note that justices J_3, J_4, and J_5 could not agree on a common proposal to replace SQ.

And if the proposal under consideration is in Region I, justices J_2, J_3, and J_4 would all defect to the other side: the coalitions on the final vote would become $\{J_1\}$ against $\{J_2J_3J_4J_5\}$, and SQ would be maintained on a 1−4 vote. Note that justices J_2, J_3, J_4, and J_5 could not agree on a common proposal to replace SQ.

In Figure 6.6, where SQ lies to the right of J_5, we show two different configurations that differ in the extent to which a justice's ideal point lies inside the preferred-to set of the next justice to the right; in particular, the ideal points in diagram A are more dispersed than in diagram B. In diagram A, consider the set of points that justice J_5 prefers to SQ, that is, $W_{J5}(SQ)$. Note that $W_{J5}(SQ)$ falls inside $W_{J4}(SQ)$, $W_{J3}(SQ)$, $W_{J2}(SQ)$, and $W_{J1}(SQ)$; that is, the points that justice J_5 prefers to SQ are also preferred to SQ by everyone to the left of J_5 (that is, by justices J_1, J_2, J_3, and J_4). Call this Region V.

Next, consider the set of points that justice J_4 prefers to SQ but that justice J_5 does not prefer to SQ. Call this Region IV. Note that $W_{J4}(SQ)$ falls entirely inside $W_{J3}(SQ)$, $W_{J2}(SQ)$, and $W_{J1}(SQ)$ but not entirely inside $W_{J5}(SQ)$. Hence, the points in Region IV that justice J_4 prefers to SQ are also preferred to SQ by everyone to the left of J_4 (that is, by J_1, J_2, and J_3).

Next, consider the set of points that justice J_3 prefers to SQ but that justices J_4 and J_5 do not prefer to SQ. This is Region III. This set of points is preferred to SQ by justices J_1, J_2, and J_3 but not by justices J_4 or J_5.

Now consider the set of points that justice J_2 prefers to SQ but that justices J_3, J_4, and J_5 do not prefer to SQ. This is Region II. This set of points is preferred to SQ by justices J_1 and J_2 but not by justices J_3, J_4, or J_5.

Finally, consider the set of points that justice J_1 prefers to SQ but that justices J_2, J_3, J_4, and J_5 do not prefer to SQ. Call this Region I. This set of points is preferred to SQ by justice J_1 but not by justices J_2, J_3, J_4, or J_5.

If the proposal under consideration is in Region V, all five justices—J_1, J_2, J_3, J_4, and J_5—would support any such policy over SQ because such a policy would lie inside all their preferred-to sets. Hence, the coalitions on the final vote here would be $\{J_1J_2J_3J_4J_5\}$ against $\{\varnothing\}$.[6] If the proposal under consideration is in Region IV, the first four justices—J_1, J_2, J_3, and J_4—would support any such policy over SQ, but would be opposed by justice J_5, who prefers SQ. Hence, the coalitions on the final vote here would be $\{J_1J_2J_3J_4\}$ against $\{J_5\}$. If the proposal under consideration is in Region III, the first three justices—J_1, J_2, and J_3—would support any such policy over SQ, but any such policy would be worse than SQ for justices J_4 and J_5, so these two justices would defect in support of SQ. Hence, the coalitions on the final vote for a policy in Region III here would be $\{J_1J_2J_3\}$ against $\{J_4J_5\}$. If the proposal under consideration is in Region II, then the proposal would be rejected, with a coalition of $\{J_1J_2\}$ in favor of the proposal and a coalition of $\{J_3J_4J_5\}$ against. Finally, if the proposal under consideration is in Region I, the coalitions on the final vote would become $\{J_1\}$ against $\{J_2J_3J_4J_5\}$.

Diagram B in Figure 6.6 is much easier to describe because the ideal points of justices J_1, J_2, J_3, and J_4 now all lie inside $W_{J5}(SQ)$. This means that each justice could write an opinion at his or her own ideal point: because these opinions would all lie inside $W_{J5}(SQ)$, which is Region V in the diagram, the resulting coalitions would all be $\{J_1J_2J_3J_4J_5\}$ to $\{\varnothing\}$, with final votes of 5–0. Opinions that gain majority support could be written in Regions III and IV, but no one would have an incentive to make any such proposal.

These examples in Figures 6.4, 6.5, and 6.6 were constructed to illustrate three important points. First, notice that whereas $W_{Jmed}(SQ)$ constrains the set of politically feasible policies, different policies within $W_{Jmed}(SQ)$ may gain support from different numbers of justices; that is, the majority coalitions supporting the various policies in $W_{Jmed}(SQ)$ can differ in size. For example, diagram A in Figure 6.6 shows that $W_{Jmed}(SQ)$—that is, $W_{J3}(SQ)$—contains three distinct regions with politically feasible policies: Region V contains policies preferred to SQ by all five justices, Region IV contains policies preferred to SQ by four justices (J_1 through J_4), and Region III contains policies preferred to SQ by just three justices (J_1 through J_3). In other words, we have the following:

PROPOSITION 6.11. Support by J_{med} for some proposal does not tell us how many other justices will support the proposal as well; depending on the locations of the justices' ideal points relative to SQ, the possible coalitions could range in size from a bare majority to unanimity.

Second, as long as the justices have unique ideal points, the farther J_{med} is from SQ (in terms of the number of intervening justices), the greater the number of distinct regions of politically feasible policies there will be within $W_{Jmed}(SQ)$. In Figure 6.4, for example, J_{med} is adjacent to SQ, and there is just one region—Region III—with politically feasible policies: a proposal anywhere in Region III would defeat SQ on a 3–2 vote. In Figure 6.5, J_{med} is farther from SQ (justice J_4 lies in between), and now there are two regions with politically feasible policies: a proposal in Region III would defeat SQ on a 3–2 vote, and a proposal in Region IV would defeat SQ on a 4–1 vote. In Figure 6.6, J_{med} is even farther from SQ (both justices J_4 and J_5 lie in between), and now there are three regions with politically feasible policies: in both diagrams A and B, a proposal in Region III would defeat

SQ on a 3–2 vote, a proposal in Region IV would defeat SQ on a 4–1 vote, and a proposal in Region V would defeat SQ on a 5–0 vote. In other words, the following holds:

PROPOSITION 6.12. The farther SQ is from J_{med} (in terms of the number of intervening justices), the greater the range of possible sizes for the majority coalition.

Third, as long as the justices have unique ideal points, we can calculate the number of politically feasible regions in a simple way. Let R denote the number of regions that contain politically feasible policies of different sizes, and let K denote the total number of justices to the majority side of SQ. Then we can compute R from the following formula:

PROPOSITION 6.13. $R = K - maj + 1$.

For example, in Figure 6.4, K = 3 (that is, there are three justices to the majority side of SQ), and because maj 3, then R = 3 − 3 + 1 = 1, which we have already identified as Region III; it is the only region that contains policies that could gain majority support against SQ. In Figure 6.5, K = 4 (there are four justices to the left of SQ), and because maj = 3, then R = 4 − 3 + 1 = 2, which we have already identified as Regions III and IV. In Figure 6.6, K = 5 (there are five justices to the left of SQ), and because maj = 3, then R = 5 − 3 + 1 = 3, which we have already identified as Regions III, IV, and V.

How Do Justices Behave When They Dislike the Majority Opinion?

Our analysis has focused thus far on the sets of opinions that various justices prefer to the status quo. However, for any one opinion that is selected by the majority opinion writer, there will almost always be a majority of justices who prefer some other policy. Only when the majority opinion is written at the ideal point of the median justice—at J_{med}—will there not be a majority of justices who prefer an alternative policy.

How these dissatisfied justices respond to a draft majority opinion can affect what policy is ultimately selected by the Court. We will formulate three different versions of our model of coalition formation and the final vote on the basis of three different sets of assumptions about how actively various groups of justices respond to a draft majority opinion that they consider to be less than ideal.

First, in what we call the "agenda-control" version of our model, we assume that the dissatisfied justices respond passively to the majority opinion writer's draft opinion. In particular, we assume that if the draft majority opinion is better than SQ for a justice, he or she will simply join the opinion, whereas if the draft majority opinion is worse than SQ for a justice, he or she will not support the draft opinion. In neither case do any of the justices who are not the majority opinion writer try to get an alternative to the draft majority opinion selected. A reading of the literature on opinion writing leads us to suspect that many students of Supreme Court decision-making have something like this agenda-control version of our model in mind, albeit perhaps only implicitly.

Second, in what we call the "open-bidding" version of our model, the justices who are dissatisfied with the draft majority opinion are assumed to respond in a very active manner. If a draft majority opinion is not at J_{med}, this means—see Proposition 6.2—that there always exists some majority of justices (always including the median justice) who could write an alternative opinion that they like better and that attracts majority support. But if actually drafted, this alternative opinion would be worse than the original majority opinion for at least some of the justices who had supported the original majority opinion. These latter justices would be forced to defend themselves by crafting their own counterproposal that could regain majority support, but the only way to do this is to craft a proposal closer to J_{med}. This back-and-forth process of proposal and counterproposal will converge on a policy at J_{med}. Even the minority-side justices would have an incentive to participate actively in this back-and-forth process because they would prefer a policy at J_{med} to any policy farther away than (that is, to the outside of) J_{med}.

Third, in what we call the "median-holdout" version of our model, we assume that the median justice, at J_{med}, will respond to the draft majority opinion in a moderately active manner simply by withholding her vote unless the majority opinion writer selects a policy at J_{med}; if she withholds her vote, the justices on the other side of J_{med} from the majority opinion writer will join with her and withhold their votes as well because they also prefer an opinion at J_{med} to any opinion on the other side of J_{med}. Because J_{med} and the remaining justices comprise a majority of the Court, the draft opinion not at J_{med} cannot become the final majority opinion without the support of at least J_{med}. In this median-holdout version of our model, as in the open-bidding version, the only policy that is in equilibrium is a policy at J_{med}. We thus conclude that a draft opinion at J_{med} will eventually be produced by the majority opinion writer, and such an opinion will always be able to gain majority support against SQ (see Proposition 6.4).

In the next three sections we describe in detail these three different versions of our model and then determine what opinions and what size coalitions each version of the model would produce. In the subsequent sections we then compare the results from the three different versions of our model.

FIGURE 6.7

Outcomes from the Agenda-Control and Open-Bidding Models

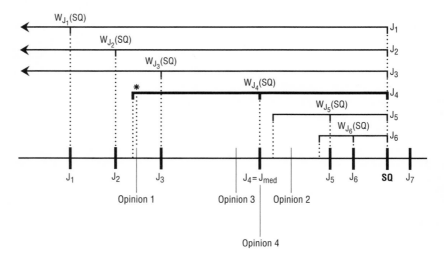

The Agenda-Control Version

The agenda-control version of our model is based on the following two assumptions:

ASSUMPTION 6.1. The writer of the majority opinion will write an opinion that meets two criteria:

(a) It lies inside the median justice's preferred-to set, $W_{Jmed}(SQ)$.
(b) It is as close as possible to his or her own ideal point.

ASSUMPTION 6.2. Justices not writing the majority opinion will support the majority opinion if it is better for them than SQ but will not support the majority opinion if it is worse for them than SQ.

For example, in Figure 6.7 note that justice J_4 is the median justice in this seven-person Court, and assume that justice J_2 has become the majority opinion writer. The best opinion for justice J_2 that could also gain majority support would be the opinion at *, labeled Opinion 1; it is the policy just inside $W_{Jmed}(SQ)$, which is closest to his own ideal point at J_2. However, notice that Opinion 1 lies outside the preferred-to sets of justices J_5, J_6, and J_7. Hence, justices J_1 through J_4 would support the majority opinion (Opinion 1 lies inside all their preferred-to sets) and justices J_5 through J_7 would not support the opinion (Opinion 1 lies outside all their preferred-to sets), yielding coalitions of $\{J_1J_2J_3J_4\}$ vs. $\{J_1J_2J_3\}$, for a 4-to-3 final vote for Opinion 1.

In this Figure 6.7 example, we emphasize that the justices who prefer SQ to Opinion 1 (justices J_5, J_6, and J_7) are passively accepting their defeat and are not proposing any alternative to Opinion 1. Moreover, even though each of the justices who prefers Opinion 1 to SQ (justices J_1 through J_4) also prefers his or her own ideal point to Opinion 1, they too are passively accepting Opinion 1 and are not proposing any alternative. Of course, justices J_1 and J_2 could not find majority support for any policy closer to them than Opinion 1 (because any policy to the left of Opinion 1 would lie outside $W_{Jmed}(SQ)$), hence they have no incentive to propose a policy other than Opinion 1. But whereas justices J_3 through J_6 could find majority support for some policy to the right of Opinion 1 but to the left of SQ, the agenda-control version of our model assumes that they make no effort to advance any such policy: justices J_3 and J_4 would simply join justices J_1 and J_2 in support of Opinion 1, and justices J_5 and J_6, as well as minority-side justice J_7, would not join the opinion.

In the agenda-control version of our model, then, as long as the majority opinion writer selects a policy that is preferred to SQ by a majority of the justices, none of the other justices will propose any alternative, even though most or all of them may prefer some other policy to what the majority opinion writer has selected. In effect, then, these other justices are voluntarily ceding control of the Court's decision-making agenda to the majority opinion writer. That is, they are treating their own decision-making agenda as containing just two options: the majority opinion writer's draft opinion and SQ. This is why we refer to this model as the *agenda-control* version of our model: the justices are ceding complete control of the Court's agenda to the majority opinion writer.

WHAT OPINIONS ARE ADOPTED AND WHAT COALITIONS RESULT?

The example in Figure 6.7 is not the only possible illustration, so we must present a more general assessment of what opinions will be adopted and what size coalitions will form in support of these opinions. The opinions adopted and the sizes of the coalitions supporting and opposing them in the agenda-control version of our model will depend on the conjunction of three variables: the location of the justices' ideal points relative to SQ, the locations of the justices' ideal points relative to each other's preferred-to sets of SQ, and which justice is writing the majority opinion.

In our analysis of what policies different majority coalitions prefer to SQ (involving Figures 6.4, 6.5, and 6.6) we have already shown how the first two variables interact. Here we systematically analyze the third variable—which justice is writing the majority opinion?—to show what policy each possible opinion writer would select.

FIGURE 6.8

Coalition Sizes with SQ to the Right of J₅

A.

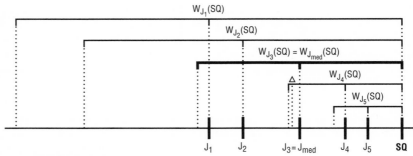

Agenda Control Model			
Opinion Writer Is	Opinion Is At	Coalition Lineups	Coalition Sizes
J_1	J_1	$J_1 + J_2 + J_3$ vs. $J_4 + J_5$	3-2
J_2	J_2	$J_1 + J_2 + J_3$ vs. $J_4 + J_5$	3-2
J_3	Open-Bidding→J_3	$J_1 + J_2 + J_3 + J_4$ vs. J_5	4-1
J_4	J_4	$J_1 + J_2 + J_3 + J_4 + J_5$ vs. Ø	5-0
J_5	J_5	$J_1 + J_2 + J_3 + J_4 + J_5$ vs. Ø	5-0

B.

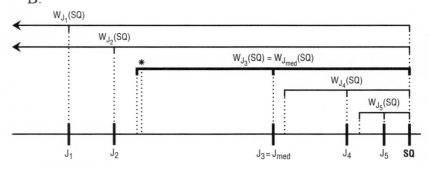

Agenda Control Model			
Opinion Writer Is	Opinion Is At	Coalition Lineups	Coalition Sizes
J_1	✳	$J_1 + J_2 + J_3$ vs. $J_4 + J_5$	3-2
J_2	✳	$J_1 + J_2 + J_3$ vs. $J_4 + J_5$	3-2
J_3	Open-Bidding→J_3	$J_1 + J_2 + J_3$ vs. $J_4 + J_5$	3-2
J_4	J_4	$J_1 + J_2 + J_3 + J_4$ vs. J_5	4-1
J_5	J_5	$J_1 + J_2 + J_3 + J_4 + J_5$ vs. Ø	5-0

We noted in Assumption 6.1 that the rational strategy for the majority opinion writer is to select that policy that lies inside the preferred-to set of the median justice, $W_{Jmed}(SQ)$, and that is also as close as possible to his or her own ideal point. In general, this has the following implications:

PROPOSITION 6.14. In the agenda-control version of our model, the majority opinion writer will write one of three different opinions, depending on the location of his or her ideal point:

(a) if the opinion writer's ideal point lies outside $W_{Jmed}(SQ)$, the opinion writer will draft an opinion just inside the outside boundary of $W_{Jmed}(SQ)$;

(b) if the opinion writer's ideal point lies inside $W_{Jmed}(SQ)$, the opinion writer will draft an opinion at his or her own ideal point;

(c) if the opinion writer's ideal point is on the minority side, the opinion writer will draft an opinion just inside the SQ boundary of $W_{Jmed}(SQ)$.

The opinion drafted at one of these three locations is the best opinion for the opinion writer that could gain majority support. Because the agenda-control version assumes that the other justices will respond passively, either by endorsing the opinion (if the majority opinion lies inside their preferred-to sets) or by not endorsing it (if the majority opinion lies outside their preferred-to sets), one of the opinions specified in Proposition 6.14 will become the final outcome.

An important aspect of this strategy by the majority opinion writer is the fact that every possible coalition size can be produced in support of the resulting opinion. What determines any particular coalition size is simply how many justices' preferred-to sets contain the majority writer's opinion. This number will depend on where SQ is located, on where the justices' ideal points are located, and on where the ideal point of the majority opinion writer is. With some configurations of these variables, a minimum-winning coalition on a nine-member Court—a 5–4 vote—will be produced; with other configurations, larger winning coalitions—for example, 6–3, 7–2, or 8–1 votes—will be produced; with still other configurations, a unanimous coalition—a 9–0 vote—will be produced.

To illustrate these arguments with a five-member Court, consider Figures 6.8, 6.9, and 6.10. In Figure 6.8 all five justices lie to the left of SQ. There are two diagrams in this figure, and they differ only in the extent of the overlap between each justice's ideal point and the preferred-to set of the next justice to the right; these varying degrees of overlap will affect the coalition sizes that are generated for the opinions written by different opinion writers. In diagram A there is a moderate amount of overlap; in particular, the ideal points of justices J_1 and J_2 fall inside the preferred-to set of justice J_3, the ideal point of justice J_3 falls inside the preferred-to set of justice J_4, and the ideal point of justice J_4 falls inside the preferred-to set of justice J_5. In dia-

FIGURE 6.9

Coalition Sizes with SQ between J₄ and J₅

A.

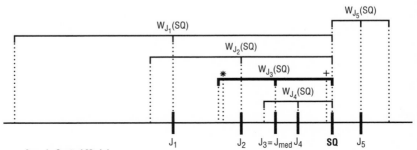

Agenda Control Model

Opinion Writer Is	Opinion Is At	Coalition Lineups	Coalition Sizes
J_1	✳	$J_1 + J_2 + J_3$ vs. $J_4 + J_5$	3-2
J_2	J_2	$J_1 + J_2 + J_3$ vs. $J_4 + J_5$	3-2
J_3	Open-Bidding→J_3	$J_1 + J_2 + J_3 + J_4$ vs. J_5	4-1
J_4	J_4	$J_1 + J_2 + J_3 + J_4$ vs. J_5	4-1
J_5	+	$J_1 + J_2 + J_3 + J_4 + J_5$ vs. Ø	5-0

B.

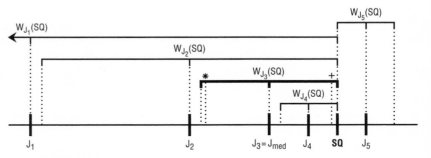

Agenda Control Model

Opinion Writer Is	Opinion Is At	Coalition Lineups	Coalition Sizes
J_1	✳	$J_1 + J_2 + J_3$ vs. $J_4 + J_5$	3-2
J_2	✳	$J_1 + J_2 + J_3$ vs. $J_4 + J_5$	3-2
J_3	Open-Bidding→J_3	$J_1 + J_2 + J_3$ vs. $J_4 + J_5$	3-2
J_4	J_4	$J_1 + J_2 + J_3 + J_4$ vs. J_5	4-1
J_5	+	$J_1 + J_2 + J_3 + J_4 + J_5$ vs. Ø	5-0

gram B, there is less of this overlap: justice J_1 falls inside justice J_2's preferred-to set but outside justice J_3's, justice J_2 falls outside justice J_3's preferred-to set, justice J_3 falls outside justice J_4's preferred-to set, and justice J_4 falls outside justice J_5's preferred-to set. Note that justice J_3 is the median justice, J_{med}, in both diagrams (and in Figures 6.9 and 6.10 below).

Underneath each diagram is a table listing the possible majority opinion writers, the location of the opinion that each opinion-writing justice would write, which other justices would support and oppose this opinion over SQ, and what the resulting coalition sizes are.

For example, in diagram A in Figure 6.8, if justice J_1 writes the opinion, he would rationally write the opinion at his own ideal point of J_1 because J_1 lies inside $W_{Jmed}(SQ)$, the preferred-to set of justice J_3, the median justice. Because an opinion at J_1 falls inside the preferred-to sets of justices $J_1, J_2,$ and J_3 but outside the preferred-to sets of justices J_4 and J_5, the resulting coalitions for and against the opinion at J_1 will be $\{J_1 J_2 J_3\}$ vs. $\{J_4 J_5\}$. Hence, the coalition sizes here will be 3–2.

If justice J_2 writes the opinion, he can write it at his own ideal point of J_2 because J_2 lies inside justice J_3's preferred-to set. As with the opinion at J_1, an opinion at J_2 falls inside the preferred-to sets of justices $J_1, J_2,$ and J_3 but outside the preferred-to sets of justices J_4 and J_5. Hence, the coalitions for and against the opinion at J_2 will again be $\{J_1 J_2 J_3\}$ vs. $\{J_4 J_5\}$, with coalition sizes of 3–2 as before.

If the median justice, J_3, writes the opinion, she can write it at her own ideal point of J_3. This opinion at J_3 falls inside the preferred-to sets of justices $J_1, J_2, J_3,$ and J_4 but outside the preferred-to set of justice J_5. Hence, the coalitions for and against the opinion at J_3 will be $\{J_1 J_2 J_3 J_4\}$ vs. $\{J_5\}$, so the coalition sizes here will be 4–1.

If justice J_4 writes the opinion, he can write it at his own ideal point of J_4 because J_4 lies inside justice J_3's preferred-to set. In fact, this opinion at J_4 falls inside the preferred-to sets of all five justices. Hence, the coalitions for and against the opinion at J_4 will be $\{J_1 J_2 J_3 J_4 J_5\}$ vs. $\{\emptyset\}$, so the coalition sizes here will be 5–0.

Finally, if justice J_5 writes the opinion, he can write it at his own ideal point of J_5 because J_5 also lies inside justice J_3's preferred-to set. In fact, because this opinion at J_5 falls inside the preferred-to sets of all five justices, the coalitions for and against the opinion at J_5 will again be $\{J_1 J_2 J_3 J_4 J_5\}$ vs. $\{\emptyset\}$, hence the coalition sizes here will also be 5–0.

In diagram B in Figure 6.8, the ideal points and SQ are in the same relative locations, but the ideal points are dispersed more to the left, with less overlap between each justice's ideal point and the preferred-to set of the next justice to the right. This alignment produces more of the minimum-winning coalitions (3–2) and fewer of the larger (4–1 and 5–0) coalitions.

FIGURE 6.10

Coalition Sizes with SQ between J_3 and J_4

A.

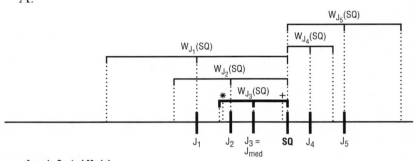

Agenda Control Model

Opinion Writer Is	Opinion Is At	Coalition Lineups	Coalition Sizes
J_1	✳	$J_1 + J_2 + J_3$ vs. $J_4 + J_5$	3-2
J_2	J_2	$J_1 + J_2 + J_3$ vs. $J_4 + J_5$	3-2
J_3	Open-Bidding→J_3	$J_1 + J_2 + J_3$ vs. $J_4 + J_5$	3-2
J_4	+	$J_1 + J_2 + J_3 + J_4$ vs. J_5	4-1
J_5	+	$J_1 + J_2 + J_3 + J_5$ vs. J_4	4-1

B.

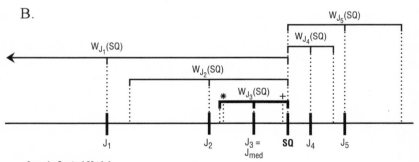

Agenda Control Model

Opinion Writer Is	Opinion Is At	Coalition Lineups	Coalition Sizes
J_1	✳	$J_1 + J_2 + J_3$ vs. $J_4 + J_5$	3-2
J_2	✳	$J_1 + J_2 + J_3$ vs. $J_4 + J_5$	3-2
J_3	Open-Bidding→J_3	$J_1 + J_2 + J_3$ vs. $J_4 + J_5$	3-2
J_4	+	$J_1 + J_2 + J_3 + J_4$ vs. J_5	4-1
J_5	+	$J_1 + J_2 + J_3 + J_5$ vs. J_4	4-1

For example, if justice J_1 writes the opinion, he will have to write it at the policy indicated by the * just inside the left-hand boundary of justice J_3's preferred-to set, $W_{J3}(SQ)$, in order to gain the support of justice J_3, and thus of a majority. Because an opinion at * falls inside the preferred-to sets of justices J_1, J_2, and J_3 but outside the preferred-to sets of justices J_4 and J_5, the coalitions for and against the opinion at * will be $\{J_1J_2J_3\}$ vs. $\{J_4J_5\}$, hence the coalition sizes here will be 3–2.

If justice J_2 writes the opinion, he must also write it at * for the same reason as when justice J_1 writes the opinion: to gain the support of justice J_3, and thus of a majority. As before, then, an opinion at * falls inside the preferred-to sets of justices J_1, J_2, and J_3 but outside the preferred-to sets of justices J_4 and J_5. Hence, the coalitions for and against the opinion at * will again be $\{J_1J_2J_3\}$ vs. $\{J_4J_5\}$, with coalition sizes of 3–2.

If justice J_3 writes the opinion, she can write it at her own ideal point of J_3. An opinion at J_3 falls inside the preferred-to sets of justices J_1, J_2, and J_3 but outside the preferred-to sets of justices J_4 and J_5. Hence, the coalitions for and against the opinion at J_3 will again be $\{J_1J_2J_3\}$ vs. $\{J_4J_5\}$, so the coalition sizes here will again be 3–2.

If justice J_4 writes the opinion, he can write it at his own ideal point of J_4 because J_4 lies inside justice J_3's preferred-to set. An opinion at J_4 falls inside the preferred-to sets of justices J_1, J_2, J_3, and J_4 but outside the preferred-to set of justice J_5. Hence, the coalitions for and against the opinion at J_4 will be $\{J_1J_2J_3J_4\}$ vs. $\{J_5\}$, so the coalition sizes here will be 4–1.

Finally, if justice J_5 writes the opinion, he can write it at J_5 because J_5 lies inside justice J_3's preferred-to set. Because an opinion at J_5 falls inside the preferred-to sets of all five justices, the coalitions for and against the opinion at J_5 will be $\{J_1J_2J_3J_4J_5\}$ vs. $\{\emptyset\}$, hence the coalition sizes here will be 5–0.

Notice in Figure 6.8 that with all five justices' ideal points lying to the left of SQ, all possible coalition sizes are produced (recall Propositions 6.11 and 6.12), depending on who the opinion writer is: coalitions can be 3–2, 4–1, or 5–0. This results from the fact that in both diagrams there is still some degree of dispersion in the justices' ideal points. If there is little dispersion, however, as in diagram B in Figure 6.6, all coalitions would be $\{J_1J_2J_3J_4J_5\}$ vs. $\{\emptyset\}$, with 5–0 votes.

Next consider Figure 6.9, in which SQ lies between J_4 and J_5. In this configuration, the same range of coalition sizes is possible (recall Proposition 6.12): coalition sizes of 3–2 and 4–1 can still occur, although 5–0 coalitions are possible only if justice J_5, a minority-side justice, writes the majority opinion (see below); if justice J_5 (whose ideal point is to the right of SQ here) does not write the majority opinion, he will always vote against the majority opinions because they will all lie to the left of SQ. Now consider the possible coalition sizes in diagram A, in which ideal points and the adjacent preferred-to sets moderately overlap. Justice J_1 will have to write an opinion at *; the resulting coalitions are $\{J_1J_2J_3\}$ vs. $\{J_4J_5\}$, with coalition sizes of 3–2. Justice J_2 can write an opinion at J_2; the resulting coalitions are $\{J_1J_2J_3\}$ vs. $\{J_4J_5\}$, with coalition sizes of 3–2. Justice J_3 can write an opinion at J_3; the resulting coalitions are $\{J_1J_2J_3J_4\}$ vs. $\{J_5\}$, with coalition sizes of 4–1. Finally, justice J_4 can write an opinion at J_4; the resulting coalitions are also $\{J_1J_2J_3J_4\}$ vs. $\{J_5\}$, so the coalition sizes here will be 4–1 as well.

For the preference configuration in Figure 6.9, however, it will also be important to identify what opinion a minority-side justice would write. A minority-side justice could end up writing the majority opinion only if he or she votes with the majority on the conference vote (stage 2); as we will see in Chapters 7 and 8, there are conditions in which a justice has sound strategic reasons for doing this. In diagram A of Figure 6.9, then, the question is what opinion the minority-side justice J_5 would write. Because he voted with the majority on the conference vote, our expectation is that he would write a majority-side opinion. The best majority-side opinion for this minority-side justice would be an opinion at +, which lies slightly to the left of SQ and just inside $W_{J3}(SQ)$, the preferred-to set of the median justice. An opinion at + would do the least amount of damage to justice J_5's concerns. (As we will demonstrate in the next two chapters, an opinion at + will sometimes be better for minority-side justices than the final opinion that would otherwise be produced, hence minority-side justices will sometimes have an incentive to behave in this general manner.) Because an opinion at + lies inside the other four justices' preferred-to sets, and because justice J_5 would vote for his own opinion, the resulting coalition would be $\{J_1J_2J_3, J_4J_5\}$ vs. $\{\varnothing\}$, so the coalition sizes will be 5–0 here.

In diagram B in Figure 6.9, the ideal points and adjacent preferred-to sets are more dispersed. Justice J_1 will have to write an opinion at *; the resulting coalitions are $\{J_1J_2J_3\}$ vs. $\{J_4J_5\}$, with coalition sizes of 3–2. Justice J_2 must also write an opinion at *; the resulting coalitions are again $\{J_1J_2J_3\}$ vs. $\{J_4J_5\}$, with coalition sizes of 3–2. Justice J_3 can write an opinion at J_3; the resulting coalitions are again $\{J_1J_2J_3\}$ vs. $\{J_4J_5\}$, with coalition sizes of 3–2. Justice J_4 can write an opinion at J_4; the resulting coalitions are also $\{J_1J_2J_3J_4\}$ vs. $\{J_5\}$, so the coalition sizes here will be 4–1. Finally, justice J_5 would again have to write an opinion at +; as in diagram A, the resulting coalition would thus be $\{J_1J_2J_3, J_4J_5\}$ vs. $\{\varnothing\}$, so the coalition sizes will be 5–0 here.

In Figure 6.10, SQ now lies between J_3 and J_4, and when a majority-side justice writes the opinion, the coalition lineups will all be $\{J_1J_2J_3\}$ vs. $\{J_4J_5\}$, and the coalition sizes will all be 3–2. This is because both justices J_4 and J_5 (whose ideal points are to the right of SQ) will always vote against the majority opinions that will all fall to the left of SQ. In diagram A, if justice J_1 writes the opinion, the opinion will have to be at ∗, and the resulting coalitions will be $\{J_1J_2J_3\}$ vs. $\{J_4J_5\}$, with coalition sizes of 3–2. If justice J_2 writes the opinion, the opinion can be at his own ideal point of J_2, and the resulting coalitions will again be $\{J_1J_2J_3\}$ vs. $\{J_4J_5\}$, with coalition sizes of 3–2. If justice J_3 writes the opinion, the opinion can be at her own ideal point of J_3, and the resulting coalitions will again be $\{J_1J_2J_3\}$ vs. $\{J_4J_5\}$, with coalition sizes of 3–2. However, if minority-side justice J_4 writes the majority opinion, he would write it at +, just inside $W_{J3}(SQ)$, and the resulting coalitions will be $\{J_1J_2J_3J_4\}$ vs. $\{J_5\}$, with coalition sizes of 4–1.[7] Similarly, if minority-side justice J_5 writes the majority opinion, he would also write it at +, just inside $W_{J3}(SQ)$, and the resulting coalitions will be $\{J_1J_2J_3J_5\}$ vs. $\{J_4\}$, with coalition sizes of 4–1 as well.

In diagram B, if justice J_1 writes the opinion, the opinion will have to be at ∗, and the resulting coalitions will be $\{J_1J_2J_3\}$ vs. $\{J_4J_5\}$, with coalition sizes of 3–2. If justice J_2 writes the opinion, the opinion will also have to be at ∗, and the resulting coalitions will again be $\{J_1J_2J_3\}$ vs. $\{J_4J_5\}$, with coalition sizes of 3–2. If justice J_3 writes the opinion, the opinion can be at her own ideal point of J_3, and the resulting coalitions will again be $\{J_1J_2J_3\}$ vs. $\{J_4J_5\}$, with coalition sizes of 3–2. If minority-side justice J_4 writes the majority opinion, he would write it at +, just inside $W_{J3}(SQ)$, and the resulting coalitions will be $\{J_1J_2J_3J_4\}$ vs. $\{J_5\}$, with coalition sizes of 4–1. Similarly, if minority-side justice J_5 writes the majority opinion, he would write it at +, just inside $W_{J3}(SQ)$, and the resulting coalitions will be $\{J_1J_2J_3J_5\}$ vs. $\{J_4\}$, with coalition sizes of 4–1 as well.

We can summarize the implications of these illustrations in the following five propositions. The diagrams in Figure 6.8 demonstrate that the entire range of coalition sizes can be produced by rational, policy-maximizing justices on a five-member Court, and a similar set of examples could easily be generated for a nine-member Court. These observations can be advanced as a general result:

PROPOSITION 6.15. In the agenda-control version of our model, a rational, policy-maximizing majority opinion writer could write a majority opinion that would generate every possible coalition size—ranging from minimum winning, at one extreme, to unanimity, at the other extreme—on the final vote, depending on the location of his or her own ideal point, on the location of SQ, and on the locations of the justices' ideal points.

One implication of this proposition is that there is no reason to expect coalitions of any one particular size—such as minimum-winning coalitions (as predicted, e.g., by Rohde 1972a)—to be produced. Instead, the opinion selected by a rational, policy-maximizing majority opinion writer could be supported by a coalition of any size, depending on the configuration of the three key variables.

Although it would difficult to list all the different ways in which any one coalition size could be produced, it is useful to characterize the conditions under which the extremes—minimum-winning coalitions, on the one hand, and unanimous coalitions, on the other—could be produced. Our next argument, then, is a general statement about the conditions under which minimum-winning coalitions will occur (assuming that no justices have identical ideal points):

PROPOSITION 6.16. In the agenda-control version of our model, a minimum-winning coalition can be produced if and only if either of the two following conditions holds:

(a)   the majority side of SQ contains only a bare majority of the justices' ideal points and a majority-side justice is the opinion writer; or

(b)   the majority side of SQ contains more than a bare majority of the justices' ideal points but the opinion writer's ideal point lies outside the preferred-to set of the next justice closer to SQ from J_{med}.

For part (a), the rationale should be obvious: if the majority side of SQ contains only a bare majority of the justices' ideal points and if the majority opinion writer is a majority-side justice, then the only majority coalitions that are possible are a bare majority in size. (If the majority opinion writer is a minority-side justice, then this justice would vote for his own opinion at + as well, hence the winning coalition would be more than a bare majority.) For a proof of part (b), we examine all possible locations for the majority opinion writer's ideal point and show that only for the specified condition will minimum-winning coalitions be produced. We begin by noting that if the majority opinion writer's ideal point lies outside the preferred-to set of J_{med} (which necessarily means that his ideal point lies outside the preferred-to set of the next justice closer to SQ from J_{med}), the opinion writer will not be able to select his or her own ideal point but will have to select a policy just inside the outside boundary of $W_{Jmed}(SQ)$. This policy will pick up the vote of J_{med} plus the *maj* − 1 justices to the outside of J_{med}, for a total of *maj* votes, which is a bare majority (and thus a minimum-winning coalition) of all the justices; however, this policy will lie outside the preferred-to set of the justices closer to SQ than J_{med}, hence the policy will not pick up the votes of any justices with ideal points closer to SQ than J_{med}. Next, if the opinion writer's ideal point lies inside the preferred-to set of J_{med} but outside the preferred-to set of the next justice closer to SQ from J_{med}, a policy at his or her own ideal point will gain the support of J_{med} plus the *maj* − 1 justices to the outside of J_{med}, for a total of *maj* votes (a bare majority). But because this policy lies outside the preferred-to set of the next justice closer to SQ from J_{med}, this justice and all remaining justices even closer to SQ (and on the other side of SQ) will prefer SQ to the policy. Hence, only *maj* justices—a bare majority—will support the opinion, which means they constitute a minimum-winning coalition. In contrast, if the opinion writer's ideal point lies inside the preferred-to set of the next justice closer to SQ from J_{med}, he can write an opinion at his own ideal point; this opinion will necessarily lie inside the preferred-to sets of J_{med} and of all justices to the outside from J_{med}, for a total of at least *maj* + 1 justices who support the policy, which is more than minimum-winning in size. Thus, of all the possible locations for the majority opinion writer's ideal point, only the location specified in condition (b) will necessarily generate minimum-winning coalitions.

We also note that for some locations of the opinion writer's ideal point, the only way to create a minimum-winning coalition is for the opinion writer to write an opinion farther away from his or her ideal point than is necessary, which is to say that the writer is behaving irrationally. In diagram A in Figure 6.6, for example, assume that justice J_5 is the opinion writer. By writing an opinion at his own ideal point of J_5, he can automatically generate a unanimous 5–0 vote for this opinion; no compromises are necessary. In order to generate a minimum-winning 3–2 vote, the opinion writer would have to draft an opinion in Region III, which is to the left of his ideal point. Of course, this strategy would make no sense for justice J_5.

The conditions under which a unanimous coalition will be produced can also be specified:

PROPOSITION 6.17. In the agenda-control version of our model, a unanimous coalition can be produced if and only if one of the following two conditions hold:

   (a) the justices' ideal points all lie to one side of SQ and the majority opinion writer's opinion lies inside the preferred-to set of the justice closest to SQ; or,

   (b) there are one or more minority-side justices, one of them is the majority-opinion writer and writes a majority-side opinion just inside the SQ end of $W_{Jmed}(SQ)$, and all the minority-side justices vote for this majority-side opinion.

For condition (a), the rationale is that, for a unanimous coalition to support some opinion, it must be possible for all the justices to want to move in the same direction from SQ; this is possible only when the justices' ideal points all lie to one side of SQ. And for a particular opinion to gain the support of all justices, the opinion must lie inside the preferred-to set of the justice closest to SQ, which means the opinion will necessarily also lie inside the preferred-to sets of all other justices to that side of SQ (see Proposition 6.9). If either of these conditions in (a) is not met, the resulting coalition will not be unanimous. For condition (b), the minority-side justice who is writing the majority opinion will write it just inside the SQ end of $W_{J_{med}}(SQ)$, as with the opinion at + in diagram A of Figure 6.9, which necessarily means that the opinion will lie inside the preferred-to set of the majority-side justice closest to SQ. This in turn means that the opinion will necessarily lie inside the preferred-to sets of all the majority-side justices, but only if all the minority-side justices support this majority-side opinion as well (for example, to prevent something even worse for them on the majority side from being adopted) will the resulting coalition be unanimous.[8]

It will sometimes be possible for a majority-side opinion writer to increase the size of the coalition supporting his or her opinion but only by drafting an opinion closer to SQ than what would be needed to gain the support of just a bare majority. In diagram A in Figure 6.6, for example, assume that justice J_1 is the majority opinion writer. If he were to write an opinion in Region III (for example, just inside the outside boundary of $W_{J_3}(SQ)$), he could gain the support of a bare majority of justices for his opinion. However, should he want unanimous support for the opinion he writes, he would have to write the opinion in Region V, which is farther to the right from Region III. Although there is nothing in our model that predicts such behavior, there may be reasons lying outside the Court—for example, concerns about the Court's legitimacy with the public—for an opinion writer to diverge from a policy-maximizing strategy and adopt a vote-maximizing strategy instead.

Propositions 6.16 and 6.17 imply that as SQ moves from an extreme location (that is, from a location to one side of all the justices' ideal points) toward J_{med}, unanimous coalitions will no longer be possible (assuming that a majority-side justice is the majority opinion writer). Hence, we can also state the following:

PROPOSITION 6.18. In the agenda-control version of our model, as SQ moves closer to J_{med} from an extreme location (in terms of the number of intervening justices), the maximum possible size of any winning coalition will decrease (assuming that a majority-side justice is the majority opinion writer).

We should note that this decrease will not be a continuous function as SQ moves inward. Instead, it will be a step function: a decrease in the maximum possible coalition size will occur each time SQ passes some justice's ideal point as it moves toward J_{med}; the maximum possible coalition size will not change as SQ moves between any two justices' ideal points.

Because a more extreme SQ allows a wider possible range of coalition sizes, this also means that the choice of the opinion writer can have a greater impact on the actual outcomes and coalition sizes. For example, in diagram A in Figure 6.8, which has an extreme SQ (that is, all justices lie to the same side of SQ), note that if justice J_1 or J_2 is the opinion writer, a 3–2 coalition is produced for an opinion at J_1 or J_2 respectively; if justice J_3 is the opinion writer, a 4–1 coalition is produced for an opinion at J_3; and if justice J_4 or J_5 is the opinion writer, a 5–0 coalition is produced for an opinion at J_4 or J_5 respectively. In contrast, in both diagrams in Figure 6.10, where SQ is at its least extreme, only 3–2 or 4–1 coalitions can be produced. In general, then, as SQ moves closer to the median justice (in terms of the number of intervening justices), an increasing proportion of all possible coalitions will be minimum-winning.

Our final topic involves an inversion of the propositions advanced thus far. We have argued, in effect, that "If such-and-such is the configuration of the locations of the justices' ideal points, the location of SQ, and who the majority opinion writer is, then the following coalition lineups and coalition sizes will emerge: . . . ". However, we can also invert this argument and ask: For any given winning coalition size that might be observed (for example, 9–0, 8–1, and so forth down to 5–4), is there any unique configuration of the three variables that would have produced this winning coalition size? The answer is "no":

PROPOSITION 6.19. In the agenda-control version of our model, for any particular winning coalition lineup and winning coalition size, there will always be multiple configurations of the justices' ideal points, the location of SQ, and the identity of the opinion writer who will be able to produce that winning coalition size.

In other words, one cannot observe some coalitional outcome and work backward to what the particular configuration must have been that generated that outcome. There is not a unique configuration that could have produced any one coalitional outcome.

To illustrate, consider the nine-member Court in the diagrams in Figure 6.11. Assume that justice J_7 is the majority opinion writer, and we arbitrarily select a coalition lineup of $\{J_1J_2J_3J_4J_5J_6J_7\}$ vs. $\{J_8J_9\}$, with the resulting winning coalition size of 7–2, to investigate. We will show that there are several different configurations that could have produced this particular coalition lineup and winning coalition size.

In diagram (a), SQ lies to the right of all nine justices. The ideal point of justice J_7 here lies outside the preferred-to sets of both justices J_8 and J_9. An opinion written at his own ideal point of J_7 (which lies inside $W_{J5}(SQ)$, the preferred-to set of the median justice) will thus gain the support of justices J_1 through J_7 (because an opinion at J_7 falls inside all their preferred-to sets), but this opinion will lose the support of justices J_8 and J_9 (because it falls outside their preferred-to sets). Hence, these coalition lineups of $\{J_1J_2J_3J_4J_5J_6J_7\}$ vs. $\{J_8J_9\}$ and coalition sizes of 7–2 will be produced.

In diagram (b), SQ lies between J_8 and J_9. Here justice J_7 lies outside jus-

FIGURE 6.11

Multiple Ways of Producing a 7–2 Coalition

A. SQ to the right of all nine justices

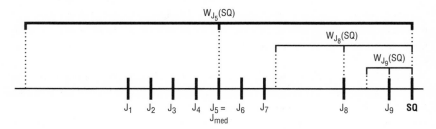

B. SQ between J_8 and J_9

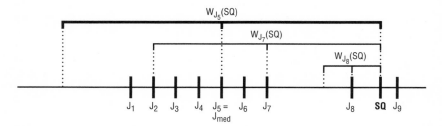

C. SQ between J_7 and J_8

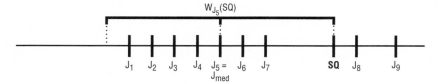

NOTE: J_7 is always the opinion writer. All coalitions produced are $\{J_1, J_2, J_3, J_4, J_5, J_6, J_7\}$ vs. $\{J_8, J_9\}$ for 7–2 final votes.

tice J_8's preferred-to set, so the opinion at J_7 will gain the support of justices J_1 through J_7 because an opinion at J_7 falls inside all their preferred-to sets, but the opinion at J_7 will be opposed by justices J_8 and J_9. Hence, these coalition lineups of $\{J_1 J_2 J_3 J_4 J_5 J_6 J_7\}$ vs. $\{J_8 J_9\}$ and coalition sizes of 7–2 will again be produced.

In diagram (c), now SQ lies between justices J_7 and J_8. Here justice J_7 is adjacent to SQ, so an opinion at J_7 will gain the support of justices J_1 through J_7 because an opinion at J_7 falls inside all their preferred-to sets but will be opposed by justices J_8 and J_9. Hence, the coalition lineups of $\{J_1 J_2 J_3 J_4 J_5 J_6 J_7\}$ vs. $\{J_8 J_9\}$ and coalition sizes of 7 to 2 will be produced yet again.

The Open-Bidding Version

The agenda–control version of our model assumes passive behavior by the justices not writing the majority opinion (see Assumption 6.2). In contrast, the open-bidding version assumes that the justices not writing the majority opinion will actively participate in the construction of an alternative opinion that is more favorable to themselves than the draft majority opinion (assuming that this initial draft majority opinion is not at J_{med}). Because the critical member of any coalition is justice J_{med}, the open-bidding process necessarily centers on efforts by justices on either side of justice J_{med} to attract her support for their preferred opinion. As they bid for her vote by making their respective proposals more and more attractive to her, the end result of this bidding process will be a final opinion at J_{med}.

There are two possible ways in which the open-bidding process might work. For example, a justice on each side of the median justice could act as a coalition leader, each proposing a draft opinion (whether simultaneously or sequentially) designed to attract the support of the median justice. Alternatively, the median justice herself might organize majority support for an opinion at her own ideal point. To cover both of these possibilities, we will advance the following as the foundation of the open-bidding version of our model:

ASSUMPTION 6.3. In the open-bidding version of our model, a justice who is not the majority opinion writer and who is dissatisfied with the draft majority opinion (that is, it is not at his or her ideal point) will behave in at least one of the following ways:

(a) If the median justice offers a draft opinion at J_{med} (or closer to J_{med} than the draft majority opinion), this justice will support it if it is closer to his or her own ideal point.

(b) If no other justice offers an alternative to the draft majority opinion, this justice will offer a draft majority opinion that is closer to his or her ideal point and that is closer to J_{med} than the draft majority opinion.

Although in the agenda-control version of our model, the minority-side justices will normally just dissent, in the open-bidding version it is rational for the minority-side justices to support an alternative to the draft majority opinion and even to participate actively in the construction and adoption of this alternative opinion. The reason is that although the minority-side justices all prefer SQ to every majority-side policy, they nonetheless have preferences over which majority-side policy is adopted. If their actions and votes could help defeat some very unfavorable majority-side policy and replace it with a less unfavorable majority-side policy, these justices would have an incentive to help establish this less unfavorable policy, even though it will remain worse for them than SQ. Nonetheless, as we will discuss below, how we should expect the minority-side justices to actually cast their final votes is not entirely clear.

To illustrate why the activism posited by Assumption 6.3 would lead to a final majority opinion at J_{med}, consider Figure 6.7 once again. Recall that justice J_4 is the median justice on this seven-member Court. Assume that justice J_2 is the majority opinion writer and that he initially writes Opinion 1 at *, which is just inside the left-hand edge of $W_{J4}(SQ)$. Justices J_1, J_2, J_3, and J_4 would all prefer Opinion 1 to SQ. However, any of the three justices who prefer SQ to Opinion 1—justices J_5, J_6, and J_7—could propose an alternative to Opinion 1, such as the policy labeled Opinion 2: Opinion 2 is closer to their ideal points than Opinion 1 and it is also closer to justice J_4's ideal point than Opinion 1. Opinion 2 would thus defeat Opinion 1 with the support of a majority of the justices, including J_4, the median justice. Hence, Opinion 2 would replace Opinion 1 as the provisional majority opinion.

However, justices J_1, J_2, and J_3 would be worse off with Opinion 2 than with Opinion 1, hence they would have an incentive to pull the opinion back toward themselves if they can. Because what turned Opinion 2 into a majority opinion was the fact that justice J_4 switched her vote from Opinion 1 to Opinion 2, justices J_1, J_2, and J_3 would have to pull justice J_4 back to their side by identifying a policy that is not only closer to their own ideal points than Opinion 2 but that is also better for justice J_4 than Opinion 2. A policy such as the one at Opinion 3 meets these needs: because Opinion 3 is closer to the ideal points of justices J_1, J_2, J_3, and J_4 than is Opinion 2, it could replace Opinion 2 as the provisional majority opinion.

But even this would not be the end of the story: because justices J_5, J_6, and J_7 all find themselves worse off with Opinion 3 than with Opinion 2, they would have an incentive to pull the opinion back rightward toward themselves yet again. Because what turned Opinion 3 into a majority opinion was the fact that justice J_4 switched her vote to it from Opinion 2, justices J_5, J_6, and J_7 would have to identify a policy that is not only closer to their own ideal points than Opinion 3 but that is also better for justice J_4 than Opinion 3. Among the set of policies that meet these needs is Opinion 4, which is located at justice J_4's own ideal point. Because Opinion 4 is closer to the ideal points of justices J_5, J_6, and J_7 than is Opinion 3, and Opinion 4 is at the ideal point of justice J_4, Opinion 4 will be preferred to Opinion 3 by a majority of the justices (J_4 through J_7). The policy of Opinion 4, located at J_4, would thus become the provisional majority opinion.

And in fact, the adoption of Opinion 4 would finally end this story. The reason is that an opinion at J_4, which is the ideal point of the median justice, is invulnerable to upset by any further counteroffers: because the median justice is getting a policy at her ideal point, she has no desire to switch her support to any other policy, and without her support, no other proposal could gain majority support.

In sum, the policy-maximizing incentives of the justices will drive policy, via this back-and-forth process, to J_{med}. It is for this reason that we refer to it as the "open-bidding" version of our model: for any draft opinion that is not at J_{med}, there are two coalitions (one on each side of J_{med}), which are openly engaged in competitive bidding, via their opinions and counteropinions, for the support of the median justice.[9]

Of course, although our illustration has emphasized the back-and-forth character of this bidding process, the majority opinion writer would presumably foresee (because of our perfect information assumption) the vulnerability of every draft opinion except J_{med}, and so would write the initial draft opinion—Opinion 4—at J_{med} at the outset: none of the back-and-forth bidding process need actually occur.[10]

An unresolved question is how any minority-side justices would vote on a final opinion at J_{med}, given the open-bidding logic. One possibility is that if the majority opinion writer begins by drafting a proposal at J_{med} (precisely because he understands the logic of the open-bidding process), then the minority-side justices will simply dissent because an opinion at J_{med} is worse for them than SQ. The outcome would thus be J_{med}, and the minority-side justices will dissent.

A second possibility stems from the nature of any back-and-forth bargaining that actually occurs: because the minority-side justices would be instrumental in helping get a policy at J_{med} adopted (rather than something to the outside of J_{med}), they might feel obliged to vote for this final policy at J_{med} to ensure that something worse does not get adopted.

A third possibility, also involving back-and-forth bargaining, is that although the minority-side justices would be instrumental in getting a policy at J_{med} adopted, they might nonetheless end up voting against what they had helped create; after all, an opinion at J_{med} is still worse for them than SQ. As long as J_{med} can be maintained as the final opinion, it will not need their votes in order to become the majority opinion; after all, an opinion at J_{med} can always gain the support of at least *maj* majority-side justices.

A fourth possibility is that if the members of the Court actually engage in the back-and-forth open-bidding process, how any minority-side justices end up voting might depend on the particular sequence by which an opinion at J_{med} is reached. For example, if at the last stage of bargaining, J_{med} is reached by a move away from the minority-side justices' ideal points (as with a move from Opinion 2 directly to a final opinion at Opinion 4 in Figure 6.7), these minority-side justices might then dissent because Opinion 4 is worse for them than the draft opinion—Opinion 2—adopted at the previous stage of bargaining. However, if at the last stage of bargaining, J_{med} is reached by a move toward the minority-side justices (as with a move from Opinion 3 to Opinion 4 in Figure 6.7), these minority-side justices might then join the majority opinion at J_{med} because J_{med} (Opinion 4) is better for them than the draft opinion (Opinion 3) adopted at the previous stage of bargaining.

It is not clear to us which of these four possible kinds of responses would be exhibited by the minority-side justices; each seems to have at least some degree of plausibility.

WHAT OPINIONS ARE ADOPTED?

There is always just one opinion that should be expected from the open-bidding version of our model: an opinion at J_{med}, the ideal point of the median justice. No matter what opinion is initially proposed by the majority opinion writer, the logic of the open-bidding process will force a convergence on a policy at J_{med}. Thus we have the following:

PROPOSITION 6.20. In the open-bidding version of our model, the only equilibrium opinion is at J_{med}.

WHAT COALITION LINEUPS AND COALITION
SIZES RESULT?

The final coalition lineups and coalition sizes that should be expected from the open-bidding version of our model depend in good part on what the minority-side justices are expected to do. Given that the final majority opinion will be at J_{med}, it seems reasonable to assume that each majority-side justice would base his or her vote simply on whether the opinion at J_{med} falls inside or outside his or her preferred-to set. However, the final coalition lineups and sizes will also depend on how the minority-side justices are assumed to vote, and as noted above, it is not clear what to expect from them.

Even so, it is clear that a wide range of coalition lineups and coalition sizes can be produced by the open-bidding version. We state this as:

PROPOSITION 6.21. In the open-bidding version of our model, a final majority opinion at J_{med} can gain the support of a majority coalition of every possible size, depending on the location of J_{med} relative to SQ.

In particular, everything from minimum-winning coalitions to unanimous coalitions can be produced. In diagram B in Figure 6.6, for example, an opinion at J_3 (the ideal point of the median justice) will be supported by a

5–0 final vote: the opinion at J_3 falls inside the preferred-to sets of justices J_1, J_2, J_3, J_4, and J_5. In diagram A in Figure 6.6, an opinion at J_3 will be supported by a 4–1 final vote: the opinion at J_3 falls inside the preferred-to sets of justices J_1, J_2, J_3, and J_4 but outside the preferred-to set of justice J_5. And in diagram B in Figure 6.8, when the opinion is at J_3 (the ideal point of the median justice), this opinion will be supported by a 3–2 final vote: the opinion at J_3 falls inside the preferred-to sets of justices J_1, J_2, and J_3, but outside the preferred-to sets of justices J_4 and J_5. Thus, for a five-member Court, 5–0, 4–1, and 3–2 final votes are all possible. Similar examples could be easily developed for a nine-member Court.

We also note the following, which is similar to Proposition 6.18 (regarding the agenda-control version of our model):

PROPOSITION 6.22. In the open-bidding version of our model, as SQ moves closer to J_{med} from an extreme location (in terms of the number of intervening justices), the maximum possible size of any winning coalition will decrease.

As with Proposition 6.18, this decrease is characterized by a step-function.

Because the outcomes from the open-bidding version will always be at J_{med}, there is likely to be a smaller set of configurations, compared to the agenda-control model, which can produce the full range of coalition lineups and sizes. Given the location of SQ in diagram A in Figure 6.6, for example, the agenda-control version can produce three different coalition sizes (3–2, 4–1, 5–0), as a result of the three different policies that can gain majority support, whereas the open-bidding version can produce just one coalition size (4–1, in Region IV where J_3, the median justice's ideal point, is located) from this particular configuration.

The Median-Holdout Version

In contrast to the entirely passive behavior assumed by the agenda-control version of our model, and in contrast to the very active behavior assumed by the open-bidding version, the median-holdout version of our model assumes that when justices are dissatisfied with the draft majority opinion (because it is not located at their ideal points), they will respond in a moderately active manner. Although neither the median justice nor any other justice will actively construct an alternative to the draft majority opinion, she and perhaps some other justices (depending on the configuration of preferences relative to SQ) will simply withhold their votes unless the majority opinion writer selects a policy at J_{med}.[11]

In fact, if justice J_{med} withholds her vote, the justices on the other side of J_{med} from the draft majority opinion will have an incentive to withhold their votes as well because they also prefer an opinion at J_{med} to a draft majority opinion on the other side of J_{med}. Because J_{med} and these justices comprise a majority of the Court, a draft majority opinion not at J_{med} cannot become the final majority opinion without the support of J_{med} or these other justices. Hence, the majority opinion writer will have to revise his opinion by locating it at J_{med} in order to gain majority support. We thus make the following assumption as the basis for the median-holdout version of our model:

ASSUMPTION 6.4. In the median-holdout version of our model, the median justice and all justices on the other side of J_{med} from the draft majority opinion will withhold their votes from the draft majority opinion until an opinion at J_{med} is drafted by the majority opinion writer.[12]

Given a draft majority opinion at J_{med}, this version of our model would then function as with the agenda-control version: if J_{med} is better than SQ for a justice, he or she will support the opinion, but if J_{med} is worse than SQ for a justice, he or she will not support it. Of course, with a draft opinion at J_{med}, there will always be a majority of justices who prefer this opinion to SQ (recall Proposition 6.4), and if the draft majority opinion starts out at J_{med}, the median justice would endorse it without hesitation. However, if the draft majority opinion at J_{med} is worse than SQ for a justice (this necessarily includes any minority-side justices), it is not clear how these justices will vote: as was the case for the open-bidding version of our model, there are plausible reasons both for why they would support the final majority opinion (for example, because their withheld votes may be essential to its adoption) and for why they would oppose the final majority opinion (it is worse for them than SQ).

To illustrate these arguments, consider diagram B in Figure 6.8. Recall that in this five-member Court, the median justice is J_3. Assume that justice J_2 is the majority opinion writer. Justice J_2 would initially be inclined to draft an opinion at the point indicated by *, just inside the left end of $W_{J3}(SQ)$. This policy at * falls within the preferred-to sets of a bare majority of justices (J_1, J_2, and J_3), and so is preferred by a majority of justices to SQ. However, suppose that justice J_3 withholds her support unless the draft opinion is rewritten at her own ideal point of J_3. Because the opinion at * falls outside the preferred-to sets of justices J_4 and J_5, this draft opinion at * could not become the majority opinion with the support of justices J_1 and J_2 alone. Hence, the opinion writer would have to redraft the opinion so that it meets the median justice's demand for a policy at J_3. This draft opinion at J_3 could then gain the support of a majority of justices over SQ (justices J_1, J_2, and J_3 would all support it), so a policy at J_3 would be the final outcome.

However, the final coalition lineup depends on how justices J_4 and J_5 would vote. Note that with a draft opinion at J_3, no further holdouts could move the draft policy from J_3. For example, if either justices J_1 or J_2 (or both of them) hold out so as to move policy leftward back toward themselves, a majority of justices—J_3, J_4, and J_5—would still prefer to keep policy at J_3 and so would vote to keep it as the majority's policy. The same holds for justices J_4 and J_5: if they hold out so as to move policy farther rightward toward themselves, a majority of justices—J_1, J_2, and J_3—would vote to keep policy at J_3. In other words, a policy at J_3 is the only equilibrium policy in this case. And because they can have no further impact on this outcome at J_3, justices J_4 and J_5 would presumably not join in support of this opinion (because it is worse for them than SQ).

For a second illustration, consider diagram A in Figure 6.6. Note again that justice J_3 is the median justice, and assume that justice J_4 is the majority opinion writer. Justice J_4 might initially think that he could write a majority opinion at his own ideal point of J_4 because it lies inside the preferred-to sets of four of the five justices (including that of J_{med}). However, justices J_1 through J_3 all prefer some policies to the left of J_4, including a policy at J_3. Hence, justice J_3, supported by justices J_1 and J_2, could hold out for a policy at J_3, thereby denying a majority to the draft policy at J_4. If justice J_4 were to draft a policy at J_3, however, no further justice or group of justices could move policy in either direction by withholding their votes. Again, J_3 would be the only equilibrium policy. Because a final policy at J_3 falls within the preferred-to sets of justices J_1, J_2, J_3, and J_4, the final majority coalition here would include these four justices. Because justice J_5 can have no further impact on the outcome at J_3, justice J_5 would presumably not join in support of this opinion (because it is worse for him than SQ).

Finally, for a somewhat more complicated example, consider diagram A in Figure 6.8. The median justice is J_3, as before, and assume that justice J_2 is the majority opinion writer. In this case, the opinion writer would initially consider whether he could write the draft opinion at his own ideal point of J_2: a policy at J_2 would fall within the preferred-to sets of a majority of justices—J_1, J_2, and J_3. However, justices J_3, J_4, and J_5 would all like to move policy at least as far rightward as J_3. Hence, these three justices would withhold their support unless the opinion was rewritten at the median justice's ideal point of J_3. The majority opinion writer, justice J_2, might think that if he moved the opinion not quite as far as J_3 but only as far as the left-hand edge of $W_{J4}(SQ)$, to the policy indicated by the Δ in the diagram, he could get justice J_4's support even without justice J_3's: justice J_4 would of course prefer an opinion in $W_{J4}(SQ)$, such as the policy at Δ, to an opinion at J_2. Nonetheless, justice J_4 would have an incentive to move policy even farther rightward to J_3 just as justice J_3 does. Hence, we conclude that he would not support an opinion at Δ inside the left-hand edge of $W_{J4}(SQ)$; the reason is that he too would have an incentive to support justice J_3 in holding out for an opinion at J_3. As before, then, the opinion writer would have to redraft the opinion at J_3 to gain justice the support of justices J_3, J_4, and J_5. Because the resulting policy at J_3 lies inside the preferred-to sets of justices J_1, J_2, J_3, and J_4, and outside the preferred-to set of justice J_5, the final coalition lineup for the policy at J_3 would include the first four justices, although it is unclear how justice J_5 would vote.

WHAT OPINIONS ARE ADOPTED?

The preceding three examples illustrate the basic logic of the median-holdout version of our model. We now consider what opinions could be adopted under this model and what coalition lineups and coalition sizes should be expected. Our general conclusion is this:

PROPOSITION 6.23. In the median-holdout version of our model, the only majority opinion in equilibrium is at J_{med}.

That is, no matter what opinion is initially drafted by the majority opinion writer, the logic of the median-holdout version of our model forces convergence on a policy at J_{med}. Various justices might consider engaging in this holdout strategy, in hopes of getting the final majority opinion moved to their own ideal point, but only an opinion at J_{med} will be invulnerable to such threats. For example, if a justice with an ideal point to the left of J_{med} holds out in hopes of getting policy moved leftward from J_{med}, a majority of justices—J_{med} plus those justices to the right of J_{med}—will support an opinion at J_{med} over any opinion to its left; similarly, if a justice with an ideal point to the right of J_{med} holds out in hopes of getting policy moved rightward from J_{med}, a majority of justices—J_{med} plus those justices to the left of J_{med}—will support an opinion at J_{med} over any opinion to its right.

Note that our illustrations have all presented a process-related story of how an opinion at J_{med} would come to be selected: the majority opinion writer first proposes some opinion not at J_{med}, and then the median justice withholds her vote (other justices will do so as well) in order to force the opinion writer to move the draft policy to J_{med}. However, our model assumes that justices have complete information about each other's ideal points. Hence, the majority opinion writer would presumably foresee that this holdout strategy will be able to undermine any draft opinion that is not at J_{med}. As a result, the majority opinion writer should be expected to select an opinion at J_{med} at the outset; no explicit negotiations with holdout justices would actually occur.[13]

WHAT COALITION LINEUPS AND COALITION SIZES RESULT?

There are three parts to our answer to the question of what coalition lineups and coalition sizes result from the median-holdout version of our model.

The first part of the answer is that who votes for the final policy at J_{med} depends simply on whether the opinion at J_{med} falls inside or outside a majority-side justice's preferred-to set. Of course, an opinion at J_{med} will always be able to gain majority support against SQ.

The second part of the answer is this:

PROPOSITION 6.24. In the median-holdout version of our model, a final majority opinion at J_{med} can gain the support of a majority coalition of every possible size.

That is, as wide a range of coalition sizes can be produced by the median-holdout version as by the agenda-control version: everything from minimum-winning coalitions to unanimous coalitions can be produced. This is demonstrated by the three illustrations that we have just considered. Thus, for this five-member Court, 3–2, 4–1, and 5–0 final votes would all be possible. Similar examples could be developed for a nine-member Court.

The third part of our answer is similar to Proposition 6.18 (for the agenda-control version of our model) and Proposition 6.22 (for the open-bidding version of our model):

PROPOSITION 6.25. In the median-holdout version of our model, as SQ moves closer to J_{med} from an extreme location (in terms of the number of intervening justices), the maximum possible size of a winning coalition will decrease.

As with Propositions 6.18 and 6.22, this decrease is characterized by a step function.

Because the outcomes from the median-holdout version will always be at J_{med}, Proposition 6.25 means that there is likely to be a smaller set of configurations, compared to the agenda-control version, which can produce this wide range of coalition lineups and sizes. Given the location of SQ in diagram A in Figure 6.8, for example, the agenda-control version can produce three different coalition sizes (3–2, 4–1, 5–0), as a result of the three different policies that can gain majority support, whereas the median-holdout version may be able to produce just one coalition size (for example, 4–1), which would form in support of J_3.

Comparison of the Agenda-Control, Open-Bidding, and Median-Holdout Versions

We can now compare and contrast the results—the opinions adopted, the coalitions that form, and the coalition sizes which result—that should be expected from these three versions of our model.

We begin by noting that, in the agenda-control version, if the median justice is appointed the majority opinion writer, she will be able to write the majority opinion at her own ideal point of J_{med}. Because the open-bidding and median-holdout versions would also produce majority opinions at J_{med}, there would be no difference in the policies chosen by the three versions here.

However, if someone other than the median justice is appointed the majority opinion writer in the agenda-control version, the majority opinion will not be at J_{med}. Of course, the majority opinion is always constrained to lie within $W_{Jmed}(SQ)$; see Propositions 6.5 and 6.6. But whereas the open-bidding and median-holdout versions will always produce an opinion at J_{med}, which lies at the center of $W_{Jmed}(SQ)$, the agenda-control version can produce an opinion anywhere inside $W_{Jmed}(SQ)$, depending on the location of the opinion writer's ideal point. Hence, the size of $W_{Jmed}(SQ)$ establishes an upper bound on how different the outcomes from the agenda-control version can be from the outcome at J_{med} expected from the other two versions. With a large $W_{Jmed}(SQ)$, the agenda-control version could produce a rather different policy from the open-bidding and median-holdout versions (although what particular policy the agenda-control version will produce depends on the ideal point of the majority opinion writer). However, with a small $W_{Jmed}(SQ)$, which would occur only when J_{med} is close to SQ, all three versions will necessarily produce similar policies.

Because the final majority opinion in the open-bidding and median-holdout versions will be at J_{med}, these two versions may generate identical coalition lineups and coalition sizes. (There is some ambiguity in our statement here as a result of our uncertainty about what behavior to expect from the minority-side justices in the open-bidding and median-holdout versions.) However, if the majority opinion from the agenda-control version differs from J_{med}, then the coalition lineups and coalition sizes from the agenda-control model may differ (although they will not necessarily differ) from those of the open-bidding and median-holdout versions. Whether they differ, and to what extent, depends on the locations of the justices' ideal points, on the location of SQ, and on who the majority opinion writer is.

In all three versions the median justice will be a member of the final majority coalition. The reason is that the final majority opinion will be either J_{med}, for the open-bidding and median-holdout versions, or will fall inside

$W_{Jmed}(SQ)$, for the agenda-control version; in all three versions, this final majority opinion will be better than SQ for the median justice.

In addition, the justices whose ideal points lie to the outside of the median justice will support the majority opinion in all three versions: whether the majority opinion is at J_{med}, to the outside of J_{med} (but still inside $W_{Jmed}(SQ)$), or to the inside of J_{med}, this opinion will still fall inside the preferred-to sets of the median justice and all justices whose ideal points lie outside of hers.

Where the three versions may differ is in the votes of the majority-side justices whose ideal points lie to the inside of the median justice: whether these justices support or oppose the majority opinion depends simply on whether this opinion falls inside or outside their preferred-to sets. Regarding the minority-side justices, the expectation from the agenda-control version is that they will vote against the majority opinion. However, as we have already noted, it is not clear how the minority-side justices will cast their final votes in the open-bidding and median-holdout versions.

Aside from these potential differences in outcomes and coalition sizes, there is some potential for significant differences among the three versions in the processes by which the final outcomes are reached. The reason, of course, is that the three versions are distinguished by the extent of the "activism" of the justices who are dissatisfied with the draft majority opinion. The agenda-control version is characterized by dissatisfied justices who nonetheless remain completely passive; they let the majority opinion writer set the Court's agenda. The open-bidding version is characterized by dissatisfied justices who are the most active; they actively formulate counteropinions in an effort to get a policy more to their liking. The median-holdout version is characterized by dissatisfied justices who are moderately active; they withhold their votes in order to induce the majority opinion writer to draft a policy more to their liking but they do not construct their own counterproposal.

As we have already argued, however, a rational and fully informed majority opinion writer in both the open-bidding and median-holdout versions should be expected to select a draft policy at J_{med} at the outset. In this case, there would be no observable process-related differences—for example, no signs of bargaining and negotiation—between the opinion-selection processes of either of these two versions. And because the agenda-control version would not be characterized by any bargaining and negotiation either (the rational and perfectly informed opinion writer would go directly to his best politically feasible policy in $W_{Jmed}(SQ)$), we concluded that none of the three versions should be expected to exhibit any signs of bargaining and negotiation. However, if there is some deviation from the perfect-information assumption (at least for the majority opinion writer's knowledge of other justices' ideal points), some of the process-related distinctions among the three versions might empirically manifest themselves.

Finally, we would emphasize that the open-bidding and median–holdout versions of our model have several important implications for the current literature. One implication is that because the final majority opinion will always be at the ideal point of the median justice, this means that it does not matter who writes the majority opinion: in order to gain a majority on the Court the opinion writer will be forced to write it at J_{med}. From this perspective, the emphasis in the empirical literature on the importance of the opinion assignment process may be misplaced; what is most important is not who the opinion writer is but who the median justice is and where her ideal point is located.

Moreover, if it does not matter who the opinion writer is for the open-bidding and median–holdout versions, it would not matter who the opinion assigner is. Nor would it even matter what strategy the opinion assigner uses to assign opinions: because the outcome would always be at J_{med}, criteria completely unrelated to the potential opinion writers' policy views (such as the opinion assigner's concerns about equity and workload among the justices) could be used to guide the assignments,.

In fact, most or all of the strategizing that is said to go on at earlier stages of the decision-making process (e.g., Epstein and Knight 1998) should not be expected to occur in the open-bidding and median–holdout versions because it would be pointless: no matter how the justices behaved at the earlier stages, the final outcome would always be at J_{med}. Indeed, strategizing should not even be expected at the certiorari stage. The reason is that if the final outcome will always be at J_{med}, then the critical issue at the certiorari stage is simply whether SQ is at J_{med} or not: if SQ is already at J_{med}, there would be no reason to accept the case because policy cannot be changed; and if SQ is not at J_{med}, then there automatically exists a majority that prefers J_{med} to SQ, and hence this majority will accept the case and subsequently ensure that the final opinion is at J_{med}. In either case, any efforts at strategizing would have no impact on the final opinion or on how the justices behave en route to that final opinion.[14]

Hence, we might conclude that precisely because Epstein and Knight (1998) assume justices to be strategically rational and well-informed policy-maximizers, their own argument about the importance of strategizing in the Court's decision-making process may be undercut by the open-bidding and median–holdout versions of our model: the rational, policy-maximizing justices will always drive policy to J_{med}, and because all the justices would understand this from the outset, it means that strategizing at the earlier stages would be irrelevant. In other words, the assumption that justices are strategically rational policy-maximizers may not be logically compatible, in the context of the open-bidding and median-holdout versions of our model, with the assumption that the justices' strategic behavior will affect the final opinion.[15]

Is Agenda-Control Behavior Unstable?

Despite these arguments, we suspect that many students of judicial politics have the agenda-control version in mind, at least implicitly, when they describe the Supreme Court's decision-making process. But if the agenda-control version of our model produces a majority opinion that is not at J_{med}, then there will always exist an alternative opinion that some majority prefers to the opinion drafted by the majority opinion writer. And if even just one or two of these dissatisfied justices behave in something other than a passive manner (for example, by drafting a counteropinion), they may be able to turn the agenda-control version of our model into something approximating the open-bidding or median-holdout versions. The reason is that the only way the remaining passive justices might be able to defend their preferred policies against a counterproposal of these more active justices would be by joining in the more active game themselves. This suggests that the behavioral passivity adopted by the justices in the agenda-control version of our model may not be an equilibrium strategy: if just one or two strategically located justices adopt a more active strategy, in short order everyone else may be forced to behave this way as well.

In other words, the control of the Court's decision-making agenda, which the literature on opinion assignment rather explicitly ascribes to the majority opinion writer, may rest on precarious and unstable foundations. In the context of our general approach, this agenda control can exist only if all the other justices behave in a self-denying manner. In Figure 6.7, for example, justice J_2's choice of Opinion 1 can be maintained only if justices J_4 through J_7 deliberately refrain from proposing and voting for an opinion at J_4, the ideal point of the median justice, even though these four justices all prefer Opinion 4 at J_4 to Opinion 1. And if a justice is voluntarily refraining from proposing and voting for an alternative that is better for him or her than some initial draft opinion, the implication would seem to be that the justice is acting irrationally. Because the most fundamental assumption of our model is that all justices are rational policy-maximizers, one possible implication is that the justices in the open-bidding and median-holdout versions are behaving much more in accordance with this assumption than they are in the agenda-control version.[16]

However, if majority opinion writers are actually granted the kind of agenda control by their fellow justices that the agenda-control version of our model assumes, then the key question for future research is this: why would rational, policy-maximizing justices who are not writing the majority opinion behave in this ostensibly irrational and self-denying manner? We address this question in Chapter 11.

Summary of Major Results

We can summarize our major results on coalition formation and the final vote as follows:

1. If J_{med} is not located at SQ, then there always exists policies that a majority of justices prefer to SQ.

2. The set of politically feasible policies is $W_{Jmed}(SQ)$.

3. The median justice, J_{med}, is a necessary member of any coalition that replaces the status quo policy with some new Court policy; if the median justice does not prefer some proposal to the status quo policy, this proposal cannot gain majority support.

4. If the median justice prefers some proposal to the status quo, there will always exist a Court majority that prefers this new policy to the status quo.

5. In the agenda-control version of our model, the decision-making process can produce a wide range of coalition sizes, from minimum-winning to unanimity.

6. If no such agenda control is granted to the majority opinion writer, the final opinion should be expected to converge on the ideal point of J_{med} (as in the open-bidding and median-holdout versions of our model).

7. If the decision-making process forces the final opinion to converge on the ideal point of J_{med} (as in the open-bidding and median-holdout versions of our model), a wide range of coalition sizes can still be produced.

8. Any given set of coalitions on the final vote can be produced by several different sets of circumstances; one cannot look at a given coalitional outcome and work backward to determine what the decision-making circumstances (that is, who had what ideal point and where was the status quo policy?) must have been.

Opinion Assignment

In the previous chapter, we developed three versions of our model of coalition formation and the final vote. For each version, we derived what opinion would be drafted by the justice who was given the assignment to write for the majority.

For both the open-bidding and median-holdout versions of our model, we found that the final majority opinion would always be at J_{med}, the ideal point of the median justice. This means that the selection of the majority opinion writer would not affect the location of the final opinion. For the agenda-control version of our model, however, we found that the selection of the majority opinion writer could affect where the final opinion was located.

In this chapter, we adopt the agenda-control assumptions—Assumptions 6.1 and 6.2—and use our agenda-control results to determine who would be assigned the authority to write the final opinion. In particular, we address the following question: for each justice who might be the majority opinion assigner, to which justice would this opinion assigner delegate the authority to write the majority opinion?

We begin our analysis with a discussion of self-assignment as an opinion-assignment strategy. No other opinion-assignment strategy can produce final opinions that are superior to those produced by self-assignment. But we also show that, under some conditions, other opinion-assignment strategies will produce final opinions that are equivalent in value to those produced by self-assignment (even when the opinion writer's ideal point differs from that of the opinion assigner). For other conditions, however, even the best opinion-assignment strategies will produce final opinions that are inferior to what would be produced by self-assignment.

One of our results is that what the literature has generally considered to be "strategic" opinion assignment—assign the opinion to the justice with the closest ideal point—does not necessarily produce the best possible majority opinion for the opinion assigner. In fact, there are conditions under which a strategically rational opinion assigner gets the best final opinion for himself by assigning the opinion to someone who does not have the closest ideal point. For this reason, assigning the opinion to the justice with the closest ideal point should not always be considered a strategically rational opinion-assignment strategy.

Even when it can be demonstrated that opinion assignment can affect the final outcome in the agenda-control model, this is different from showing how much opinion assignment can affect the final outcome. Drawing on our results from Chapter 6, we argue that there are conditions under which opinion assignment, although it matters some, does not matter very much. Under other conditions, however, opinion assignment can matter substantially more.

We conclude the chapter with a brief summary of our results on opinion assignment.

Self-Assignment as an Opinion-Assignment Strategy

The central argument in this section is that by self-assigning the opinion, the opinion assigner ensures that majority support can be gained for an opinion that is as close as possible to the assigner's ideal point. The basic reason is obvious: a policy-maximizing opinion assigner will pursue a policy at his or her own ideal point, whereas assignment of the opinion to another justice would allow that justice to pursue a policy at his or her own ideal point. Hence, we will begin by asserting the following:

PROPOSITION 7.1. The opinion assigner has no assignment strategy that produces final outcomes that are superior to those produced by self-assignment.

However, there are three sets of conditions under which outcomes equal to the self-assignment strategy for the opinion writer can be produced. First, and most obviously, if there is another justice with an ideal point identical to that of the opinion assigner, the opinion could be assigned to this justice in full confidence that he or she would produce the same opinion that the assigner would produce. Second, a final outcome equal to that produced by the self-assignment strategy will also be produced when the opinion assigner and at least one other justice (who is assigned the majority opinion) have ideal points that fall outside the median justice's preferred-to set, $W_{Jmed}(SQ)$. Third, a final outcome equal to that produced by the self-assignment strategy will be produced when the opinion assigner and at least one other justice (who could be assigned the majority opinion) have ideal points that lie on the minority side.

FIGURE 7.1

What Majority Opinion Would Each Justice Write?

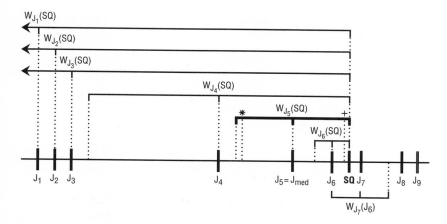

The first of these conditions needs no illustration. For the second and third conditions, consider the nine-member Court in Figure 7.1.[1] Justice J_5 is the median justice, and note that justices J_1, J_2, J_3, and J_4 all have ideal points that lie outside $W_{J5}(SQ)$. Assume that justice J_4 is the majority opinion assigner. Because J_4 lies outside $W_{J5}(SQ)$, justice J_4 cannot write an opinion at his own ideal point; the best policy for which justice J_4 can gain majority support is located at *, which is just inside the outside (left-hand) boundary of $W_{J5}(SQ)$. If self-assignment by justice J_4 is not possible, assignment to justices J_1, J_2, or J_3 would produce exactly the same opinion at *: even though these other three justices have ideal points that are more extreme than justice J_4's ideal point, each of them would rationally select precisely the same policy at * in order to gain majority support. Hence, justice J_4 would lose nothing by assigning the majority opinion to any of them.

Similarly, consider any minority-side justice, such as J_7, J_8, and J_9 in Figure 7.1. Assume that justices J_7 and J_8 previously voted on the majority side on the conference vote, and so are eligible to write the majority opinion.[2] Each of these minority-side justices would write an opinion at the point labeled +, which lies just to the left of SQ and thus inside $W_{Jmed}(SQ)$. If justice J_7 is the opinion assigner, for example, this means that assigning the majority opinion to justice J_8 would produce the same final majority opinion, at +, that would be produced by self-assignment.

In sum, then, we can state:

PROPOSITION 7.2. The majority opinion assigner can assign the opinion to another justice and get the same final opinion as from self-assignment under three conditions:

(a) If the ideal points of the opinion assigner and the other justice are identical.

(b) If the ideal points of the opinion assigner and the other justice both lie outside $W_{Jmed}(SQ)$.

(c) If the ideal points of the opinion assigner and the other justice both lie on the minority side.

Of course, the empirical literature suggests that self-assignment is often not possible. Moreover, the opinion assigner may not always be able to find another justice who will produce a final opinion at the opinion assigner's own ideal point. Hence, in the next section we discuss what alternative opinion-assignment strategies the rational opinion assigner would have to adopt.

Alternative Opinion-Assignment Strategies

Analysis of majority opinion assignment strategies when self-assignment is not possible must begin with our arguments, from Chapter 6, regarding what majority opinion would be drafted by each justice. The key arguments are summarized in Proposition 6.14, which we repeat here as Proposition 7.3 because of its importance for opinion assignment:

PROPOSITION 7.3. In the agenda-control version of our model, the majority opinion writer will write one of three different opinions, depending on the location of his or her ideal point.

(a) If the opinion writer's ideal point lies outside $W_{Jmed}(SQ)$, the opinion writer will draft an opinion just inside the outside boundary of $W_{Jmed}(SQ)$.

(b) If the opinion writer's ideal point lies inside $W_{Jmed}(SQ)$, the opinion writer will draft an opinion at his or her own ideal point.

(c) If the opinion writer's ideal point is on the minority side, the opinion writer will draft an opinion just inside the SQ boundary of $W_{Jmed}(SQ)$.

To illustrate, consider Figure 7.1 again. Part (a) of the proposition refers to justices J_1, J_2, J_3, and J_4: each would write an opinion at the point labeled * just inside the left-hand boundary of $W_{J5}(SQ)$, where it would gain the support of a majority of the justices. Part (b) of the proposition refers to justices J_5 and J_6: each would write an opinion at his or her own ideal point and the opinion would automatically gain the support of at least a majority of justices because the opinion would lie inside $W_{J5}(SQ)$, the preferred-to set of the median justice. Part (c) of the proposition refers to justices J_7, J_8, and J_9: each would write an opinion at the point labeled +, which is located just inside the SQ boundary of $W_{J5}(SQ)$.

We will present our results about majority opinion assignment in terms of these three categories established by Proposition 7.3. In particular, we first examine cases in which the majority opinion assigner's ideal point lies outside $W_{Jmed}(SQ)$. Next we examine cases in which the majority opinion assigner's ideal point lies inside $W_{Jmed}(SQ)$. Then we examine cases in which the majority opinion assigner's ideal point lies on the minority side of $W_{Jmed}(SQ)$.

Our fundamental argument about majority opinion assignment for all three categories is easily stated:

PROPOSITION 7.4. The strategically rational majority opinion assigner will assign the opinion to the justice whose final majority opinion would be closest to the assigner's own ideal point.

One might plausibly argue that this proposition is so directly implied by the definition of strategic opinion assignment that it should not be considered any kind of result at all. However, because the literature has long been confused about this point (the literature erroneously considers assignment to the nearest justice to be indicative of strategically rational behavior), we state it as an explicit proposition here.

Opinion Assignment by a Justice Outside $W_{Jmed}(SQ)$

We begin our assessment of opinion assignment strategies by examining cases in which the opinion assigner's ideal point lies outside $W_{Jmed}(SQ)$. There are three conditions to examine here:

(1) Only the opinion assigner lies outside $W_{Jmed}(SQ)$.

(2) The opinion assigner and just one other justice lie outside $W_{Jmed}(SQ)$.

(3) The opinion assigner and two or more other justices lie outside $W_{Jmed}(SQ)$.

First, consider the condition in which only the opinion assigner lies outside $W_{Jmed}(SQ)$; this means that any other justice to whom the assignment might be made lies inside $W_{Jmed}(SQ)$ or to the minority side. In the seven-member Court in Figure 7.2, for example, assume that justice J_1 is the opinion assigner, and note that J_1 is the only ideal point outside $W_{J4}(SQ)$, the median justice's preferred-to set. Justice J_2 is the closest other justice to assigner J_1, but because justice J_2's ideal point lies inside $W_{J4}(SQ)$, his opinion could be written at J_2. Any other justice to the right of justice J_2 would write an opinion even farther to the right; justice J_3, for example, would write an opinion at J_3. Hence, assigner J_1's best strategy would be to assign the opinion to justice J_2, with the result that the final opinion would be at J_2. Hence, we can assert:

PROPOSITION 7.5. If only the opinion assigner lies outside $W_{Jmed}(SQ)$ and does not self-assign, then the opinion assigner will assign the opinion to the adjacent justice.

FIGURE 7.2

Only the Opinion Assigner Lies Outside $W_{Jmed}(SQ)$

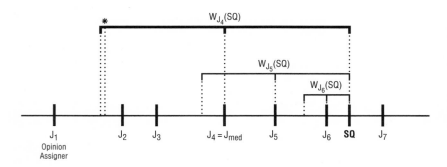

Note that if assigner J_1 were to self-assign, he would write an opinion at *
at the left-hand end of $W_{J4}(SQ)$. Because assignment to justice J_2 would
produce an opinion at J_2, which is farther away from J_1 than the opinion at
*, assigner J_1 would prefer to self-assign if possible. However, if justice J_2's
ideal point were located precisely at * (not shown), opinion assigner J_1's
assignment of the opinion to justice J_2 would produce an outcome, at *,
which would be the same as from self-assignment. Hence, we can also assert:

PROPOSITION 7.6. If only the opinion assigner lies outside $W_{Jmed}(SQ)$, and

(a)   if the closest justice inside $W_{Jmed}(SQ)$ has an ideal point that does not lie just
      inside the outside boundary of $W_{Jmed}(SQ)$, then the opinion assigner's best
      strategy is self-assignment; or,

(b)   if the closest justice inside $W_{Jmed}(SQ)$ has an ideal point that lies just inside
      the outside boundary of $W_{Jmed}(SQ)$, then assignment to this justice will pro-
      duce the same final opinion as from self-assignment.

Second, consider the set of conditions in which the opinion assigner and
just one other justice lie outside $W_{Jmed}(SQ)$. In Figure 7.3, for example,
assume for both diagrams A and B that justice J_2 is the majority opinion
assigner. Note that opinion assigner J_2 and the justice farther outside, justice
J_1, both lie outside $W_{J4}(SQ)$, the preferred-to set of the median justice, and
note also that the closest justice to the inside, justice J_3, lies inside $W_{J4}(SQ)$.
Because justice J_1's ideal point lies outside $W_{J4}(SQ)$, he would have to write
an opinion at *, just inside the outside boundary of $W_{J4}(SQ)$. However,
because justice J_3's ideal point lies inside $W_{J4}(SQ)$, he would write an opinion at J_3. Hence, in both diagrams opinion assigner J_2 has only two effective
opinion assignment choices (if he does not self-assign): an assignment to justice J_1, who would produce an opinion at *, and an assignment to justice J_3,
who would produce an opinion at J_3.[3]

FIGURE 7.3

*The Opinion Assigner and Just One Other Justice Lie
Outside $W_{Jmed}(SQ)$*

A.

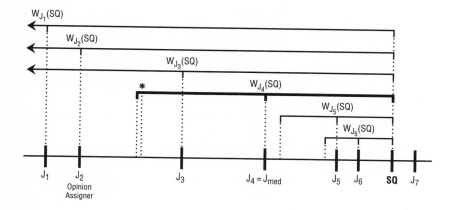

B.

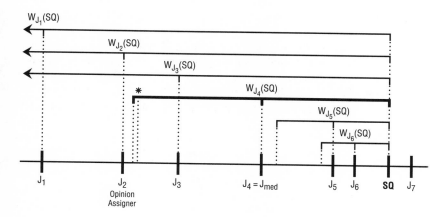

Now compare opinion assigner J_2's assignment strategies in diagrams A and B. We can see in both diagrams that assigner J_2's ideal point is closer to * (produced by an assignment to justice J_1) than to J_3 (produced by an assignment to justice J_3). Hence, in each diagram assigner J_2 would assign the opinion to justice J_1 rather than to justice J_3. But although in diagram A assigner J_2's ideal point is closer to justice J_1's ideal point, note in diagram B that assigner J_2's ideal point is closer to justice J_3's ideal point. In other words, in diagram A it is rational for assigner J_2 to assign the opinion to the closer justice, but in diagram B it is rational for assigner J_2 to assign the opinion to the farther justice.

We can thus see that it is not necessarily the best strategy for the opinion assigner to assign the opinion to the justice with the closest ideal point. Instead, what the opinion assigner wants, as Proposition 7.4 emphasizes, is a final majority opinion that is as close as possible to his or her own ideal point, and the closest justice will not necessarily produce the closest final opinion: as diagram B in Figure 7.3 demonstrates, justice J_3 is the closest justice to assigner J_2 but justice J_1 would write the closest opinion to assigner J_2's ideal point.

There is one minor caveat to this line of argument: if the closest justice lying inside $W_{Jmed}(SQ)$ has an ideal point (not shown) that is at *, just inside the outside boundary of $W_{Jmed}(SQ)$, then assignment to this justice will produce an opinion that is the same as the opinion, also at *, which would be produced by assignment to the justice whose ideal point lies outside $W_{Jmed}(SQ)$; in fact, self-assignment by justice J_2 would produce this same opinion as well.

For the second condition, then, we can summarize the results as follows:

PROPOSITION 7.7. If the majority opinion assigner's ideal point and the ideal point of just one other justice lie outside $W_{Jmed}(SQ)$, then the opinion assigner has two assignment strategies.

   (a)   If the closest justice inside $W_{Jmed}(SQ)$ has an ideal point that does not lie just inside the outside boundary of $W_{Jmed}(SQ)$, then the opinion assigner's best strategy is to assign the opinion to the other justice whose ideal point lies outside $W_{Jmed}(SQ)$—this also produces the same opinion as self-assignment.

   (b)   If the closest justice inside $W_{Jmed}(SQ)$ has an ideal point that lies just inside the outside boundary of $W_{Jmed}(SQ)$, then assignment to this justice will produce the same final opinion as from assignment to the justice whose ideal point lies outside $W_{Jmed}(SQ)$ and from self-assignment.

Third, consider the set of conditions in which the opinion assigner and at least two or more other justices have ideal points outside $W_{Jmed}(SQ)$. In Figure 7.4, for example, assume that justice J_2 is the opinion assigner. Assigner J_2 would consider assigning the opinion either to justice J_1 or justice J_3. Because justices J_1 and J_3 both have their ideal points to the left of $W_{J4}(SQ)$, each would write his opinion at * just inside the left-hand boundary of $W_{J4}(SQ)$. Because these two potential assignees would write the same opinion at *, it makes no difference to assigner J_2 which one to select: he could select the closer one, justice J_3, to write the opinion, or the more distant one, justice J_1. In fact, if assigner J_2 could self-assign here, he would also

FIGURE 7.4

*The Opinion Assigner and at Least Two Other Justices Lie
Outside $W_{Jmed}(SQ)$*

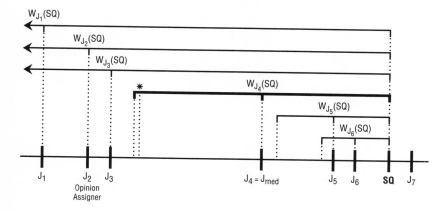

write an opinion at * at the left-hand end of $W_{J4}(SQ)$. Hence, self-assignment here would do no better than assignment to either potential assignee.
Moreover, the same basic observations hold no matter which of these outside justices is the opinion assigner and which justice is the opinion writer.

For this third basic set of conditions, then, we can assert:

PROPOSITION 7.8. If the majority opinion assigner's ideal point and the ideal points
of two or more other justices lie outside $W_{Jmed}(SQ)$, then the opinion assigner has
two assignment strategies.

(a) If the closest justice inside $W_{Jmed}(SQ)$ has an ideal point that does not lie
     just inside the outside boundary of $W_{Jmed}(SQ)$, then the opinion assigner's
     best strategy is to assign the opinion to any of the other justices whose ideal
     points lie outside $W_{Jmed}(SQ)$—this also produces the same opinion as self-
     assignment.

(b) If the closest justice inside $W_{Jmed}(SQ)$ has an ideal point that lies just inside
     the outside boundary of $W_{Jmed}(SQ)$, then assignment to this justice will pro-
     duce the same final opinion as from assignment to any of the other justices
     whose ideal points lie outside $W_{Jmed}(SQ)$ and from self-assignment.

Opinion Assignment by a Justice Inside $W_{Jmed}(SQ)$

Next we consider majority opinion assignment by a justice whose ideal
point lies inside $W_{Jmed}(SQ)$. There are five basic sets of conditions that we
must examine when the assigner's ideal point lies inside $W_{Jmed}(SQ)$:

(1) The majority opinion assigner has an ideal point inside $W_{Jmed}(SQ)$ and all

other justices' ideal points are inside $W_{Jmed}(SQ)$ but closer to SQ or on the minority side.

(2)   The majority opinion assigner has an ideal point inside $W_{Jmed}(SQ)$ that is the closest ideal point to the outside boundary of $W_{Jmed}(SQ)$, but there is at least one justice outside $W_{Jmed}(SQ)$ and at least one justice inside $W_{Jmed}(SQ)$ whose ideal point is closer to SQ than the assigner's ideal point.

(3)   The majority opinion assigner and at least two other justices (at least one on each side of the assigner) all lie inside $W_{Jmed}(SQ)$.

(4)   The majority opinion assigner is adjacent to SQ, and all other justices lie to the outside.

(5)   The majority opinion assigner is adjacent to SQ, at least one other justice lies inside $W_{Jmed}(SQ)$ but farther from SQ than the assigner, and at least one other justice lies on the minority side of SQ.

Consider the first set of conditions, in which the majority opinion assigner has an ideal point inside $W_{Jmed}(SQ)$ and all other justices' ideal points are either inside $W_{Jmed}(SQ)$ but closer to SQ or on the minority side. In Figure 7.5, for example, assume that justice J_1 is the opinion assigner, and note that all other justices' ideal points are either closer to SQ (as with justices J_2, J_3, J_4, and J_5) or on the minority side (as with justices J_6 and J_7). Recall that any justice with an ideal point inside $W_{Jmed}(SQ)$ could write an opinion at his or her ideal point.

So if opinion assigner J_1 cannot self-assign (which would give him the best outcome, because he could write the opinion at J_1), he will have to assign the opinion inward, and because justice J_2's opinion at J_2 would be closer than any other justice's opinion, the assignment would go to justice J_2 and so the final opinion would be at J_2. In this case, then, the opinion assigner would be assigning the opinion to the justice with the closest ideal point. Hence we have:

PROPOSITION 7.9. When the majority opinion assigner has an ideal point inside $W_{Jmed}(SQ)$ and all other justices' ideal points are either inside $W_{Jmed}(SQ)$ but closer to SQ or on the minority side, then the opinion assigner will assign the opinion to the next justice closer to SQ, if he does not self-assign.

Now consider the second set of conditions, in which the majority opinion assigner has an ideal point inside $W_{Jmed}(SQ)$ that is the closest ideal point to the outside boundary of $W_{Jmed}(SQ)$, but there is at least one justice outside $W_{Jmed}(SQ)$ and at least one justice inside $W_{Jmed}(SQ)$ whose ideal point is closer to SQ. To illustrate see Figure 7.6. In all the diagrams here, assume that justice J_2 is the majority opinion assigner, and note that justice J_4 is the median justice. Assigner J_2 could assign the opinion rightward to justice J_3, who of course lies inside $W_{J4}(SQ)$, or to justice J_1, who

FIGURE 7.5

*The Opinion Assigner Has an Ideal Point Just Inside
the Outside Boundary of $W_{Jmed}(SQ)$, and All Other Justices Have
Ideal Points Closer to SQ or on the Minority Side*

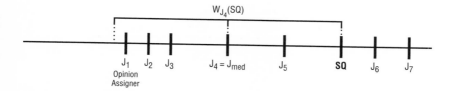

lies outside $W_{J4}(SQ)$. If justice J_3 were assigned the opinion, he would write the opinion at his own ideal point of J_3. If justice J_1 were assigned the opinion, he would write the opinion at * just inside the outside boundary of $W_{J4}(SQ)$. Hence, in each diagram assigner J_2 faces a choice between an opinion at J_3, produced by justice J_3, and an opinion at *, produced by justice J_1. Whether assigner J_2 is closer to an opinion at J_3, produced by justice J_3, or to an opinion at *, produced by justice J_1, will thus determine the assignment.

In diagram A in Figure 7.6, assigner J_2's ideal point is closer to J_3 than to *, so assigner J_2 would assign the opinion to justice J_3, who would write the final majority opinion at his ideal point of J_3. In diagrams B and C in Figure 7.6, however, assigner J_2's ideal point is closer to * than to J_3, so assigner J_2 would assign the opinion to justice J_1, who would write the final opinion at *.

Note that in diagrams A and B in Figure 7.6, assigner J_2 would assign the majority opinion to the closest justice (that is, to justice J_3 in diagram A, to justice J_1 in diagram B). In diagram C, however, assigner J_2 would assign the opinion to justice J_1 (because the opinion at * is closer than the opinion at J_3) even though justice J_1's ideal point is now farther from J_2 than is justice J_3's ideal point. In this case, we again find that the assigner, justice J_2, would strategically assign to someone who is not the closest justice.

For this second set of conditions, then, we can assert:

PROPOSITION 7.10. If the majority opinion assigner has an ideal point inside $W_{Jmed}(SQ)$ that is the closest ideal point to the outside boundary of $W_{Jmed}(SQ)$, but there is at least one justice outside $W_{Jmed}(SQ)$ and at least one justice inside $W_{Jmed}(SQ)$ whose ideal point is closer to SQ, then the opinion assigner has the following three strategies.

(a) If the assigner's ideal point is closer to a policy just inside the outside boundary of $W_{Jmed}(SQ)$ than to the policy chosen by the next justice toward SQ, the assigner will assign the opinion to a justice whose ideal point lies outside $W_{Jmed}(SQ)$, if he does not self-assign.

FIGURE 7.6

*The Opinion Assigner Has an Ideal Point Just Inside SQ that Is
Closest to the Outside Boundary of $W_{Jmed}(SQ)$, At Least One
Justice Lies Outside $W_{Jmed}(SQ)$, and At Least One Justice Lies
Closer to SQ*

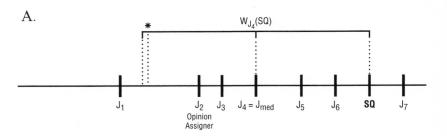

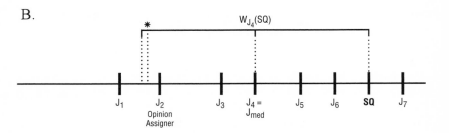

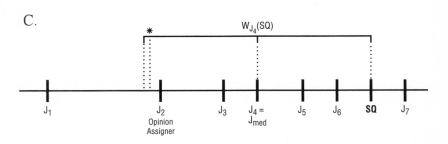

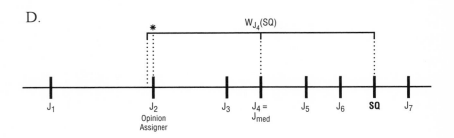

FIGURE 7.7

*The Opinion Assigner Has an Ideal Point in $W_{Jmed}(SQ)$, and
At Least Two Other Justices (At Least One on Each Side of the
Assigner) Have Ideal Points in $W_{Jmed}(SQ)$*

A.

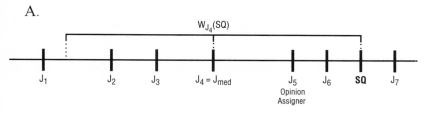

B.

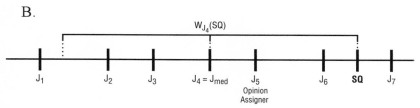

(b) If the assigner's ideal point is closer to the policy chosen by the next justice toward SQ than to a policy just inside the outside boundary of $W_{Jmed}(SQ)$, the assigner will assign the opinion to this next justice toward SQ, if he does not self-assign.

(c) If the assigner's ideal point is equidistant between the policy chosen by the next justice toward SQ and a policy just inside the outside boundary of $W_{Jmed}(SQ)$, the assigner will be indifferent between assigning to the inside justice or to a justice outside $W_{Jmed}(SQ)$.

We can also assert:

PROPOSITION 7.11. If the majority opinion assigner has an ideal point inside $W_{Jmed}(SQ)$ that is the closest ideal point to the outside boundary of $W_{Jmed}(SQ)$, but there is at least one justice outside $W_{Jmed}(SQ)$ and at least one justice inside $W_{Jmed}(SQ)$ whose ideal point is closer to SQ, then the opinion assigner would prefer to self-assign (unless the assigner's ideal point lies just inside the outside boundary of $W_{Jmed}(SQ)$, in which case the assigner would be indifferent between self-assignment and assignment to the justice outside $W_{Jmed}(SQ)$).

The reason for this result is that neither the justice outside $W_{Jmed}(SQ)$ nor the next justice to the inside would write an opinion at the assigner's ideal point. The specified exception, illustrated by diagram D in Figure 7.6, states that if assigner J_2's ideal point lies precisely at justice J_1's opinion at *, then assigner J_2 would be indifferent between self-assignment and assignment to justice J_1.

FIGURE 7.8

*The Opinion Assigner's Ideal Point Is Adjacent to SQ and
All Other Ideal Points Lie to the Outside*

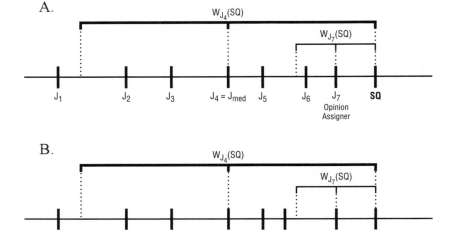

For the third set of conditions, the opinion assigner and at least two other justices, at least one to each side of the assigner, lie inside $W_{Jmed}(SQ)$. In Figure 7.7, for example, assume that justice J_5 is the opinion assigner and cannot self-assign. The two other justices with ideal points inside $W_{Jmed}(SQ)$ are justices J_4 and J_6, and so they could write majority opinions at their own respective ideal points. No other justice's opinion would be closer to assigner J_5's ideal point than the opinions of justice J_4 (at J_4) and justice J_6 (at J_6).

In diagram A in Figure 7.7, J_6 is closer to assigner J_5's ideal point than is J_4, hence assigner J_5 would assign the majority opinion to justice J_6, who would then write an opinion at J_6. In diagram B, J_4 is closer to assigner J_5's ideal point than is J_6, hence assigner J_5 would assign the majority opinion to justice J_4, who would then write an opinion at J_4. In either case, assigner J_5 is simply assigning to the justice with the closest ideal point. Of course, in both cases assigner J_5 would prefer to self-assign if possible: because justice J_4 would write at J_4 and justice J_6 would write at J_6, self-assignment would be the only way for justice J_5 to get an opinion at J_5.

For this third set of conditions, then, we can assert:

PROPOSITION 7.12. If the majority opinion assigner has an ideal point inside $W_{Jmed}(SQ)$ and at least two other justices (at least one to each side of the assigner) lie inside $W_{Jmed}(SQ)$, then the opinion assigner will assign the opinion to the justice with the closer ideal point to the assigner, if he does not self-assign.

Now consider the fourth set of conditions, in which the majority opinion assigner is adjacent to SQ, and all other justices lie to the outside. For example, consider Figure 7.8. In this seven-member Court, justice J_7 is the majority opinion assigner, and all other justices lie to the outside of J_7. Recall that any justice with an ideal point inside $W_{Jmed}(SQ)$, which is $W_{J4}(SQ)$ here, would write an opinion at his or her ideal point. In diagram A, if opinion assigner J_7 cannot self-assign, he will have to assign the opinion outward, and because justice J_6's opinion at J_6 would be closer than any other justice's opinion, the assignment would have to go to justice J_6 and the final opinion would be at J_6. In this case, then, the opinion assigner would be assigning the opinion to the justice with the closest ideal point to her own. Note that J_6 falls inside the assigner's preferred-to set, $W_{J7}(SQ)$, which means that this opinion at J_6 would be better for assigner J_7 than SQ.

For the fourth set of conditions, then, we have:

PROPOSITION 7.13. When the majority opinion assigner has an ideal point that is adjacent to SQ, all other justices' ideal points lie to the outside, and self-assignment is not possible, then the opinion assigner will assign the opinion to the adjacent justice outward from SQ.

However, as shown in diagram B of Figure 7.8, opinion assigner J_7's assignment of the opinion to anyone else can produce an opinion worse for himself than SQ. In diagram B, an opinion at J_6 lies outside $W_{J7}(SQ)$, which means that justice J_6's opinion at J_6 would be worse for assigner J_7 than SQ. In this case, then, assigner J_7 would have a strong preference to self-assign.

Finally, consider the fifth set of conditions, in which the majority opinion assigner is adjacent to SQ, at least one other justice lies inside $W_{Jmed}(SQ)$ but farther from SQ than the assigner, and at least one other justice lies on the minority side of SQ. The assignment decision here will depend on two factors: whether the next justice to the outside of the opinion assigner falls inside or outside the assigner's preferred-to set of SQ, and whether any of the minority-side justices is eligible for assignment. (Of course, a minority-side justice becomes an eligible opinion writer only by voting on the majority side on the conference vote.)

We initially examine a case in which this next justice to the outside of the assigner falls outside the assigner's preferred-to set of SQ. In diagram A in Figure 7.9, for example, assume that justice J_6 is the opinion assigner for this nine-member Court. Note that justice J_5 is the next justice to justice J_6's left, and note that if justice J_5 writes the opinion, she could write this opinion at her own ideal point of J_5 (because justice J_5 is the median justice). Note also

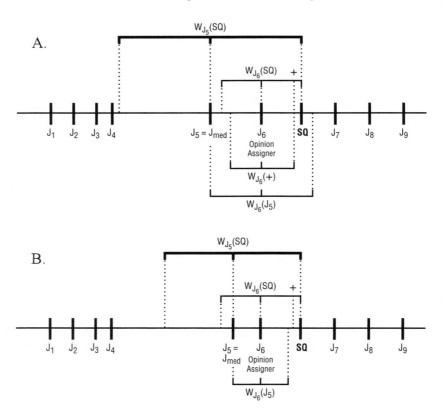

FIGURE 7.9

The Opinion Assigner Is Adjacent to SQ, At Least One Other
Justice Lies Inside SQ But Farther from SQ Than the Assigner,
and At Least One Justice Lies on the Minority Side

that an opinion at justice J_5's ideal point here falls outside assigner J_6's pre-ferred-to set of SQ. And note that if any of the minority-side justices (justices J_7, J_8, or J_9) is eligible to write a majority opinion (because of their voting on the majority side on the conference vote), each of their opinions would be written at + just inside the SQ boundary of $W_{J5}(SQ)$. For example, if only justice J_7 is eligible, assigner J_6 could assign either to justice J_5 or justice J_7. Because justice J_7's opinion at + is closer to assigner J_6's ideal point than is justice J_5's opinion at J_5 (note that J_5 lies outside the $W_{J6}(+)$ pre-ferred-to set in diagram A), assigner J_6 would prefer to assign to justice J_7; the resulting opinion would be at +. In fact, assigner J_6 would prefer to assign to justice J_7 rather than to justice J_5 even if justice J_7's ideal point lay much farther to the right of SQ than shown: justice J_7's majority opinion would still have to be at +.

Note also in diagram A in Figure 7.9 that assigner J_6 would prefer to assign to justice J_7 here even though justice J_7's ideal point is farther from J_6 than is justice J_5's ideal point (note that J_7 lies outside the $W_{J6}(J_5)$ preferred-to set in the diagram). The reason is that justice J_7's opinion at + is closer to assigner J_6's ideal point than is J_5's opinion at J_5; once again, it is where the other justices' opinions would be that matters, not where their ideal points are.

Of course, if none of the minority-side justices is eligible to write the majority opinion, and if assigner J_6 cannot self-assign, he would have no choice but to assign the opinion to justice J_5, who would write the majority opinion at J_5, which is worse than SQ for assigner J_6. Clearly, assigner J_6's preference here is to self-assign, because any other assignment (assuming justice J_7, J_8, or J_9 is not available) will produce an opinion worse for him than SQ.

Now consider the corresponding case in which the next justice to the opinion assigner's left falls inside the assigner's preferred-to set of SQ. In diagram B in Figure 7.9, for example, the ideal points are identical to those in diagram A except that justice J_5's ideal point is now farther to the right and falls inside assigner J_6's preferred-to set, $W_{J6}(SQ)$. If justice J_5 were the opinion writer, she would write her opinion at J_5, and as before, if any of the minority-side justices (justices J_7, J_8, or J_9) are eligible, each of their opinions would be written at +, just inside the SQ boundary of $W_{J5}(SQ)$. So if justice J_7 is eligible, for example, assigner J_6 could assign the opinion either to justice J_5 or justice J_7. Because justice J_5's opinion at J_5 now falls substantially inside justice J_6's preferred-to set of SQ, whereas justice J_7's opinion at + now falls just inside the SQ boundary of justice J_6's preferred-to set of SQ, assigner J_6 would prefer to assign to justice J_5 (note that the opinion at + in the diagram lies outside the $W_{J6}(J_5)$ preferred-to set); the resulting opinion would be at J_5. In this case, then, the strategically rational opinion assigner would assign the opinion to the justice with the closest ideal point, but only because the final opinion would be closer to the assigner's ideal point. Of course, if none of the minority-side justices is eligible to write the majority opinion, assigner J_6 would have no choice but to assign the opinion to justice J_5, who would then write the majority opinion at her ideal point of J_5.

For this fifth set of conditions, then, we can assert:

PROPOSITION 7.14. If the majority opinion assigner is adjacent to SQ, at least one other justice lies inside $W_{Jmed}(SQ)$ but farther from SQ than the assigner, and at least one other justice lies on the minority side of SQ, to whom the assigner makes the assignment depends on whether there is an eligible minority-side justice and on whether the ideal point of the next justice to the outside (away from SQ) falls inside or outside the assigner's preferred-to set of SQ.

(a) If there is no eligible minority-side justice, and if the assigner does not self-assign, then the opinion assigner will assign the opinion to the adjacent justice to the outside of the assigner.

(b) If there is at least one eligible minority-side justice but the ideal point of the adjacent justice to the outside of the assigner falls farther inside the assigner's preferred-to set of SQ than a minority-side justice's opinion, and if the assigner does not self-assign, then the opinion assigner will assign the opinion to this adjacent justice to the outside.

(c) If there is at least one eligible minority-side justice and the ideal point of the adjacent justice to the outside falls outside the assigner's preferred-to set of SQ, and if the assigner does not self-assign, then the opinion assigner will assign the opinion to a minority-side justice.

If self-assignment is possible for justice J_6 in Figure 7.9, it would be the best strategy: assigner J_6 could write the opinion at J_6, whereas none of the other justices to whom the assignment might have to be given—majority-side justice J_5 and minority-side justices J_7, J_8, or J_9—would write an opinion at J_6. Hence, as previously noted, justice J_6 would prefer self-assignment here if possible; the only exceptions would be if J_6 were identical to J_5, or if J_6 were identical to $+$. In general, then, we can assert:

PROPOSITION 7.15. *If the majority opinion assigner is adjacent to SQ, at least one other justice lies inside* $W_{Jmed}(SQ)$ *but farther from SQ than the assigner, and at least one other justice lies on the minority side of SQ, then self-assignment is preferable to assignment to either of these other justices (unless the assigner's ideal point is identical to the ideal point of the adjacent justice to the outside, or the assigner's ideal point is identical to the minority-side justice's opinion, in which case the assigner is indifferent between self-assignment and assignment to one of those justices).*

Opinion Assignment by a Minority-Side Justice

There are three sets of conditions to examine when a minority-side justice is the opinion assigner. When we refer to a minority-side justice who is an "eligible opinion assigner," we mean a justice whose ideal point is on the minority-side but who voted with the majority on the conference vote and so is eligible to assign the majority opinion. And as before, when we refer to a minority-side justice who is an "eligible opinion writer," we mean a justice whose ideal point is on the minority side but who voted with the majority on the conference vote and so is eligible to write the majority opinion.

For assignments by an eligible minority-side opinion assigner, the three sets of conditions we must consider are as follows:

(1)   The opinion assigner and two or more eligible opinion writers all lie on the minority side of $W_{Jmed}(SQ)$.

(2)   The opinion assigner and just one eligible opinion writer lie on the minority side of $W_{Jmed}(SQ)$.

(3)   The opinion assigner lies on the minority side of $W_{Jmed}(SQ)$ but there are no eligible opinion writers (besides the assigner) on the minority side of $W_{Jmed}(SQ)$.

Consider the first set of conditions, in which the ideal points of the opinion assigner and two or more eligible opinion writers all lie on the minority side of $W_{Jmed}(SQ)$. Returning to Figure 7.1, for example, assume that justice J_9 is an eligible opinion assigner and that justices J_7 and J_8 are eligible opinion writers. Assigner J_9 could assign either to justice J_8, who would then write a majority side opinion at + just inside the SQ boundary of $W_{J5}(SQ)$, the preferred-to set of the median justice, or to justice J_7, who would also write an opinion at +. Because both justices would write an opinion at +, assigner J_9 would be indifferent over which justice is given the assignment; in either case, the final opinion will be at +.

In fact, if opinion assigner J_9 were to self-assign, he would also write an opinion at +. Because this opinion of his at + is no better for him than if justice J_8 or justice J_7 writes the opinion, self-assignment here does no better than assignment to any of the potential minority-side opinion writers.

Next, consider the second set of conditions, in which the opinion assigner and just one eligible opinion writer lie on the minority side of $W_{Jmed}(SQ)$. In Figure 7.1, for example, assume that justice J_9 is the assigner and that justice J_7 is the only eligible opinion writer on the minority side (for example, because justice J_8 was on the minority side on the conference vote). Justice J_7 would write an opinion at + at the SQ boundary of $W_{J5}(SQ)$. The only other justice who would be considered for opinion assignment is justice J_6; because justice J_6 lies inside $W_{J5}(SQ)$, the preferred-to set of the median justice, justice J_6 could write an opinion at his own ideal point of J_6. For assigner J_9, then, the choice is between an opinion at + (from justice J_7) and an opinion at J_6 (from justice J_6). Assigner J_9 would thus assign the opinion to justice J_7 because the opinion at + is closer to his own ideal point than an opinion at J_6.

In fact, if opinion assigner J_9 were to self-assign, he would also write an opinion at +. Because this opinion of his at + is no better for him than if justice J_7 writes the opinion at +, self-assignment does no better than assignment to the eligible minority-side opinion writer, justice J_7.

Now consider the third set of conditions, in which the opinion assigner lies on the minority side of $W_{Jmed}(SQ)$ but there are no eligible opinion writers on the minority side. In Figure 7.1, for example, assume that justice

J_9 is the assigner and that justices J_7 and J_8 are not eligible to write the majority opinion (for example, because they were both on the minority side on the conference vote). Note that justice J_6, whose ideal point lies inside $W_{J5}(SQ)$, is the nearest possible assignee. Assigner J_9 would thus assign the opinion to the closest majority-side justice, who is justice J_6, and justice J_6 would write a majority opinion at his own ideal point of J_6.

However, if opinion assigner J_9 were to self-assign, he would write an opinion at $+$. Because this opinion of his at $+$ is better for him than if he had to assign the opinion to justice J_6, he would prefer to self-assign in this case.

For these three sets of conditions, then, we can summarize our arguments as follows:

PROPOSITION 7.16. A minority-side opinion assigner who does not self-assign will assign the opinion to any other minority-side justice who is eligible to write the majority opinion; if no other minority-side justice is eligible, the opinion assigner will assign the opinion to the majority-side justice who is closest to the minority-side opinion assigner.

Regarding self-assignment, we can also state:

PROPOSITION 7.17. For any minority-side opinion assigner, if no other minority-side justices is an eligible assignee, the minority-side opinion assigner will prefer to self-assign; if at least one minority-side justice is eligible, the minority-side opinion assigner will be indifferent between self-assignment and assignment to one of the eligible minority-side justices.

Finally, note again that assignment to the justice with the closest ideal point does not necessarily produce the best outcome for the minority-side opinion assigner. In Figure 7.1, for example, if justice J_7 is the assigner, he would prefer to assign to justice J_8 or J_9, if they are eligible, rather than to justice J_6, even though J_6 is closer to J_7 than is either J_8 or J_9 (note that J_8 and J_9 both lie outside $W_{J7}(J_6)$ in Figure 7.1). In this case, then, the assigner does better with an assignment to the more distant justice. The reason, of course, is that justice J_6 would write an opinion at J_6, whereas justices J_8 and J_9 would write opinions at $+$; because an opinion at $+$ is closer to assigner J_7's ideal point than is an opinion at J_6, assigner J_7 would prefer to assign to either justice J_8 or J_9 rather than to justice J_6. Of course, justice J_7's ideal point could be located closer to J_8 and J_9 than to J_6 (not shown). In this case, assignment to justices J_8 or J_9 would go to one of the closer justices.

Would an Opinion Assigner Prefer Larger Coalitions?

When two potential majority opinion writers would write opinions that are equidistant from the ideal point of the majority opinion assigner, thereby yielding identical utilities for the assigner, the logic of our argument is

FIGURE 7.10

*Choosing an Opinion Assignment When the Resulting
Coalition Sizes May Differ*

A.

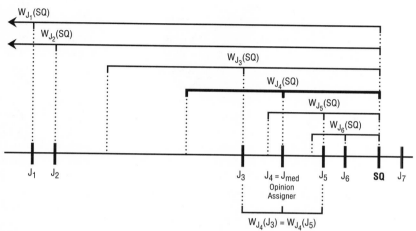

B.

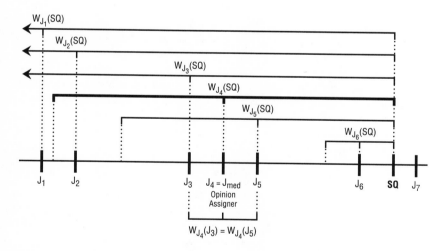

that the assigner would be indifferent between the two assignments. However, it is important to note that one of these two opinions may attract the support of a larger coalition than the other opinion. Although we have not incorporated a concern for the size of the majority in our justices' utility functions (see Assumption 5.3), a revised model might be designed with this in mind. The result would be that the assigner will assign the majority opinion to the justice who would write the opinion that generates the larger majority.

To illustrate, consider the two diagrams in Figure 7.10; there are seven justices here. Assume that the median justice, J_4, is the opinion assigner. The potential assignees are then justices J_3 and J_5. Because both of these potential assignees have ideal points that lie inside $W_{J4}(SQ)$, each could write a majority opinion at his or her own ideal point. Note in both diagrams that the ideal points of justices J_3 and J_5 are equidistant from J_4's own ideal point; that is, $W_{J4}(J_3) = W_{J4}(J_5)$. This means that the policies that justices J_3 and J_5 would respectively write would be equidistant from assigner J_4's ideal point. Hence, assigner J_4 would be indifferent between an opinion at J_3 and an opinion at J_5.

However, for diagram A in Figure 7.10 one might argue that opinion assigner J_4 would prefer to assign the opinion rightward to justice J_5 rather than leftward to justice J_3. The reason is that the opinion written by justice J_5 would attract more support than the opinion written by justice J_3. In particular, an opinion at J_5 would attract the support of justices J_1 through J_6 because J_5 lies inside the preferred-to sets of all six of these justices; only justice J_7 would fail to support an opinion at J_5. In contrast, an opinion at J_3 would attract the support of justices J_1 through J_4, but would fail to attract the support of justices J_5, J_6, and J_7. Thus, a majority opinion at J_5 would gain the support of six justices, for a 6–1 vote, whereas a majority opinion at J_3 would gain the support of only four justices, for a 4–3 vote.

So even though the opinions at J_3 and J_5 are equidistant from J_4, and thus of equivalent value to justice J_4, the revised utility function would imply that opinion assigner J_4 should assign the opinion to the justice whose opinion can gain a larger majority against SQ; a larger majority, for example, might have greater value as a precedent for the Supreme Court and for the lower courts. In general, then, this concern for the size of the majority means that the assignment would go to the potential assignee whose ideal point is closer to SQ. (We again emphasize that this is not part of the justices' utility functions as we have modeled them.)

However, it is not necessarily the case that two potential opinions that are equidistant from the opinion assigner's ideal point will generate different-sized majorities. Consider diagram B in Figure 7.10. Justice J_4 is again the opinion assigner and justices J_3 and J_5 have ideal points that are equidistant from J_4. Now, however, J_3 and J_5 both lie inside $W_{J5}(SQ)$ but outside $W_{J6}(SQ)$. With this configuration, then, majority opinions at J_3 and J_5 would both gain the support of five justices, J_1 through J_5, and fail to gain the support of two justices, J_6 and J_7, for a 5–2 vote in each case. Hence, we would pose the following proposition about the potential for a majority-increasing choice by an opinion assigner:

PROPOSITION 7.18. Two potential opinions, both of which can gain majority support, both of which are equidistant from the opinion assigner's ideal point, and both of which are thus of equal utility to the opinion assigner, may be able to gain the support (but will not necessarily gain the support) of different-size majorities.

A concern for the size of the majority may extend beyond this kind of case in which two potential opinions are equidistant from the assigner's ideal point. In Chapter 6, for example, we discussed the possibility that an opinion writer might, in the pursuit of a larger majority, deliberately choose to write an opinion closer to SQ than is required to gain just a bare majority. To illustrate this argument, assume again that justice J_4 in diagram A in Figure 7.10 is the opinion writer. If she writes the opinion at her own ideal point, she will gain the support of five justices, J_1 through J_5. But with a revised utility function, she might instead decide to write her opinion just inside the left-hand boundary of justice J_6's preferred-to set, $W_{J6}(SQ)$, thereby giving up the utility from an opinion at J_4 (which would automatically gain the support of five of the seven justices) in exchange for the support of justice J_6; the resulting opinion (not shown) would thereby gain the support of all six majority-side justices.

In sum, then, just like the opinion writer who is willing to put up with a less desirable opinion in order to gain more support, the opinion assigner may be willing to make a less desirable opinion assignment in order to generate more support for the final opinion. Again, though, the justices' utility functions in our model would have to be revised to allow this kind of trade-off.

How Much Does Opinion Assignment Matter?

The premise of the preceding analysis of opinion assignment in the agenda-control version of our model has been that it can affect outcomes. But if we ask the question, "How much can opinion assignment affect outcomes?", the answer is simply, "It varies." In Chapter 6, we argued that opinion writing is always constrained by the size of the median justice's preferred-to set, $W_{Jmed}(SQ)$. But the closer J_{med} is to SQ, the closer the outside boundary of $W_{Jmed}(SQ)$ will be to SQ. Hence, as J_{med} moves closer and closer to SQ, the range of majority opinions that could be written gets smaller and smaller. This means that as J_{med} moves closer and closer to SQ, to whom the opinion is assigned would make less and less difference to what majority opinion is ultimately adopted. When $W_{Jmed}(SQ)$ is small, then, this would allow the opinion assigner to give more weight to decision criteria not included in our model, such as workload and equity considerations.

We end by reemphasizing that opinion assignment only matters in the context of the agenda-control model. Under either the open-bidding model or the median-holdout model, which justice writes the opinion is irrelevant: the final opinion will always be at J_{med}. If either of these two models is an accurate characterization of behavior on the Court, this suggests that many of the empirical results on opinion assignment in the literature may also be irrelevant: the same opinion would result, regardless of who writes it.

Summary of Major Results

We can summarize our most important results on opinion assignment with the following observations:

1. The majority opinion assigner has no opinion assignment strategy that is superior to self-assignment.

2. If the majority opinion assigner cannot self-assign, to whom the assignment is made depends on two variables. First, does the opinion assigner's ideal point lie (a) outside $W_{Jmed}(SQ)$, (b) within $W_{Jmed}(SQ)$, or (c) to the minority side of $W_{Jmed}(SQ)$? And second, do the ideal points of the potential assignees lie (a) outside $W_{Jmed}(SQ)$, (b) within $W_{Jmed}(SQ)$, or (c) to the minority side of $W_{Jmed}(SQ)$? Different answers to these two questions will lead to different assignment strategies for the opinion assigner.

3. If the ideal points of the majority opinion assigner and two or more other justices lie outside $W_{Jmed}(SQ)$, then it does not matter to the opinion assigner which of these possible outside assignees writes the opinion: the opinions will all lie just inside the outside boundary of $W_{Jmed}(SQ)$.

4. If the ideal points of the majority opinion assigner and two or more other justices lie inside $W_{Jmed}(SQ)$, at least one on each side of the assigner, the assigner will assign the opinion to the justice with the closest ideal point.

5. If the ideal points of the majority opinion assigner and all eligible assignees lie to the minority side of SQ, then it does not matter to the opinion assigner which of these eligible minority-side assignees writes the opinion: the opinions will all lie just inside the SQ boundary of $W_{Jmed}(SQ)$.

6. How much opinion assignment affects the final opinion in the agenda-control model depends on how close J_{med} is to SQ: the closer J_{med} is to SQ, the less opinion assignment can affect what final opinion is written.

7. Given two majority opinions of equivalent distance on either side of the opinion assigner's ideal point, there exist conditions under which the rational opinion assigner may assign to the next justice inward, rather than outward, and thereby attract the support of a larger majority coalition.

CHAPTER 8

The Conference Vote

In Chapter 6, we determined what final policy would be endorsed by the writer of the majority opinion for the Supreme Court, and we also identified what coalition of justices would form in support of this opinion writer's policy. Then in Chapter 7 we determined, for any justice who might become the majority opinion assigner, which justice this opinion assigner would designate as the majority opinion writer. Here in Chapter 8, we identify the justice who would become this opinion assigner.

The opinion assigner is selected via a conference that the justices hold soon after oral argument on a case. For each case considered in conference, each justice briefly discusses what general policy he or she thinks the Court should adopt for the case and also states whether he or she thinks the lower-court opinion (which had been appealed to the Supreme Court) should be affirmed or reversed. At least in recent decades, the Chief Justice has gone first in announcing his views on the case, and then the associate justices follow with their own statements, made in decreasing order of seniority on the Court.[1]

When the justices have completed their statements, it is usually apparent how many justices want a policy that affirms the lower-court ruling and how many justices want a policy that reverses it. Who becomes the majority opinion assigner depends on which side received the most support. If the Chief Justice supported the majority side, he becomes the assigner; if the Chief Justice supported the minority side, the most senior associate justice on the majority side becomes the assigner.[2]

In Chapter 5, we observed that "strategic" behavior in the Supreme Court's decision-making process often has a clearer meaning than "sincere"—that is, nonstrategic—behavior. However, on the conference vote, it is sincere behavior that seems to have the clearer meaning and strategic behavior that seems to allow alternative predictions of how strategic justices would behave.

On the conference vote, it seems most reasonable to think that a sincere justice will simply endorse a policy at his or her own ideal point. Hence, we have:

ASSUMPTION 8.1. On the conference vote for a case, a sincere justice will express support for a policy located at his or her ideal point.

If all justices behave sincerely in this way, then the selection of the opinion assigner follows directly:

PROPOSITION 8.1. Assuming that all justices behave sincerely on the conference vote, one of the following will occur:

(a)   *If* the ideal point of the Chief Justice lies on the majority side of SQ, *then* the Chief Justice will become the opinion assigner.

(b)   *If* the Chief Justice's ideal point lies to the minority side of SQ, *then* the most senior associate justice whose ideal point lies on the majority side of SQ will become the opinion assigner.

Once the majority opinion assigner is selected, the opinion assignment process can proceed as discussed in Chapter 7.

In contrast, if we assume that all justices behave strategically on the conference vote, it is far more difficult to determine whom we should expect to become the opinion assigner. Of course, a very general view of how a strategic justice will behave on the conference vote can be easily drawn from our Chapter 5 definition of what it means to be strategic. Hence, we can advance:

ASSUMPTION 8.2. On the conference vote, a strategic justice will express support for that policy that leads the Court to adopt a final policy that is as close as possible to the justice's ideal point.

Unfortunately, this assumption tells us very little about what particular policy a strategically rational justice should be expected to endorse on the conference vote. Nor does knowing what any one justice might do necessarily tell us how the strategically calculated choices of all the justices will interact to produce an opinion assigner.

Of course, we have already argued that if the open-bidding version of our model accurately characterizes coalition formation and the final vote (stages 4 and 5), who assigns the majority opinion (stage 3) will not affect what final policy is chosen. The reason is that no matter who writes this majority opinion, the final policy adopted will end up at J_{med}, the ideal point of the median justice. Hence, any strategizing on the conference vote (stage 2) would be irrelevant to the final outcome.

However, if the agenda-control version of our model accurately characterizes stages 4 and 5, then the strategic considerations that arise in stage 2 here can affect the final policy. We have already shown in Chapter 7 that a Chief Justice with a minority-side ideal point can engage in strategic behavior on the conference vote by endorsing some majority-side policy, which ensures that he will become the majority opinion assigner. In this chapter, we present several additional results regarding the conference vote.

For example, under some conditions, what final opinion emerges will not be affected by any strategic behavior by the justices on the conference vote. However, under other conditions, a justice will find it advantageous to engage in strategic position-taking—that is, endorsing something other than his or her most preferred policy in order to attract the opinion assignment from the Chief Justice. In fact, the aggregate result of strategic position-taking by multiple justices on the conference vote is that the justices should be expected to express support for policies that converge on the ideal point of the Chief Justice.

This convergence behavior has a further implication. If at least one justice endorses a position on the conference vote that is identical to the Chief Justice's own ideal point, and if the Chief Justice trusts this justice to write a final majority opinion as close as possible to the position that the justice had endorsed, then the Chief Justice can assign the opinion to this justice and get a final opinion that is as good as if the Chief Justice were to self-assign. Hence, a Chief Justice who is concerned solely about his own policy goals may still be willing to assign the opinion to other justices on a regular basis. In fact, at the end of this chapter, we will suggest that whenever the Chief Justice suffers no policy losses by assigning the majority opinion to other justices, he could then make these assignments on the basis of other criteria, such as equity or workload.

We begin our analysis of strategic behavior on the conference vote by initially assuming that just one justice behaves strategically while everyone else behaves sincerely. Once we have clarified key aspects of strategic behavior by just one justice on the conference vote, we then broaden our analysis by considering what happens when all the justices behave strategically on the conference vote; this is where our "convergence" results emerge.

After these analyses are completed, we will review the role played by commitment, reputation, trust, and trustworthiness in the opinion-assignment and opinion-writing process. Our analysis will focus on those justices who, for strategic reasons aimed at attracting the opinion assignment, endorse something other than their most preferred policy on the conference vote. But then the following problem arises: what reason would the opinion assigner have to trust any other justice to write a final majority opinion that is as close as possible to the policy this other justice endorsed on the conference vote? Or will this other justice, having gained control of the majority opinion, write the final opinion as close as possible to his own ideal point, despite having publicly endorsed some other policy on the conference vote?

For this reason, the majority opinion assigner must somehow determine whether this potential opinion writer is trustworthy or instead will renege on what he or she said on the conference vote. If the opinion assigner believes this potential opinion writer will renege, the opinion assigner will assign the opinion just as we indicated in Chapter 7—that is, to that justice who, in the pursuit of a policy as close as possible to his or her own ideal point, would be writing a final majority opinion that also happens to be closest to the opinion assigner's own ideal point. But if the opinion assigner believes instead that some potential assignee would write a final opinion as close as possible to the policy that the potential assignee endorsed on the conference vote, then the opinion assigner might find it advantageous to base opinion assignment on this position that the justice endorsed rather than on what the justice's ideal point is.

We conclude the chapter with a brief summary of our major results.[3]

Different Kinds of Strategic Behavior from Different Kinds of Justices

There are three different categories of justices whose behavior must be understood before we can draw any general conclusions about how strategic behavior on the conference vote will affect who becomes the majority opinion assigner. First, whether the Chief Justice endorses a majority-side policy on the conference vote will be critical in determining who becomes the majority opinion assigner. Second, we must consider the behavior of what we call the "high-seniority" associate justices, one of whom could become the majority opinion assigner if the Chief Justice does not endorse some majority-side policy. Third, we must consider the behavior of the justices who have such low seniority that they can never become the majority opinion assigner; this route to influence is completely foreclosed to them. We will also show how to identify these low-seniority justices.

In the next three sections we examine strategic behavior on the conference vote by these three different kinds of justices. In each section, our analysis involves a comparison of the different outcomes that can result from the different strategies a justice could adopt. In particular, each justice has available just three different kinds of strategies on the conference vote:

To express support for some policy on the majority side of SQ.

To express support for the policy at SQ.

To express support for some policy on the minority side of SQ.

On the conference vote, each strategically rational justice will decide which policy to support by comparing outcomes from these three different kinds of strategies. The rational justice will then choose the strategy that leads to the best outcome.

Whatever strategy a justice chooses, any influence that the justice might exercise over the final outcome of a case will take place through one of three different routes. One route is that some justice can become the majority opinion assigner. This route to influence is dominated by the behavior of the Chief Justice: if he votes with the majority side, he automatically becomes the majority opinion assigner. Only if the Chief Justice votes with the minority side can one of the high-seniority associate justices become the majority opinion assigner. As already noted, none of the low-seniority justices can ever become the majority opinion assigner.

A second route to influence is that any of the justices can become the majority opinion writer. Of course, if the Chief Justice becomes the majority opinion assigner and also self-assigns, then this route to influence is foreclosed to the remaining justices, whether high or low seniority. But if the Chief Justice does not self-assign, others will have an opportunity to become the majority opinion writer. High-seniority justices have no advantage here over the low-seniority justices: the rational Chief Justice (or whoever becomes the opinion assigner) will, in the manner we have described in Chapter 7, simply select that justice who will write that final majority opinion that is closest to the Chief Justice's (or other opinion assigner's) ideal point.

Of course, only one justice can become the majority opinion assigner, and only one justice can become the majority opinion writer. But there might conceivably be a third route to influence that some of the seven remaining justices might consider on the conference vote. If the policy that would be selected by the majority opinion writer would be worse than the status quo policy for one or more of the seven remaining justices, these justices could try to behave in a way that undermines the majority opinion writer's ability to gain the support of a Court majority. In particular, their goal would be to reduce the Court majority for the opinion to a Court plurality. These justices could try to achieve their goal by defecting from the majority side and expressing support instead either for SQ or for some minority-side policy. As we will demonstrate, however, this strategy of trying to undermine majority support for the opinion writer's policy is unlikely to work. We show that if the opinion writer behaves rationally, by writing the majority opinion inside $W_{Jmed}(SQ)$, there will never be enough dissatisfied justices to make this strategy of defection a successful one.

In each of the following three sections, we assume that the justice of interest—the Chief Justice, a high-seniority associate justice, and a low-seniority associate justice—behaves strategically but that all other justices behave sincerely. In a subsequent section, we then consider what happens when all justices behave strategically.

Strategic Behavior by the Chief Justice

There are two conditions that we must analyze in order to understand how the Chief Justice can affect the results of the conference vote. In the first condition, the Chief Justice's ideal point is on the majority side of SQ; in the second condition, the Chief Justice's ideal point is on the minority side of SQ. For each condition, the three different kinds of strategies outlined above will be available to the Chief Justice: (a) express support for some policy on the majority side of SQ, (b) express support for the policy at SQ, and (c) express support for some policy on the minority side of SQ. To determine what the Chief Justice would do, for each condition we must compare the final outcome from his pursuit of strategy (a) to the final outcomes from his pursuit of strategies (b) and (c). The rational Chief Justice would adopt that strategy that leads to the best final majority opinion for him.

CONDITION I: THE CHIEF JUSTICE HAS A MAJORITY-SIDE IDEAL POINT

When the Chief Justice has a majority-side ideal point, he need only express support for some policy on the majority side in order to become the opinion assigner. In effect, he should pursue strategy (a). Indeed, a Chief Justice with a majority-side ideal point would have no reason to express support for any policy other than his own ideal point. Moreover, we will later demonstrate that if another justice tries to attract the opinion assignment from the Chief Justice, he or she will have to do so on the conference vote by expressing support for a policy that is close to or even at the policy that the Chief Justice endorsed. If the Chief Justice were to express support for something other than his own ideal point, it would not be clear to the other justices what policy they would find it advantageous to endorse as each tries to attract the opinion assignment from him: should they endorse the policy he endorses, or endorse a policy at or close to his ideal point? Endorsing a policy at his own ideal point allows them to endorse policies that benefit him the most.

There would certainly be no reason for the Chief Justice to pursue strategies (b) or (c), which involve expressing support for some policy not on the majority side: some other justice on the majority side would then become the opinion assigner, which could then lead to a policy that is worse for the Chief Justice than what he could get by expressing support for a policy at his majority-side ideal point.

When the Chief Justice has a majority-side ideal point, then, we conclude that strategic behavior and sincere behavior by the Chief Justice will be identical. Hence, we have:

PROPOSITION 8.2. On the conference vote, a Chief Justice with a majority-side ideal point will express support for a policy at his own ideal point.

With the majority-side Chief Justice thus becoming the opinion assigner, the logic of opinion assignment developed in Chapter 7 can then be used to characterize how the Chief Justice would assign the opinion.

CONDITION 2: THE CHIEF JUSTICE HAS A
MINORITY-SIDE IDEAL POINT

When the Chief Justice has a minority-side ideal point, he can again adopt one of three different strategies, examined here in reverse order because the Chief Justice's ideal point is now on the minority side: (c) to express support for some policy on the minority side of SQ, (b) to express support for the policy at SQ, and (a) to express support for some policy on the majority side of SQ. To determine what strategy he would adopt, we must compare the final outcomes from the Chief Justice's pursuit of strategies (c) and (b) to the final outcome from his pursuit of strategy (a).

With strategy (c), this minority-side Chief Justice would express support for a policy on the minority side (presumably at his own ideal point, although it does not matter which minority-side policy he endorses). The consequence is that the most senior associate justice on the majority side would become the opinion assigner. The result would be a majority-side opinion lying within $W_{Jmed}(SQ)$, and of course, any opinion on the majority side will be worse than SQ for this minority-side Chief Justice.

If the Chief Justice follows strategy (b), the result is the same as from strategy (c): opinion assignment would be managed by the most senior associate justice on the majority side. This again means that a majority-side opinion lying within $W_{Jmed}(SQ)$ would be produced, and this majority-side opinion would again always be worse than SQ for the minority-side Chief Justice.

In contrast, the minority-side Chief Justice can almost always get the best outcome for himself by following strategy (a), that is, by expressing support for some opinion on the majority side. To illustrate, consider Figure 8.1. Assume that the Chief Justice is minority-side justice J_7, and note that the median justice is J_4. If the Chief Justice behaves sincerely on the conference vote, by expressing support for a policy at his own ideal point of J_7, the most senior associate justice on the majority side (that is, one of justices J_1 through J_5) will become the opinion assigner; the resulting opinion would then be written somewhere inside $W_{J4}(SQ)$, the preferred-to set of the median justice.

FIGURE 8.1

*Strategic Behavior by a Chief Justice with
a Minority-Side Ideal Point*

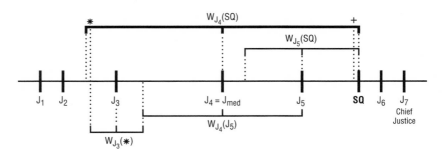

To understand more precisely what would happen, we first establish a sincere-behavior baseline of what policy would result if all justices behave sincerely. In particular, we determine what would happen if each of justices J_1 through J_5 were to become the opinion assigner. For example, if justice J_5 becomes the opinion assigner and self-assigns, he could write an opinion at his own ideal point of J_5 because his ideal point lies inside $W_{J4}(SQ)$. If he does not self-assign, he would assign outward to justice J_4, the median justice, who would write an opinion at her own ideal point of J_4.

If justice J_4 becomes the opinion assigner and self-assigns, she could write an opinion at J_4. If she does not self-assign, she would assign either inward to justice J_5, who would write an opinion at J_5, or outward to justice J_3, who could write an opinion at J_3 because his ideal point also lies inside $W_{J4}(SQ)$. Because justice J_4 prefers an opinion at J_5 to an opinion at J_3 (note in the diagram that J_4 is closer to J_5 than to J_3), she would assign inward to justice J_5, with the result being an opinion at J_5.

If justice J_3 becomes the opinion assigner and self-assigns, he could write an opinion at J_3. If he does not self-assign, he could assign either inward to justice J_4, who would write an opinion at J_4, or outward to justice J_2 or J_1, each of whom would have to write an opinion at *, which is just inside the outside boundary of $W_{J4}(SQ)$. Because justice J_3 prefers an opinion at * to an opinion at J_4 (note in the diagram that J_3 is closer to * than to J_4), he would assign outward to justice J_2 or J_1, with the result being an opinion at *.

If justice J_2 becomes the opinion assigner and self-assigns, he would write an opinion at *. If justice J_2 does not self-assign, he would assign to justice J_1 rather than to J_3: justice J_1's opinion would be at *, whereas justice J_3's opinion would be at J_3, which is farther away than *. Finally, if justice J_1 becomes the opinion assigner and self-assigns, he would write an opinion at *. But if he does not self-assign, he would assign to justice J_2, who would write an opinion at *.

Now consider what a strategically rational Chief Justice with a minority-side ideal point at J_7 would do, given these possible outcomes when everyone is sincere. If he votes on the minority side on the conference vote, the final opinion will be at J_5, J_4, J_3, or * (depending on who becomes the majority opinion assigner and majority opinion writer), all of which are clearly worse for him than SQ. Hence, the best strategy for the Chief Justice would be to become the majority opinion assigner himself by expressing support for a policy at +, just inside the SQ boundary of $W_{J4}(SQ)$. This policy at + is the policy closest to SQ (and thus closest to his own ideal point), which the majority-side justices would still support over SQ. If he were to adopt this strategy and then self-assign, he could then write the final majority opinion at +. This policy at + would gain the votes of justices J_1 through J_5 (it lies inside all their preferred-to sets) plus the Chief Justice's own vote.

Of course, a final policy at + would be worse for the Chief Justice than a final policy at SQ. However, if he were to vote sincerely by endorsing a policy at his own minority-side ideal point, he would end up with a policy either at J_5 or somewhere to the left of J_5. Thus, by behaving strategically and then self-assigning, he would produce the policy at +, which would be better for him than the policy that would otherwise be selected by any of the majority-side opinion writers. Endorsement of a policy at + is, in effect, a damage-limitation strategy.[4]

If the Chief Justice expresses support for the policy at + on the conference vote but feels that he cannot self-assign, he could try to persuade a fellow minority-side justice to vote with the majority as well and then assign the opinion to this other minority-side justice.[5] In Figure 8.1, for example, assume that the Chief Justice at J_7 has voted with the majority by expressing support for the policy at +, and assume that he persuades justice J_6 to express support for the policy at + as well. With both the Chief Justice and justice J_6 now voting with the majority on the conference vote, the Chief Justice would become the opinion assigner and could assign the opinion to justice J_6, who would then write the majority opinion at +.[6]

If the Chief Justice cannot self-assign and cannot persuade any other minority-side justice to join him in expressing support for the policy at + on the majority side, he must assign the majority opinion to some majority-side justice. The best the Chief Justice could do is to assign to the closest majority-side justice—justice J_5 in this case—who would then produce an opinion at J_5. This majority-side opinion at J_5, although unavoidable by the minority-side Chief Justice, would be even worse for him than the majority-side opinion at +.[7]

Of course, if justice J_5 were the senior associate justice on the majority side, he would have become the opinion assigner even if the Chief Justice had behaved sincerely on the conference vote (that is, by endorsing his own minority-side ideal point). If justice J_5 were thus the opinion assigner and were to self-assign, he would write the final opinion at J_5. Similarly, if median justice J_4 were the senior associate justice on the majority side, she would have become the opinion assigner if the Chief Justice had behaved sincerely on the conference vote. If justice J_4 were thus the opinion assigner but did not self-assign, she would prefer to assign the opinion inward to justice J_5, who would write the final opinion at J_5. In either case, the final opinion would be at J_5. But as we have just seen, this final opinion at J_5 is what would result if the minority-side Chief Justice became the opinion assigner by endorsing a majority-side policy at + but then had to assign leftward to justice J_5. In either of these circumstances, then, strategic behavior by the Chief Justice would not yield any improvement in outcomes: he would get a final outcome at J_5, which is what he would get if he behaved sincerely. We would thus expect sincere behavior from him in these kinds of situations.

To summarize these arguments, we can thus state:

PROPOSITION 8.3. On the conference vote, if a minority-side Chief Justice expresses support for that majority-side policy that is closest to SQ, there are three strategies for opinion assignment:

(a) *If* he self-assigns, *then* he will write a final majority opinion endorsing the majority-side policy closest to SQ.

(b) *If* he does not self-assign *and if* he can assign the opinion to some other minority-side justice who also expresses support for the majority-side policy which is closest to SQ, *then* he will assign the opinion to that minority-side justice, who will then write a final majority opinion endorsing the majority-side policy closest to SQ.

(c) *If* he does not self-assign *and if* there is no other minority-side justice to whom he can assign the opinion, *then* he will have to assign the opinion to the majority-side justice whose ideal point is closest to SQ and who will thus write a final majority opinion at his or her own ideal point.[8]

PROPOSITION 8.4. *If* a minority-side Chief Justice could become the opinion assigner by expressing support for the majority-side policy closest to SQ but would have to assign the opinion to the majority-side justice whose ideal point is closest to SQ *and if* this majority-side justice would be assigned the majority opinion if the Chief Justice were to vote sincerely on the conference vote, *then* the Chief Justice would gain no benefit from behaving strategically (that is, from expressing support for a majority-side policy) and so would behave sincerely on the conference vote.

Because the conditions in Proposition 8.4 are relatively restrictive, this suggests that a minority-side Chief Justice will normally find it beneficial to engage in strategic behavior on the conference vote.

Table 8.1 summarizes how the strategically rational Chief Justice should be expected to behave when he has a majority-side ideal point and when he has a minority-side ideal point.

TABLE 8.1

Strategic Behavior by the Chief Justice

If the Chief Justice has...	a majority-side ideal point, **Condition 1**	then he will endorse a policy at his own majority-side ideal point, and thus become the majority opinion assigner.
	a minority-side ideal point **Condition 2**	then he will endorse the majority-side policy closest to SQ and thus become the majority opinion assigner. (Exception: The Chief Justice will endorse his own minority-side ideal point when the justice who would become the majority-side opinion assigner would assign the opinion to someone who would write the same opinion that the Chief Justice's assignee would write if the Chief Justice became the majority opinion assigner.)

Strategic Behavior by an Associate Justice Who Could Become the Opinion Assigner

We now consider the second category of justices, involving those associate justices who have enough seniority that they could, at least in principle, become the opinion assigner if a minority-side Chief Justice votes sincerely, despite the preceding arguments, on the conference vote.

Who are these associate justices who could become an opinion assigner? We can identify them by first determining which associate justices have such low seniority that they could never become an opinion assigner (assuming all justices on the Court participate in the conference vote). If we eliminate both the Chief Justice and those associate justices with such low seniority that they could never become an opinion assigner, we are left with the associate justices who could become the opinion assigner.

To identify the justices who have such low seniority that they cannot become the opinion assigner, we examine the possible lineups on the conference vote in a nine-member Court. In each possible lineup (that is, 9–0, 8–1, 7–2, 6–3, and 5–4) we will place the Chief Justice and the most senior of the associate justices on the minority side so that they cannot become the opinion assigner; the remaining justices will be placed on the majority side. It would thus be the most senior of these lower-seniority associate justices remaining on the majority side who would become the assigner; the remaining lower-seniority justices would not become the assigner. In this way, we can identify those justices who can never become the opinion assigner, even when the Chief Justice and the most senior associate justice are on the minority side.

We begin with a lineup in which all justices have ideal points to the same side of SQ and then work our way downward to a lineup in which at most five justices have ideal points to the same side of SQ:

> First consider a lineup in which all nine justices have ideal points to the same side of SQ. Because the Chief Justice is necessarily in the majority here, he will become the opinion assigner. Given this lineup, none of the eight associate justices could become the opinion assigner.

> Next, consider a lineup in which there are eight justices in the majority and just one in the minority, and assume that the Chief Justice is the lone justice in the minority. The eight associate justices would thus form the majority, and the most senior justice of the eight would assign the opinion. Given this lineup, none of the seven least senior associate justices could become the opinion assigner.

> Now consider a lineup in which there are seven justices in the majority and two in the minority, and assume that the Chief Justice and the most senior associate justice are in the minority. The seven least senior associate justices would thus form the majority, and the most senior justice of the seven would assign the opinion. Given this lineup, none of the six least senior associate justices could become the opinion assigner.

> Next, consider a lineup in which there are six justices in the majority and three in the minority, and assume that the Chief Justice and the two most senior associate justices are in the minority. The six least senior associate justices would thus form the majority, and the most senior justice of the six would assign the opinion. Given this lineup, none of the five least senior associate justices could become the opinion assigner.

> Finally, consider a lineup in which there are just five justices in the majority and four in the minority, and assume that the Chief Justice and the three most senior associate justices are in the minority. The five least senior associate justices would thus form the majority, and the most senior justice

of the five would assign the opinion. Given this lineup, none of the four least senior associate justices could become the opinion assigner.

In sum, we see that even under this last condition, which is most favorable for low-seniority associate justices to become the majority opinion assigner, it is still the case that the four lowest-seniority associate justices will not have any opportunity to become the opinion assigner.

Generalizing this pattern to a Court with J members, we can assert:

PROPOSITION 8.5. On the conference vote by a J-member Court (with J an odd number), none of the $[(J + 1)/2] - 1$ associate justices with the lowest seniority can possibly become the opinion assigner, assuming all J justices participate in the conference vote.

For example, we just demonstrated that on a nine-member Court the four lowest-seniority justices can never become the opinion assigner, and this same result could have been derived from the formula as follows: $[(9 + 1)/2] - 1 = 5 - 1 = 4$ lowest-seniority associate justices who can never become the opinion assigner. For a seven-member Court, the calculation is: $[(7 + 1)/2] - 1 = 4 - 1 = 3$ lowest-seniority associate justices who can never become the opinion assigner.[9]

We can now determine which of the associate justices could become the opinion assigner. Given J justices on the Court, we can subtract the single justice who is the Chief Justice and also subtract the $[(J + 1)/2] - 1$ justices with the lowest seniority who could never become the opinion assigner; what remains are the associate justices who could become the opinion assigner. Algebraically, this is $J - 1 - \{[(J + 1)/2] - 1\} = J - 1 - [(J + 1)/2] + 1 = J - (J + 1)/2$ of these justices. Hence, we have:

PROPOSITION 8.6. On the conference vote by a J-member Court (with J an odd number), any of the $J - [(J + 1)/2]$ associate justices with the highest seniority could potentially become the opinion assigner, assuming all J justices participate in the conference vote.

For a nine-member Court, this means that any of the four highest-seniority associate justices could conceivably become the opinion assigner. For a seven-member Court, any of the three highest-seniority associate justices could conceivably become the opinion assigner.

For the analysis that follows in the remainder of this section, we will focus primarily on the behavior of the most senior associate justice.[10] Given the centrality of the Chief Justice to how the senior associate justice will rationally behave, there are two basic conditions that we must examine.

In Condition 1, the Chief Justice votes with the majority (either because his ideal point is on the majority side or because his ideal point is on the minority side but he is voting strategically for a majority-side position). When the Chief Justice votes with the majority, we must then consider what happens if this senior associate justice has a majority-side ideal point and if this senior associate justice has a minority-side ideal point; these are subconditions 1(i) and 1(ii), respectively.

In Condition 2, the Chief Justice votes with the minority (because his ideal point is on the minority side and he votes sincerely). When the Chief Justice votes with the minority, we must then consider what happens if the senior associate justice has a majority-side ideal point and if this senior associate justice has a minority-side ideal point; these are subconditions 2(i) and 2(ii), respectively.

Whatever strategy the Chief Justice uses in voting, and wherever the most senior associate justice's ideal point is located, this justice will always be able to respond with one of the three kinds of strategies previously described: (a) to express support for some policy on the majority side of SQ, (b) to express support for the policy at SQ, and (c) to express support for some policy on the minority side of SQ. The strategically rational senior associate justice would then adopt that strategy that leads to the best final outcome for himself or herself.

CONDITION 1: THE CHIEF JUSTICE VOTES WITH THE MAJORITY SIDE

When the Chief Justice votes with the majority side, this means that he will become the opinion assigner. For the senior associate justice, this forecloses the most important route to policy influence. What is left are the other two routes to policy influence: to become the opinion writer (if possible), and to prevent (if possible) some undesirable policy from gaining the support of a Court majority. As we will demonstrate, the latter route to policy influence does not work. Hence, if the senior associate justice cannot become the opinion assigner, behaving in such a way as to become the opinion writer is the only possible way to influence the final opinion.

When the Chief Justice votes with the majority side, the two subconditions that must be considered are Subcondition (i), in which the ideal point of the senior associate justice is on the majority side of SQ, and Subcondition (ii), in which the ideal point of the senior associate justice is on the minority side of SQ. We now consider how this senior associate justice will behave under each of these two subconditions.

Subcondition (i): The Ideal Point of the Senior Associate
Justice Is on the Majority Side

When the ideal points of both the Chief Justice and the senior associate justice are on the majority side, we must determine what the final outcome will be if the associate justice pursues each of the three basic strategies: (a) to express support for some policy on the majority side of SQ, (b) to express support for the policy at SQ, and (c) to express support for some policy on the minority side of SQ. Whichever outcome is best for that justice will dictate his or her choice.

As before, we first determine the sincere-behavior baseline, which is the final policy that would result if all justices behave sincerely, by expressing support for policies at their own ideal points. Then, given this sincere-behavior outcome, we determine whether there is any other policy that the senior associate justice can strategically endorse which would lead to a better outcome.

What strategy the senior associate justice should adopt, in response to the final policy in the sincere-behavior baseline, depends on where his or her ideal point is in relation to SQ and in relation to the other justices' ideal points. Unfortunately, so many different configurations are possible that we can neither illustrate them all nor provide formal results for them all. Hence, we will only provide a few illustrations to help the reader develop some intuitions about how the senior associate justice's decision-making would proceed. For any one configuration, it is not very difficult to determine what strategy the senior associate justice should adopt; the complexity comes from the number of different configurations that could occur.

First consider the two diagrams in Figure 8.2, where we examine a seven-member Court in which the senior associate justice's ideal point lies to the right of the ideal point of any possible Chief Justice. Assume that justice J_5 is the senior associate justice, and note that justice J_4 is the median justice. Assume that the Chief Justice is the opinion assigner, which means (given all-sincere behavior) that he is either justice $J_1, J_2, J_3,$ or J_4. The question is: how will justice J_5 have to behave on the conference vote to get a final policy that is as close as possible to his own ideal point?

We first observe that if justice J_5 (sincerely) expresses support for a policy at his own majority-side ideal point, he will be eligible for selection as the majority opinion writer. However, whether he would actually be assigned the opinion depends on where the Chief Justice is located: as just noted, the Chief Justice could be either justice $J_1, J_2, J_3,$ or J_4. So let us consider what would happen if the Chief Justice is $J_1, J_2, J_3,$ or J_4 in turn.

In diagram A of Figure 8.2, we see that if the Chief Justice is justice J_4 (the median justice) and self-assigns, she could write the opinion at her own ideal point of J_4. If she does not self-assign, she would prefer to assign the opinion to justice J_3 (who would write an opinion at his own ideal point of J_3) rather than to justice J_5 (who would write an opinion at his own ideal point of J_5) because J_3 is closer to her ideal point of J_4 than is J_5; note that J_5 lies outside (to the right of) the $W_{J4}(J_3)$ preferred-to set.

FIGURE 8.2

*Strategic Behavior by a Senior Associate Justice with a
Majority-Side Ideal Point Lying to the Right of the
Chief Justice*

A.

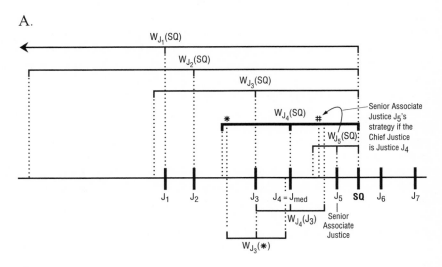

B.

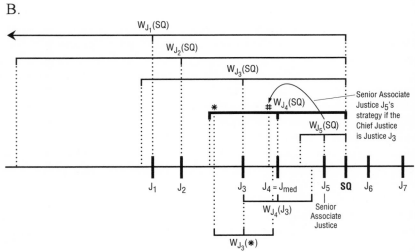

If the Chief Justice is justice J_3 and self-assigns, he could write the opinion at J_3 because J_3 lies inside $W_{J4}(SQ)$, the preferred-to set of the median justice. If Chief Justice J_3 does not self-assign, he would prefer to assign the opinion to justice J_1 or J_2 (each of whom would write an opinion at * just inside the left-hand boundary of $W_{J4}(SQ)$) rather than to justice J_4 (whose opinion would be at J_4) because * is closer to justice J_3's ideal point than is J_4; note that J_4 lies outside the $W_{J3}(*)$ preferred-to set.

If the Chief Justice is either justice J_1 or J_2 and self-assigns, he would write an opinion at * just inside the outside (left-hand) boundary of $W_{J4}(SQ)$. If Chief Justice J_1 does not self-assign, he would assign to justice J_2, and if Chief Justice J_2 does not self-assign, he would assign to justice J_1; the reason is that either opinion writer here would have to write an opinion at *.

We conclude that if each of the justices (including justice J_5) behaves sincerely by expressing support for a policy at his or her own ideal point, the resulting opinion would be at J_4, at J_3, or at *, depending on who the Chief Justice is and who is given the opinion-writing assignment. However, note that each of these opinions lies outside $W_{J5}(SQ)$, which means they are all worse for senior associate justice J_5 than SQ. So is there anything that justice J_5 can do to avoid these outcomes that are all worse than SQ for him?

Justice J_5 has the three different strategies for trying to avoid an outcome that is worse for him than SQ: (a) to express support for some policy on the majority side; (b) to express support for the policy at SQ; (c) to express support for some policy on the minority side. He would adopt the strategy that leads to the best final outcome for himself.

We first observe that strategies (c) and (b)—express support for some policy on the minority side of SQ, or for SQ—will not benefit justice J_5. The problem with these strategies is that even if justice J_5 expresses support for some minority-side policy, or for SQ, the majority-side policies that he is trying to avoid—J_4, J_3, and *—are all better than SQ for each of the other majority-side justices. As shown in diagram A of Figure 8.2, each of these three policies lies inside all their preferred-to sets of SQ, and these other majority-side justices collectively form a Court majority. Hence, a majority of this particular Court—justices J_1 through J_4—would express support for any of these majority-side policies. This means that defection by justice J_5 to the minority side, or endorsing a policy at SQ, would make no difference to the final outcome.

There remains only one strategy that our senior associate justice with a majority-side ideal point would consider on the conference vote: strategy (a), which is to express support for some policy on the majority side of SQ. Of course, we already know that endorsing a policy at his own ideal point is not the solution: the resulting policies will still be at J_4, J_3, or * rather than at his own ideal point of J_5. So is there any other policy that justice J_5 could endorse so as to get a final outcome closer to his ideal point than J_4, J_3, or *?

Because justice J_5 has no possibility of becoming the opinion assigner (recall that under Condition 1(i) here the Chief Justice is voting on the majority side), the rational policy to support would be that policy that attracts the opinion assignment.[11] For example, given the outcomes from the sincere-behavior baseline, we already know that if justice J_4 is the Chief Justice but does not self-assign, she would prefer to assign outward (leftward) to justice J_3, with an opinion at J_3 as the result.

However, if justice J_5 were to behave strategically, he could express support for an opinion at #, which is located just inside the right-hand boundary of $W_{J4}(J_3)$, the set of policies that Chief Justice J_4 prefers to the opinion at J_3, which justice J_3 would write; see diagram A in Figure 8.2. Because of justice J_5's strategically motivated endorsement of the policy at #, Chief Justice J_4 would now prefer to assign the opinion to justice J_5 (which would result in the policy at #) rather than to justice J_3 (which would result in a policy at J_3). For senior associate justice J_5, then, endorsing and eventually writing this final opinion at # yields a better outcome than the policy at J_3, which would otherwise result from voting sincerely for a policy at J_5 on the conference vote.[12]

Justice J_5 can use a similar kind of strategy if justice J_3 is the Chief Justice and so is the opinion assigner; see diagram B in Figure 8.2. In this case, if Chief Justice J_3 does not self-assign, he would have a choice between an opinion at * (if he assigns the opinion to either justice J_1 or J_2) or an opinion at J_4 (if he assigns the opinion to justice J_4). Because the opinion at * is closer to Chief Justice J_3's ideal point than an opinion at J_4, Chief Justice J_3 would prefer to assign the opinion outward (leftward) to either justice J_1 or J_2. Hence, the sincere-behavior outcome here would be a final opinion at *.

However, if justice J_5 behaves strategically in diagram B in Figure 8.2, he could express support for the policy at #, which is located just inside the right-hand boundary of $W_{J3}(*)$, the set of policies that Chief Justice J_3 prefers to the opinion at * that justice J_1 or J_2 would write. Because of justice J_5's strategic support for the policy at #, Chief Justice J_3 would now prefer to assign the opinion to justice J_5 (which results in a final opinion at #) rather than to justice J_1 or J_2 (which results in a final opinion at *). For senior associate justice J_5, then, endorsing and writing this opinion at # yields a policy that is better than the policy at *, which would otherwise result.

In contrast to these two examples in which senior associate justice J_5 can improve outcomes for himself by strategic position-taking, there is nothing that justice J_5 can do to improve outcomes for himself if either justice J_1 or J_2 is the Chief Justice. For example, if justice J_2 is the Chief Justice and so is the opinion assigner, he would assign to justice J_1, and if justice J_1 is the Chief Justice, he would assign to justice J_2; in either case, the resulting opin-

FIGURE 8.3

Strategic Behavior by a Senior Associate Justice with a Majority-Side Ideal Point Lying to the Left of the Chief Justice

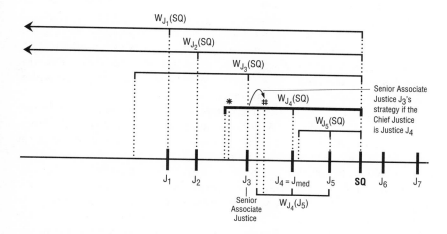

ion would be at *; see diagram A in Figure 8.2. Because * lies to the right of both J_1 and J_2, there is nothing that justice J_5 can do to attract the opinion assignment from them: no policy to the left of * could gain majority support (justice J_5 would not want to move policy leftward from * anyway), and no policy to the right of * (a movement that justice J_5 would like to see) could attract the opinion from Chief Justice J_1 or J_2. Hence, justice J_5 could do nothing to improve outcomes for himself here: he would simply have to endure a final policy at *.

Precisely the same kind of strategies—but now going in the opposite direction—can be adopted if the senior associate justice lies outside the Chief Justice. For example, in Figure 8.3 assume that our high-seniority justice is justice J_3. The question is: how should justice J_3 behave?

As before, we first establish what would happen if all justices behave sincerely. Then, given this sincere-behavior baseline for our analysis, we determine whether there is any policy that justice J_3 can strategically endorse that leads to a better outcome for him. Because by assumption justice J_3 is not the Chief Justice, either justice $J_1, J_2, J_4,$ or J_5 will be the Chief Justice and so will be the opinion assigner. Now consider what would happen when the Chief Justice is each of these other justices in turn.

If justice J_5 is the Chief Justice and self-assigns, he could write the majority opinion at his own ideal point of J_5. If Chief Justice J_5 does not self-assign, he would have to assign the majority opinion leftward, to justice $J_4,$

who would then write the majority opinion at her own ideal point of J_4.

If justice J_4 is the Chief Justice and self-assigns, she could write the majority opinion at her own ideal point of J_4. If Chief Justice J_4 does not self-assign, she would prefer to assign inward to justice J_5 rather than outward to justice J_3; the reason is that J_4 is closer to J_5 than to J_3 (note that J_3 lies outside the $W_{J4}(J_5)$ preferred-to set).

If justice J_2 is the Chief Justice and self-assigns, or if justice J_1 is the Chief Justice and self-assigns, each such Chief Justice would write an opinion at *. If Chief Justice J_2 does not self-assign, he would assign to justice J_1, and if Chief Justice J_1 does not self-assign, he would assign to justice J_2; in either case, the opinion writer would write an opinion at *.

Note that each of these possible outcomes—opinions at J_5, J_4, and *—is better than SQ for senior associate justice J_3: these opinions all lie inside $W_{J3}(SQ)$. However, although justice J_3 thus gets outcomes that are better for him than SQ when everyone behaves sincerely, the question is whether he can get an even better outcome from strategic behavior. As before, three different strategies are available: (a) to express support for some policy on the majority side of SQ, (b) to express support for the policy at SQ, and (c) to express support for some policy on the minority side of SQ. To determine what strategy justice J_3 would choose, for each condition we must compare the final outcome from his pursuit of strategy (a) to the final outcomes from his pursuit of strategies (b) and (c). He would then adopt that strategy that leads to the best final outcome for himself.

If justice J_3 pursues strategy (c) and expresses support for a minority-side policy, or pursues strategy (b) and expresses support for SQ, he would gain nothing because policies J_5, J_4, and * could each gain majority support even without his vote. Moreover, he prefers each of the policies that would be chosen anyway—J_5, J_4, and *—to SQ. Hence, he would not pursue strategies (c) or (b) by defecting from the majority side. But is there some majority-side policy that he could strategically endorse that would lead to a better outcome than what would otherwise be adopted?

For one of the possible Chief Justices here—Chief Justice J_4—a better outcome is indeed possible for justice J_3 if he votes strategically. Note that if Chief Justice J_4 does not self-assign, she would prefer to assign inward to justice J_5: the opinion at J_5 is closer to Chief Justice J_4's ideal point than is the opinion at J_3, the senior associate justice's ideal point—note that J_3 lies outside $W_{J4}(J_5)$. But there is also a set of points that Chief Justice J_4 prefers to J_5: this is $W_{J4}(J_5)$. The existence of the points inside $W_{J4}(J_5)$ means that senior associate justice J_3, who lies to the left of J_4, can attract the opinion assignment if he expresses support for a policy inside $W_{J4}(J_5)$. The best policy inside $W_{J4}(J_5)$ for justice J_3 is the policy at #, just inside the outside (left-hand) boundary of $W_{J4}(J_5)$. Because this policy at # is closer to Chief Justice J_4's ideal point than the policy at J_5 that would otherwise result, she would as-sign the opinion to justice J_3, who would then write an opinion at #. In this way, by acting strategically, senior associate justice J_3 can get a policy at # in-stead of a policy at J_5, which is even farther from his ideal point of J_3.

However, for the possible Chief Justices other than justice J_4 here, justice J_3 cannot obtain a better outcome from strategic position-taking on the conference vote. If justice J_5 is the Chief Justice and self-assigns, there is nothing justice J_3 can do to attract the opinion assignment. If Chief Justice J_5 does not self-assign, he would assign the opinion to justice J_4, who would write the final opinion at her own ideal point of J_4. If justice J_4 were Chief Justice J_5's assignee, there is nothing that justice J_3 could do to attract the opinion from Chief Justice J_5: the only way to do this would be to endorse a policy closer to J_5 than J_4, but this would leave justice J_3 worse off than with justice J_4's opinion at J_4. And if either justice J_1 or J_2 is the Chief Justice, each would assign the opinion to the other, with the result that the final opinion would be written at *, which is what self-assignment would pro-duce as well. But there is nothing that justice J_3 can do here that would pro-duce a better outcome for justice J_1 or J_2 than the policy at *: no policy to the left of * could gain majority support (justice J_3 would not want to move leftward from * anyway), and no policy to the right of * could attract the opinion from Chief Justice J_1 or J_2. In this case, then, strategic behavior by senior associate justice J_3 could not produce a better policy for himself than a policy at *.

What distinguishes the cases in which our senior associate justice can at-tract the opinion assignment from the cases in which he cannot? In the dia-grams in Figure 8.2, we observe that the opportunities for strategic behavior by senior associate justice J_5 on the conference vote stem from the conjunc-tion of two factors: first, justice J_5 lies inward (closer to SQ) from whoever might be the Chief Justice; and second, although the Chief Justice could as-sign either to the next justice inward (toward justice J_5), and thus get a more inward policy, or to one of the next justices outward (away from justice J_5), and thus get a more outward policy, he finds it preferable to assign outward (away from justice J_5). For a senior associate justice like justice J_5 in Figure 8.2, with an ideal point that lies inward from the Chief Justice's ideal point, the Chief Justice's outward assignment preference (away from justice J_5) means that there exists a set of policies inward from the Chief Justice's ideal point (toward justice J_5) that the Chief Justice prefers to the policy that the outward assignee would otherwise adopt. It is the existence of this set of pre-ferred policies inward from the Chief Justice's ideal point that allows inward-lying justice J_5 here to strategically express support for a policy that would attract the opinion from the Chief Justice; justice J_5 could then write an opinion that he prefers to the opinion that would otherwise be written by an assignee outward from the Chief Justice.

A similar set of arguments, although reversed in direction, hold for the diagram in Figure 8.3. Hence, we can summarize the implications of these Figure 8.2 and 8.3 diagrams in the following three propositions:

PROPOSITION 8.7. If every associate justice except the senior associate justice votes sincerely on the conference vote, when a majority-side Chief Justice is the opinion assigner and would prefer to assign the opinion to a justice to the outside (inside), a senior associate justice with a majority-side ideal point to the inside (outside) of the Chief Justice's ideal point can attract the opinion assignment by strategically expressing support for some policy that the Chief Justice prefers to the policy that the potential outside (inside) assignee would endorse.

PROPOSITION 8.8. If every associate justice except the senior associate justice votes sincerely on the conference vote and a majority-side Chief Justice is the opinion assigner, there does not necessarily exist a policy that a senior associate justice with a majority-side ideal point could strategically endorse and thereby attract the opinion assignment from the Chief Justice.

PROPOSITION 8.9. If every associate justice except the senior associate justice votes sincerely on the conference vote, the senior associate justice with a majority-side ideal point will never benefit from voting for the policy at SQ or for a policy on the minority side.

This concludes our analysis and discussion of how the senior associate justice with a majority-side ideal point will behave when the Chief Justice votes on the majority side. Next we must consider how a strategically rational minority-side associate justice would behave when the Chief Justice votes on the majority side.

Subcondition (ii): The Ideal Point of the Senior Associate Justice Is on the Minority Side

When the senior associate justice's ideal point lies on the minority side but the Chief Justice votes on the majority side on the conference vote, if the senior associate justice behaves sincerely he cannot become either the opinion assigner or the opinion writer: both are prerogatives of justices who vote with the majority side. Moreover, the majority side will be able to move policy away from SQ, which means that this sincere minority-side senior associate justice would be unable to prevent policy from moving away from his own ideal point. Hence, the question facing this minority-side senior associate justice is this: can he prevent the policy from being moved quite as far from his own ideal point as it otherwise would be? The answer is that, in some situations, there are strategies that can limit the loss that he will suffer.

FIGURE 8.4

Strategic Behavior by a Senior Associate Justice with a Minority-Side Ideal Point

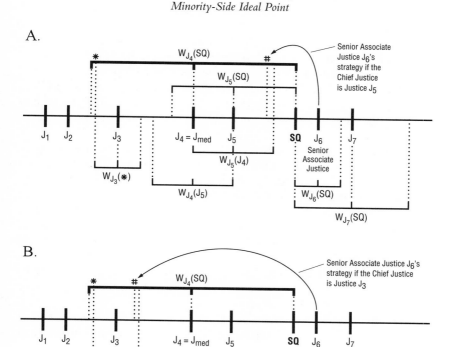

As before, we conduct our analysis by first identifying the sincere-behavior baseline, that is, what policy would be adopted if all justices behave sincerely. We then compare that outcome to what policy would be adopted if the senior associate justice behaves strategically. As before, there are three different strategies that are available to this justice: (a) to express support for some policy on the majority side of SQ, (b) to express support for the policy at SQ, and (c) to express support for some policy on the minority side of SQ.

To illustrate, consider diagram A in Figure 8.4. Assume that the senior associate justice on the Court is minority-side justice J_6. Note that the median justice is J_4, which means that all final majority opinions must lie inside her preferred-to set, $W_{J_4}(SQ)$. The Chief Justice could be any one of majority-side justices J_1 through J_5. Now let us identify how senior associate justice J_6 should behave if the Chief Justice is each of these other justices in turn, assuming everyone else behaves sincerely.

If justice J_5 is the Chief Justice and self-assigns, he could write the opinion at J_5. If he does not self-assign, he would have to assign the opinion outward to median justice J_4, who would then write the opinion at her ideal point of J_4.

If justice J_4 is the Chief Justice and self-assigns, she could write the opinion at J_4. If she does not self-assign, she would assign the opinion either to justice J_3 or justice J_5, each of whom could write the opinion at his own ideal point; both J_3 and J_5 lie inside $W_{J4}(SQ)$. Because J_5 is closer to Chief Justice J_4's ideal point than is J_3 (note that J_3 lies outside $W_{J4}(J_5)$), Chief Justice J_4 would assign the opinion to justice J_5, who would then write the final opinion at J_5.

If justice J_3 is the Chief Justice and self-assigns, he could write the opinion at J_3. If he does not self-assign, he could assign the opinion either to justice J_4 (who would write the final opinion at J_4) or to either justice J_1 or J_2, each of whom would write the final opinion at * just inside the outside (left-hand) boundary of $W_{J4}(SQ)$. Because an opinion at * is closer to justice J_3's ideal point than is J_4 (note that J_4 lies outside $W_{J3}(*)$), Chief Justice J_3 would assign the opinion outward to either justice J_1 or justice J_2, with the result being a final opinion at *.

If justice J_2 is the Chief Justice, he would assign the opinion to justice J_1, and if justice J_1 is the Chief Justice, he would assign the opinion to justice J_2; in either case, the final opinion would be at *.

Given these sincere-behavior final outcomes, the question is whether senior associate justice J_6 can improve outcomes for himself by pursuing any of the three possible strategies.

It is clear that strategies (b) and (c) would produce no gain for this associate justice. Endorsing a policy at SQ or some minority-side policy (such as his own ideal point) would leave unchanged the sincere-behavior outcomes on the majority side. Hence, the only strategy worth considering is strategy (a), which involves expressing support for some majority-side policy.

There are two situations under which a high-seniority minority-side justice can improve outcomes for himself by expressing support for some majority-side position. The first situation involves a lineup in which the Chief Justice's ideal point is adjacent to SQ, which means that the only majority-side justice available for opinion assignment is the next justice outward. In this situation, our minority-side justice can attract the opinion assignment by expressing support for a policy that is closer to the Chief Justice's ideal point than the policy that would be written by the next justice outward from the Chief Justice.

In diagram A in Figure 8.4, for example, consider a lineup in which justice J_5 is the Chief Justice. Of course, if Chief Justice J_5 self-assigns (and thus writes an opinion at J_5), there is nothing justice J_6 can do to improve outcomes for himself; he would then have no reason to vote other than sincerely. But if Chief Justice J_5 does not self-assign, he would have to assign outward to justice J_4, who would write an opinion at J_4. But there is a set of policies that Chief Justice J_5 prefers to this opinion at J_4: this is $W_{J5}(J_4)$, part of which lies to the right of Chief Justice J_5's ideal point. This means that justice J_6 could express support for a policy that lies inside $W_{J5}(J_4)$, and for justice J_6 the best policy inside $W_{J5}(J_4)$ is a policy at #, just inside its right-hand boundary. Because Chief Justice J_5 would prefer the policy at # to an opinion at J_4, he would thus assign the opinion to justice J_6, who would then write the final majority opinion at #. This opinion at # would be better for justice J_6 than the opinion at J_4 that would otherwise result. Hence, justice J_6 would strategically endorse the policy at # rather than (sincerely) express support for any minority-side policy, such as his own ideal point of J_6.

Although justice J_6 would certainly prefer SQ to the policy at #, if he behaves sincerely he will get something worse than SQ and worse even than #, such as an opinion at J_4. So behaving strategically enables him to reduce the size of the policy loss that he is inevitably going to suffer: he gets a bad (for him) policy at # rather than an even worse policy at J_4. The senior associate justice here is thus forced to adopt a damage-limitation strategy.

In the second situation under which a minority-side senior associate justice can attract the opinion assignment, the Chief Justice has two possible choices: he can assign the opinion either to the next justice outward (away from SQ) or the next justice inward (toward SQ). When the Chief Justice gets a better outcome by assigning the opinion to the next justice outward, this means that the opinion written by this next justice outward is closer to the Chief Justice's ideal point than the opinion written by the next justice inward. As a result, a minority-side justice could take advantage of this situation by expressing support for a policy that lies inward from the Chief Justice's ideal point and that is closer to the Chief Justice's ideal point than the policy that would be written by an outward assignee.

To illustrate, consider diagram B in Figure 8.4. Assume justice J_3 is the Chief Justice here and is considering whether to assign the opinion inward to justice J_4 or outward to justices J_1 or J_2. If justice J_4 writes the opinion, she could write it at her own ideal point of J_4; if either justice J_1 or justice J_2 writes the opinion, each would write the opinion at *, which lies just inside the outside (left-hand) boundary of $W_{J4}(SQ)$. Chief Justice J_3 would prefer to assign to either justice J_1 or J_2 rather than to justice J_4: because J_4 lies outside $W_{J3}(*)$, it follows that an opinion at * (from justice J_1 or J_2) is better for Chief Justice J_3 than an opinion at J_4 (from justice J_4). The final majority opinion would thus be at *.

However, there is a set of policies that Chief Justice J_3 prefers to *: this is $W_{J3}(*)$. If minority-side justice J_6 behaves strategically, the best policy for which he could express support is a policy at # just inside the right-hand boundary of $W_{J3}(*)$. Because Chief Justice J_3 prefers # to *, he would thus assign the opinion to justice J_6, who would then write the opinion at #; this opinion at # would be better for justice J_6 than the opinion at * that would otherwise result if justice J_6 behaves sincerely.

Again, we emphasize that although the policy at # is worse for justice J_6 than SQ, justice J_6 is nonetheless unable to protect SQ. By behaving strategically he gets a bad (for him) policy at # rather than an even worse policy at *. As before, this is only a damage-limitation strategy, but it is the best he can do.

We can summarize the implications of these Figure 8.4 diagrams as follows:

PROPOSITION 8.10. On the conference vote, given that the Chief Justice has a majority-side ideal point, the senior associate justice with a minority-side ideal point can gain a better final policy for himself by expressing support for some majority-side policy in two situations:

(a) *If* the Chief Justice has an ideal point that is adjacent to SQ, and so can only assign the opinion to the next justice outward (assuming he does not self-assign), *then* the minority-side senior associate justice can attract the opinion assignment by expressing support for a majority-side policy that is closer to the Chief Justice's ideal point than the policy that would be written by the next justice outward from the Chief Justice.

(b) *If* the Chief Justice can assign the opinion either to the next justice outward or the next justice inward, *and if* the opinion that would be written by the next justice outward is closer to the Chief Justice's ideal point than the opinion that would be written by the next justice inward, *then* the minority-side senior associate justice can attract the opinion assignment by expressing support for a majority-side policy that is closer to the Chief Justice's ideal point than the policy that would be written by the next justice outward from the Chief Justice.

As before, we must raise the question as to whether, for a minority-side senior associate justice (such as justice J_6 in Figure 8.4), there will necessarily be this kind of opportunity to improve outcomes by expressing support for some majority-side policy. And as before, the answer is that there is not. In Figure 8.4, for example, if either justice J_1 or J_2 is the Chief Justice, the final opinion will be at *, and there is nothing that any other justice (such as justice J_6) can do about this.

Overall, then, for Condition 1, in which the Chief Justice votes with the majority side, we can draw two broad conclusions about strategic behavior by a high-seniority associate justice. First, whether the associate justice's ideal point is on the majority side or the minority side, there exist conditions under which the justice can get a better outcome (compared to sincere behavior) by strategically endorsing some majority-side policy, and thereby attracting the opinion assignment from the Chief Justice. Second, there also exist conditions under which this high-seniority associate justice cannot improve outcomes for himself at all by behaving strategically.

All of the previous analysis in this section has assumed that the Chief Justice expresses support for some policy on the majority side; this is Condition 1. We now consider what happens if the Chief Justice votes with the minority side, which is Condition 2.

CONDITION 2: THE CHIEF JUSTICE VOTES WITH THE MINORITY SIDE

If the Chief Justice has a minority-side ideal point and actually votes with the minority side on the conference vote (that is, he does not behave strategically), there are two subconditions that must be considered: (i) the ideal point of the senior associate justice is on the majority side; and (ii) the ideal point of the senior associate justice is on the minority side. We consider each of these in turn.

Subcondition (i): The Ideal Point of the Senior Associate Justice Is on the Majority Side

Under Condition 2(i), with the Chief Justice voting on the minority side on the conference vote and with the ideal point of the most senior associate justice on the majority side, this associate justice need only express support for his or her own ideal point on the conference vote and he or she will automatically become the opinion assigner. At this point, opinion assignment can proceed as described in Chapter 7, with the senior associate justice rather than the Chief Justice acting as opinion assigner. For the senior associate justice in this case, strategic behavior is indistinguishable from sincere behavior.

Subcondition (ii): The Ideal Point of the Senior Associate Justice Is on the Minority Side

Now consider Condition 2(ii), with the Chief Justice voting on the minority side on the conference vote and with the ideal point of the senior associate justice on the minority side as well. To determine what the associate justice would do here, we again construct the sincere-behavior baseline. We then identify what would happen if he pursued each of the three different kinds of strategies that are available: (c) to express support for some policy on the minority side of SQ, (b) to express support for a policy at SQ, and (a) to express support for some policy on the majority side of SQ.

FIGURE 8.5

*Strategic Behavior by a Minority-Side Senior Associate Justice,
with a Minority-Side Chief Justice*

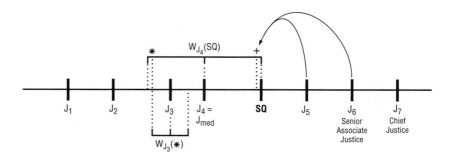

It is essential to note that the strategic situation that this minority-side associate justice is facing here is essentially identical to that which a minority-side Chief Justice faces when he considers endorsing some majority-side policy.[13] For an example, consider Figure 8.5, with justices J_1 through J_4 on the majority side and justices J_5, J_6, and J_7 on the minority side. Assume that justice J_6 is the senior associate justice on the Court, and assume that justice J_7 is the Chief Justice. Note that justice J_4 is the median justice. Hence any majority opinion will have to fall inside $W_{J4}(SQ)$.

To identify the sincere-behavior baseline here, we first note that one of the four majority-side justices—J_1 through J_4—will become the majority opinion assigner, and one of them will also become the opinion writer. If justice J_4 becomes the opinion assigner and self-assigns, she could write the opinion at her own ideal point of J_4. If she does not self-assign, she would have to assign outward to justice J_3, who could write an opinion at his own ideal point of J_3. If justice J_3 becomes the opinion assigner and self-assigns, he could write the opinion at his own ideal point of J_3. If he does not self-assign, he would assign either inward to justice J_4, who could write an opinion at J_4, or outward to either justice J_1 or J_2, each of whom would write an opinion at *, which is just inside the outside (left-hand) boundary of $W_{J4}(SQ)$. Because justice J_3 prefers * to J_4 (note that J_4 lies outside $W_{J3}(*)$), he would assign the opinion to either justice J_1 or J_2, with an opinion at * as the result. If either justice J_1 or J_2 becomes the opinion assigner, each would assign the opinion to the other, with the result being an opinion at *. Hence, if senior associate justice J_6 behaves sincerely (as does the Chief Justice), final policies at J_4, J_3, or * will be the outcome, depending on who the opinion writer is. The question is: can justice J_6 do anything to get a better outcome?

Senior associate justice J_6 would gain no benefit at all from pursuing strategy (c) or strategy (b): they would leave these possible outcomes—J_4, J_3, or ∗—unchanged. However, he can improve the outcome for himself by pursuing strategy (a), that is, by expressing support for some policy on the majority side. If he does this, as senior associate justice he would become the opinion assigner (even though his ideal point lies on the minority side), and his best strategy would be to express support for a policy at +, which is located just to the left of SQ.

If justice J_6 expresses support for a policy at + on the conference vote and then self-assigns, he could then write his opinion at +, and this policy at + would gain the support of five of the seven justices on the Court, that is, from justices J_1 through J_4 plus his own vote. Of course, this final policy at + would be worse for justice J_6 than a final policy at SQ. However, if he supports only a minority-side policy, he will end up with some policy ranging from J_4 leftward as far as ∗. Hence, his chosen policy at + would be an improvement over the policy that would otherwise be selected by one of the majority-side justices.

If this minority-side senior associate justice J_6 votes with the majority and so becomes the opinion assigner but feels that he cannot self-assign, he could try to persuade a fellow minority-side justice to vote with the majority too and then assign the opinion to this other minority-side justice. For example, in Figure 8.5 he can try to persuade justice J_5 to express support for the policy at + as well. (The Chief Justice is still justice J_7 here, and we are continuing to assume that he votes sincerely.) With justices J_6 and J_5 both voting with the majority, justice J_6 would have the authority to make the opinion assignment and could then assign the opinion to justice J_5, who could then write the majority opinion at +.

However, if no other minority-side justice can be persuaded to join with him in endorsing a policy at +, justice J_6 would have to assign leftward to justice J_4, who could then write an opinion at her own ideal point of J_4. Of course, because it is possible that justice J_4 would become the opinion assigner when everyone is sincere, in this case justice J_6 would gain no benefit from voting strategically for the majority-side policy at +, and so would vote sincerely on the minority side.

Regarding the behavior of the senior associate justice, then, we would assert:

PROPOSITION 8.11. On the conference vote, if a minority-side senior associate justice expresses support for that majority-side policy that is closest to SQ, there are three strategies for opinion assignment:

(a)   *If* he self-assigns, *then* he will write a final majority opinion endorsing the majority-side policy closest to SQ.

(b)   *If* he does not self-assign *and if* he can assign the opinion to some other minority-side justice who also expresses support for the majority-side policy that is closest to SQ, *then* he will assign the opinion to that minority-side justice who will write a final majority opinion endorsing the majority-side policy closest to SQ.

(c)   *If* he does not self-assign *and if* there is no other minority-side justice to whom he can assign the opinion, *then* he will have to assign the opinion to the majority-side justice whose ideal point is closest to SQ and who will thus write a final majority opinion at his or her own ideal point.

PROPOSITION 8.12. *If the minority-side senior associate justice could become the opinion assigner by expressing support for the majority-side policy closest to SQ but would have to assign the opinion to the majority-side justice whose ideal point is closest to SQ and if this majority-side justice would be assigned the majority opinion if the senior associate justice were to vote sincerely on the conference vote, then the senior associate justice would gain no benefit from behaving strategically (that is, from expressing support for a majority-side policy) and so would behave sincerely on the conference vote.*

These two propositions are exactly parallel to Propositions 8.3 and 8.4 regarding a Chief Justice with a minority-side ideal point.

We can now summarize our results for Condition 2, when the Chief Justice votes on the minority side. If the senior associate justice's ideal point is on the majority side, he can gain control of opinion assignment simply by endorsing a policy at his own majority-side ideal point. If his ideal point is on the minority side, he can gain control of opinion assignment by expressing support for that majority-side policy that is closest to SQ; under some conditions he gains a better final outcome from this strategy, but under other conditions strategic behavior produces no improvement in the final outcome.

Table 8.2 summarizes how the strategically rational senior associate justice should be expected to behave under these two conditions.

Strategic Behavior by a Low-Seniority Justice Who Cannot Become the Opinion Assigner

Finally, we consider strategic behavior by a low-seniority justice who has no possibility of becoming the opinion assigner. No matter whether this low-seniority justice has a majority-side ideal point or a minority-side ideal point, and no matter whether he or she expresses support for a majority-side policy, or for the policy at SQ, or for a minority-side policy, some other justice—either the Chief Justice or a more senior associate justice—will become the opinion assigner. However, a low-seniority justice could

TABLE 8.2

Strategic Behavior by the Senior Associate Justice

If the Chief Justice endorses . . .	a majority-side policy,	and the senior Associate Justice has a majority-side ideal point,	then the senior Associate Justice will endorse a majority-side policy intended to attract the majority opinion assignment from the Chief Justice.
		Condition 1(i)	
		and the senior Associate Justice has a minority-side ideal point,	then the senior Associate Justice will endorse a majority-side policy intended to attract the majority opinion assignment from the Chief Justice.
		Condition 1(ii)	
	a minority-side policy,	and the senior Associate Justice has a majority-side ideal point,	then the senior Associate Justice will endorse a policy at his own ideal point, and thus will become the majority opinion assigner.
		Condition 2(i)	
		and the senior Associate Justice has a minority-side ideal point,	then the senior Associate Justice will endorse the majority-side policy closest to SQ.
		Condition 2(ii)	(Exception: The senior Associate Justice will endorse his own minority-side ideal point when the justice who would thus become the majority-side opinion assigner would assign the opinion to someone who would write the same opinion that the senior Associate Justice's assignee would write if the senior Associate Justice became the majority opinion assigner.)

become the majority opinion writer, and high-seniority justices have no advantage over low-seniority justices in becoming the opinion writer.

As it turns out, there is little new that can be said about strategic position-taking by a low-seniority justice who cannot become the majority opinion assigner but who could become the majority opinion writer. Assuming as before that all the other justices act sincerely on the conference vote, a low-seniority justice will want to identify and endorse a majority-side policy that attracts the majority opinion assignment from whoever becomes the majority opinion assigner. This general strategy holds whether the low-seniority justice has a minority-side ideal point or a majority-side ideal point. What

TABLE 8.3

Strategic Behavior by a Low-Seniority Associate Justice

If the Chief Justice endorses…	a majority-side policy,	and the senior Associate Justice endorses a majority-side policy, **Condition 1(i)**	then the low-seniority Associate Justice with either a majority-side or minority-side ideal point will endorse a majority-side policy intended to attract the majority opinion assignment from the Chief Justice.
		and the senior Associate Justice endorses a minority-side policy, **Condition 1(ii)**	then the low-seniority Associate Justice with either a majority-side or minority-side ideal point will endorse a majority-side policy intended to attract the majority opinion assignment from the Chief Justice.
	a minority-side policy,	and the senior Associate Justice endorses a majority-side policy, **Condition 2(i)**	then the low-seniority Associate Justice with either a majority-side or minority-side ideal point will endorse a majority-side policy intended to attract the majority opinion assignment from the senior Associate Justice.
		and the senior Associate Justice endorses a minority-side policy, **Condition 2(ii)**	then the low-seniority Associate Justice with either a majority-side or minority-side ideal point will endorse a majority-side policy intended to attract the majority opinion assignment from the more senior Associate Justice who becomes the majority opinion assigner.

particular policy the low-seniority justice would have to endorse to attract the majority opinion assignment depends on who would be given the majority opinion and what policy this majority opinion writer would adopt. However, the logic of what the low-seniority justice would do in each situation is virtually identical to what the senior associate justice would do in these situations, and this has already been covered in the previous section. Of course, just as with the senior associate justice, there may exist no policy that a strategically rational low-seniority justice could endorse that would attract the opinion assignment.

In Table 8.3, we summarize the basic conditions that a strategically rational low-seniority associate justice might face and how this justice should in general be expected to behave, assuming everyone else behaves sincerely. The table does not describe precisely what strategy this low-seniority justice would adopt, because as just noted, all the relevant details involving what particular policy to endorse have already been covered in the previous section.

In general, as we can see from Table 8.3, under any of the conditions that the low-seniority associate justice might face, and no matter whether his or her ideal point is on the majority side or on the minority side, his or her best strategy is simply to identify and endorse that majority-side policy that attracts the opinion assignment from whoever the opinion assigner happens to be (that is, from the Chief Justice, from the senior associate justice, or from one of the three next most senior associate justices). Of course, as we have already emphasized for high-seniority associate justices on the conference vote, there may exist no policy that a strategically rational low-seniority justice can endorse and that would produce a better outcome for the justice than if the justice behaves sincerely.

What If Everyone Behaves Strategically?

Our analysis to this point has presumed that strategic behavior is exhibited only by one justice at a time.[14] That is, only the Chief Justice behaves strategically and no one else, or only the senior associate justice behaves strategically and no one else, or only a single low-seniority justice behaves strategically and no one else. Because there may be some variation among real-world justices on whether they choose to behave strategically, it is important to have conducted this analysis. However, as a general research strategy, if we assume that one justice behaves strategically, we should assume that all the other justices will behave strategically as well. In this section, then, we will determine what would happen if all justices on the Court behave strategically on the conference vote.

We begin by noting that one of our results about strategic behavior by single justices, with everyone else sincere, generalizes immediately to multiple justices. In particular, consider our argument that no justice with a majority-side ideal point—whether the Chief Justice, the senior associate justice, or a low-seniority associate justice—will be able to change the outcome by defecting from the majority side (that is, by expressing support for SQ or for some minority-side policy). In each case, the reason is either that this majority-side justice actually preferred the opinion writer's proposed policy to SQ or that a majority-side justice who endorses a minority-side policy would be unable to undermine the majority's support for the opinion writer's majority-side proposal.

This argument generalizes to the all-strategic context in the following way. When the majority-side opinion writer writes what he or she considers the best majority opinion inside $W_{Jmed}(SQ)$, this means that the median justice and all justices to the outside of the median justice will necessarily find this opinion better than SQ. Of course, if the median justice and all justices to the outside of the median justice prefer the opinion to SQ, it follows that even if all justices closer to SQ than the median justice defect from the majority side and endorse SQ or even some minority-side policy, there will remain a majority of justices who prefer the opinion to SQ. Hence, we have:

PROPOSITION 8.13. On the conference vote, *if* the majority opinion writer's opinion falls inside $W_{Jmed}(SQ)$, *then* a Court majority will support this opinion over SQ even if each majority-side justice who prefers SQ to this opinion defects from the majority side (by endorsing either SQ or some minority-side policy).

In other words, the final outcome will never be changed by majority-side defections to SQ or to the minority side on the conference vote as long as the majority opinion is inside $W_{Jmed}(SQ)$. Hence, the individual strategies that make any difference in the final outcome will be confined to the endorsement of majority-side policies. This conclusion considerably simplifies our analysis of the all-strategic problem.

We now present some additional results on the impact of strategic behavior by all the justices. First, we show that under what we call the "convergence conditions," strategic behavior by all the justices can be expected to affect the final outcome (and in a rather interesting way), compared to a sincere-behavior baseline. Second, we show that under what we call the "nonconvergence conditions," strategic behavior by all the justices can be expected not to affect the final outcome, compared to a sincere-behavior baseline. We discuss these two conditions in turn, providing illustrations of each argument involved.

THE CONVERGENCE CONDITIONS

We define the convergence conditions as follows:

DEFINITION 8.1. On the conference vote, the convergence conditions hold if all the following conditions hold:

(a)   The Chief Justice has an ideal point inside $W_{Jmed}(SQ)$.

(b)   There is at least one other justice on each side of the Chief Justice.

(c)   The Chief Justice does not self-assign.

We now assert:

PROPOSITION 8.14. If the convergence conditions hold on the conference vote, then in an effort to attract the opinion assignment from the Chief Justice, other justices will express support for opinions that converge, in the limit, on the ideal point of the Chief Justice.

We provide several examples that illustrate the rationale for this proposition.

In diagrams A through E in Figure 8.6, we assume that the Chief Justice is justice J_4. Because Chief Justice J_4 is also the median justice and so has an ideal point inside $W_{Jmed}(SQ)$, this means that Convergence Condition (a) in Definition 8.3 holds. And because there is at least one other justice on each side of the Chief Justice, this means that Convergence Condition (b) in Definition 8.3 holds. Because the Chief Justice has a majority-side ideal point, she will be the majority opinion assigner, but we also assume—see Condition (c)—that she does not self-assign. We now show what will happen if all justices behave strategically.

Consider diagram A in Figure 8.6. Chief Justice J_4 would initially prefer to assign the opinion inward to justice J_5 (who could write an opinion at his own ideal point of J_5) rather than outward to justice J_3 (who could write an opinion at his own ideal point of J_3). The reason for this preference is that J_5 is closer to Chief Justice J_4's ideal point than is J_3 (note that J_3 lies outside $W_{J4}(J_5)$). Hence, the final outcome here would be an opinion at J_5. However, this opinion at J_5 is not identical to Chief Justice J_4's ideal point, so there is a set of points—$W_{J4}(J_5)$—that the Chief Justice prefers to the opinion at J_5. Hence justice J_3, who is located on the other side of $W_{J4}(J_5)$ from opinion writer J_5's ideal point, could endorse a policy at # just inside the left-hand boundary of $W_{J4}(J_5)$; because Chief Justice J_4 prefers # to J_5, she would now prefer to assign the opinion to justice J_3 rather than to justice J_5. However, this opinion at # is not identical to the Chief Justice's ideal point either, so there is a set of points—$W_{J4}(\#)$—that the Chief Justice prefers to this opinion at #. So justice J_5 could attract the opinion back by endorsing a policy at Δ just inside the right-hand boundary of $W_{J4}(\#)$; because Chief Justice J_4 prefers Δ to #, she would again prefer to assign the opinion to justice J_5 rather than to justice J_3. However, this opinion at Δ is not identical to the Chief Justice's ideal point either, so there is a set of points—$W_{J4}(\Delta)$—that the Chief Justice prefers to this opinion at Δ. So justice J_3 could attract the opinion back by now endorsing a policy at □ just inside the left-hand boundary of $W_{J4}(\Delta)$; because Chief Justice J_4 prefers □ to Δ, she would again prefer to assign the opinion to justice J_3 rather than to justice J_5.

This illustrates the basic logic of the convergence process: on the conference vote, the strategically rational justices on either side of the Chief Justice will express support for opinions that, in the limit, converge on the Chief Justice's ideal point. The only equilibrium policy in this process—that is, the only policy that is not vulnerable to upset—is a policy at the Chief Justice's ideal point. Hence, we conclude that on the conference vote some justice, on one side or the other side of the Chief Justice, will end up endorsing a policy at the Chief Justice's ideal point.

In diagram B in Figure 8.6, much the same process goes on, except that Chief Justice J_4 initially prefers to assign to justice J_3 (who could write an

FIGURE 8.6

The All-Strategic Convergence Condition

A.

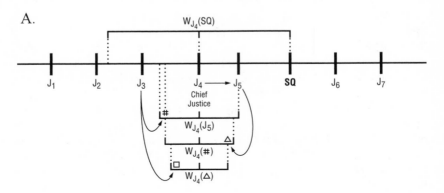

B.

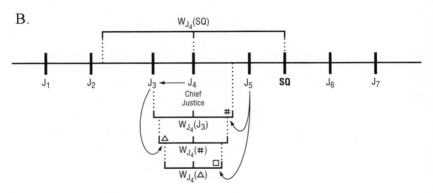

C.

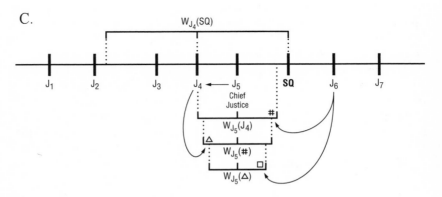

FIGURE 8.6

The All-Strategic Convergence Condition (cont.)

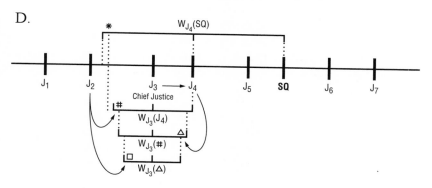

D.

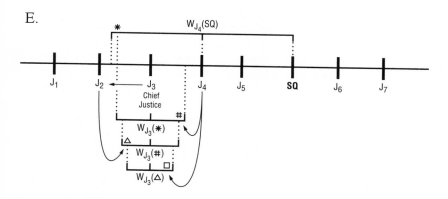

E.

opinion at J_3) rather than to justice J_5 (who could write an opinion at J_5); in this diagram, J_3 is closer to Chief Justice J_4's ideal point than is J_5. However, justice J_5 would counter with an opinion at # inside $W_{J4}(J_3)$, justice J_3 would then counter with an opinion at Δ inside $W_{J4}(\#)$, justice J_5 would then counter with an opinion at $\square$ inside $W_{J4}(\Delta)$, and so forth, with this process ultimately converging again on Chief Justice J_4's ideal point.

In diagram C in Figure 8.6, we demonstrate that this convergence process is not affected even if one of the justices involved is on the minority side. In this diagram, justice J_5 is the Chief Justice, and if he does not self-assign, he would initially prefer to assign outward (leftward) to justice J_4, who could write an opinion at her own ideal point of J_4. The opinion at J_4 would thus be the all-sincere outcome. The set of points that Chief Justice J_5 prefers to this opinion at J_4 is $W_{J5}(J_4)$. However, minority-side justice J_6 would have an incentive to counter with an opinion at # inside $W_{J5}(J_4)$, justice J_4 would then counter with an opinion at Δ inside $W_{J5}(\#)$, justice J_6 would then counter with an opinion at $\square$ inside $W_{J5}(\Delta)$, and so forth, ultimately converging again on Chief Justice J_5's ideal point.

In diagrams D and E in Figure 8.6, we demonstrate that this convergence process is not affected even if one of the justices lies to the outside of $W_{Jmed}(SQ)$. In diagram D, justice J_3 is the Chief Justice, and if he does not self-assign, he would prefer to assign inward (rightward) to justice J_4, who could write an opinion at her own ideal point of J_4, rather than to justice J_1 or J_2, each of whom would write an opinion at * just inside the left-hand boundary of $W_{J4}(SQ)$; the opinion at J_4 is closer to Chief Justice J_3's ideal point than is the opinion at *. The set of points that Chief Justice J_3 prefers to this opinion at J_4 is $W_{J3}(J_4)$. Hence, justice J_2 would counter with an opinion at # inside $W_{J3}(J_4)$, justice J_4 would then counter with an opinion at Δ inside $W_{J3}(\#)$, justice J_2 would counter with an opinion at $\square$ inside $W_{J3}(\Delta)$, and so forth, ultimately converging on Chief Justice J_3's ideal point.

In diagram E, much the same process goes on as in diagram D, except that Chief Justice J_3 here would initially prefer to assign the opinion outward to justice J_2 (who would write an opinion at *) than to justice J_4 (who would write an opinion at J_4); the opinion at * is closer to Chief Justice J_3's ideal point than is the opinion at J_4. The set of points that Chief Justice J_3 prefers to this opinion at * is $W_{J3}(*)$. However, justice J_4 would counter with an opinion at # inside $W_{J3}(*)$, justice J_2 would then counter with an opinion at Δ inside $W_{J3}(\#)$, justice J_4 would then counter with an opinion at $\square$ inside $W_{J3}(\Delta)$, and so forth, ultimately converging on Chief Justice J_5's ideal point.

In sum, as long as the convergence conditions are met on the conference vote, strategic justices on either side of the Chief Justice's ideal point will, in their efforts to attract the opinion-writing assignment from the Chief Justice, express support for policies that are increasingly close to the Chief Justice's ideal point. In fact, the only equilibrium policy from this process—that is, the only policy that someone could endorse and that is not vulnerable to a counterendorsement from some other justice—is a policy at the Chief Justice's ideal point. The Chief Justice would then assign the opinion to whichever justice proposed a policy at the Chief Justice's own ideal point.

Although we have emphasized the fundamental logic of the process by which this convergence might occur, strategically rational justices with complete information would understand this logic and would endorse the Chief Justice's ideal point at the outset, without actually having to go through this full back-and-forth convergence process.

However, there are some aspects of this convergence process that our model cannot adequately resolve. Note that the convergence process in our examples is driven by just three of the justices on the Court: the Chief Justice who is the opinion assigner, a justice who is on one side of the Chief

Justice, and a justice who is on the other side of the Chief Justice. But the process could be driven by several different justices on each side of the Chief Justice. Moreover, the final endorsement of a policy at the Chief Justice's ideal point could be made by just one justice or it could be made by virtually all of the associate justices, as each tries to attract the opinion from the Chief Justice. Our model is not capable of telling us how many of the justices will express support for an opinion at the Chief Justice's ideal point. The model predicts that there is only one equilibrium outcome from this convergence process on the conference vote (someone will endorse an opinion at the Chief Justice's ideal point), and it tells us something about how this final outcome could be reached (for example, the logic of convergence), but the model cannot tell us precisely who will be involved in this convergence process, who would ultimately express support for the Chief Justice's ideal point, or who would ultimately write the final majority opinion (although because this final majority opinion will always be at the Chief Justice's ideal point, the identity of the opinion writer may not matter).

Despite these indeterminacies it is important to note that if several justices are endorsing policies at the Chief Justice's ideal point, the Chief Justice could base his assignment decisions on something other than policy outcomes. For example, equity or workload considerations might then become the basis for the Chief Justice's assignment decisions.

THE NONCONVERGENCE CONDITIONS

The convergence conditions involve circumstances on the conference vote in which strategic behavior by all justices will result in some justice endorsing a policy at the Chief Justice's ideal point. However, there are some corresponding conditions in which strategic behavior by all the justices will not produce this result. We call these the "nonconvergence conditions," and they have the following characteristics:

DEFINITION 8.2. On the conference vote, the nonconvergence conditions hold if any of the following conditions hold:

(a) The Chief Justice has an ideal point inside $W_{Jmed}(SQ)$ *and* there is no justice on one side of the Chief Justice's ideal point.

(b) The Chief Justice has an ideal point outside $W_{Jmed}(SQ)$.

(c) The Chief Justice self-assigns (having behaved in a way that makes him the opinion assigner).

Given this definition, we now assert:

PROPOSITION 8.15. If any of the nonconvergence conditions hold on the conference vote, the Chief Justice will assign the opinion to some justice who endorsed a policy that is not identical to the Chief Justice's ideal point (unless he self-assigns).

We first provide the rationale for Nonconvergence Condition (a). This condition means that the Chief Justice has an ideal point that lies inside $W_{Jmed}(SQ)$ and that is located at one end or the other of the line of judges on the issue dimension. Assuming as before that the Chief Justice does not self-assign, he will have to assign the opinion to the adjacent justice (that is, the first justice in the direction of all the other justices). Because the Chief Justice is at the end of the line, there is no other justice who will try to attract the opinion in the direction away from the other justices. This leaves the opinion assignment with the initial assignee (the adjacent justice), who would then write a policy as close as possible to his or her own ideal point. In effect, the logic of opinion assignment and opinion writing here will be just as described in Chapters 6 and 7.

For example, consider the seven-member Court in diagram A in Figure 8.7. In this diagram, the Chief Justice is justice J_7, and justice J_4 is the median justice. Note that Chief Justice J_7 has an ideal point inside $W_{J4}(SQ)$, so the first part of Nonconvergence Condition (a) is met. Note also that Chief Justice J_7 has an ideal point at the right-hand end of the line of justices, closest to SQ, so the second part of Nonconvergence Condition (a) is met. Assuming that Chief Justice J_7 does not self-assign, he would have to assign the opinion leftward to the adjacent justice, justice J_6, who could write an opinion at his own ideal point of J_6. But because J_6 is not at the Chief Justice's ideal point of J_7, there is a set of policies, $W_{J7}(J_6)$, which Chief Justice J_7 prefers to this opinion at J_6. However, there is no justice to the right of J_7, so there is no justice who would endorse a policy that is inside $W_{J7}(J_6)$ and that is closer to Chief Justice J_7's ideal point than is J_6. Instead, justices J_1 through J_7 would all like to move the opinion leftward from J_6, and no other justice (besides Chief Justice J_7) would like to move the opinion rightward from J_6. Because no one besides Chief Justice J_7 wants to move the opinion rightward from J_6, no one will propose an alternative opinion inside $W_{J7}(J_6)$ that is closer to the Chief Justice's ideal point of J_7. Hence, justice J_6 will remain the opinion writer (assuming, as noted, that the Chief Justice does not self-assign), and the final majority opinion will remain at J_6.

Diagram B in Figure 8.7 illustrates the same logic for Nonconvergence Condition (a), but for a Chief Justice who is the justice at the end of the lineup farthest from SQ. Note that Chief Justice J_1 here has an ideal point inside $W_{J4}(SQ)$, so the first part of Nonconvergence Condition (a) is met, and Chief Justice J_1 is at an end of the lineup of justices, so the second part of Nonconvergence Condition (a) is met. Assuming that Chief Justice J_1 does not self-assign, he will assign to justice J_2, the adjacent justice to the right, who could write an opinion at his own ideal point of J_2. The set of policies that Chief Justice J_1 prefers to this opinion at J_2 is thus $W_{J1}(J_2)$. However, there is no justice to the left of J_1, so there is no justice who would en-

FIGURE 8.7

The All-Strategic Nonconvergence Condition (a)

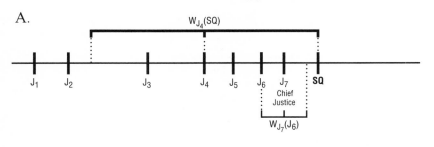

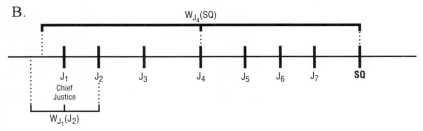

dorse a policy, inside $W_{J1}(J_2)$, which is closer to J_1 than J_2. That is, justices J_3 through J_7 would all like to move the opinion rightward from J_2, and no other justice (besides Chief Justice J_1) would like to move the opinion leftward from J_2. Because no one else wants to move the opinion leftward from J_2, no one will propose an alternative opinion, inside $W_{J1}(J_2)$, which is closer to the Chief Justice's ideal point of J_1. Hence, justice J_2 will remain the opinion writer, and the final majority opinion will remain at J_2.

Next, we illustrate Nonconvergence Condition (b), which involves a Chief Justice with an ideal point that lies outside $W_{Jmed}(SQ)$. A Chief Justice's ideal point that lies outside $W_{Jmed}(SQ)$ can be either a majority-side ideal point or a minority-side ideal point.

First consider a Chief Justice with a majority-side ideal point outside $W_{Jmed}(SQ)$. In diagram A in Figure 8.8, the Chief Justice is justice J_2, and the median justice is justice J_4. Assume that Chief Justice J_2 does not self-assign. Note that J_2 lies outside $W_{J4}(SQ)$, so Nonconvergence Condition (b) is met. Chief Justice J_2 can assign either outside to justice J_1, who would have to write an opinion at * just inside the outside (left-hand) boundary of $W_{J4}(SQ)$, or to justice J_3, who could write an opinion at his own ideal point of J_3. Because the policy at * is closer to Chief Justice J_2's ideal point than is the policy at J_3, the Chief Justice would prefer to assign the opinion outward to justice J_1, with the result being an opinion at *. The set of policies that

FIGURE 8.8

The All-Strategic Nonconvergence Condition (b):
The Chief Justice Has a Majority-Side
Ideal Point Outside $W_{Jmed}(SQ)$

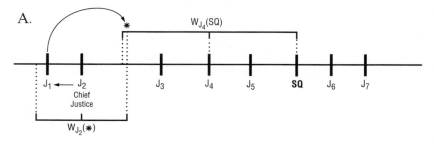

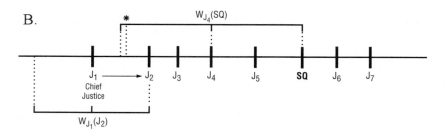

Chief Justice J_2 prefers to the opinion at * is $W_{J_2}(*)$, and notice that justices J_3 through J_7 would all like to move the opinion rightward from *. Notice also that only opinion writer J_1 and Chief Justice J_2 would like to move the opinion leftward from *, but this leftward move in policy would be politically impossible because the policy at * is the leftmost policy inside $W_{J_4}(SQ)$. Hence, justice J_1 will remain the opinion writer, and the opinion will remain at *. In effect, then, justices J_3 through J_7 could do nothing to prevent an outcome at * even if all these justices are strategic. (An essentially identical story follows if justice J_1 is the Chief Justice and assigns the opinion to justice J_2: even if all justices are strategic, justice J_2 will remain the opinion writer, and the opinion will remain at *.)

A slightly different story is shown in diagram B in Figure 8.8. The Chief Justice is again justice J_1, but because now there are no other justices to the left of $W_{J_4}(SQ)$, he would have to assign inward to justice J_2, who could write an opinion at his own ideal point of J_2. The set of policies that Chief Justice J_1 prefers to the opinion at J_2 is $W_{J_1}(J_2)$, and notice that all justices (other than Chief Justice J_1) would like to move the opinion rightward from J_2. Notice also that no other justice besides Chief Justice J_1 would like to

FIGURE 8.9

The All-Strategic Nonconvergence Condition (b):
The Chief Justice Has a Minority-Side
Ideal Point

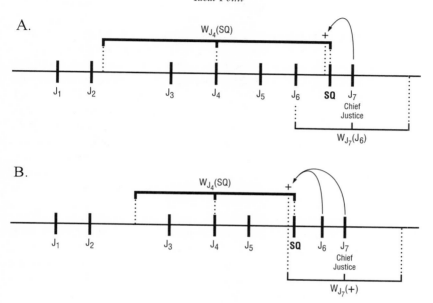

move the opinion leftward from J_2. Hence, justice J_2 will remain the opinion writer, and the opinion will remain at J_2, even if all justices are strategic.

Now consider the alternative situation, in which the Chief Justice has a minority-side ideal point. In diagram A in Figure 8.9, the Chief Justice is justice J_7, and the median justice is justice J_4. Because Chief Justice J_7 lies outside $W_{J_4}(SQ)$, this meets Nonconvergence Condition (b). Notice that there are no other minority-side justices. On the conference vote, Chief Justice J_7 would express support for an opinion at +, which is the majority-side opinion closest to SQ, in order to become the majority opinion assigner. However, if the Chief Justice does not self-assign, he would have to assign the opinion to justice J_6, who is the majority-side justice closest to SQ; justice J_6 would then write an opinion at his own ideal point of J_6. The set of points that Chief Justice J_7 prefers to the opinion at J_6 is $W_{J_7}(J_6)$. Notice that justices J_1 through J_5 would all like to move the opinion leftward from J_6, and no other justice (besides Chief Justice J_7) would like to move the opinion rightward from J_6. Because no one else wants to move the opinion rightward from J_6, no one will propose an alternative opinion that is inside $W_{J_7}(J_6)$ and that is closer to the Chief Justice's ideal point of J_7. Hence, justice J_6 will remain the opinion writer, and the opinion will remain at J_6.

Finally, in diagram B, the Chief Justice is again justice J_7, and the median justice is again justice J_4. Notice that there is now another minority-side justice, justice J_6. Because Chief Justice J_7 lies outside $W_{J4}(SQ)$, this again meets Nonconvergence Condition (b). Chief Justice J_7 would express support for an opinion at +, which is the majority-side opinion closest to SQ, in order to become the majority opinion assigner. In an effort to attract the opinion assignment, associate justice J_6 would also express support for an opinion at +, and Chief Justice J_7 would then assign the opinion to justice J_6, who would in turn write an opinion at +. The set of points that Chief Justice J_7 prefers to the opinion at + is $W_{J7}(+)$. Notice that justices J_1 through J_5 would all like to move the opinion leftward from +, and no other justices (besides justice J_6 and Chief Justice J_7) would like to move the opinion rightward from +. Because no one else wants to move the opinion rightward from +, no one will propose an alternative opinion that is inside $W_{J7}(+)$ and that is closer to the Chief Justice's ideal point of J_7. Hence, justice J_6 will remain the opinion writer, and the opinion will remain at +.

For Nonconvergence Condition (c), we simply note that no matter where the Chief Justice's ideal point is located, if he self-assigns, having gained control of the opinion assignment on the conference vote, there will be no convergence by the other justices on the Chief Justice's ideal point. The reason is obvious: if he is going to self-assign, there is nothing any of the other justices can do to attract the opinion assignment from him.

In summary, our analysis of what happens when all justices are strategic leads us to two broad conclusions. If the convergence conditions hold on the conference vote, then in an effort to attract the opinion assignment from the Chief Justice, competition among the associate justices on either side of the Chief Justice will lead them to express support for opinions that are, in equilibrium, located at the Chief Justice's ideal point. In effect, these other justices are competing for the favor of the Chief Justice on the conference vote.

Moreover, justices would usually be forced to engage in this competition even if they do not initially want to compete: given the opinion that might otherwise be written on one side of the Chief Justice's ideal point (for example, an opinion at J_5 in diagram A in Figure 8.6), the justices on the other side (for example, justices J_1, J_2, and J_3 in this same diagram) would benefit from the final outcome (for example, an opinion at J_4 rather than an opinion at J_5) that results from the competition involved in trying to attract the opinion assignment from the Chief Justice. The justices on the original side are hurt by the outcome of this competition (for example, the final opinion at J_4 is worse for justices J_5, J_6, and J_7 than the opinion at J_5), but these justices cannot prevent the competition. Instead, all they can do is participate in it in order to prevent the final opinion from being as bad for them as it could otherwise be: by joining in the competition they ensure that the final outcome is at J_4 rather than at #, for example). If the associate justices on one side of the Chief Justice's ideal point were to refrain from this competition (for example, if none of justices $J_5, J_6,$ or J_7 responds to justice J_3's counteroffer of an opinion at #), the resulting ideal point will be farther away from them (for example, at #) than it would otherwise ultimately be (for example, at J_4, the Chief Justice's ideal point).

In sum, when the convergence conditions hold, justices on both sides of the Chief Justice have an incentive to engage in this competition for the opinion assignment: the justices on one of the sides will have an incentive to initiate the competition, and the justices on the other side will then have an incentive to respond so as to protect themselves. And of course, the consequence of this competition is that the Chief Justice will be able to assign the opinion to someone who ultimately endorses an opinion at his own ideal point. In contrast, when any of the nonconvergence conditions hold, the basic result is that nothing changes from what would happen either when all justices are sincere, or when just the Chief Justice is strategic. That is, even when all justices are strategic on the conference vote, the Chief Justice would get the opinion he would have gotten even if everyone were sincere or if he were the only justice to behave strategically.

When Does the Chief Justice Self-Assign?

One key aspect of the conference vote is the question of whether the Chief Justice, as opinion assigner, will self-assign the majority opinion or will assign it to some other justice instead. The results in the previous section on the convergence conditions have a rather striking implication: if all justices behave strategically and if the convergence conditions hold, then the Chief Justice need not self-assign at all. The reason is that one or more other justices will, in the pursuit of their own policy goals, endorse and pursue the Chief Justice's most preferred policy, and so might be expected to write a final majority opinion at this point.

Moreover, consider what happens even when the nonconvergence conditions hold: for several of the cases covered by these conditions, the result is the same—the Chief Justice would have no need to self-assign. For example, consider what happens when the Chief Justice has a majority-side ideal point that lies outside $W_{J4}(SQ)$, the preferred-to set of the median justice, as illustrated in the diagrams in Figure 8.8. In diagram A, Chief Justice J_2 assigns the opinion outward to justice J_1 who would endorse a policy at *, whereas if the Chief Justice self-assigned, he would select this same policy at *; like assignee J_1, he would have to select this policy at * in order to gain the support of a majority of the justices. Hence, he would not have to self-assign here: assigning to justice J_1 would do just as well.

For another example, consider what happens when the Chief Justice has a minority-side ideal point, as illustrated in diagram B in Figure 8.9. Like Chief Justice J_7 here, justice J_6 also has a minority-side ideal point and would (strategically) express support for a policy at +, the majority-side policy closest to his own ideal point. Of course, this policy at + is what Chief Justice J_7 would endorse if he self-assigned. Hence, he would not have to self-assign here.[15]

However, for several other cases covered by the Nonconvergence Conditions (a) and (b), the Chief Justice would prefer to self-assign. For example, consider what happens when the Chief Justice has an ideal point inside $W_{Jmed}(SQ)$ but there are not other justices on both sides of his ideal point. This means that there will not be a competitive process that forces the other justices to converge on the Chief Justice's ideal point. In each diagram in Figure 8.7, for example, the Chief Justice is located at one end of the lineup of justices, and if he assigns to anyone else (for example, to justice J_6 in diagram A, or to justice J_2 in diagram B), he will get some final policy other than his own ideal point. Hence, in these two cases, he would prefer to self-assign.

Similarly, he would prefer to self-assign in diagram B in Figure 8.8. The reason is that, in this case, no other justice besides Chief Justice J_1 has an ideal point outside $W_{J4}(SQ)$. This means that he would have to assign the policy all the way inward to justice J_2, who would write the final opinion at J_2, whereas if the Chief Justice self-assigned, he could write the final opinion at *.

The Chief Justice would likewise prefer to self-assign in diagram A in Figure 8.9. In this diagram, there is no other minority-side justice, and so if Chief Justice J_7 does not self-assign, he would have to assign leftward all the way to justice J_6, who would write a majority-side opinion at J_6, whereas if he were to self-assign, he would write an opinion at +, the majority-side policy closest to his own ideal point. Hence, he would prefer to self-assign here as well.

Overall, then, we can draw two conclusions about the need for self-assignment by the Chief Justice. First, if the convergence conditions hold when all justices are strategic on the conference vote, the Chief Justice should never have to self-assign because he should always expect to get his ideal point anyway; and when the nonconvergence conditions hold, he might expect to get his ideal point in at least some of the possible cases here as well.

Second, this discussion makes some clear predictions about when a Chief Justice (or other opinion assigner) will self-assign and when assignment will be made to others. In particular, we can now formulate a general proposition:

PROPOSITION 8.16. Given the policy views expressed by the associate justices on the conference vote,

(a)   The Chief Justice will self-assign when that is the only way to get the final majority opinion that is the closest possible to his own ideal point.

(b)   The Chief Justice need not self-assign when some other justice is expected to write a final majority opinion that is the closest policy to his own ideal point that is politically possible.

In other words, when self-assignment yields the best policy he can possibly get, he will self-assign. But when assignment to someone else yields as good a policy (for him) as self-assignment, he need not self-assign.[16]

Will the Chief Justice Trust What Other Justices Say on the Conference Vote?

We began this chapter with an analysis of how sincere—that is, non-strategic—justices should be expected to behave on the conference vote. The argument we made there, in Proposition 8.1, was simple: if the ideal point of the Chief Justice lies on the majority side of SQ, then the Chief Justice will become the majority opinion assigner, but if the Chief Justice's ideal point lies on the minority side of SQ, then the most senior associate justice whose ideal point lies on the majority side of SQ will become the majority opinion assigner. Once the majority opinion assigner has been selected in this manner, majority opinion assignment will then proceed as described in Chapter 7.

However, if one or more of the justices behaves in a strategically rational manner on the conference vote, describing what should be expected to happen has been far more complex. Of course, if the Chief Justice behaves strategically on the conference vote, then this will settle the question of who becomes the majority opinion assigner: whether he has a majority-side ideal point or a minority-side ideal point, the Chief Justice will always endorse some majority-side policy and so will automatically become the majority opinion assigner. How he assigns the majority opinion will again proceed as described in Chapter 7.

But if the other justices are strategically rational on the conference vote as well, what our model says about opinion assignment by the Chief Justice appears to depend on whether the Chief Justice actually expects the other justices to write final opinions at the positions they endorsed on the conference vote. Note that in our section on the convergence and nonconvergence conditions, we assumed that if a justice endorses some position on the conference vote and thereby successfully attracts the opinion assignment, the justice will then write the final majority opinion at the position he or she endorsed on the conference vote (or at least an opinion that is as close as possible to the position he or she endorsed but that can also gain majority support). Thus, our analysis presumed that if this justice receives the opinion assignment, he or she would write a final opinion as close as possible to the Chief Justice's ideal point.

However, there is a potentially serious problem with this line of analysis, stemming from two of our original assumptions in Chapter 5. Assumption 5.8 asserts that each justice knows the ideal point of every other justice, and that all justices know and understand what the decision-making procedures are. Assumption 5.9 asserts that each justice considers policies that might be adopted in any future case to have no relevance to his or her choice of a policy on the current case. For our analysis of the conference vote, Assumption 5.8 implies that the Chief Justice will know when the ideal point of a strategically rational justice differs from what policy that justice endorsed on the conference vote. If as a result of the convergence process, the justice has endorsed a policy at the Chief Justice's ideal point that is different from his or her own ideal point, it follows that the Chief Justice should be concerned that if he gives the majority opinion assignment to this justice, the justice will then proceed to write a final majority opinion as close as possible to his or her own ideal point rather than as close as possible to the Chief Justice's ideal point.

In other words, the Chief Justice should rationally fear that the justice will renege on what may be seen as an implicit commitment to the Chief Justice on the conference vote. The justice may have endorsed a policy at the Chief Justice's ideal point on the conference vote, but then, having successfully attracted the majority opinion from the Chief Justice, the justice will have an incentive to renege on this initial endorsement by writing an opinion at his or her own ideal point (or something as close to it as possible, given the need to attract majority support) on the final vote.

In our model, this incentive to renege is heightened by Assumption 5.9, which in effect treats decision-making on each Supreme Court case as a one-period game that has no consequences for policy-making in future cases. But because the Chief Justice, like all the justices, knows that Assumption 5.9 is governing decision-making (this knowledge is an implication of the second part of Assumption 5.8, which is that all justices know and understand the decision-making procedures), he should expect the justice to whom he assigns the opinion to renege on what he or she said on the conference vote. It follows that a rational Chief Justice will not base his opinion-assignment decisions on what policies any justice endorses on the conference vote. Instead, the rational Chief Justice will base his opinion-assignment decisions just on what the other justices' ideal points would lead them to do on the final vote.

Ironically, then, if the other justices behave in a strategically rational fashion on the conference vote, the Chief Justice will ignore what they say on the conference vote and base his opinion assignment only on what their own ideal points would lead them to do on the final vote. And because these justices know the Chief Justice will ignore any endorsement of a policy other than their own respective ideal points, they may as well simply endorse their own ideal points. In other words, precisely because the Chief Justice will be rationally concerned about the strategically rational behavior of the other justices, these other justices will end up behaving sincerely on the conference vote (albeit for strategically rational reasons). Hence, we should conclude (a) that the Chief Justice will always be the majority opinion assigner because of his strategic behavior, and (b) that because of the other justices' incentives to behave in a strategically rational fashion, the Chief Justice will base his opinion-assignment decisions just on the other justices' ideal points, as described in Chapter 7, rather than on whatever policies they had endorsed on the conference vote, as described here in Chapter 8.

Nonetheless, for future revisions of our model, it seems reasonable to relax Assumption 5.9 in some fashion, so that a justice can somehow commit to writing a final majority opinion as close as possible to the policy he or she endorsed on the conference vote. This commitment might even take the form of a concern that the justice might have for his or her own reputation as a trustworthy colleague. For example, a justice concerned about his own reputation would not want to renege in the manner just described, because reneging might possibly impair his future efforts to attract opinion assignments from future opinion assigners. That is, if the justice behaves in a trustworthy fashion on the current case, future opinion assigners would be more likely to trust this justice to write the opinion he endorsed on the conference vote on future cases. In effect, then, a strategically rational justice might plausibly wish to distinguish between short-term rationality (which could lead to reneging on the current case) and long-term rationality (which could lead to trustworthy behavior even in the short term, as a result of a concern for his or her long-term reputation regarding his or her likely behavior on future cases).

If we make this alternative assumption, which implies that a justice will write a final opinion as close as possible to what he or she actually endorsed on the conference vote, the Chief Justice could then base his opinion assignment on the policies the other justices endorsed on the conference vote, and as a result we should expect to see convergence on the Chief Justice's ideal point (or, more generally, on the majority opinion assigner's ideal point) whenever the convergence conditions hold. With this alternative assumption involving commitment, trustworthiness, trust, and long-term rationality, we should thus conclude (a) that the Chief Justice will always be the majority opinion assigner because of his strategic behavior on the conference vote, and (b) that the Chief Justice's opinion assignment decisions will be on the basis of what policies the other justices endorsed on the conference vote, which means that opinion assignment will precede as described in the section on the convergence and nonconvergence conditions earlier in this chapter.

It is ultimately an empirical question as to which set of assumptions most accurately characterizes the behavior of real-world justices on the conference vote and beyond. If strategically rational justices care only about the short-term consequences of their current behavior, then Chapter 7 should be expected to characterize the Chief Justice's (or, more generally, the majority opinion assigner's) opinion-assignment practices. But if these strategically rational justices care about the long-term consequences of their current behavior, then our section on the convergence and nonconvergence conditions should be expected to characterize the Chief Justice's (or, more generally, the majority opinion assigner's) opinion-assignment practices.

Of course, it may be that either the open-bidding or median-holdout version of our model more accurately characterizes Supreme Court decision-making. If so, then the Chief Justice will not have to be concerned about any of these issues involving commitment, trust, trustworthiness, and long-term rationality. The reason, of course, is that the opinion writer—whoever that turns out to be—will always be forced to write the final opinion at J_{med}. In that case, the complex logic that we have developed in this chapter will be largely irrelevant.

Summary of Major Results

We can now summarize our major results on the conference vote with the following observations:

1. Assuming that all justices behave sincerely on the conference vote, if the ideal point of the Chief Justice lies on the majority side of SQ, then the Chief Justice will become the majority opinion assigner, but if the Chief Justice's ideal point lies on the minority side of SQ, then the most senior associate justice whose ideal point lies on the majority side of SQ will become the majority opinion assigner.

2. A strategically rational Chief Justice will always vote on the majority side on the conference vote and so will always become the majority opinion assigner.

3. A strategically rational Chief Justice whose ideal point is on the majority side will become the majority opinion assigner simply by expressing sup-

port for an opinion at his or her own ideal point on the conference vote.

4. A strategically rational Chief Justice whose ideal point is on the minority side will become the majority opinion assigner by expressing support on the conference vote for that majority-side opinion that is closest to SQ.

5. If all justices on a nine-member Court participate in the conference vote, the Chief Justice or any of the four most senior associate justices could become the opinion assigner, whereas the four least senior justices can never become the opinion assigner.

6. On the conference vote, justices with majority-side ideal points will have no reason to endorse a minority-side policy or the policy at SQ.

7. If the Chief Justice becomes the majority opinion assigner, the strategic behavior of the other justices (whether high-seniority or low-seniority) will be aimed at attracting the opinion assignment from the Chief Justice.

8. If all justices behave strategically and the convergence conditions hold, one or more of the associate justices will express support for an opinion at the Chief Justice's ideal point.

9. If all justices behave strategically and the nonconvergence conditions hold, the final outcome will not differ from what would happen if only the Chief Justice behaves strategically and all other justices behave sincerely.

10. A Chief Justice who is the majority opinion assigner will self-assign when only self-assignment yields the best possible policy for him; when assignment to someone else yields a policy as good for him as from self-assignment, he need not self-assign.

11. If all justices behave strategically, and if a justice's decision-making behavior on each case has no consequences for his or her decision-making behavior in any subsequent case, then the justice given the majority opinion assignment will write an opinion that is as close as possible to his or her own ideal point (given the need to attract majority support on the final vote) rather than an opinion that is as close as possible to the position he or she endorsed on the conference vote. Hence, the Chief Justice (or other majority opinion assigner) will base majority opinion assignment on the justices' ideal points rather than on what positions they endorse on the conference vote. As a result, the justices will only endorse policies at their ideal points on the conference vote, which means that opinion assignment will proceed as described in Chapter 7.

12. If strategically rational justices can commit themselves to the policies they endorsed on the conference vote, then the Chief Justice will base his majority opinion assignment on what policies the justices endorsed rather than on what the justices' ideal points are. Hence, when the convergence

conditions hold, we should expect some justice to endorse a policy at the Chief Justice's ideal point, attract the opinion assignment from him, and write an opinion as close as possible to his (the Chief Justice's) ideal point; but when the nonconvergence conditions hold, we should expect opinion assignment to proceed as described in Chapter 7.

CHAPTER 9

Certiorari

We have finally worked our way back to the first stage of the Supreme Court's decision-making process. This stage involves whether the Court should grant some petitioner a writ of certiorari and thereby accept the petitioner's case for review.[1]

When received by the Court, petitions for certiorari are distributed to all the justices. The Court usually makes its decisions on these certiorari petitions in regularly scheduled conferences. Shortly before each conference, the Chief Justice circulates a "discuss list" that indicates the petitions he would like the Court to discuss. Each of the other justices is allowed to add petitions to this list (Rehnquist 1987, 265). A petition is considered to be "dead listed" if no justice puts it on the discuss list; a dead-listed petition receives no further consideration by the Court.

For a writ of certiorari to be granted, Court practice since passage of the Certiorari Act of 1925 has been that at least four justices—one less than a majority—must indicate at the certiorari conference that they want the case to receive a full review; this four-justice requirement for a grant of certiorari is often called "the rule of four." On some occasions, especially in recent years, grants of certiorari may be made without the justices being in each other's physical presence; instead, the justices apparently reach agreement on a certiorari decision via telephone, fax, or e-mail (Biskupic 2000).

In this chapter, we specify the conditions under which the justices on the Supreme Court will and will not grant a petition for certiorari. We first present several propositions describing the conditions under which a Court populated by sincere justices will and will not grant certiorari. We then present several more propositions describing the conditions under which a Court populated by strategic justices will and will not grant certiorari. For both sincere and strategic decision-making, we also analyze how individual justices will vote. We then discuss the implications of our results for what the literature has called "aggressive granting" and "defensive denials" in certiorari decisions.

We end the chapter with a brief summary of our major results.

Sincere Behavior on Certiorari Decisions

For decision-making on a petition for certiorari, it seems most reasonable to make the following assumptions about sincere behavior on certiorari:

ASSUMPTION 9.1. A sincere justice will vote for certiorari if some improvement over the policy status quo is possible for the justice; a sincere justice will vote against certiorari if no policy improvement is possible for the justice.

The implications of these assumptions about sincere behavior are straightforward:

PROPOSITION 9.1. A sincere justice will vote to grant certiorari on a case if SQ is not located at his or her ideal point; a sincere justice will vote to deny certiorari on the case if SQ is located at his or her ideal point.[2]

As noted above, the nine-member Supreme Court requires the votes of at least four justices for certiorari to be granted; if there are three or fewer votes for certiorari, it will be denied. We can generalize this requirement by assuming that a Court with J members (assuming J is odd) will grant certiorari to a petitioner if at least $maj - 1$ justices wish to grant certiorari (recall that maj is a bare majority of J). We can thus deduce that certiorari will be granted by sincere justices if at least $maj - 1$ justices have ideal points not at SQ. But if certiorari is granted whenever at least $maj - 1$ sincere justices have ideal points not at SQ, this implies that certiorari will be granted whenever maj or fewer justices have ideal points at SQ. The reason is simply that if at least $maj - 1$ justices have ideal points not at SQ, it must be that all the remaining justices—that is, maj or fewer justices—do have ideal points at SQ. Hence we can assert:

PROPOSITION 9.2. Assuming J is odd, a Court with sincere justices will grant certiorari if at least $maj - 1$ justices have ideal points not at SQ; equivalently, the Court will grant certiorari if maj or fewer justices have ideal points at SQ.[3]

For example, given a nine-member Court, it follows that $maj = 5$ (that is, 5 is a bare majority of 9), and $maj - 1 = 4$. Assuming for some case that there are four or more justices who have ideal points not at SQ, the Court would then grant certiorari because there are four or more justices who would vote for certiorari.

Most of our examples in this chapter will involve a Court with seven members. In this case, *maj* = 4 (that is, 4 is a bare majority of 7), and *maj* − 1 = 3. Assuming for some case that there are three or more justices who have ideal points not at SQ, the Court would then grant certiorari because there are three or more justices who would vote for certiorari.

The preceding analysis focused on grants of certiorari, but the same logic can be used to describe denials of certiorari. In particular, a Court populated by J sincere justices (assuming J is odd) will deny certiorari if fewer than *maj* − 1 justices have ideal points not at SQ. But if certiorari is denied whenever fewer than *maj* − 1 justices have ideal points not at SQ, this implies that certiorari will be denied whenever at least *maj* + 1 justices have ideal points at SQ. The reason is simply that if fewer than *maj* − 1 justices have ideal points not at SQ, it must be that all the remaining justices—that is, at least *maj* + 1 justices—have ideal points at SQ. Hence we can assert:

PROPOSITION 9.3. Assuming J is odd, a Court with sincere justices will deny certiorari if fewer than *maj* − 1 justices have ideal points not at SQ; equivalently, the Court will deny certiorari if at least *maj* + 1 justices have ideal points at SQ.[4]

For example, given a nine-member Court, if fewer than four justices (that is, three justices or fewer) have ideal points not at SQ, there must be at least six justices with ideal points at SQ. The Court will deny certiorari here because there are fewer than four votes for certiorari; at least four votes are needed. For a seven-member Court, if fewer than three justices (that is, two justices or fewer) have ideal points not at SQ, there must be at least five justices with ideal points at SQ. The Court will deny certiorari here because there are fewer than three votes for certiorari; at least three votes are needed.

The five diagrams involving a seven-member Court in Figure 9.1 illustrate Proposition 9.2 on the granting of certiorari by sincere justices. In each diagram the *maj* − 1 standard for granting certiorari is met because there are at least three justices with ideal points not at SQ: diagram A has three justices to the left of SQ; diagram B has two justices to the left of SQ and one justice to the right; diagram C has two justices to each side of SQ; diagram D has four justices to the left of SQ; and diagram E has four justices to the left of SQ and three to the right. Because the *maj* − 1 standard is met in each case, certiorari would be granted in each case.

The two diagrams involving a seven-member Court in Figure 9.2 illustrate Proposition 9.3 on the denial of certiorari by sincere justices. In each diagram, the *maj* + 1 standard for denying certiorari is met because there are five justices with ideal points at SQ and only two justices with ideal points not at SQ. Whether these two justices have ideal points to the same side of SQ, as in diagram A, or on opposite sides of SQ, as in diagram B, is irrelevant: certiorari will be denied in either case because at least three justices are

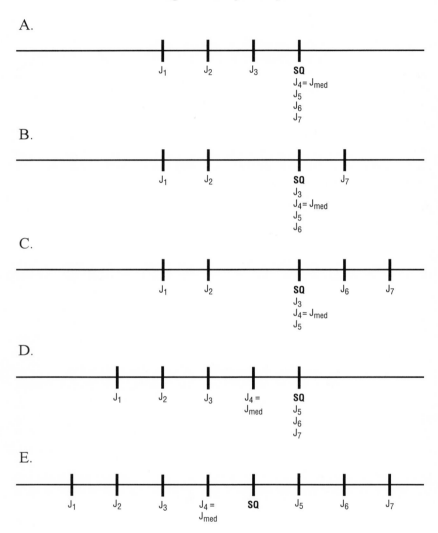

FIGURE 9.1

Granting Certiorari by Sincere Justices

FIGURE 9.2

Denying Certiorari by Sincere Justices

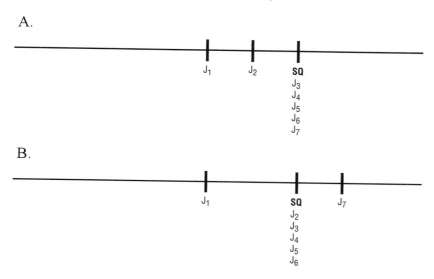

needed to grant certiorari and only two would vote to do so.

For a Court populated by sincere justices, one noteworthy implication of the *maj* − 1 rule for granting certiorari is that even if there are at least *maj* − 1 justices who would vote to grant certiorari in a case, this does not necessarily mean that there will be enough justices to change policy on the case. For example, in diagram A in Figure 9.1, the *maj* − 1 standard for granting certiorari is met because justices J_1, J_2, and J_3 all have ideal points not at SQ: they would all vote to grant certiorari. However, a majority of the justices in this case—J_4 through J_7—have ideal points at SQ and so would vote to keep policy at SQ. Similarly, in diagram B, the *maj* − 1 standard for granting certiorari is met because justices J_1, J_2, and J_7 all have ideal points not at SQ: they would again all vote to grant certiorari; however, a majority of the justices— J_3 through J_6—have ideal points at SQ and so would vote to keep policy at SQ. In diagram C, certiorari would also be granted because the *maj* − 1 standard is met. In fact, a majority of the justices in this case—J_1, J_2, J_6, and J_7— have ideal points not at SQ and so would all vote for certiorari. However, these four justices with ideal points not at SQ would be unable to agree on a direction for a change in policy: although the total of four justices is sufficient to change policy, only two justices—J_1 and J_2—want to move policy leftward from SQ, and only two justices—J_6 and J_7—want to move policy rightward from SQ. Hence, policy would remain at SQ.

In these first three diagrams in Figure 9.1, then, sincere behavior on the certiorari vote by just *maj* − 1 justices can waste the time and energy of all the justices, including those voting to grant certiorari. In effect, the Court would be forced to hold a full review of each case even though the Court would be unable to change the status quo policy in any of the cases.

Only in diagrams D and E in Figure 9.1 could certiorari be granted and policy then be changed. The reason is that in both of these cases there exists a majority of justices—J_1 through J_4—who all want to move policy the same direction—leftward in each case—from SQ. Hence, we can assert:

PROPOSITION 9.4. For sincere justices, certiorari can be granted *and* policy can then be changed only when there exists some policy that a majority of justices prefer to SQ.

In other words, one less than a majority (that is, *maj* − 1) can force the Court to hear a case but it still takes a majority (*maj*) to change policy.

In fact, for sincere justices, only when the median justice has an ideal point not at SQ will there exist some policy that a majority of justices prefer to SQ. Hence, we can assert:

PROPOSITION 9.5. For sincere justices, certiorari can be granted *and* policy can be changed only when J_{med} is not at SQ.

Certiorari can be granted and policy changed in diagrams D and E in Figure 9.1 because the ideal point of the median justice (who is justice J_4 here) is not at SQ. If J_{med} is at SQ, certiorari can still be granted, as in diagrams A, B, and C in Figure 9.1, but policy cannot be changed in these cases because J_{med} is at SQ.

Strategic Behavior on Certiorari Decisions

If the justices behave strategically rather than sincerely, there are two key questions that we must address. First, under what conditions would the Court grant and deny a petition for certiorari? Second, how would each of the strategic justices vote on the petition?

We begin by specifying the essential characteristic of strategic behavior on the certiorari vote. Recall our argument in Chapter 5 that a strategic justice is concerned solely with the final policy in a case: he or she wants a better final outcome than the status quo policy. And although the costs of decision-making on a case (for example, the time and energy expended and the other case or cases that could be heard foregone) are not explicitly taken into account in our model, it seems reasonable to think that if the final outcome from a case will be no improvement in policy, then the strategically rational justice will vote against certiorari. For our model, then, the implications are straightforward:

PROPOSITION 9.6. A strategic justice will vote to grant certiorari on a case if the final outcome will be closer to his or her ideal point than SQ; the justice will vote to deny certiorari on the case if the final outcome is expected to be either at SQ or farther from his or her ideal point than SQ.

In other words, our argument about strategic behavior on certiorari decisions assumes an asymmetry in decision-making behavior: it is not sufficient for the final outcome to be better than or equal to SQ for a strategic justice to vote for certiorari; instead, the final outcome will have to be strictly better than SQ for the strategic justice to vote for certiorari. The rationale is simply that the justices' time and energy would be consumed on the case even though SQ would be unchanged, whereas SQ could be retained if the justices merely deny certiorari in the first place.

WHEN WILL THE COURT GRANT OR DENY A PETITION FOR CERTIORARI?

We can now consider the question as to when a Court populated by strategic justices would grant a petition for certiorari and when it would deny a petition for certiorari.

The condition under which a petition for certiorari will be granted by strategic justices is easily characterized:

PROPOSITION 9.7. A Court with strategic justices will grant a petition for certiorari if and only if there exists a set of policies that a majority of justices prefer to SQ.

In other words, if there exists a set of policies that a majority of justices prefer to SQ, the members of this majority should be expected to adopt one of these policies as the final outcome of the case. Moreover, if there is a majority of justices (that is, *maj* or more justices) who can agree on a change in policy, this necessarily implies that there is at least one less than a majority of justices (that is, at least $maj - 1$ justices) who also want to change policy and who would thus vote to grant certiorari. In fact, the proposition asserts that it is only when there exists some set of policies that a majority of justices prefer to SQ that certiorari will be granted by strategic justices; if no policy change is possible, strategic justices will vote to deny certiorari.

We can also specify when there will exist a set of policies that some majority of justices prefer to SQ:

PROPOSITION 9.8. In a Court with strategic justices, there exists a set of policies that a majority of justices prefer to SQ if and only if J_{med} is not at SQ.

In effect, it is only when the ideal point of the median justice is not at SQ that there will exist a set of policies that some majority of strategic justices prefer to SQ.

Combining Propositions 9.7 and 9.8, we can thus assert:

PROPOSITION 9.9. A Court with strategic justices will grant a petition for certiorari if and only if J_{med} is not at SQ.

That is, only if the ideal point of the median justice is not at SQ will a Court with strategic justices grant a petition for certiorari.

The conditions under which certiorari will be denied by strategic justices is also easily characterized. We have already argued that if there exists no policy that a majority of justices prefer to SQ, then the members of the Court will be unable to change policy; that is, SQ will remain in effect. For strategic justices, if a policy cannot be changed, then there is no purpose in granting certiorari for a case. Hence, certiorari will be denied when the following condition holds:

PROPOSITION 9.10. A Court with strategic justices will deny a petition for certiorari if there exists no policy that a majority of justices prefer to SQ.

And we can in turn specify when there exists no policy that is preferred to the status quo by some majority of justices. This condition is simply the following:

PROPOSITION 9.11. In a Court with strategic justices, there exists no policy that a majority of justices prefer to SQ if and only if J_{med} is at SQ.

Combining Propositions 9.10 and 9.11, we can thus assert:

PROPOSITION 9.12. A Court with strategic justices will deny a petition for certiorari if and only if J_{med} is at SQ.

That is, if the ideal point of the median justice is at SQ, the Court will deny a petition for certiorari. And in fact, this is the only condition in our model under which a Court with strategic justices will deny a petition for certiorari.

We end this section by noting that all our results on certiorari, given strategic justices, apply not only to the agenda-control version of our model but also to the open-bidding and median-holdout versions as well. All that matters for any of these three versions of our model is whether J_{med} is at SQ: if J_{med} is at SQ, certiorari will be denied, whereas if J_{med} is not at SQ, certiorari will be granted.

HOW WILL INDIVIDUAL STRATEGIC JUSTICES VOTE ON PETITIONS FOR CERTIORARI?

There is an interesting difference between how strategic justices should be expected to vote when they grant a petition for certiorari and how they should be expected to vote when they deny a petition for certiorari. For the granting of certiorari we should not necessarily expect unanimity, whereas for the denial of certiorari we should always expect unanimity.

To explain, recall that a strategic justice will vote to deny certiorari if the final outcome would be at SQ. But if the final outcome is at SQ, we can then assert:

PROPOSITION 9.13. In a Court with strategic justices, if there exists no policy that a majority of justices prefer to SQ, then every justice will vote to deny a petition for certiorari.

The basic reason goes back to Proposition 9.6: if the final outcome of a case will be at SQ, then no strategic justice has any reason to spend time and energy holding a hearing or making a decision on the case because policy cannot be changed. This logic holds for every justice. Hence, whenever a petition for certiorari is denied by strategic justices, which will occur whenever SQ is expected to be the final outcome, the petition will be denied unanimously.

However, unanimous behavior is not to be expected on petitions that are granted. These petitions for certiorari would be granted because there exists a set of policies that some majority of justices prefer to SQ. But even if a majority of justices prefers some policy to SQ, this does not mean that all justices prefer some particular policy to SQ. Instead, how any individual justice will vote on certiorari depends on what the final outcome is expected to be.

In the previous three chapters we discussed what policy outcome should be expected to emerge on the final vote. In particular, we know from Chapter 6 that an opinion written by a rational justice should always be expected to lie inside $W_{Jmed}(SQ)$. And from Chapters 6, 7, and 8 we know that several different outcomes inside $W_{Jmed}(SQ)$ are possible, depending on which version of our model characterizes Supreme Court decision-making (that is, is it the agenda-control version or the open-bidding or median-holdout version?), who the opinion assigner is (is it the Chief Justice or some other justice?), who the opinion writer is (is it someone with an ideal point inside $W_{Jmed}(SQ)$ or someone with an ideal point outside $W_{Jmed}(SQ)$?), and of course where the justices' ideal points are located relative to each other and relative to SQ.

For example, if either the open-bidding or median-holdout version of our model accurately characterizes Supreme Court decision-making, then the final outcome will be at J_{med}, and each justice will then base his or her certiorari vote simply on whether J_{med} is better or worse for him or her than SQ. But if the agenda-control model characterizes Supreme Court decision-making, then these other factors can lead to a final outcome in $W_{Jmed}(SQ)$ that is different from J_{med}. For instance, if the opinion writer has an ideal

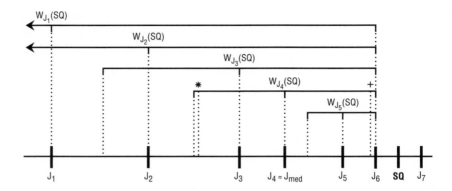

FIGURE 9.3

Voting on Certiorari by Strategic Justices

point that lies outside $W_{Jmed}(SQ)$, then he or she will write the opinion just inside the outside boundary of $W_{Jmed}(SQ)$. Or if the opinion writer has an ideal point that lies inside $W_{Jmed}(SQ)$, he or she can write the opinion at his or her own ideal point. Or if the opinion writer has a minority-side ideal point but has voted with the majority on the conference vote, he or she can write the opinion just inside the SQ boundary of $W_{Jmed}(SQ)$ (and thus as close as possible to his or her own minority-side ideal point).

In fact, unless we specify a particular final outcome on a case, given the agenda-control version of our model, we cannot be any more specific regarding how any particular justice will vote on the petition for certiorari. In Figure 9.3, however, we show how the several different final outcomes that are possible for a case under consideration by a seven-member Court will lead different justices to vote in different ways on their initial certiorari decisions.

For example, in Figure 9.3 if either justice J_1 or J_2 is the opinion writer, then the opinion will be written at the policy at *, just inside the outside (left-hand) boundary of $W_{J4}(SQ)$, the preferred-to set of the median justice. This opinion at * is better than SQ for justices J_1 through J_4, hence they would all vote to grant certiorari, but the opinion at * is worse than SQ for justices J_5 through J_7, so they would all vote to deny certiorari. Certiorari would thus be granted (only three votes are needed, but the petition gets four), and so the final outcome would be the policy at *.

If the opinion writer is justice J_3, justice J_3 would write the opinion at his own ideal point of J_3 because J_3 lies inside $W_{J4}(SQ)$. As with the opinion at *, this opinion at J_3 is better than SQ for justices J_1 through J_4, hence they would all vote to grant certiorari, but the opinion at J_3 is worse than SQ for justices J_5 through J_7, so they would all vote to deny certiorari. Certiorari would thus be granted (only three votes are needed, but the petition gets four), and the final outcome would be the policy at J_3.

If the opinion writer is justice J_4, justice J_4 could write the opinion at her own ideal point of J_4 because she is the median justice. As with the opinions at * and at J_3, this opinion at J_4 is better than SQ for justices J_1 through J_4, hence they would all vote to grant certiorari, but the opinion at J_4 is worse than SQ for justices J_5 through J_7, so they would all vote to deny certiorari. Certiorari would thus be granted (only three votes are needed, but the petition gets four), and the final outcome would be the policy at J_4.

If the opinion writer is justice J_5, justice J_5 could write the opinion at his own ideal point of J_5 because J_5 lies inside $W_{Jmed}(SQ)$. This opinion at J_5 is better than SQ for justices J_1 through J_5, hence they would all vote to grant certiorari, but the opinion at J_5 is worse than SQ for justices J_6 and J_7, so they would both vote to deny certiorari. Certiorari would thus be granted (only three votes are needed, but the petition gets five), and the final outcome would be the policy at J_5.

If the opinion writer is minority-side justice J_6 or J_7, each justice would write the opinion at the policy at +, which is the policy inside $W_{J4}(SQ)$ that is closest to SQ. As with the opinion at J_5, this opinion at + is better than SQ for justices J_1 through J_5, hence they would all vote to grant certiorari, but the opinion at + is worse than SQ for justices J_6 and J_7, so they would both vote to deny certiorari. However, certiorari would still be granted (only three votes are needed, but the petition would get five), and the final outcome would be the policy at +.

These illustrations from Figure 9.3 lead us to our final three propositions:

PROPOSITION 9.14. In a Court with strategic justices, if the final opinion for a case is not at SQ (which means the case will be granted certiorari), then the justices for whom the final opinion will be better than SQ will all vote for certiorari, and the justices for whom the final outcome will be worse than SQ will all vote against certiorari.

PROPOSITION 9.15. In a Court with strategic justices, the justices who support certiorari will be the same as the justices who support the final opinion, and the justices who oppose certiorari will be the same as the justices who do not support the final opinion.

PROPOSITION 9.16. In a Court with strategic justices, the number of justices actually voting for certiorari (at least *maj* justices) will always be larger than the number of justices required by Court rules to grant certiorari (at least *maj* − 1 justices).

"Aggressive Granting" and "Defensive Denial" When Justices Are Strategic

Our arguments about whether a petition for certiorari will be granted or denied by strategic justices, as summarized in Propositions 9.7 through 9.12, have some implications for discussions in the literature regarding "aggressive granting" and "defensive denials" (e.g., Boucher and Segal 1995; Epstein and Knight 1998). In our view, these discussions are logically incomplete and thus open to misinterpretation.

We first note that, as long as SQ is not at J_{med}, what is sometimes called an aggressive granting strategy will always work. We have already presented the basic reasons in our discussions of Propositions 9.7, 9.8, and 9.9: when SQ is not at J_{med}, there will always exist a set of policies that a majority of justices prefer to SQ. Because this majority of justices will want to adopt one of the policies that is better for them than SQ, they will always vote for certiorari; because they are a majority, certiorari will be granted. And because they are a majority of the Court, they can then proceed to adopt one of the policies that they prefer to SQ.

In fact, we are inclined to suggest that the phrase, aggressive granting, is superfluous: whenever SQ is not at J_{med}, there will automatically exist a Court majority that prefers some other policy—any of the policies in $W_{Jmed}(SQ)$—to SQ. If the Court majority that wants something other than SQ decides to hear the case, they can do so. There is nothing that distinguishes aggressive granting from any other kind of granting.

Moreover, precisely because aggressive granting as a strategy will always succeed when J_{med} is not at SQ, it follows that defensive denial as a strategy will always fail. It is certainly the case that individual justices will sometimes have an incentive to vote defensively against a grant of certiorari. In Figure 9.3, for example, given a final opinion at J_3, it is rational for three justices— J_5, J_6, and J_7—to vote against granting certiorari because granting it would ultimately lead to a new policy at J_3, and this policy at J_3 is worse for all three than SQ. But even though these three justices are engaging in defensive denial, they will be on the losing end of this certiorari vote. The reason is that, given the final opinion at J_3, justices J_1 through J_4 all prefer J_3 to SQ and so would all support certiorari, hence certiorari will be granted and all four of these justices would then vote to replace SQ by J_3.

In other words, defensive denial is basically an individual-level strategy that does not yield a successful Court-level outcome. That is, as long as J_{med} is not at SQ, there will automatically be a Court majority that prefers some policy to SQ, and precisely because this Court majority is a majority, its members will have the votes to grant certiorari and then adopt the policy they prefer to SQ. In fact, the only times when defensive denial will succeed in any sense—that is, when a petition for certiorari will be successfully denied—is when J_{med} is at SQ. However, by the logic of Proposition 9.12, when J_{med} is at SQ, the petition will be unanimously denied: everyone will vote for denial. And note also that the petition is being denied in this case not because some justices are managing to avoid an outcome worse for them than SQ. Instead, the petition is being denied simply because SQ cannot be changed at all.

Justices who find it necessary to practice defensive denial are thus doomed to failure: although defensive denial may be a rational strategy, it is not an effective strategy except when SQ is at J_{med}. In contrast, aggressive granting (which is indistinguishable from granting) as an individual-level strategy will always yield a successful Court-level outcome when SQ is not at J_{med}.

Summary of Major Results

We can summarize our major results on certiorari with the following observations:

1. Assuming sincere behavior, justices with ideal points not at SQ will vote to grant certiorari; justices with ideal points at SQ will vote to deny certiorari.

2. Assuming sincere behavior (and assuming J is odd), the Court will grant certiorari if at least *maj* − 1 justices have ideal points not at SQ; equivalently, the Court will grant certiorari if *maj* or fewer justices have ideal points at SQ.

3. Assuming sincere behavior (and assuming J is odd), the Court will deny certiorari if fewer than *maj* − 1 justices have ideal points not at SQ; equivalently, the Court will deny certiorari if at least *maj* + 1 justices have ideal points at SQ.

4. Assuming strategic behavior, there is one condition under which the Court will grant certiorari: when J_{med} is not at SQ (that is, when $W_{Jmed}(SQ) \neq \varnothing$). When this condition holds, it means that there exists some policy that a majority of justices prefer to SQ, and this majority will vote for certiorari in pursuit of a policy that they prefer to SQ.

5. Assuming strategic behavior, there is one condition under which the Court will deny certiorari: when J_{med} is at SQ (that is, when $W_{Jmed}(SQ) = \varnothing$). When this condition holds, it means that SQ will remain the outcome, hence all strategic justices will vote against certiorari because no improvement in outcomes is possible.

6. Assuming strategic behavior, the justices who prefer the final outcome to SQ will all vote for certiorari; the justices who prefer SQ to the final outcome will all oppose certiorari. This means that the lineup of justices sup-

porting and opposing a grant of certiorari will be the same as the lineup of justices supporting and opposing the final majority opinion.

7. Aggressive granting on certiorari decisions by strategic justices will always succeed when SQ is not at J_{med}; defensive denial on certiorari decisions by strategic justices will always fail when SQ is not at J_{med}.

PART THREE

Future Directions for Theories of
Supreme Court Decision-Making

In Part II of this book, we developed a formal model of multistage Supreme Court decision-making by strategically rational justices. In Part III, we now attempt to assess the significance and implications of this model. Chapter 10 highlights, summarizes, and discusses some of the empirical implications of this model. Chapter 11 ends the book by reexamining a variety of the model's most fundamental assumptions and by discussing some alternative assumptions that might help our model accommodate potential empirical problems. The chapter also considers several possible extensions of our model.

CHAPTER 10

Empirical Implications

In Chapters 5 through 9, we developed a formal model of multistage decision-making by strategically rational Supreme Court justices. The model produced a full set of expectations regarding how these justices would behave in each stage of the Supreme Court's decision-making process, given a wide range of initial conditions involving the justices' ideal points and the location of the status quo policy. Most importantly, the model produced a full set of expectations regarding where the final opinion would be located in relation to the justices' ideal points and the status quo policy.

These results suggest that the judicial politics literature on Supreme Court decision-making requires substantial revision. Some aspects of the conventional wisdom appear to be incompatible with other aspects of the conventional wisdom, and some of the conventional wisdom in the literature simply appears to be incorrect. Although additional aspects of the conventional wisdom do appear to be correct, our model provides a much clearer and more logical explanation for why strategically rational justices might behave in these particular ways.

As we constructed our model, some questions emerged about the conventional wisdom that, to our knowledge, had not previously been asked. In particular, it became apparent that strategically rational justices might plausibly interact with each other in several different ways as they pursued their policy goals. For this reason, we developed the agenda-control, open-bidding, and median-holdout versions of our model. These different versions present different interpretations of how decision-making on the Court proceeds, and it will be essential to understand which version most accurately characterizes Supreme Court decision-making.

Many of our results have clear empirical implications that should be tested. To assist the development of a program of empirical research, this chapter will summarize and highlight some of the contributions that we think our model makes to an understanding of Supreme Court decision-making. Although many of these contributions have already been noted in Chapters 6 through 9, we think it will be useful to discuss them and elaborate on their significance in one central place.

We focus on four key sets of issues that are especially relevant to empirical tests of hypotheses stimulated by our model. First, we discuss the implications of our model's results for an understanding of each of the five stages of Supreme Court decision-making. For the last two stages, involving coalition formation and the final vote, we evaluate the three different versions of our model. We also consider the implications of our results on coalition sizes for earlier research suggesting that Supreme Court coalitions will generally be minimum winning in size.

Second, we review the ongoing debate in the recent Supreme Court literature over whether justices are "sincere" or "strategic" in their decision-making behavior. We consider sincere and strategic behavior at each of the five stages of Court decision-making, and we show how our model helps clarify this debate.

Third, we discuss an important question raised by recent empirical research on the Court: what are the causes of vote switching, involving whether a justice supports the same policy on the conference vote (stage 2) and on the final vote (stage 5)? We argue that empirical evaluation of this question requires greater theoretical sophistication than is currently available in the literature. Our model helps clarify some of the key issues.

Fourth, we briefly mention some methodological problems involved in testing predictions from our model. Especially critical will be the development of techniques for estimating the dimensionality of Supreme Court decision-making: is it single dimensional, in some sense, as we have assumed in this book, or is the dimensionality of Supreme Court decision-making more complex? Understanding this issue of dimensionality will also be an important factor in developing techniques for estimating the locations of the justices' ideal points and the status quo policy.

Whatever these empirical tests show about the validity of our model, the results from the tests will provide an essential foundation for future improvements in the model. In fact, because our model is perhaps the simplest possible model of multistage decision-making by strategically rational justices, it will almost certainly fail to explain some important aspects of the justices' behavior. Knowing just where the model falls short empirically will thus be helpful in determining how to improve it theoretically. In Chapter 11, we will highlight some of the issues that are especially relevant to improving our theory and model.

Understanding the Five Stages of Supreme Court Decision-Making

We have distinguished five stages of Supreme Court decision-making, and our model provides an improved understanding and some new interpretations of the justices' behavior in each of these stages. We begin by first considering the implications of our model for certiorari, then the conference vote, then opinion assignment, and finally coalition formation and the final vote.

IMPLICATIONS FOR CERTIORARI (STAGE 1)

Our most basic result on certiorari is that, if the ideal point of the median justice is not at the status quo, then there always exists a Court majority that can move policy in some direction from the status quo. And if there is a Court majority—five votes on a nine-member Court—that can move policy in some direction from SQ, then there certainly exist the four votes needed to grant certiorari so that this majority can move policy in the desired direction. In contrast, if the ideal point of the median justice is at SQ, then there is no Court majority that can move policy in any direction from the status quo: although there may exist sufficient votes for certiorari even if the median justice is at SQ, there would not be enough votes to change policy, and hence it would make no sense for any strategically rational justice to support a grant of certiorari on the case.

These simple and straightforward results have important implications for the distinction in the literature between "aggressive granting" and "defensive denial." If there is a Court majority that wants to replace SQ by some alternative policy, then this Court majority can replace SQ by some alternative policy precisely because it is, by definition, a majority. To use the phrase *aggressive granting* here adds nothing to an understanding of who would support a grant of certiorari or what the Court's final decision on certiorari would be. Similarly, if there is a Court majority that prefers SQ to every other possible policy, then this Court majority can protect SQ precisely because it is, by definition, a majority. To use the phrase *defensive denial* here adds nothing to an understanding of who would oppose a grant of certiorari or what the Court's final decision on certiorari would be.

The basic problem with these two phrases that our model highlights is that the phrases fail to distinguish between what may be *individually rational* strategies, on the one hand, and what are *institutionally effective* strategies, on the other hand. For example, although it may be rational for some individual justice to adopt a defensive-denial strategy (that is, to oppose a grant of certiorari), it will nonetheless be a losing strategy if there is a Court majority that wants to replace the status quo with some alternative policy. In fact, whenever there exists a Court majority that wants to upset the status quo (that is, whenever J_{med} is not at SQ), then the aggressive granting strategy will always work and the defensive denial strategy will always fail. Only when there exists no Court majority that can upset the status quo (that is, whenever J_{med} is at SQ) could it be said that the defensive denial strategy will work and the aggressive granting strategy will fail. For these reasons, then, we think that the phrases aggressive granting and defensive denial could be abandoned without any significant loss in our understanding of the Supreme Court's decisions on certiorari.[1]

We should mention one possible limitation of our analysis of certiorari: it may overpredict what petitions for certiorari will be accepted by the Court. Of course, on most cases for which applications for certiorari are made, the median justice and perhaps several other justices may well have ideal points at SQ. Hence, these applications would be rejected because there is no possibility of policy change. However, there may still be numerous petitions for certiorari for which J_{med} is not at SQ, and our model asserts that all such petitions will be granted. Nonetheless, the Court may refuse to accept some of these otherwise desirable cases as a result of time constraints and workload reasons, factors that are not part of our model.

IMPLICATIONS FOR THE CONFERENCE VOTE (STAGE 2)

Our most interesting results on the conference vote involve the incentive that all justices have to support—or at least consider supporting—positions other than their respective ideal points. Our analysis makes clear that this incentive is very strong for a minority-side Chief Justice because he can gain control of opinion assignment only if he sides with the majority on the conference vote. And in fact, the Supreme Court literature has often mentioned that Chief Justice Warren Burger would occasionally delay making his views known in conference until the other justices had reported theirs (see, e.g., the discussion in Epstein and Knight 1998, 128–35). The presumption is that Chief Justice Burger was thereby ensuring that his vote would be on the majority side so that he could control the opinion assignment.[2]

This strategy of announcing support on the conference vote for some policy other than one's own ideal point has been less often mentioned with regard to the associate justices, although Epstein and Knight (1998, 28) do briefly discuss how these justices can "misrepresent their sincere preferences" when participating in the conference discussion. In fact, after remarking that "the institution governing opinion assignment ensures that the power rests almost exclusively with the chief justice and the senior associate," Epstein and Knight go on to say that if the junior justices want to influence the decision-making process,

> they must consider mechanisms other than the power to assign opinions. Perhaps that is why some scholars have observed the Court's most junior members tending to align "their political preferences with the Court's ideological center of gravity."[3] By so doing, they can offset their inability to assign opinions with the power to serve as pivots. (Epstein and Knight 1998, 128)

Our own analysis of strategically calculated endorsements on the conference vote provides a clear logical foundation for Epstein and Knight's discussion. Even more significantly, this passage from Epstein and Knight suggests that there may be some empirical evidence for the kind of strategic behavior by associate justices that is predicted by our convergence condition (see Proposition 8.14 in Chapter 8). Although the convergence condition does state that convergence will occur on the ideal point of the majority opinion assigner rather than on the ideal point of the median justice (the latter is what seems to be implied by the quotation cited by Epstein and Knight, that the junior members will align themselves "with the Court's ideological center of gravity"), the logic of convergence does seem to have at least some empirical manifestation.

What seems to be absent from the literature, however, is any explicit discussion of the critical but complex issue of whether the opinion assigner (such as the Chief Justice) will actually trust what other justices say on the conference vote and therefore base his opinion assignment on the policies they endorse there. As we argued in our analysis at the end of Chapter 8, if a justice is concerned only about the current case and is not concerned about the implications of his current behavior for outcomes in future cases (see Assumption 5.9), he would endorse whatever policy would be most likely to attract the opinion assignment, but having gained control of the opinion, he would then write the opinion at his own ideal point, ignoring the policy he had endorsed in conference. Of course, because a rational opinion assigner would realize all this, the opinion assigner would simply assign the opinion on the basis of the justices' ideal points, ignoring whatever policies they had endorsed on the conference vote. Hence the other justices, concluding that their strategic policy endorsements in conference would be ignored, would simply behave sincerely (although for these strategically calculated reasons) on the conference vote and just endorse policies at their respective ideal points.

In contrast, if a justice does care about the consequences of his current behavior for the outcomes of future cases (that is, if Assumption 5.9 does not hold), then he may be more likely to write a final opinion at (or as close as politically possible to) the policy he endorsed on the conference vote. If the opinion assigner considers him to be trustworthy for this reason, the assigner may then be willing to base opinion assignment on what policies the justice endorsed in conference. And because these previously endorsed policies would become the basis of opinion assignment, the other justices would then make their strategically calculated policy endorsements on the conference vote. The evidence that Epstein and Knight cite on strategic behavior by junior justices suggests that this dynamic (involving the violation of Assumption 5.9) may indeed be at work on the conference vote.

In sum, how justices behave in conference may be affected by the complex set of issues involving commitment, trustworthiness, trust, and long-term versus short-term rationality that we discussed at the end of Chapter 8. Of course, if either the open-bidding or median-holdout version of our model accurately characterizes Supreme Court decision-making (more on this below), then these issues of commitment and trust are moot because every majority opinion writer will be forced to write the final majority opinion at J_{med}, no matter what policy he or she may have endorsed on the conference vote.

Although we cannot completely resolve these kinds of issues here (see Chapter 11 for further analysis), we note that it was only via the modeling process that we even recognized the existence of such issues in the conference vote and the opinion assignment process. Subsequent empirical research on the conference vote will have to take these complex theoretical issues into account.

IMPLICATIONS FOR OPINION ASSIGNMENT
(STAGE 3)

We have two sets of remarks about the implications of our results for opinion assignment. Our first set of remarks begins with the observation that it is easy to find references in the literature to the importance of opinion assignment. In fact, there seems to be substantial agreement, among justices and judicial scholars alike, that because it matters who writes the final opinion, a strategically rational majority opinion assigner will use opinion assignment to further his or her own policy goals. So if it is observed empirically that majority opinions do not all end up at J_{med}, then this would seem to indicate that something like the agenda-control version of our model may be at work. This in turn would suggest that opinion assignments may have affected what final opinions were adopted.

In contrast, if all justices are strategically rational in the manner assumed by the open-bidding and median-holdout versions of our model, then it follows that the opinion writer's final opinion will be driven to the ideal point of the median justice. But if the final opinion is driven to the ideal point of the median justice, then it does not matter who the opinion writer is: the opinion assigner could assign the opinion to anyone and the final opinion will still end up at J_{med}. If opinion assignments do not have any policy implications because the majority opinions always end up at J_{med}, this might be a reason why the Chief Justice, as the primary opinion assigner, appears able to distribute opinions reasonably equitably among the other justices, as suggested by at least some of the empirical literature.

Thus, what we think are plausible arguments about how the Supreme Court makes its decisions (that is, the three different versions of our model) have very different implications for how opinion assignments are handled. Clearly, substantial empirical work, informed by the theoretical perspectives we have developed, is needed to clarify what the justices are actually doing here.

Our second set of remarks involves the commonly made claim in the opinion-assignment literature that a strategically rational opinion assigner will assign the opinion to that justice who is ideologically closest to the assigner. Our model shows that this particular claim rests on a logical error. Under some conditions, as we showed in Chapter 7, it is rational for the opinion assigner to assign the opinion to some justice who is not the closest ideologically. Thus, assigning to the closest justice under these conditions can leave the opinion assigner worse off than he or she might otherwise be. This suggests that many empirical tests of opinion assignment theories will have to be reformulated: what is usually being tested is a logically incorrect hypothesis.

IMPLICATIONS FOR COALITION FORMATION AND THE FINAL VOTE (STAGES 4 AND 5)

We begin by noting that our model is almost unique in the literature in that it predicts the location of the final majority opinion relative to the locations of the justices' ideal points and the status quo policy; as we noted in Chapters 1, 2, and 3, the previous literature primarily emphasizes who would vote with whom. Thus, our model cannot be said to challenge the conventional wisdom on the location of the final opinion because there is very little conventional wisdom to challenge.

Our model also has a number of other implications that should be mentioned. We discuss three of these implications here.

The Role of the Median Justice

Our model highlights the central importance of the median justice on the Court and the set of policies that she prefers to SQ. Notice in particular that all three versions of our model revolve around the median justice: in the agenda-control version the final majority opinion must lie inside the median justice's preferred-to set, $W_{Jmed}(SQ)$, whereas the final opinion converges on the median justice's ideal point, J_{med}, in the open-bidding and median-holdout versions. Although the popular press often refers to the "swing justice" on a case, the judicial politics literature on Supreme Court decision-making less often makes the swing justice (whom we assume to be the median justice) the central figure in its analyses. In fact, it is our view that the judicial politics literature does not give the median justice anything like the importance that is deserved.

Which Version of Our Model?

We have just noted the different final outcomes that might be expected from the three different versions of our model, and it is an empirical issue as to which of these versions most accurately characterizes Supreme Court decision-making. However, if something like the agenda-control version of our model does turn out to characterize Supreme Court decision-making, it will force us to think more deeply about the nature of the justices' rationality.[4]

For example, it may be that justices are not, in fact, as strategically rational as some of the literature (e.g., Epstein and Knight 1998) appears to suggest. Perhaps the justices are unable to be fully strategic on any one case, or perhaps they are choosing not to be fully strategic.

If the justices are unable to behave in a fully strategic manner on some cases, then the strategic-rationality assumption must be substantially modified. Perhaps the justices feel they lack sufficient information about each other's goals and strategies to make a strategically rational decision (although there certainly do exist formal models of strategic behavior under uncertainty). Or perhaps the justices lack the personal computational capacity (for example, they are boundedly rational) to fully use whatever information about the other justices they do happen to have. After all, it might be difficult to figure out, at the certiorari stage, what will happen at all four of the next stages (that is, who will take what position in conference, who will become the opinion assigner, who will be assigned the majority opinion, what policy will the final majority opinion endorse, and who will support or oppose this policy?). So perhaps real-world justices are simply incapable of behaving according to the dictates of strategic rationality in our model.

On the other hand, if the justices are capable of behaving in a fully strategic manner on each case but choose not to do so, as with the agenda-control version of our model, then we must explain why they would make this choice. That is, why might it be rational for them not to behave in a fully strategic manner on any one case?

One possibility is that the agenda-control behavior stems from a kind of institutionalized quid pro quo involving decisions not to challenge each other's draft majority decisions. For example, each justice might think, "If I do not challenge the majority opinion writer on this case, which he cares about more than I do, he may be less inclined to challenge me when I am the majority opinion writer on some subsequent case that I care about more than he does." For each case taken in isolation, this behavior might look simply like a "norm of deference" to the majority opinion writer, but such a norm might actually represent a rational strategy of mutual cross-case accommodation that all or most of the justices adopt.

Unfortunately, because the current literature does not seem to recognize these very different patterns of decision-making that the Court could exhibit, this means that the literature provides little help in determining which pattern we should expect to observe empirically. Although our model cannot answer these empirical questions by itself, we should point out that it was the modeling process that highlighted these questions in the first place and that also suggested where to begin looking for empirical answers.[5]

Are Coalitions on the Court Minimum Winning?

One of the earliest applications of rational-choice theory to coalition formation on the Court involved David Rohde's arguments—see Rohde (1972a)—that (a) Supreme Court justices should normally be expected to construct minimum-winning coalitions on the final vote, but that (b) coalitions that are larger than minimum winning should be expected when the justices feel the Court is threatened by external political pressures. However, as we demonstrated in Chapter 6, if each case is assumed to have a status quo policy in some unidimensional policy space, there is no reason to think that the justices will construct only those coalitions that are minimum winning in size (at least for the nonthreat cases). Instead, the size of the final coalitions will depend simply on how many justices consider the opinion writer's final opinion to be better than the status quo policy.

Of course, if only five justices have majority-side ideal points, then the final winning coalition will necessarily be minimum winning in size: no matter who writes the final majority opinion here, a 5–4 vote will be produced. However, this minimum-winning coalition does not stem from any kind of bargaining or compromising by the opinion writer. In fact, there is nothing that the opinion writer could do here that would increase the size of the majority coalition: the 5–4 vote results from the basic structure of the situation rather than from any deliberate strategy by the opinion writer.

Furthermore, it can easily happen that some particular policy will be unanimously preferred by the justices to the status quo policy even though the opinion writer makes no compromises at all. For example, consider the case illustrated in diagram B in Figure 6.8. Note that the status quo policy lies to the right of every justice's ideal point. Now assume that justice J_5 is the opinion writer and so can write an opinion at his own ideal point. A unanimous vote in favor of this opinion at J_5 will be the result here, and this unanimity will result even though the opinion writer, justice J_5, does not have to compromise his views in the slightest. Of course, it would be possible for justice J_5 to write an opinion that generates a 3–2 minimum-winning coalition: it would require a policy at * just inside the outside boundary of $W_{J3}(SQ)$. However, it would be completely irrational for justice J_5 to write such an opinion at * because he can get unanimous support for a policy at his own ideal point. In sum, we would argue that there is no good reason to expect that only minimum-winning coalitions will form on the Court, or even that there should be a tendency in this direction.

Although the expectation from the theory of minimum-winning coalitions should be that 5–4 lineups will form in all of the nonthreat cases, it is significant that these 5–4 lineups formed in Rohde's data set in just 39.9% of the nonthreat cases (see Rohde's table 1), which means that in 60.1% of the nonthreat cases the coalitions were not minimum winning in size. Only when 6–3 coalitions were included in Rohde's tabulation did even a majority of lineups (a total of 63.0%) turn out to be minimum winning in size.

Rohde's justification for the inclusion of the 6–3 lineups along with the 5–4 lineups (see Rohde 1972a, 218–19) is that the opinion writers may have been uncertain about whether a majority of justices would support their opinions, hence they might have written their opinions so as to attract an additional justice just to be safe. However, it is not clear to us how valid this justification regarding uncertainty actually is. As Maltzman, Spriggs, and Wahlbeck (2000) demonstrate, for example, there is extensive and explicit communication and bargaining among the justices as to who will support any particular final opinion; in the end, it appears that relatively little uncertainty may remain about who will support what opinion. Hence, there may not be great justification for including the 6–3 votes in the tabulation. And if these lineups are excluded, the minimum-winning coalition theory does not fare very well.[6]

In our view, the key empirical variable for explaining the distribution of coalition sizes may simply be the distribution of the locations of the status quo policies in the set of Court cases in which one is interested. If there is any kind of central tendency in the locations of SQ in the cases the Court accepts (that is, if there are more cases in which SQ is located relatively close to the median justice than in which SQ is located closer to the extreme justices at either end), then coalition sizes will tend, on average, to be smaller rather than larger. In contrast, if there is no such central tendency for the locations of SQ, then coalition sizes will tend, on average, to be somewhat larger. Without knowing the initial distribution of the locations of SQ in the cases in the data set, it may well be that Rohde's empirical results on coalition sizes tell us primarily that the status quo policy was located in a wide variety of different locations, relative to the justices' ideal points, in the cases in his data set.

Rohde's empirical data do appear to suggest that coalitions are bigger in the threat situations than in the nonthreat situations. Even here, however, there is a possible alternative explanation: perhaps the justices' ideal points in the threat cases tended to cluster on the same side of the status quo policy (for some unknown reason). This would have allowed a wider range of winning coalition sizes, including unanimous and close-to-unanimous coalitions, than would have been possible in cases in which the median justice's ideal point was adjacent to the status quo policy (see our discussion in the first sections of Chapter 6). This alternative hypothesis—a bias in the locations of the status quo—should be ruled out before the empirical data are interpreted as validating Rohde's hypothesis about the influence of external threats on Supreme Court decision-making.

"Nonstrategic" or "Sincere" Behavior on the Supreme Court

As we pointed out in Chapters 2 and 3, one important issue in the recent literature on strategic behavior on the Supreme Court has involved the question of whether the justices are "strategically" rational or "sincerely" rational (that is, "nonstrategically" rational). However, our analyses in Chapters 6 through 9 suggest that references to sincere rationality sometimes have substantial ambiguities; that is, what constitutes sincere behavior is often unclear. In this section we will review our arguments about sincere and strategic behavior.

For the first stage of Supreme Court decision-making involving certiorari, we observed in Chapter 9 that what constitutes sincere rationality for a justice might initially seem to be clear: a sincere justice would support certiorari if the status quo policy for the case is not at his or her own ideal point, whereas this justice would reject certiorari if the status quo policy for a case is at the justice's own ideal point. However, we also pointed out that if five of the nine justices have ideal points at the status quo but four justices would like to move policy in some agreed-upon direction and so would support a grant of certiorari, this grant of certiorari might actually seem to be irrational, or at least wasteful, because it could lead these four justices to expend their time and energy on a case for which no policy improvements are possible for them. Hence, it remains unclear how to characterize such behavior.

For the second stage of Supreme Court decision-making involving the conference vote, our analysis in Chapter 8 suggested that both sincere rationality and strategic rationality would have the same behavioral manifestation: the justice would endorse a policy at his or her own ideal point. Thus a justice might behave sincerely but for strategic reasons.[7]

For the third stage of Supreme Court decision-making involving opinion assignment, we pointed out in Chapter 7 (and reiterated earlier in this chapter) that what is considered strategic opinion assignment in the literature—the majority opinion assigner should assign the opinion to the justice whose ideal point is closest to the assigner's own ideal point—does not necessarily lead to the best possible final outcome for the assigner. Instead, there are conditions under which this decision rule produces outcomes for the assigner that are inferior to what could be obtained by assigning the opinion to a more distant justice. In fact, the optimal decision rule for the strategically rational opinion assigner is simply that he or she should always assign the opinion to the justice whose final opinion would be closest to the assigner's own ideal point.

But if strategic opinion assignment means that the opinion should be assigned to the justice whose final opinion will be closest to the assigner's ideal point, then what would sincere opinion assignment be? One possibility is that the decision rule of "assign to the closest other justice" should actually be considered the sincere behavior. Or it might instead be argued that self-assignment should be considered the most sincere behavior because self-assignment could be done without paying any attention at all to any kind of political considerations. Thus, there remains some ambiguity about what would constitute sincere behavior at the opinion-assignment stage.

Finally, for the fourth and fifth stages of Supreme Court decision-making involving coalition formation and the final vote, we suggested in Chapter 2 that the purest form of sincere, nonstrategic rationality might be expected to lead each justice to write an opinion at his or her own ideal point; with nine different opinions, there would be no process by which a majority of justices would coalesce around some majority-side opinion. However, we also demonstrated in Chapter 2 that writing an opinion at his or her own ideal point could lead to an inferior outcome for the justice (because only a plurality opinion might be produced) compared to the outcome from compromising on some kind of majority opinion. Because a plurality opinion will not generally set any kind of precedent, and thus not change Court policy, this kind of sincere opinion writing means that possible policy improvements are being foregone. This would seem to negate the very meaning of the term *rationality*.

In sum, then, it is strategically rational behavior that generally seems to have clearer meanings and sincerely rational behavior that more often seems to have unclear or ambiguous meanings. The basic reason for this difference, we suspect, is that the phrase *sincerely rational* is generally an oxymoron. *If* the goal of rational behavior for a justice is assumed to be the best possible final outcome on a case, *then* rationality automatically implies strategic rationality. If sincere behavior does not achieve the best possible final outcome on a case, or (in a world with some uncertainty) is at least not expected to achieve the best possible final outcome, then such behavior cannot be considered rational (in the sense of maximizing achievement of one's policy goal on the case). Only when sincere and strategic behavior lead to the same outcome, or are at least expected to lead to the same outcome, can sincere behavior be considered rational.

Vote Switching between the Original and Final Votes

Although much of the empirical literature on Supreme Court decision-making behavior has focused on just one stage of decision-making at a time (for example, just on certiorari, or just on opinion assignment, or just on the final vote), one recurring issue in the literature has involved vote switching between the conference vote (stage 2) and the final vote (stage 5). Three questions in particular have been raised about vote switching: first, under what conditions should a justice be expected to switch his or her vote between the original and final votes?; second, how often do justices actually switch their votes in this fashion?; and third, why do justices actually switch their votes?[8]

The second question is an empirical one that we cannot address here. However, the first and third questions turn out to involve some complex theoretical issues, and we would argue that it is primarily within the context of our model, or something like it, that understanding of this phenomenon of vote switching can be advanced. In fact, we would argue that without an adequate theoretical understanding of the strategically calculated reasons for vote switching (that is, when and why would a justice benefit from it?), it will be difficult to conduct adequate empirical research on the phenomenon.

We begin our analysis by observing that vote switching will not necessarily change the outcome of a case. If a justice who endorses a minority-side policy on the conference vote switches to the majority side on the final vote, the outcome will not change; instead, the majority will merely get larger. And if a justice with a majority-side ideal point that lies to the inside of the median justice (that is, between J_{med} and SQ) switches to the minority side on the final vote, the outcome again will not change; the majority on the final vote may shrink, compared to the conference vote, but the majority will still remain the majority. It is primarily when the median justice switches her vote from the majority side to the minority side that the majority coalition on the conference vote would lose its majority on the final vote. In other words, there is not always a tight link between behavior and outcome here: most of the vote switching that is possible will not change the final outcome.

Whether the outcome changes or does not change, explaining vote switching at the individual level requires that we determine the conditions under which a strategically rational justice would switch his or her vote from the conference vote to the final vote. In Chapter 8 we argued that if justices are strategically rational and if their behavior on one case has no relevance to outcomes on subsequent cases, then on the conference vote we should expect them to endorse policies at their own ideal points (that is, their strategic behavior will look like it is sincere). The reason is that the Chief Justice (or other majority opinion assigner) will not trust any other justice to write the final opinion at the position this other justice endorsed on the conference vote; instead, the opinion assigner will expect any other justice to renege by writing the final opinion as close as possible (constrained by the need to attract majority support on the final vote) to his or her own ideal point. Hence, the opinion assigner will base the assignment on the other justices' ideal points, rather than on the policies they endorse on the conference vote, which means that these other justices might as well vote sincerely on the conference vote.

However, on the final vote, the majority opinion will be written by some particular justice, and this opinion writer may write a final opinion that another justice with a majority-side ideal point finds to be worse than SQ; hence, this other justice would not join the majority opinion on the final vote.[9] For example, consider diagram B in Figure 6.8, and assume that the agenda-control version of our model holds. Because all five justices' ideal points lie to the left of SQ, the coalition lineup and sizes on the conference vote will be $\{J_1, J_2, J_3, J_4, J_5\}$ to $\{\varnothing\}$, for a 5–0 vote (assuming strategically sincere voting). However, if justice J_1 becomes the opinion writer, he will write a final majority opinion at *, just inside the outside boundary of $W_{J3}(SQ)$, the preferred-to set of the median justice here, and note that this final opinion at * lies outside the preferred-to sets of justices J_4 and J_5. Hence, the coalition lineups and sizes on the final vote will be $\{J_1, J_2, J_3\}$ to $\{J_4, J_5\}$, for a 3–2 vote. As a result, justices J_4 and J_5 will have switched their votes from the conference vote to the final vote, and for entirely rational reasons: the opinion that became available to them on the final vote was worse for them than SQ.[10]

The same dynamic can occur with the open-bidding version of our model. For example, again consider diagram A in Figure 6.8. For the same reasons as before, the coalition lineups and sizes on the conference vote will be $\{J_1, J_2, J_3, J_4, J_5\}$ to $\{\varnothing\}$, for a 5–0 vote. However, with the open-bidding version, the opinion at justice J_3's ideal point is the only equilibrium opinion. Nonetheless, a final majority opinion at J_3 lies outside (and to the left of) the preferred-to sets of justices J_4 and J_5. So justices J_4 and J_5 will switch their votes on the final vote, producing coalition lineups of $\{J_1, J_2, J_3\}$ to $\{J_4, J_5\}$, for a 3–2 final vote.

Notice that the vote switching that is predicted in both of these examples here goes from the original majority side to the final minority side. In other words, the original majority coalition would be larger than the final majority coalition.

In fact, even if it turns out that the majority opinion assigner does trust each other justice to write a final opinion as close as possible to the policy he or she endorsed on the conference vote, our conclusions about vote switching will remain the same: even if there is convergence on the ideal point of the opinion assigner (recall the convergence and nonconvergence conditions in Chapter 8), the final opinion may be worse than the status quo for some majority-side justices, and if so, these justices would join the minority side. Thus, any vote switching will again go from the majority side to the minority side.

However, strategically motivated vote switching can go in the other direction, from the minority side on the conference vote to the majority side on the final vote. In fact, the empirical evidence (see, e.g., Dorff and Brenner 1992)—appears to show that most vote switching involves switches by some minority-side justices to the majority side. The interpretation of this behavior is generally that these vote-switching minority-side justices have either been persuaded by the arguments of the majority or else are joining the majority for other reasons, such as increasing the Court's legitimacy by producing larger majorities for the Court's policies. But there is a possible alternative explanation: in the open-bidding and median-holdout versions of our model, some minority-side justices may be joining the majority so as to ensure that a majority-side opinion at J_{med} is adopted rather than a majority-side opinion that is even farther from their minority-side ideal points than J_{med}. These justices would have voted sincerely on the minority side on the conference vote, for reasons we discussed at the end of Chapter 8, but then ended up supporting a majority-side opinion at J_{med} to prevent something worse than J_{med} from being adopted.

Our model's clearest predictions do seem to involve movement from the majority side on the conference vote to the minority side on the final vote. The open-bidding and median-holdout processes may involve movement from the minority side on the conference vote to the majority side on the final vote, as our last example suggests, but the logic is not quite as clear. As we just noted, empirical research on vote switching appears to show that vote switching more often involves movement from the minority side on the conference vote to the majority side on the final vote rather than the reverse. But whether this reflects outcomes from the open-bidding or median-holdout processes or from some other kind of process is not clear. Indeed, as discussed earlier in this chapter, if there is a quid pro quo among the justices (for example, "I'll support you on the opinions you write if you support me on the opinions I write"), it may be that the minority-side-to-majority-side vote switching that is empirically observed stems from this kind of cross-case decision-making process.

In our view, the phenomenon of vote switching requires further theoretical development and more empirical explorations before adequate hypothesis testing will be possible.

Problems of Empirical Measurement

Our model of Supreme Court decision-making assumes that there is a single issue dimension for each case, that each justice has an ideal point on this dimension, and that there is a status quo policy on this dimension. Empirical tests of our propositions from Chapters 6 through 9 will thus require verification that each case is effectively unidimensional and will require identification of each justices' ideal point and the status quo policy on this dimension.

Regarding the unidimensionality assumption, we pointed out in Chapter 5 that there are at least three different interpretations of what "a single issue dimension" might mean. One interpretation is that every case that the Court considers can be placed on a single common dimension, such as the standard "liberal/conservative" issue dimension that underlies much of the research stimulated by the attitudinal model.

A second interpretation is that every Supreme Court case can be placed on its own unique dimension. Even though each case's dimension may be different from every other case's dimension, all that matters for our model is that each case has just a single dimension.

A third interpretation is that various groups of cases share a single common dimension. Thus, there might be a single "civil liberties" dimension that is distinct from a single "criminal rights" dimension, which is in turn distinct from a single "federalism" dimension, and so forth.

In contrast, it could be that some cases—indeed, perhaps all cases—are unavoidably multidimensional. In this case, a multidimensional version of our model would have to be constructed. Although we have already sketched out one possible interpretation of Supreme Court decision-making in two dimensions (see Hammond, Bonneau, and Sheehan 1999), we leave this problem for further consideration in Chapter 11; as we will demonstrate there, several additional theoretical issues must be considered when decision-making takes place in a multidimensional setting.

Empirical research on the dimensionality of Supreme Court decision-making is an ongoing enterprise, and there is no consensus on an answer. Some research (e.g., Grofman and Brazill 2002) suggests that there is one primary dimension. Other research (e.g., Brazill and Grofman 2002; Martin and Quinn 2002) suggests that there are two primary dimensions (a "civil liberties" dimension and an "economics" dimension). It is not clear, though, whether this latter body of research implies that every case is two dimensional, or whether it simply indicates that some cases are unidimensional on the "civil liberties" dimension while the other cases are unidimensional on the "economics" dimension. (This is, in effect, our third interpretation of what unidimensionality might mean.)

Whatever the outcome of this empirical research, it is essential to understand the nature of the dimensionality of Supreme Court decision-making before we can know what kind of decision-making model to develop and test. Meanwhile, there is enough evidence of unidimensionality that we find it reasonable to construct a one-dimensional model.

A closely related empirical problem involves estimation of the ideal points of the justices. Through the use of multidimensional scaling techniques, it is usually possible to estimate not only the dimensionality of the issue space but also the locations of the justices' ideal points on the resulting dimensions. Much work has been done in recent years on estimating ideal points of legislators, especially representatives and senators in the U.S. Congress, given their votes on roll calls. Many of these techniques could be applied to the votes of the Supreme Court justices; indeed, some of this work has already been conducted (e.g., Bailey and Chang 2001; Grofman and Brazill 2002; Martin and Quinn 2002).[11]

A third empirical problem involves the estimation of the location of the status quo policy in each case in the data set of interest.[12] One technique would involve coding each final opinion and locating it in relation to the justices' ideal points. Some of the coding decisions made by Harold Spaeth for his Supreme Court databases (e.g., is a Court decision in a criminal rights case a "pro-police" decision or a "pro-defendant" decision?) may be usable for this purpose.[13]

To test hypotheses from our model against a database of Supreme Court decisions would require that all these estimates—of dimensionality, of ideal points, and of status quo locations—be incorporated in the analysis. Hence, it appears that some advances in theoretically grounded empirical estimation techniques will be needed.

Conclusion

Our model of multistage decision-making by strategically rational Supreme Court justices has many implications for the current generation of literature on Supreme Court decision-making. Ultimately, it will take rigorous empirical research to test these implications and address the further questions that our model has raised.

However, we expect that there will be at least some discrepancies between what is predicted by our model and what is empirically observed. Our model will thus have to be modified to resolve these problems. In Chapter 11, we consider what some of these modifications might be.

CHAPTER 11

Future Research

The previous generations of theories of Supreme Court decision-making have left much to be desired in terms of their clarity, coherence, consistency, and scope of application. Our model of Supreme Court decision-making by strategically rational justices shows that substantial improvement is possible. In particular, by constructing our model on a solid foundation—a clear, coherent, and consistent set of assumptions drawn from the metaphor of rational choice—we have demonstrated how judicial politics scholars can build more satisfactory theories and models for use in their empirical research. And the fact that the propositions derived from our model could be used to generate numerous empirically testable hypotheses about each stage in the Court's decision-making process suggests that this model also has a wide scope of application.

Although we have not conducted a systematic empirical assessment, the plausibility of many of our results suggests to us that our model will find substantial empirical support. Nonetheless, there will undoubtedly be some discrepancies between the hypotheses derived from our model and what the empirical evidence actually shows. This will require that our model be revisited in an effort to determine where it may have gone astray. In this final chapter, we consider some of the modifications that might prove useful or necessary.

We begin with an analysis of five of the most critical assumptions on which our model rests. First, we review our assumption that justices have perfect information about each other's preferences, and we consider some modifications involving uncertainty about the justices' preferences. Second, we review our assumption that justices always have clear policy preferences on a case, and we consider modifications in which the justices are unsure of their own preferences. Third, we review our assumption that what happens on one case has no influence on any subsequent cases, and we consider modifications in which the Court's decision on one case might affect what cases subsequently arise and what the justices do with them. Fourth, we review our assumption that each case is characterized by just one issue dimension, and we consider some possible modifications involving multiple issue dimensions. Fifth, we review our assumption that writing the majority opinion is a costless enterprise, and we consider modifications assuming that opinion writing is a costly enterprise instead.

After discussing these theoretical refinements, we discuss the fact that justices not only write or join majority opinions but also may write or join regular or special concurrences. We then suggest some ways of predicting when justices might engage in these other activities.

Next we describe a possible extension of our model involving the incorporation of a lower court (such as a federal appeals court) populated by judges who, like the Supreme Court justices themselves, are also strategically rational. We also discuss the application of our model to other collegial courts and similar multimember institutions.

Then we briefly reexamine the primary interpretation we have given to our formal model, considering whether an alternative interpretation involving legal concerns rather than personal policy preferences might be appropriate.

After that, we consider what role "the law" and other legal issues might play in the justices' policy preferences and in their decision-making practices on the Court.

We end this final chapter with a brief discussion of the implications of our model both for those who claim that the attitudinal model accurately characterizes Supreme Court decision-making as well as for those who are skeptical of this claim. Both groups, we will argue, need our model. The proponents of the attitudinal model would have to predict that in an empirical test of our model, most of the variance will be explained, whereas the skeptics would have to predict that much of the variance will be left unexplained.

Do the Justices Have Perfect Information about Each Other's Preferences?

Our model assumes that the justices have perfect information about each other's policy preferences; see Assumption 5.8, which states that "Each justice knows the ideal point of every other justice, and all justices know and understand what the Supreme Court's decision-making procedures are." Although we acknowledge that this perfect-information assumption makes formal analysis simple and straightforward, we adopted the assumption in good part because we think that it describes the context of Supreme Court decision-making reasonably well.

In fact, to the extent that the individuals in any American political institution have perfect information about each other's policy preferences, it is probably the justices on the Supreme Court who have it. Although the senior justices may have some uncertainty about the policy preferences of a justice who has only recently joined the Court, this uncertainty may last just a short time: as the new justice announces her views on the many dozens of cases on the docket in her first term or two on the Court, her more senior colleagues will quickly develop an understanding of her preferences and thus learn to predict her views. Although the newcomer may arrive somewhat uncertain about the views of her more senior colleagues, we suspect that, having actively served as a lawyer and perhaps as a judge for the previous two or three decades, she will arrive at the Court with substantial knowledge about the policy preferences of the sitting justices.

Nonetheless, there is evidence that uncertainty about the justices' preferences does have an impact on at least some aspects of Supreme Court decision-making. Regarding the granting of certiorari, for example, coalitions of just four justices sometimes grant certiorari not in the certainty but more in the hope that a fifth vote can be found in support of their joint position (e.g., Perry 1991). Justices in this kind of situation appear to base their behavior on a guess as to whether their policy preferences are more likely to be achieved by granting certiorari or by denying it.

Regarding the conference vote, we mentioned in Chapter 10 that Chief Justice Burger would occasionally delay announcing his own policy views until all the other justices had announced theirs. The reason for this delay was apparently that the Chief Justice was unsure how one or more other justices would vote, which left him uncertain as to what the majority side was going to be on the case. This in turn meant that he was unsure about what position he would have to endorse so as to gain control of opinion assignment. By waiting until the other justices had announced their views, he could determine how he would have to vote so as to control opinion assignment. But if the Chief Justice had always started with perfect knowledge of the other justices' policy preferences, he would never have had to delay announcing his own views.

The final vote also shows evidence of the impact of uncertainty about the justices' preferences. For example, Maltzman, Spriggs, and Wahlbeck (2000) show that there are extensive negotiations between majority opinion writers and other justices whose support is needed for Court majorities. Of course, if a majority opinion writer has perfect information about the other justices' policy preferences, he would not have to negotiate at all: he could simply calculate in advance precisely what opinion he would have to write so as to attract the votes of at least four other justices. This suggests that the negotiations that Maltzman et al. found on the Court are a byproduct of uncertainty: the majority opinion writer was seeking information about what it would take to attract the other justices' votes, and as the negotiations proceeded the other justices were gradually revealing information about what concessions would be required to win their votes. If the majority opinion writer had started with perfect information about the others' preferences, the transaction costs entailed by these negotiations could have been avoided.

An additional kind of uncertainty that may affect the justices' ability to be strategically rational in the early stages of decision-making is that the justices may have difficulty predicting who will become the majority opinion writer. The reason stems from the complexity of the issues involving how the justices should be expected to vote on the conference vote (stage 2), and whether the ultimate opinion assigner will choose (in stage 3) to self-assign or to assign the majority opinion to someone else. If these choices are difficult for the justices to predict, it will be difficult for them to predict what the final outcome will be, hence it will also be difficult for them to determine how to be strategically rational at the earlier stages of decision-making.

The empirical evidence, combined with the preceding arguments about uncertainty, suggest that it would be desirable to construct a model involving how strategic justices make decisions under uncertainty. If this kind of expected-utility model were formulated, whether the justice is risk averse or risk acceptant can be expected to influence his or her strategic behavior. In fact, although the phrases *aggressive granting* and *defensive denial* are uninformative about decision-making on certiorari when there is perfect information (as we argued in Chapters 9 and 10), these terms may not be completely inappropriate for situations in which four justices who want policy to move in a particular direction are uncertain as to whether a fifth vote can be found for their desired policy change. As mentioned in Chapter 10 (see note 1), for example, it might be that a justice's "aggressive granting" strategy—we suggested that "risky granting" would be a better label—indicates that the justice is risk acceptant when faced with uncertainty: even if only three other justices initially support certiorari, the risk-acceptant justice might be willing to support certiorari (thereby giving it the needed fourth vote) in the expectation that a fifth vote can be found for the policy change that the justice desires. Similarly, a justice's "defensive denial" strategy might indicate that the justice is risk averse when faced with uncertainty: even if three justices are already willing to grant certiorari, the risk-averse justice might be unwilling to support certiorari (thereby denying it the needed fourth vote) in fear that a fifth vote could not be found for the policy change the justice desires. Even if the "objective" probabilities of what is likely to happen are judged to be the same by both the risk-acceptant and the risk-averse justices, their differing levels of risk acceptance and risk aversion may induce them to behave in different ways.

In general, then, we think that relaxing the perfect-information assumption by incorporating uncertainty about each other's policy preferences would be a fruitful modification of our model. We suspect that any discrepancies between our current model's predictions and the empirical evidence would be substantially reduced by this kind of modification.

Do the Justices Always Have Clear and Fixed Preferences?

A different kind of uncertainty involving the justices' preferences is that a justice may sometimes be unsure at the outset of a case just what his or her own policy preferences are. In fact, the justice might even lack any preferences at all at the outset and develop preferences only as the case unfolds. Lack of preferences, or even just having some uncertainty about one's own preferences, can be seen as violating Assumption 5.1, which states that "Each justice has preferences over the legal policies that might be considered by the Supreme Court on each case."

For one case in which the justices' preferences were probably quite unclear at the outset, consider *New Jersey v. New York* (1998; 523 U.S. 767), which involved a dispute between New York and New Jersey over what parts of Ellis Island (the site of the Statue of Liberty) lay in which state. It seems unlikely that, at the outset of this case, any of the justices had clear preferences over the various possible outcomes. Although this may be an extreme example, it is certainly not uncommon for a justice's policy preferences over the possible options in a given case to become clearer and more nuanced as the case works its way through the Court's decision-making process. The Court's oral arguments stage, which we have omitted from our model because no collective decisions are made in it, may be a significant part of the process by which a justice develops and clarifies his or her own policy preferences (and also learns about the preferences of the other justices from their questions and comments).

Of course, a justice initially lacking clear preferences on a case would find it difficult to make strategic calculations because he would not know precisely what policy goal he is trying to achieve. And if this justice does not know how to behave at the outset, because of the uncertainty of his own policy preferences, other justices will find it even more difficult to make their own strategic calculations. The reason, of course, is that they would not initially know—indeed could not know—what the first justice would do. Thus, the existence of unclear preferences would seem to affect whether the justices can be expected to behave in a strategically calculated manner.

Another important observation about the justices' preferences is that their preferences sometimes change. This sometimes happens rather quickly: there are well-known instances in which a justice begins a case with one set of views on what would be a desirable policy but then concludes during the Court's decision-making process that some other policy is more desirable. It is also clear that some justices show evidence of having undergone long-term preference changes, and there is a scholarly literature that tries to assess how much this has happened for various justices (see, e.g., Epstein et al. 1998).

Either kind of preference change could cause problems in testing our model. A short-term change in preferences can cause what might appear to be a logical inconsistency in a justice's behavior during the decision-making on a case. In fact, this kind of within-case preference change is a possible cause of the vote switching discussed in Chapter 10. And a long-term change in preferences means that if we are estimating the location of a justice's ideal point on the basis of votes from early in his Court career but the justice then experiences some fundamental preference changes, use of these early career estimates may lead to mistaken predictions about how he will behave on the Court, and how the Court itself will thus behave, later in his career.

Modeling preference formation, preference clarification, or preference change is likely to lead a theorist in the direction of various kinds of psychological models (such as models from cognitive psychology, learning theory, or social psychology). Nonetheless, we think that such a psychological model would eventually have to be unified with a model of strategic rationality. The reason is that a model of how a justice forms, clarifies, or changes his or her initial policy preferences will not necessarily tell us how the justice should be expected to behave throughout the Court's multistage decision-making process on any one case.

Are Supreme Court Cases Independent from Each Other?

A third key assumption in our model is that the justices' behavior on one case is completely independent from their behavior on all subsequent cases. This is a direct implication of Assumption 5.9, which states that "Each justice considers policies that might be adopted in any future case to have no relevance to his or her choice of a policy on the current case."

In one sense, this is certainly a justifiable assumption: Supreme Court justices are independent actors who can freely exercise their own individual judgments on each legal case as it arises. Nonetheless, strategically rational justices may find it beneficial to consider how the case currently under consideration might affect their own future behavior on the Court's future decisions. There are at least two different kinds of future consequences that a justice might want to take into account on the current case: what the future stream of Court cases might be, as influenced by the Court's decision in the current case, and whether the justice's behavior on the current case will influence whether he or she is seen as a trustworthy opinion writer on future cases.

THE FUTURE STREAM OF COURT CASES

If some particular policy is adopted on the current case, it seems reasonable to think that the justice will expect this new policy to affect what future cases are likely to come before the Court. If a current Court decision can indeed be expected to affect the kinds of cases that the Court will have to consider in the future, this may lead the current justices to respond to the current case in terms of the possible future decisions.

For example, if a justice would like to have these future cases heard because she wants to move policy in the direction desired by the likely plaintiffs in these cases, and because she predicts that, if given the opportunity, the future Courts would actually move policy in the direction she and these plaintiffs desire, then she will want the current case decided in a way that would invite this kind of future litigation. In contrast, if another justice would prefer not to have these future cases heard because he does not want to move legal policy in the direction that the future Courts are likely to take in these cases, he would want the current case handled in a way that forecloses this kind of future litigation.

Furthermore, precisely because a Court decision moves policy in a particular direction, or forecloses a particular direction of policy change, potential litigants are likely to interpret the decision as signaling what direction, if any, some future Court majority may be willing to move. These potential litigants will then choose their legal strategies accordingly, and the justices on the Court may eventually have to respond to some of the legal cases that result.

We provide two illustrations of these arguments. In the first, the justices in the Court majority may have desired the future stream of cases that seemed likely to result from their decision. In the second, the justices in the Court majority may have disliked the future stream of cases that seemed likely to result from one possible decision they could have made, and for this reason rejected this particular decision.

In the first illustration, the Supreme Court ruled in *PGA Tour v. Martin* (2001; 532 U.S. 661) that the Americans with Disabilities Act (ADA) applied to the Professional Golfers Association (PGA) Tour. Golf courses were deemed places of public accommodation, and because walking the course was not considered by the Court to be integral to the game of golf, the PGA Tour had to accommodate the request of disabled golfers to use a cart. This decision was widely regarded as expanding the scope of coverage of the ADA. As a result, both the PGA Tour and the United States Golf Association (USGA), which runs a variety of golf tournaments, have received applications from other disabled golfers requesting other kinds of accommodations. Thus, the Court's decision in *PGA Tour v. Martin* was clearly not the "final" vote on this general issue, and the justices in the majority may have based their decisions partly on what they considered to be the desirability of the future stream of cases that seemed likely to materialize.

In the second illustration, the Supreme Court ruled in *Dickerson v. United States* (2000; 530 U.S. 428) that it was not going to weaken the requirements of the "Miranda warning," established in *Miranda v. Arizona* (1966; 384 U.S. 436), which police officers are required to give suspects. For the Court majority, a key problem was what would replace the Miranda warning. One possibility, advanced in 18 U.S.C. §3501 (originally passed into law in 1968), was that the "voluntariness" of the suspect's statement or confession should be the critical issue. In fact, it was section §3501 that was the focus of the litigation in the *Dickerson* case, and section §3501 specified that a trial judge, in determining the voluntariness of a statement or confession,

shall take into consideration all the circumstances surrounding the giving of the confession, including

(1) the time elapsing between arrest and arraignment of the defendant making the confession, if it was made after arrest and before arraignment,

(2) whether such defendant knew the nature of the offense with which he was charged or of which he was suspected at the time of making the confession,

(3) whether or not such defendant was advised or knew that he was not required to make any statement and that any such statement could be used against him,

(4) whether or not such defendant had been advised prior to questioning of his right to the assistance of counsel; and

(5) whether or not such defendant was without the assistance of counsel when questioned and when giving such confession.

The presence or absence of any of the above-mentioned factors to be taken into consideration by the judge need not be conclusive on the issue of voluntariness of the confession.

However, the Court majority in *Dickerson* seemed uncomfortable with what it referred to as this section's "totality-of-the-circumstances test," arguing in their opinion that this test "is more difficult than Miranda for officers to conform to, and for courts to apply consistently." Thus, the justices in the majority may have been worried about the future stream of cases that seemed likely to arise as various aspects of this totality-of-the-circumstances test were challenged and came to the Court for adjudication. For these justices, maintaining the Miranda warning and foreclosing this future stream of cases may have seemed the best resolution of this dispute.[1]

This discussion suggests that instead of analyzing Supreme Court decision-making as if it were a single-period game, as implied by Assumption 5.9 and as exemplified by our own model, Supreme Court decision-making should be analyzed as if it were a multiperiod game—that is, as one that takes place over several time periods. For example, a justice's decision-making process on the current case might have the following components:

1. The justice would begin by making an assumption about what the Court decision will be on the current case at time t (for example, "What would happen if the Court overrules *Miranda*?"); the justice would then predict the consequences of this decision at time t for the Court's probable decisions on cases likely to arise in the $t + 1$ time period; the justice would then predict the consequences of these decisions at times t and $t + 1$ for the Court's probable decisions on cases likely to arise in the $t + 2$ time period; and so forth. The value of this entire stream of decisions to the justice would be the sum of the value of the outcome assumed from the current case at time t, plus the value of the expected outcomes at time $t + 1$, plus the value of the expected outcomes at time $t + 2$, and so forth.

2. The justice would then make an alternative assumption about what the Court decision will be on the current case at time t for example, "What would happen if the Court maintains *Miranda*?"); the justice would predict the consequences of this alternative decision at time t for the Court's probable decisions on cases likely to arise in the $t + 1$ time period; the justice would then predict the consequences of these decisions at times t and $t + 1$ for the Court's probable decisions on cases likely to arise in the $t + 2$ time period; and so forth. The value of this stream of decisions to the justice would be the sum of the value of the alternative outcome from the current case at time t, plus the value of the expected outcomes at time $t + 1$, plus the value of the expected outcomes at time $t + 2$, and so forth.

3. Finally, the justice would compare the values of the two different streams of decisions, and would base his or her decision regarding the current case on the total value that he or she places not just on the Court's possible decision on the current case but also on the Court's probable decisions on the two streams of future cases likely to emerge as a consequence of the two possible Court decisions on the current case.

In multiperiod models it is usually assumed that an actor evaluates outcomes from future decisions somewhat differently than outcomes from the current decision. In particular, it is often assumed that an actor discounts the future to some degree. For example, even if the Court's decisions on different cases would be of equal value to a justice if decided at the same time, the justice would place a higher value on the Court decisions that occur closer to the present than on the Court decisions that occur further in the future.

Of course, it is possible for justices to have different discount rates: one justice may have a high discount rate, which means that he values present Court opinions relatively highly compared to future Court opinions, whereas a second justice may have a lower discount rate, which means that she weighs the impact of future Court opinions more heavily. Whatever the justice's specific discount rate, the strategically rational justice would prefer the Court opinion on the current case that would generate that particular stream of future Court cases whose opinions would have the highest total discounted value for the justice.[2]

A JUSTICE'S REPUTATION FOR TRUSTWORTHINESS

Even when justices have complete information about each other's ideal points, the Chief Justice as majority opinion assigner may have difficulty deciding whether to assign the opinion on the basis of what policies the other justices strategically endorse on the conference vote (as they try to attract the majority opinion assignment from him) or simply on the basis of the other justices' ideal points. As we emphasized in our Chapter 8 analysis of the conference vote, the Chief Justice should be concerned that if he assigns the opinion on the basis of what policy another justice endorses on the conference vote (for example, a policy at the Chief Justice's ideal point), the opinion writer he selects might later renege by writing the final opinion as close as possible to her own ideal point rather than as close as possible to the policy she endorsed on the conference vote. For a single-period game such as in our model (Assumption 5.9), we concluded that because there would be no cost to reneging, the opinion writer would always write the final opinion as close as possible to his or her own ideal point. But, anticipating precisely this behavior, the Chief Justice would respond by basing his assignment decisions just on the other justices' ideal points.

However, if the Chief Justice sees some other justice as trustworthy, this means that he would trust her to write the final opinion as close as possible to the policy she had endorsed on the conference vote. Of course, for her to develop this kind of reputation for trustworthiness, especially with regard to behavior on important cases, is something that may require multiple time periods to establish because the Chief Justice may trust her only to the extent that she has already behaved in a trustworthy manner on previous cases. But given the longevity of the justices on the Court, their repeated interactions would give each justice ample opportunities to maintain a reputation for trustworthiness. All that is required would be to repeatedly write final opinions that are as close as possible to the policy he or she endorsed on the conference vote rather than to write final opinions that are as close as possible to his or her own ideal point.

However, it is an open question as to how any justice would initially develop such a reputation for trustworthiness. After all, if the Chief Justice always assigns opinions on the basis of the other justices' ideal points, then no justice will ever be given an opportunity to demonstrate that she will write final opinions as close as possible to the policies she endorsed on the conference vote. Nonetheless, the small size of the Court and the ease of identifying who has written what kind of opinion may create an incentive for all justices to behave in a trustworthy manner from the outset (see, e.g., Axelrod 1984). Following this logic, the Chief Justice might then decide at the outset to trust the other justices to write final opinions as close as possible to the policies they endorsed on the conference vote, and so would make opinion assignments on this basis.

Of course, as we noted in Chapter 8, if either the open-bidding or median-holdout version of our model accurately characterizes Supreme Court decision-making, then this issue of trust and trustworthiness in the opinion assignment process would be irrelevant. The reason is that whoever is assigned the majority opinion will be forced to write it at the ideal point of the median justice. Hence, one might not want to invest in the development of models of reputation development on the Court until it is determined whether it matters who the majority opinion writer is.

Regular and Special Concurrences

Our model gives the justices two primary pairs of choices on the final vote: they can write or join a majority opinion, or they can write or join a dissenting opinion. However, the justices actually have a somewhat broader range of choices than this. Most importantly, on any one case a justice can write or join a regular concurrence, or write or join a special concurrence.

With a regular concurrence, the justice not only joins another justice's majority opinion but also writes or joins an additional opinion. In a sense, a regular concurrence simply presents additional thoughts that a justice considers relevant to the majority's arguments in their opinion.

With a special concurrence, the justice is agreeing with the majority's disposition of the current case (that is, with whether the Court affirms or reverses the decision of the lower court regarding which of the litigants should prevail) but is disagreeing with the majority opinion as to what the general policy should be for such cases. In writing or joining a special concurrence, a justice is not joining what the majority opinion writer is intending to be the majority opinion.

For a justice to write or join a regular concurrence does not change the outcome of a case: the majority opinion will still be the majority opinion. But for a justice to write or join a special concurrence can change the outcome of a case: if too many justices write or join special concurrences (or else dissent), the majority opinion writer will be unable to attract a majority of votes, and the plurality opinion that results will lack precedential value.

The key question here is when justices will write or join regular concurrences and why they will write or join special concurrences. And in fact, Segal and Spaeth (2002, 386–87) advance a detailed argument about which justices will do what:

Those who join the majority opinion are ideologically closer to the opinion writer than those who write regular concurrences; regular concurrers, in turn, are ideologically closer to the majority opinion writer than special concurrers; and to complete the picture, special concurrers are ideologically closer to the majority opinion writer than are justices who dissent.[3]

However, because the Segal-Spaeth argument does not take into account who wants to maintain or upset the status quo policy, we think that the argument can lead to erroneous predictions.

For an example, see Figure 7.1. Assume that justice J_6 is the majority opinion writer, and note that he can write the majority opinion at his own ideal point of J_6. Justice J_7 is obviously a minority-side justice, and note that his J_7 ideal point is closer to opinion writer J_6's ideal point (and opinion) than is justice J_4's ideal point. So Segal and Spaeth would predict that justice J_7 is more likely to join the majority opinion (or to join or write a regular concurrence) than justice J_4. Yet it seems clear that justice J_7 would write or join a dissent: he wants to move policy rightward from SQ but justice J_6's majority opinion at J_6 is moving policy to the left. And because the opinion at J_6 lies inside justice J_4's preferred-to set, it is justice J_4 who would presumably join the majority opinion (although he might also—see below—write or join a regular concurrence). Indeed, even though justices J_1, J_2, and J_3 have the ideal points that are the most distant of all from the opinion at J_6, all three would also join this opinion at J_6 (although they might also write or join a regular concurrence); these justices would certainly not dissent. So we conclude that the Segal-Spaeth argument leads to logically questionable predictions about who will do what.

In contrast, we think this question of who will do what can be more satisfactorily addressed in terms of our own model. From this perspective, there are three different categories of justices who will respond differently regarding concurrences: (a) majority-side justices for whom the draft majority opinion lies inside their preferred-to sets of SQ, (b) majority-side justices for whom the draft majority opinion lies outside their preferred-to sets of SQ, and (c) justices with minority-side ideal points.

For the first category of justices, whenever a draft majority opinion lies inside a majority-side justice's preferred-to set, our model clearly implies that such a justice will join the draft majority opinion. (In Figure 7.1, in fact, this applies to all majority-side justices: the opinion at J_6 lies inside all their preferred-to sets, so they would all join the draft majority opinion.) Even so, if a justice does not feel that the draft opinion is close enough to his own ideal point, we would expect this justice to be more likely to write a regular concurrence. By joining the majority opinion, he is helping ensure that this new policy does gain majority support (after all, it is better for him than the status quo), but he is also indicating via the concurring opinion that the new policy could be even better than it already is.

We would expect differences among these category (a) justices with regard to whether they consider a draft opinion to be close enough to their respective ideal points before they decide to write or join a regular concurrence. One justice might be very tolerant of majority opinions that differ from her ideal point: as long as the majority opinion lies inside her preferred-to set and is not too distant from her ideal point, she will join the majority opinion and not write or join a regular concurrence. This opinion could be quite far from her ideal point but she would still not insist on writing or joining a regular concurrence. In contrast, another justice might be very intolerant of majority opinions that differ from his ideal point: even though the majority opinion lies inside his preferred-to set, he will write or join a regular concurrence because the majority opinion is not close enough to his ideal point. For this justice, even a relatively close opinion might induce him to write or join a regular concurrence.

In fact, these two justices could have identical ideal points yet would respond differently to a draft majority opinion inside their preferred-to sets: both justices would join the majority opinion but the intolerant justice would also insist on writing or joining a regular concurrence. In effect, then, we are suggesting that each justice has a range of tolerance for opinions that are inside his or her preferred-to set but that differ from his or her ideal point: a justice with a wide range of tolerance will be less likely to write or join regular concurrences than a justice with a narrow range of tolerance. For each justice, though, the farther a draft opinion is from the justice's ideal point, the more likely is the justice to join or write a regular concurrence.

For the category (b) justices, we suggest that when a draft opinion lies to the outside of the preferred-to set of a majority-side justice, this justice will be more likely to write a special concurrence. This justice does want the Court's policy to move in his direction from SQ (this is also the majority's direction) but the justice thinks that the draft majority opinion goes too far because it has ended up to the outside of his preferred-to set. By writing or joining a special concurrence rather than a dissenting opinion, the justice is indicating that he likes the direction of policy change but is objecting that the policy went too far (because it ended up outside his preferred-to set). For this reason, the justice refuses to join the opinion, thereby reducing its chances of gaining a Court majority. (In Figure 7.1, if we assume the draft majority opinion is at J_5, we would predict that majority-side justice J_6 would write a special concurrence in response: he likes the fact that policy is moved leftward from SQ by the draft majority opinion, but he thinks the policy at J_5 goes too far to the left, thereby leaving it outside his $W_{J6}(SQ)$ preferred-to set.)

In general, it is the majority-side justices whose ideal points are closest to SQ who will be most likely to write or join special concurrences, although whether they actually do depends on whether the draft majority opinion is inside or outside their respective preferred-to sets of SQ. (An alternative argument here would simply be that when the draft opinion lies outside the justice's preferred-to set of SQ, he or she will write or join a dissent.)

The category (c) justices are already covered by our model: we generally expect that a minority-side justice will write or join a dissent from a draft majority opinion. The primary exception occurs (as described in Chapter 6) when a minority-side justice, by voting on the majority side in conference and thereby gaining control of the majority opinion assignment, can ensure that the majority opinion is written as close as possible to SQ, thus preventing the majority opinion from being even worse.

Our arguments here clearly focus on where the draft majority opinion lies in relation to each justice's ideal point and to the location of the status quo policy rather than simply on the ideological distances among the justices, as argued by Segal and Spaeth. Both sets of arguments should be empirically testable, at least in principle. However, our argument on regular concurrences does suggest that there may be some idiosyncratic differences among justices regarding their range of tolerance for opinions that differ from their ideal points. Such idiosyncratic differences among justices might be difficult to measure and incorporate in a systematic empirical test, although perhaps each individual's range of tolerance could be estimated empirically from one set of cases (that is, holding everything else constant, how often does a justice write or join a regular concurrence?) and then used as a parameter in empirical tests of a theory regarding opinion joining in another set of cases.

How Many Issue Dimensions Are There?

Assumption 5.5 states that "Supreme Court policy-making on each case takes place in a one-dimensional issue space." This means, in effect, that all the justices evaluate all the possible issues in each case in terms of just one common dimension. As discussed in Chapter 10, there are empirical reasons to think that Supreme Court decision-making is characterized by one primary "liberal/conservative" dimension.

Nonetheless, at least some cases undoubtedly raise multiple issues and thus entail multiple issue dimensions. Indeed, one might argue that every Supreme Court case involves at least two dimensions. The first dimension would involve what the Court should do about the lower court's disposition of the case; that is, should the Court affirm or reverse the lower court's decision regarding the litigants? This first dimension might be called the *affirm/reverse dimension*. The second dimension involves what general policy the Court should establish for the current case; it is this second dimension— we will call it the *policy dimension* here—on which our unidimensional model has focused.

At least in principle, these are two distinct dimensions, and a justice may have a most-preferred outcome on each of these dimensions. That is, he or she may have clear preferences over who should win or lose the case, and he or she may also have clear preferences over what general policy should be established for this general kind of case. The combination of these two most-preferred outcomes, one on each dimension, would define the justice's ideal point in this two-dimensional space. As before, each justice's goal would be to get the Court to make decisions on the case that are as close as possible to his or her own ideal point.

An alternative multidimensional approach is to ignore the affirm/reverse aspects of a case and focus just on the existence of multiple policy dimensions; after all, the legal fates of particular litigants may be of little consequence to the justices (especially if they are unsavory characters with substantial criminal histories). Some cases will clearly involve two or more fundamental policy issues from the outset, as when two different constitutional doctrines come head-to-head in a case. Furthermore, justices may occasionally have strategic reasons for changing the number of issue dimensions. For example, if a justice appears to be on the minority side on one policy dimension, he may have an incentive to introduce a second policy dimension on which he is on the majority side; this second policy dimension would be deliberately selected so that it breaks apart the majority coalition that was dominating decision-making on the first dimension. Epstein and Knight (1998, 88–95) discuss several examples of this kind of strategy involving Chief Justice Burger.[4]

In previous work (Hammond, Bonneau, and Sheehan 1999) we provided one possible representation, with graphical illustrations, of how Supreme Court decision-making might occur in a two-dimensional issue space. As it turned out, at least some of the propositions we have derived from our one-dimensional model here seem to have counterparts in this two-dimensional setting.

However, when a second dimension is added to what had been a unidimensional issue space, a critical issue arises: there is now the potential for majority-rule instability. That is, although there always exists an overall equilibrium policy—the ideal point of the median justice—on a single issue dimension, formal theorists have shown (see Mueller 1989, 67–73, for a survey) that it is only under very restrictive conditions that an overall equilibrium policy exists in a multidimensional setting. Only in the rare case that there is a justice who is the median justice on all possible dimensions will there be a multidimensional equilibrium. The general nonexistence of a multidimensional median means that for every draft majority opinion that might be adopted, there is almost always an alternative policy that is preferred by some other Court majority. So the question is: how can any kind of policy stability be reached on a multidimensional Court lacking a median justice? That is, what would prevent the Court from cycling endlessly from policy to policy, each preferred to its predecessor by a different Court majority?

Unfortunately, what should be expected to happen on a Supreme Court with multiple issue dimensions is not entirely clear, and the lack of a clear answer presents two closely related difficulties. First, if there is no multidimensional equilibrium outcome, it is not clear what opinion some Court majority would adopt on the final vote. What would we predict to be the final outcome if, for every policy that might be adopted, there is always an alternative policy that is preferred by some Court majority? Second, as we have made clear in our model, strategic decision-making depends on knowing what the final outcome will be. But if the final outcome is unpredictable because there is no equilibrium outcome, it is difficult to determine how strategically rational justices would behave at the earlier stages of the decision-making process.

There are three possible solutions to this problem of majority-rule instability on the Court, all involving restrictions on the set of policy alternatives that the justices impose on themselves. The first kind of self-imposed restriction involves the way the Court sequences its decisions on a case. In the second kind of restriction, the justices give sole agenda-setting power to the majority opinion writer in order to prevent bargaining and negotiation from continuing indefinitely. The third kind of restriction involves an institutionalized agreement among the justices not to challenge the majority opinions each of them may write; this norm is a kind of generalized quid pro quo involving mutual deference among those who write the majority opinion.

We discuss each of these mechanisms in more detail below, focusing in particular on why rational justices might voluntarily adopt these restrictions on their own freedom of choice.

DIMENSION-BY-DIMENSION DECISION-MAKING

The first explanation for policy stability involves the way the Supreme Court sequences the decisions that it makes on a case. Consider the distinction between the affirm/reverse dimension and the policy dimension. When the justices meet in conference after oral argument, they present their general views on how the case should be settled. Because no draft opinions are yet available, the justices' presentation of their views here tends to be organized along the lines of who wants to affirm the lower court ruling and who wants to reverse this ruling. Then, after the majority opinion writer is appointed and writes a draft majority opinion, the justices conduct the final vote, which involves deciding on the general policy to be established for this kind of case.

One possible interpretation of these decision-making practices is that the justices are first deciding how this case should be resolved (this is the affirm/reverse decision), and only then establishing what the general policy should be. From this perspective, it is interesting to note if a multidimensional decision-making problem is broken down into a sequence of dimension-by-dimension decisions, with one decision firmly established on one dimension before the actors move to the next dimension for the next decision, and so forth, a policy equilibrium is thereby established; see Mueller (1989, 89–91) for an accessible introduction to these general arguments.

In a two-dimensional model of Supreme Court decision-making, then, if the decision on the affirm/reverse dimension is initially made and subsequently treated as fixed by the justices, the decision on the policy dimension can be made without provoking any majority-rule cycling. The overall Court decision that would thereby emerge is simply the aggregate result of these dimension-by-dimension decisions.

As an empirical matter, however, it is not clear that the justices actually settle the affirm/reverse aspects of a case before deciding on a final policy. Our own view is that the justices generally use their preferences on the policy dimension to determine what to do on the affirm/reverse dimension. In fact, we suspect that the affirm/reverse dimension is usually not even an independent dimension: what outcomes the justices choose on it are likely to be determined by their preferences on the policy dimension. Furthermore, whatever is done on the conference vote regarding the affirm/reverse aspects of a case may be largely provisional and subject to change once the final majority opinion is established. Thus, this explanation may not provide an adequate explanation for majority-rule stability on a multidimensional Court.

AGENDA CONTROL AND THE COSTS OF DELAY

For the second explanation, recall that in the agenda-control version of our model the justices not writing the majority opinion voluntarily choose not to offer a counteropinion to the draft being written by the officially designated majority opinion writer. As we noted in Chapter 6, there is a potential problem here: why would these other justices protect the privileged position of the majority opinion writer by voluntarily accepting restrictions on their own ability to amend or replace the draft majority opinion?

One possible answer stems from the work of Baron and Ferejohn (1989) on legislating in a multidimensional setting that lacks a majority-rule equilibrium. The central implication of the Baron-Ferejohn argument for the Supreme Court is that if the justices place a positive value on their own time and energy, then the more time and energy it takes to make a final decision on one case as a result of majority-rule instability and the resulting endless negotiations over what the majority opinion should be, the costlier this delay becomes. There are also opportunity costs because substantial delay in completing a decision on the case, because of the ongoing negotiations, means that decisions will go unmade on subsequent cases that are of considerable interest to the justices. Each justice may thus calculate that although surrendering power to an agenda setter on the case can be costly (because it may produce a final opinion that diverges more from the justice's own ideal point than is absolutely necessary), allowing the decision-making process to continue indefinitely will be even more costly (the result of time and energy expenditures plus the opportunity costs). It follows that "impatient" justices—that is, justices who want to make a decision on the case at hand and move on to the next case—may be willing to allow a majority opinion writer to control the content the agenda of the decision-making process.

A NORM OF DEFERENCE TO THE MAJORITY OPINION WRITER

The third possible explanation for stability in Supreme Court decision-making involves a kind of mutual agreement among the justices—a quid pro quo—not to challenge each other's draft majority opinions.

One way of thinking about this is to assume that justices have preferences over the various kinds of cases that the Supreme Court will hear: although every justice presumably cares at least a little about every kind of case, each justice is likely to care more about some kinds of cases than others. For example, some justices may be particularly concerned about civil rights and civil liberties cases, other justices may be particularly concerned about economic regulation, still other justices may be particularly concerned about federalism and separation-of-powers issues, and so forth. So when a justice becomes the majority opinion writer on one kind of case that is especially important to her, she would greatly prefer that her draft majority opinion not be challenged. Similarly, when a second justice becomes the majority opinion writer on a different kind of case that is especially important to him, he would greatly prefer that his draft majority opinion not be challenged. This suggests that the two justices might be able to reach a mutual accommodation: the first justice would agree not challenge the second justice's opinions on cases about which he especially cares, whereas the second justice would agree not to challenge the first justice's opinions on cases about which she especially cares.

Of course, it would be very complicated (and perhaps unworkable) for the justices to try to make explicit deals about who will defer to whom on what particular kinds of cases. Instead, what may happen is that something like a norm of deference to the majority opinion writer may emerge over time even among rational justices interested only in their personal policy preferences. In effect, then, something that approximates the agenda-control version of our model would be established: this institutionalized norm of deference would protect the agenda-setting authority of the majority opinion writer.

Maintaining this norm of deference to the majority opinion writer may not always be easy: the temptation to defect is likely to be particularly strong on cases about which all the justices have strong policy preferences (e.g., *Bush v. Gore?*). Nonetheless, even rational justices interested only in their own policy preferences may benefit in the long run from the maintenance of a norm of deference on most cases. In fact, because it is easy to identify defectors from the norm, it may even be possible for the justices who adhere to the norm to impose sanctions on those who do not, for example, by concurring in, but not joining, the opinions the defectors are allowed to write, or by not assigning opinions to them at all.

For the Chief Justice as majority opinion assigner, maintaining an equitable distribution of opinion assignments among the justices might contribute to the stability of a norm of deference to the majority opinion writer, even if this means that the Chief Justice will not always get what he considers his own best outcome on each case. After all, if several justices almost never receive an opinion assignment, or receive only the most onerous and least interesting opinions to write, then these justices might have little to lose in organizing challenges to the majority opinion writers' drafts, as suggested by the open-bidding and median-holdout versions of our model.

Whatever the source of stability in the Court's decision-making processes, it does seem clear that there is substantial stability: the Court is able to produce a large number of decisions in each term, and endless cycling and institutional indecision do not seem to occur on most cases. So if a draft majority opinion can be produced on the final vote even when there are two or more policy dimensions, then it may be that the type of analysis we have developed for the one-dimensional setting could be appropriately replicated in a multidimensional setting. Clearly, however, much further research, both theoretical and empirical, remains to be conducted here.

Costly Opinion Writing

Assumption 5.13 states that "Writing the majority opinion is costless for the opinion writer." The fifth possible modification of our model is to assume instead that writing the majority opinion is costly, in the sense that it consumes the opinion writer's scarce time and energy. Several of our results may change if this alternative assumption were adopted.

For example, costly opinion-writing might allow the majority opinion writer somewhat greater latitude in writing his opinion. Thus, even when the opinion writer cannot write the final opinion at his own ideal point because he needs to attract majority support, he might nonetheless be able to write it somewhat closer to his own ideal point than our model allows as long as the other justices do not want to incur the costs of writing a counteropinion and organizing a coalition on its behalf. In general, the greater these costs, the closer the majority opinion writer may be able to approach his own ideal point in his opinion before the other justices will revolt. For an example of a formal model of Supreme Court decision-making when opinion writing is costly see Lax and Cameron (2001).

We would suggest that the greater these costs, the more decision-making will look like the agenda-control version of our model and the less it will look like the open-bidding version. In fact, this general logic suggests an empirical test. For complex, multifaceted cases, which thereby entail relatively high costs for writing a counteropinion, we might expect to observe decision-making processes that approximate the agenda-control version of our model. But for simple and straightforward cases, which thereby entail relatively low costs for writing a counteropinion, we might expect decision-making processes that approximate the open-bidding version of our model to be more likely.

Furthermore, note that the median-holdout version of our model requires little in the way of costly activities by the median justice as she attempts to get a final policy at her ideal point; all she needs to do is say, "I won't sign yet!" Thus, as the opinion-writing costs increase, Supreme Court decision-making may look increasingly like the median-holdout version and less like the open-bidding version.

However, these conjectures raise an interesting question: because the median-holdout strategy is always available to the median justice on a case, and because the open-bidding strategy entails higher decision-making costs than the median-holdout strategy, why would we ever see the justices resort to the open-bidding strategy?

One possible answer is that if the median-holdout strategy fails (that is, if the majority opinion writer chooses not to concede to the median justice's demand that the opinion be written at her ideal point of J_{med}), the result will be a plurality opinion with no precedential value and thus no change in the status quo policy. In fact, this outcome—the maintenance of the status quo policy—would be worse for the median justice than the opinion that the majority opinion writer initially wanted to write but that the median justice refused to support (that is, an opinion inside $W_{Jmed}(SQ)$ but not at J_{med}). In contrast, the open-bidding strategy will always produce a policy at J_{med}, and this policy at J_{med} will always be better than SQ for the median justice. Of course, adoption of this counteropinion at J_{med} would require the expenditure of the time and energy needed to write it and gather support for it.

Whether the median-holdout strategy is more valuable for the median justice (and her supporters) than the open-bidding strategy will thus depend on the relative sizes and probabilities of (a) the policy loss the median justice and her supporters will suffer if the opinion writer does not write a policy at J_{med} and so a plurality opinion results, leaving SQ unchanged, and (b) the time and energy costs that the median justice and her supporters would have to incur in writing and organizing support for a counteropinion at J_{med}. Although we would expect in general that the strategy with the higher expected value will be the one more likely to be adopted, this is a topic that clearly requires more theoretical exploration and development.

There is one other way in which costly time and energy could enter into a revised version of our model. The justices have limited time and energy to expend in each term of the Court, and this limits the number of cases they can hear. For certiorari decisions, then, each justice may have a rather large list of cases for which he or she would, in principle, like to grant certiorari, but the justice may not have sufficient time and energy to hear all such cases. This factor would limit the applicability of our argument in Chapter 9 that certiorari will be granted for every case for which J_{med} is not at SQ. What instead may happen, in effect, is that every petition for which J_{med} is not at SQ will be put on the Court's "discuss list," but only those petitions on the discuss list that some majority considers to be the most important, given their limited time and energy, will be granted certiorari.

Extensions of the Model

The five alternative kinds of assumptions just discussed—uncertainty about each other's ideal points, uncertainty about one's own ideal point, the interdependence of cases, the existence of multiple dimensions, and costly opinion-writing—represent alternatives to several of the most important assumptions that we adopted in Chapter 5. For most of these alternative assumptions there already exist formal modeling techniques that could be deployed, and well-trained formal theorists could work with students of the Court to develop and test models that are based on various combinations of these alternative assumptions. However, additional models might also be developed that incorporate other kinds of judicial institutions.

One obvious possibility involves the incorporation of a lower court with strategic judges in our model of Supreme Court decision-making. For very few kinds of cases does the Supreme Court have original jurisdiction; the major category involves disputes between the states (as in the *New Jersey v. New York* case discussed earlier). Most other cases come to the Court from some kind of lower court, usually either a federal appeals court or a state supreme court. If the judges on a lower court are strategically rational and make decisions in the same general way as the justices on the Supreme Court, then one might ask whether there are strategic interactions between the lower court and the Supreme Court. For example, we have argued in this book that the location of the status quo policy—the legal state of affairs—has a critical impact on Supreme Court decision-making. But some lower court, such as a federal appeals court or a state supreme court, may be able to affect what the status quo policy actually happens to be for the Supreme Court; by manipulating this status quo policy through their own decisions, the lower-court judges might be able to manipulate the Supreme Court's decisions.

For example, a federal appeals court may be able to impose a new policy on its own circuit on some issue, and this new policy will remain in effect on its circuit unless overruled by the Supreme Court. For example, consider *Hopwood v. University of Texas Law School* (1996; 78 F 3ᵈ 932), the decision by the Fifth Circuit Court of Appeals invalidating the affirmative-action admissions policies of the University of Texas Law School: this policy was in force in the Fifth Circuit for more than six years until the Supreme Court ruled on this topic in *Grutter v. Bollinger* (2003; 288 F 3ᵈ 732). The policy chosen by the Fifth Circuit Court could thus be considered to have changed an aspect of the status quo policy that the Supreme Court ultimately felt it had to face (because of conflict among the circuits). In fact, by the time of the *Grutter* decision, it would have been accurate to describe the status quo "policy" in this issue area as a composite, with several different policies holding in several different circuits around the country.

If a lower court can influence the status quo policy in this fashion, then it may be possible for the judges on the lower court to strategically select a policy that would affect the location of the status quo policy for the Supreme Court in such a way that the Court makes that decision that the lower-court judges want the Court to make. This is an interesting and important problem, and in other work (see Hammond, Bonneau, and Sheehan, forthcoming) we have expanded our model of Supreme Court decision-making to include a strategically rational lower court judge.

In one version of this expanded model, when the lower-court decision is appealed to the Supreme Court, the influence of the lower-court judge on the Supreme Court's choice depends on the location of the lower-court judge's ideal point vis-à-vis the justice's ideal points. With some preference configurations on the lower court and the Supreme Court, the lower-court judge has little influence on the Supreme Court's decision, whereas with other configurations, the judge can decisively influence the Supreme Court's decision. As with our model of Supreme Court decision-making itself, this expanded model requires further research, both theoretical and empirical.

Exogenous Preferences and the Impact of The Law

Our assumption that Supreme Court justices pursue their personal policy goals says nothing about the origins of the justices' preferences. Instead, we simply take the justices' ideal points as given and then determine the impact of their ideal points' locations on the location of the final majority opinion. Because we have made very little reference to "the law" in the previous chapters in this book, one might thus construe our model as implying that "the law" does not matter to the justices. For this reason, some readers may be inclined to dismiss our theory and model because the justices in our model appear completely unconcerned about the law or any other purely legal considerations.

However, this would be a serious misunderstanding of our approach. In fact, we would argue that it is the law, along with the facts of a case, the justices' personal policy preferences, and perhaps many other factors as well, which collectively determine each justice's ideal point on a case. Some justices may weigh factors like precedent and the law quite heavily on some case, whereas other justices may be more likely to follow their own personal policy preferences on the case; for some justices, an interpretation of a case from the viewpoint of "strict construction" or "original intent" may be most appropriate on some case, whereas other justices may view the Constitution as a "living document" whose application to the case that must be adapted to the times. All of these factors can influence the location of a justice's ideal point. Moreover, any one justice may have different reasons for his policy preferences on different cases.

In fact, when we refer to a justice's "personal policy preferences," it may even be that the justice has entirely altruistic motives for his or her judicial decision-making: what the justice may want is merely what he or she considers to be "good jurisprudence for the whole country." Nonetheless, we have retained the phrase *personal policy preferences* because, even with justices with the most altruistic of motives, it is the justice's personal interpretation of what is "good jurisprudence for the country" that ultimately matters. Moreover, even within a Court populated only by the most altruistic of justices, "politics" can still be expected to exist if these justices have conflicting interpretations of what is good jurisprudence for the country and each justice pursues his or her own notion of what is good jurisprudence on each case.

We are agnostic as to where the justices' policy preferences originate, and it does not matter to our model anyway. In fact, we would argue that one of the primary virtues of our model is that it is applicable to Supreme Court decision-making regardless of the particular mix of considerations that influence how each justice forms his or her preferences over the available options. As long as each justice's preferences are single-peaked on the issue dimension—that is, as long as the value of alternative policies to the justice declines monotonically the farther the policy is from the justice's ideal point—our model is appropriate.

Thus, although our model may appear to some as overly disconnected from the judicial and legal reasoning processes in which the Supreme Court justices clearly engage (at least publicly), we think our model is connected in a rather intimate fashion to this judicial and legal reasoning via the locations of what we call the justices' "ideal points."

Broader Applications

In the most abstract and general sense, our book simply develops a formal model of how a particular set of mathematical rules governs how a set of points on a line leads to the selection of another point on this line. It is only when we apply this model to the Supreme Court—defining the mathematical rules in terms of "the Court's multistage decision-making procedures," calling the line an "issue dimension," referring to some of the points as "the ideal points of the justices" and another of the points as the "status quo policy," and referring to the point that they select as "the final majority opinion"—that it becomes a model of "Supreme Court decision-making."

As an abstract and general model, however, our model of points interacting on a line could be applied to other courts, such as the multimember federal Courts of Appeals, state supreme courts, the high courts of other countries, and even to multimember regulatory commissions and other such institutions. Although particular aspects of the model would have to be modified to fit these other institutions (especially the institutional procedures—the mathematical operations—governing how one set of points on the line leads to the selection of some other point), the underlying theory would remain substantially the same.

For example, although an application of this model to the United States Courts of Appeals would require exclusion of the certiorari stage (because these courts do not have discretionary jurisdiction), the underlying theory— that a court majority has to support the final decision for the decision to be definitive, and that each judge will make those choices that lead to a final outcome that is as close as possible to his or her ideal point—would remain essentially the same. And of course, the appeals court judges may on occasion expect that their case will end up in the Supreme Court, and so they might craft their opinions strategically, as noted in the previous section, so as to induce the Court to adopt the final opinion the appeals court judges most prefer.

Another possible reinterpretation of our general model focuses on what the line represents. In this book, we have generally represented the line in our model as a "liberal/conservative" issue dimension. Indeed, for many students of judicial politics this will probably be the most obvious or plausible interpretation because this interpretation meshes well not only with previous theoretical discussions of Supreme Court decision-making but also with a large body of empirical work involving decision-making on the Court.

Strictly speaking, however, there is nothing intrinsic to our formal model that says anything at all about what this line represents. That is, the purely formal aspects of our model say nothing about what it is over which the justices have their preferences. This raises the possibility that if some key decision-making criterion in the "legal model" (such as precedent, plain meaning, original intent, or legislative history) can be represented as a line (for example, involving more or less of the criterion), and if each justice can plausibly be considered as having an ideal point and single-peaked preferences over whatever it is that the line represents, then our formal model could conceivably be viewed as a model of "legal" decision-making. If our model is at all amenable to this interpretation, this would advance a research agenda that is rather different, both theoretically and empirically, from the one that has guided most of our discussions in this book.

Conclusion

For too long, research on Supreme Court decision-making in the field of judicial politics and public law has proceeded in an overly atheoretical fashion. Although there has been considerable high-quality empirical research in the field, and although much has been learned about the

Supreme Court as a result, most of this research has been conducted without the benefit of a clear, consistent, and coherent theory of decision-making by the individual justices or of collective, multistage decision-making by the Court as a whole. In this book, we have advanced a theory and developed a formal model of multistage decision-making by strategically rational justices that we think will not only help organize and make sense of the knowledge that is already available about the Court but will also help initiate, or at least contribute to, a substantial program of theoretically guided empirical research.

If some reader is already convinced that the attitudinal model, or at least the rational-choice version of the attitudinal model, accurately describes Supreme Court decision-making, then one possible implication is that this reader should also be convinced that the propositions we have advanced in Chapters 6 through 9 accurately describe Supreme Court decision-making. The reason we make this argument is simply that the propositions stem from a model that we have deliberately constructed so as to represent, as much as we are capable, the rational-choice interpretation of the attitudinal model.

If our propositions are empirically tested and found to be solidly supported by the evidence, this could be interpreted as providing substantial validation of the attitudinal model as an explanation for Supreme Court decision-making. But if our propositions are empirically tested and found not to be supported by the evidence, this could be interpreted as raising some questions about the adequacy of the attitudinal model as an explanation of Supreme Court decision-making. Of course, it may be that the empirical test is flawed, or it may be that our interpretation of the attitudinal model— that is, our formal model—is flawed. But if the empirical tests are well done, and if our model is accepted as a valid interpretation of the attitudinal model, then any empirical problems are almost inevitably going to raise questions about the attitudinal model itself.

This is why those who are skeptical about the adequacy of the attitudinal model as an explanation of Supreme Court decision-making still need to understand and use our model (or at least some modification of it). The reason is simply that if the skeptic is correct in challenging the attitudinal model, he or she should be able to use our model to demonstrate, via a series of empirical tests on Supreme Court decision-making, that our model leaves unexplained a large proportion of the variance in the data. So if empirical tests that are based on our model do not perform very well, one possible conclusion (although only one among many) is that the problem lies not just in our own model but in the attitudinal model itself.

Of course, another possible conclusion is that our theory and model have been formulated in a conceptually sound manner but that we have simply made a substantial number of logical errors in deriving our specific propositions. This is certainly possible: although we have done our best to avoid logical errors, and although we think the use of formal theory has helped us avoid them, it is quite unlikely that our book is error-free. Of course, we hope that none of these errors is significant, but certainly one of the virtues of formal theory, as we argued in Chapter 4, is that it should make our errors easier for the reader to identify.

This book is only the beginning of what we expect will have to be a large and complex research program. The book only provides a theory and develops a model, and the empirical testing of this model has scarcely begun; much remains to be done. Indeed, like many intellectual enterprises, ours has raised as many new questions as it has answered old ones. So we hope and expect that our book will stimulate a substantial body of additional research, both theoretical and empirical, on old and new questions. This interplay between theory and evidence, repeated in an ongoing series of cycles, is what accounts for the advancement of science. And in our view, it is this repeated interplay between theory and evidence, and between theorists and empiricists, that is also most likely to push the field of judicial politics in the direction of a more adequate understanding of Supreme Court decision-making.

Notes

Chapter 1

1. For only a few kinds of cases (e.g., state-vs.-state conflicts) does the Court continue to have original jurisdiction.

2. There does exist a formal literature on the Supreme Court, but most of these studies focus on the Court's relationships with external institutions such as Congress and the president (e.g., Bergara, Richman, and Spiller 2003; Rogers 2001; Segal 1997; Spiller and Gely 1992). Only in the past few years—see, e.g., Caldeira, Wright, and Zorn (1999) and Lax and Cameron (2001)—have formal models of the Supreme Court's internal decision-making practices been developed. However, these latter models have focused only on one or two stages of the Court's decision-making process; none considers all five stages.

Chapter 2

1. The psychological theories used in the more psychologically oriented literature on Supreme Court decision-making seem to have come largely from the 1950s, or from the 1960s at the latest. Although psychological theories of individual and group decision-making were improved enormously in the subsequent decades, and the field of cognitive psychology (which one might think would be very relevant to the study of elite decision-making) was developed largely after the 1950s, there is little reference to these more advanced theories in the modern judicial politics literature.

2. Other kinds of rational-choice theories are possible, in the sense that justices might rationally pursue goals other than (or in addition to) their personal policy goals; see Baum (1997, 37–56) for an insightful discussion of these other possible motivations.

3. An ongoing dispute between the students of public law and the students of judicial politics is whether the legal theories advanced by the students of public law (involving stare decisis, etc.) are adequate. Proponents of the judicial politics theories argue that the legal theories are not very good theories, for both theoretical and empirical reasons (see, e.g., Segal and Spaeth 1993, 32–64; 2002, chap. 2). Proponents of the legal theories have their own criticisms of the judicial politics theories,

involving whether the pursuit of personal policy goals adequately accounts for the complex legal reasoning in which the justices engage as they argue over and make their decisions. Our book cannot resolve this ongoing dispute, although by making our own model of judicial politics clearer and more explicit, and thus more adequately testable, we hope to contribute to a resolution of this debate.

4. If the justice's behavior did not follow automatically when the attitude is activated, the question would then arise as to what other factors would be influencing the justice's behavior besides the attitude that has been activated.

5. Signorino (1999) and Smith (1999) provide excellent discussions of these general kinds of problems in international politics theory and how they must be dealt with methodologically. Similar arguments could be made for the judicial politics literature.

6. If two or more lower courts have issued conflicting rulings, which is one reason why the Supreme Court may choose to grant certiorari, then a somewhat wider range of options may become available. But the basic story still applies: the possible options for the Court are limited to what the lower courts provided.

7. A very similar concern has been raised about studies of congressional roll call voting on the House and Senate floors: if committees send to the floor a biased sample of bills referred to the committees, and if the content of the bills sent to the floor is biased (via the amendment process within the committees) by the partisan or ideological composition of the committees, then efforts to find patterns in the floor roll calls (see, e.g., Poole and Rosenthal 1997) may produce biased results. The argument has thus been made (e.g., Snyder 1992) that modeling the decisions made by the committees must be a component of any effort to explain the pattern of roll call votes on the floor.

8. On occasion, the justices will issue a decision that affirms in part and reverses in part, but the judicial politics literature generally refers to just two options: to affirm or to reverse.

9. See, e.g., Riker (1982, chap. 6).

10. In Chapter 8 on the conference vote, what sincere behavior would look like did seem somewhat clearer and less complex than what strategic behavior would look like.

Chapter 3

1. William Thomson (1824–1907)—Lord Kelvin—was an eminent British physicist of the 19th and early 20th centuries.

2. Parts of this book had already appeared in Schubert (1958).

3. In his chapter 2, which concerned Court decisions on whether or not to accept a case for review, Schubert (1959, 66) did hint at the possibility that justices were behaving strategically: "We are thus forced to conclude that the Supreme Court's action in granting or denying access to petitioners must be informed not only by a judgment regarding jurisdiction—which we take to imply the significance of the policy issues raised by cases; rather, the Court appears frequently to estimate what the outcome of a case would be if it were taken, i.e., to make a decision, in the psychological rather than the legal sense, on the merits."

4. Schubert's subsequent revision of *The Judicial Mind* (1965), titled *The Judicial Mind Revisited* (1974), was even more focused on theory-of-measurement issues, and it completely dropped any description or discussion of models of choice. Hence, we discuss only the former work.

5. Schubert himself did not attempt to draw any such diagram, although the rendition presented here seems to conform to his verbal discussion. The earliest versions of this diagram that we can find are in Baum (1988, 906) and in Figure 2.1 and the associated discussion in Segal and Spaeth (1993, 67–68).

6. It is interesting to note that our own model here (see Part II) is more similar to this proximity model, which Schubert rejects, than to the ordinal model, which Schubert adopts.

7. An adherent of Schubert's model might respond by saying that this matter of the stimulus levels between i_2 and j_3 would normally be considered in some future case. But we would respond that if a majority of justices did want to enunciate a general rule lying between i_2 and j_3 here, without having to consider yet another case, this attitude-activation model provides no mechanism specifying how they could do this.

8. Rohde and Spaeth (1976) did attempt to construct an approach that integrated both the rational-choice and the psychological approaches; see their chapter 4, especially pages 72–78. The basic framework that Rohde and Spaeth adopted is rational-choice theory, but they used Rokeach (1968) to develop an argument as to how "beliefs," "attitudes," and "values" are "the psychological components of personal policy preferences" (74). In other words, Rohde and Spaeth used psychological arguments regarding beliefs, attitudes, and values to provide an explanation for the origins of the justices' personal policy preferences, which are obviously a critical component of the rational-choice approach. It is not clear to us, however, that this represents a satisfactory integration of these two bodies of thought. For example, a careful reading of the quote from Rokeach, which Segal and Spaeth presented in the main text as shown above, raises questions about whether Rokeach's psychological processes can legitimately be relegated just to preference formation and so can be seen as having no direct impact on choices and decisions. And whatever the merits of this particular construction by Rohde and Spaeth, it is certainly not how Schubert conceived of individual decision-making. Nor is it a construction that appears to have fundamentally shaped subsequent development of the attitudinal model. Segal and Spaeth (1993), for example, does not make this distinction between preference formation (which Rohde and Spaeth say is to be explained by the attitude-activation theory) and rational choice (which Rohde and Spaeth say is how the final policies are to be chosen).

9. The furthest any piece of the attitudinalist literature has gone toward an integration of the psychological and rational-choice approaches is Rohde and Spaeth (1976). In general, however, we are inclined to think that this effort at integration is unsuccessful: the attitude-activation and rational-choice theories, as portrayed in the attitudinalist literature, are just too dissimilar to be combined in any coherent way.

10. In our view, even the effort at integration of the attitude-activation and rational-choice approaches in Rohde and Spaeth (1976) should be considered a theory and not any kind of explicit model.

11. Interestingly, Maltzman, Spriggs, and Wahlbeck (2000, 48) report that although the empirical support for their hypothesis is statistically significant and in the expected direction, the effect is small (which is what Rohde 1972b found as well). Perhaps one reason that the effect appears small is that the hypothesis is not logically correct under all conditions. Correcting the hypothesis—again, see our Chapter 7—might result in increased empirical support.

12. A preliminary empirical test is available in Bonneau et al. (2004).

Chapter 4

1. An earlier version of the arguments in this and the following two sections originally appeared in Hammond (1996).

2. The mathematics does not have to be abstruse. The formal model we develop in Chapters 5 through 9 relies primarily on an ability to see that one line is longer than, or shorter than, some other line. Few readers will have difficulty making such a comparison.

3. Of course, we must acknowledge that theories and informal verbal models can also play this organizing and systematizing role: Darwin's theory of evolution by natural selection was not formalized in any kind of mathematical fashion until the 1920s and 1930s, yet it had enormous organizing power from the outset.

4. For example, by formally modeling the impact of domestic veto institutions on foreign policy decision-making by chiefs of government, Hammond and Prins (1999) discovered that many of the key relationships were not monotonic. If these monotonicities are not taken into account in statistical tests of the model, biased results may be produced.

5. Perhaps the best example of this in political science comes from legislative studies over the past two decades, where very useful cycles of interaction between formal theories and empirical tests have been occurring.

6. This was one of the major arguments of Green and Shapiro (1994).

Chapter 5

1. Spatial modeling can also involve policy-making in a multidimensional issue space. In Chapter 11, we discuss the representation of policy-making when it occurs in a two-dimensional issue space.

2. For empirical evidence that Supreme Court decision-making in recent decades has largely been characterized by a single issue dimension, see Grofman and Brazill (2002).

3. However, if it is the Washington, D.C., Circuit Court of Appeals that has issued the rule (e.g., regarding the authority of some federal regulatory agency), there would not be a mixed pattern of different rulings holding in different circuits; instead, this ruling would cover the entire country.

4. An even more complex status quo policy can emerge if two or more appeals courts issue rulings that modify the current legal state of affairs in different ways. Consider the legal state of affairs on university affirmative action policies in the

country over the past decade: starting with the *Hopwood v. Texas* decision by the Fifth Circuit in 1996, different circuits issued different rulings, and it was not until the Supreme Court's decisions in *Gratz v. Bollinger* and *Grutter v. Bollinger* in 2003 that these conflicts among the circuits were resolved. During these seven years, then, the legal status quo was characterized by several different kinds of affirmative action policies that were in effect in several different regions of the country.

5. Note that a preferred-to set of SQ contains only those policies that the justice *prefers to* SQ. Because the justice is indifferent between SQ and the policy at the other end of the preferred-to set, this policy at the other end is not included in the preferred-to set.

6. We will also frequently refer to a policy that lies "just inside the SQ boundary of $W_{J3}(SQ)$." The logic of the phrase here is the same as for a policy that lies "just inside the outside boundary of $W_{J3}(SQ)$": such a policy is located inside $W_{J3}(SQ)$ at a minimally perceptible distance to the left of SQ.

7. In Chapter 11, we consider variations of our model in which the perfect-information assumption does not hold.

8. As we mentioned in Chapter 2, though, our analysis in Chapter 8 suggests that what sincere behavior on the conference vote would look like is somewhat clearer, and certainly far less complex, than what strategic behavior would look like.

Chapter 6

1. This stage should perhaps not be described as a vote because the justices are primarily just indicating, in a sequential manner (beginning with the Chief Justice and working down the roster of justices in order of decreasing seniority), what their views are on the case. Rehnquist (1987, 289–95) provides a description of the conference procedures and practices in recent decades. See also the discussion in Segal and Spaeth (1993, 210–12; 2002, 281–84).

2. To standardize the diagrams that illustrate our propositions, we will presume throughout the book that J_{med} is located to the left of SQ. Of course, a left-to-right mirror image of all our illustrations and arguments also applies for cases in which J_{med} lies to the right of SQ.

3. We will argue in our analysis of certiorari in Chapter 9 that if SQ is at J_{med}, the Court would not accept such a case in the first place. Even though there would be *maj* − 1 justices (the minimum needed to grant certiorari) who would prefer some policy other than SQ, and who could thus force the Court to grant certiorari, the only possible outcome of the case would be for the Court merely to reaffirm what is already the status quo policy. Because SQ could not be changed, no justice would gain anything (in our model) from hearing the case. On the real-world Court, some justices might see a benefit in reaffirming some status quo policy that was initially established several decades previously, although if hearing a case is costly in any sense (even due just to the opportunity cost of not being able to hear some other case), this might reduce or even eliminate any net benefits of reaffirming the old policy.

4. We use the { . . . } notation to indicate the justices who vote the same way

on a proposal to replace SQ with some alternative policy. Although we refer to the justices listed inside { . . . } as a coalition, we are not suggesting that these justices are necessarily engaging in any conscious coordination of their votes; they may be voting as they do simply because each individual justice prefers the proposal to SQ, or prefers SQ to the proposal.

5. Because $W_{J2}(SQ)$ contains all the points in $W_{J3}(SQ)$, we do not have to specify that the points in $W_{J3}(SQ)$ must be subtracted as well.

6. We indicate an empty coalition—that is, a coalition with no members—by {∅}.

7. When a minority-side justice such as justice J_4 writes a majority-side opinion at +, it is not clear how any other minority-side justice (such as justice J_5) will vote. Because the minority-side justices are all better off with an opinion at + rather than with an opinion farther to the left (which is the only other feasible option), one might expect that all of them would support the opinion at +. On the other hand, the opinion at + requires only a bare majority to be adopted, which would on occasion allow some of the minority-side justices to oppose it by dissenting, thereby behaving consistently with their minority-side ideal points. Our model does not lead to a clear prediction as to how all the minority-side justices would behave here. We will assume only that a sufficient number of minority-side justices (always including the minority-side opinion writer) will vote to ensure that the opinion at + is adopted; the rest will dissent.

8. We have previously assumed—see footnote 7—that not all minority-side justices would necessarily support an opinion at +.

9. This characterization of the open-bidding process does not resolve the potential coordination problem involving who will be the coalition leaders on each side of J_{med} (if justice J_{med} does not organize the countercoalition herself on behalf of an opinion at J_{med}). In the example just completed, justice J_2 is the majority opinion writer (by assumption), but would it be justice J_5, or justice J_6, or even justice J_7, who takes on the responsibility of writing the counteropinions labeled Opinion 2 and Opinion 4? Any inclination by these three justices to free ride on each other (e.g., if opinion writing is costly, contrary to Assumption 5.13) might leave these counteropinions unwritten, and hence it would be left to justice J_4 (the median justice) to draft an opinion at J_4. But if the cost of doing this is too high for her, then Opinion 1 will stand, and we will have reverted, in effect, to the agenda-control version of our model. We further discuss this matter in Chapter 11.

10. However, the back-and-forth bargaining might actually appear if the opinion writer had only imperfect information about the median justice's ideal point (i.e., Assumption 5.8 does not hold) and had to determine what was acceptable to her by negotiating directly with her.

11. The ultimate threat that can be exercised here by the median justice and all the justices on the other side of J_{med} from the draft majority opinion is simply to dissent (or to write or join a special concurrence). By permanently withholding their votes in this manner from what was intended to be the majority opinion, this opinion can become only a plurality opinion, which lacks precedential power. In Chapter 11, we discuss special concurrences; here our model assumes only that the

median justice and her supporters threaten not to join what was intended to be the majority opinion unless the median justice gets an opinion at her ideal point; precisely what they do if they do not get what they demand does not need to be specified here.

12. There is some anecdotal evidence that Justice Sandra Day O'Connor, who has often been the median justice on the Rehnquist Court, does withhold her vote in this fashion and does succeed in having the final opinion modified as she desires; see the general account of Justice O'Connor's decision-making practices by Rosen (2001). We should acknowledge that one of her former clerks is quoted as saying, "She's very careful to write minimalist opinions, taking each case one at a time and trying not to decide too much that's not before the court. She really has no grand constitutional theory. But that's a different sense of calculatedness than the idea that she holds out in order to dictate what the court says, which I didn't see at all." However, it seems to us that the practical impact of the behavior that Rosen describes is precisely what this former clerk denies: in many cases, by insisting on her own viewpoint, she is effectively threatening to withhold her vote, which means she effectively dictates what the Court can say.

13. As with the open-bidding version of our model, if the majority opinion writer has imperfect information about the median justice's ideal point, he may have to discover what the median justice would accept by negotiating directly with her.

14. We consider these issues in greater depth in our analysis of certiorari in Chapter 9.

15. A further implication would be that our own emphasis in Chapters 2 and 3 on the importance of strategic behavior, both at the final stage and at the earlier stages, might be incorrect.

16. A similar question can be raised about the relationship between the median-holdout and open-bidding versions of our model. That is, what would happen if the majority opinion writer refuses to concede to the median justice's insistence that the opinion be written at her ideal point; what may result is a plurality opinion that leaves the status quo policy unchanged. This may leave the median justice (and at least some of her supporters) worse off than they would be with some agreement on a majority-side opinion. To protect themselves, the median justice and her supporters may thus have to adopt the open-bidding strategy, actively writing their own opinion at J_{med}. See Chapter 11 for further discussion of this complex issue.

Chapter 7

1. It will be necessary to use seven-member and nine-member examples in this chapter to illustrate the full variety of conditions that can affect opinion assignment.

2. Just because a justice's ideal point is located on the minority side does not necessarily mean that the justice will actually vote with the minority on the conference vote. For example, assume in Figure 7.1 that justice J_7 is the Chief Justice and so would be the opinion assigner if he votes with the majority on the conference vote: in this way he could control opinion assignment and thereby influence what the final opinion would be. Similarly, justice J_8 may have good reason to think

that, if he were to vote with the majority along with the Chief Justice, the Chief Justice would assign the majority opinion to him, expecting that he would write a majority opinion that is as close to SQ as possible. We discuss this general strategy later in this chapter, and in Chapter 8 we analyze this kind of strategic behavior on the conference vote.

3. Of course, he could assign to justices J_4, J_5, or J_6, but they would also write opinions at their respective ideal points, which are worse for assigner J_2 than J_3.

Chapter 8

1. Although we call this stage the "conference vote," it is sometimes referred to as the "original vote on the merits." We rely on Rehnquist (1987, 289–95) for our discussion of these procedures. As we noted in Chapter 6, this stage is not, strictly speaking, a vote at all because the justices are primarily just indicating what their views are on the case.

2. On particularly complex cases, or on cases in which some of the justices' statements are ambiguous, determining whether the affirm side or the reverse side has the majority may require some interpretation (see Rehnquist 1987, 293–94), and it will be the Chief Justice who makes this interpretation. On occasion, this interpretation has been a matter of dispute within the Court.

3. We should explicitly acknowledge that what follows does not take into account the sequencing of the justices' actions on the conference vote. Whether the sequencing can be expected to affect outcomes, and if so, how much, remains to be determined. We conjecture that the sequencing does not matter in our complete-information model.

4. The Chief Justice could presumably endorse any majority-side policy (not just the policy at +), become the majority opinion assigner as a result, and then write the final majority opinion at +. We are implicitly assuming here that the Chief Justice places some value on consistency between what he endorses on the conference vote and what he does as a majority opinion writer.

5. Strictly speaking, discussion of this particular strategy—persuade some other minority-side justice to endorse a policy at + on the conference vote—may belong in our "What If Everyone Behaves Strategically?" section later in this chapter. However, it is most easily understood here.

6. It is an open question how the Chief Justice would behave on the final vote regarding this opinion at + written by justice J_6. Because the Chief Justice has endorsed + on the conference vote, and because he has assigned the opinion to justice J_6 here (knowing that the result would be an opinion at +), he might be expected to join the majority in support of the opinion at +. However, this opinion at + is worse for him than SQ, and because the opinion at + written by justice J_6 would gain majority support even without his (the Chief Justice's) vote, the Chief Justice could vote sincerely by writing a dissenting opinion in support of a policy at his own ideal point of J_7. It is not obvious which strategy the Chief Justice would use.

7. Note that the justice on the majority side who is closest to SQ (and who would thus become the Chief Justice's assignee in this situation) will always be able to gain majority support for an opinion at his or her ideal point because this ideal

point will always lie inside the preferred-to sets of a majority of the justices.

8. We italicize each "if" and "then" in this and most other propositions in this chapter to visually clarify and simplify what are often rather complex logical statements.

9. Of course, if the Chief Justice or one or more of the high-seniority associate justices recuses himself or herself, these results will change accordingly.

10. In this section, when we uses phrases like "the senior associate justice" or "the associate justice" or even just "the justice," we mean the most senior associate justice unless otherwise specified.

11. We will soon demonstrate that such an opinion-attracting policy does not always exist.

12. In fact, this final opinion at # is also better for justice J_5 than SQ; recall that all of the possible sincere-behavior outcomes are worse for him than SQ. However, he would benefit from this strategy of endorsing the policy at # even if the policy at # were worse for him than SQ: what matters is that the policy at # is better for him than the policy at J_3 that would otherwise result.

13. See our earlier section on "Strategic Behavior by the Chief Justice" and especially the discussion under its "Condition 2: The Chief Justice Has a Minority-Side Ideal Point" (which focuses on Figure 8.1).

14. Our only exception has involved cases when a minority-side Chief Justice or senior associate justice expresses support for that majority-side policy closest to SQ, and then tries to induce some other minority-side justice to support that same policy as well, so that the opinion could be assigned to that other minority-side justice.

15. In Chapter 7, we made essentially the same observation regarding conditions under which the Chief Justice would have no need to self-assign.

16. As we have already suggested, our conclusion here has important implications for the debate over whether a Chief Justice distributes opinion assignments with regard to the relative workload among the justices or to some kind of norm of equity (e.g., each justice gets to write roughly the same number of opinions as every other justice). However, our conclusion suggests that even if the Chief Justice distributes opinion assignments solely on the basis of maximizing achievement of his own policy goals, a wide range of justices might well receive these assignments (especially if SQ is located in a wide range of possible positions). In other words, the Chief Justice's pursuit of his own policy goals might produce a distribution of opinion assignments that appears as if it were motivated in good part by his concern for equity, or relative workload, even though equity or workload had nothing to do with his assignments. The Chief Justice's pursuit of "equity," or evenly distributed workload, may thus be relatively compatible with a single-minded pursuit of his own policy goals.

Chapter 9

1. The Supreme Court has original jurisdiction, and as late as 1988 still had some mandatory jurisdiction, over a small set of cases. For these kinds of cases, the stage of decision-making involving certiorari is (or was) simply bypassed. For an analysis

that uses our model, decision-making would thus begin at the conference vote rather than at certiorari. However, nothing else about our analysis of these cases would have to be changed.

2. In contrast, we will argue below that a strategic justice will base his or her certiorari decision on whether this possible policy improvement will actually occur.

3. If J is even (because there is a Court vacancy or a justice recuses himself or herself), the Court will grant certiorari if at least $maj - 1$ justices have ideal points not at SQ; equivalently, the Court will grant certiorari if $maj - 1$ or fewer justices have ideal points at SQ.

4. If J is even, the Court will deny certiorari if fewer than $maj - 1$ justices have ideal points not at SQ; equivalently, the Court will deny certiorari if at least maj justices have ideal points at SQ.

Chapter 10

1. The arguments advanced here depend critically on Assumption 5.8, the perfect-information assumption. If justices are uncertain about each other's views, or some justices consider other justices to be persuadable, it may sometimes make sense for four justices to force a grant of certiorari, in the hope or expectation that a fifth vote could be found to create a majority for the first four justices' preferred policy. If the four justices do this, it might be called "aggressive granting," although we think that a more descriptive phrase would be "risky granting" because it would be risk-acceptant (rather than risk-averse) justices who might want to engage in such a strategy under these conditions of uncertainty.

2. The fact that Chief Justice Burger was delaying his own announcement in order to see what positions others would take clearly suggests that Assumption 5.8, our perfect-information assumption, did not hold for him in these cases.

3. Epstein and Knight (1998) here cite Edelman and Chen (1996, 42).

4. Preliminary empirical research—see Bonneau et al. (2004)—suggests that the agenda-control version fares somewhat better than the open-bidding and median-holdout versions in accounting for individual justices' final votes during the Burger Court.

5. Bonneau et al. (2004) is an initial example of how to determine empirically whether the agenda-control version of our model explains the justices' individual votes better than the versions predicting outcomes at the median justice's ideal point (i.e., the open-bidding and median-holdout versions).

6. In fact, even if justices were voting completely randomly (e.g., by flipping coins where $p = 0.5$) on whether to support or reject some draft majority opinion, which of course is the very antithesis of rational choice, a simple application of the Binomial Theorem reveals that there would still be considerably more of the 5–4 or 4–5 lineups than any other kind of outcome. Thus, even if a higher proportion of 5–4 or 4–5 votes is empirically observed than any other kind of lineup, this does not necessarily indicate that any kind of strategically rational behavior is occurring.

7. Recall that in the "all strategic" context (and assuming that the justices' behavior on subsequent cases has no relevance), the opinion assigner will not trust any other justice to write any opinion other than the one that is as close as possi-

ble to the other justice's own ideal point. However, if the potential opinion writers' behavior on subsequent cases is relevant (i.e., Assumption 5.9 does not hold), then sincere and strategic behavior may turn out to be quite different.

8. Because vote switching involves two different stages of Supreme Court decision-making, an analysis did not fit neatly into either Chapter 8 (on the conference vote) or Chapter 6 (on the final vote), so we left it for consideration here.

9. In fact, this other justice would have voted to deny certiorari in the first place, expecting the final policy to be worse than SQ for him, but he would have been outvoted by those who wanted to hear the case (because each of them expected the final opinion to be better than SQ for himself or herself).

10. One might ask whether justices J_4 and J_5 who switch to the minority side could have prevented this opinion at * from being adopted by behaving differently on the certiorari or conference votes. The answer is no: they are simply outvoted by the $\{J_1J_2J_3\}$ coalition.

11. As we remarked in Chapter 2, however, adequate scaling methods may need to take into account the Court's internal agenda-setting process. None of the current scaling studies of the Supreme Court do this.

12. Bonneau et al. (2004) use the justices' certiorari votes to infer between which two justices' ideal points the status quo policy lies. Unfortunately, if justices are strategically rational throughout the entire decision-making process, then estimates of the location of the status quo policy from the certiorari vote may be contaminated by this strategic behavior because how the justices vote on certiorari gives only an indirect indication of the location of their ideal points.

13. Although Spaeth argues (personal communication, June 4, 2004) that these "pro-" and "anti-" coding decisions are not premised on what the current status quo policy is, there may be some way of using these coding decisions to make plausible inferences regarding the location of SQ for each case.

Chapter 11

1. In his dissent in *Dickerson*, Justice Scalia argued that the original *Miranda* decision had its own ambiguities and had actually generated more legal disputes that the Court had been required to settle than had the voluntariness standard in force between 1936 and the adoption of the *Miranda* decision in 1966. Indeed, Justice Scalia asserted that Justice Byron White, in his dissent to the original *Miranda* decision, "predicted with remarkable prescience" most of the numerous legal disputes that would ultimately be raised by the *Miranda* decision. In other words, it appears that Justice White in *Miranda* and the justices in the majority in *Dickerson* were all basing their decisions in part on their forecasts of the future stream of cases likely to emerge as a consequence of the Court's decisions. However, these justices expected rather different streams of cases to emerge, or at least they made rather different estimates of the value of the stream they considered most likely to emerge.

2. It may be possible to reinterpret our one-period model in such a way that it has at least one of the key characteristics of a multiperiod model. In particular, each justice's ideal point could be seen as that policy that, if adopted by the Court on the current case, would generate the future stream of Court decisions whose total dis-

counted value is greatest for the justice. Decision-making on the current case would then be conducted essentially as our model specifies. From this perspective, our one-period model can perhaps be interpreted as an implicit multiperiod model.

3. Segal and Spaeth (2002) here cite Westerland (2001) in support of this argument.

4. Ideas presented in Riker (1982, chap. 8–9) or Riker (1986) may be useful in depicting and analyzing strategies involving the addition of a new issue dimension to the justices' debate. Ideas presented in Hammond and Humes (1993) may be useful in depicting and analyzing the strategic elimination of an issue dimension from the justices' debate and an equally strategic redefinition of the remaining dimension.

References

Arrow, Kenneth J. 1951. *Social choice and individual values.* New York: Wiley. Rev. ed., 1963.

Axelrod, Robert M. 1970. *Conflict of interest: A theory of divergent goals with applications to politics.* Chicago: Markham.

—————.1984. *The evolution of cooperation.* New York: Basic Books.

Bailey, Michael, and Kelly H. Chang. 2001. Comparing presidents, senators, and justices: Interinstitutional preference estimation. *Journal of Law, Economics, and Organization* 17:477–506.

Baron, David P., and John A. Ferejohn. 1989. Bargaining in legislatures. *American Political Science Review* 83:1181–206.

Baum, Lawrence. 1988. Measuring policy change in the U.S. Supreme Court. *American Political Science Review* 82:905–12.

—————.1997. *The puzzle of judicial behavior.* Ann Arbor: University of Michigan Press.

Bergara, Mario, Barak Richman, and Pablo T. Spiller. 2003. Modeling Supreme Court strategic decision making: The congressional constraint. *Legislative Studies Quarterly* 28:247–80.

Biskupic, Joan. 2000. Full court press: Justices in conference: A tradition wanes. *Washington Post*, February 7, A15.

Black, Duncan. 1948a. On the rationale of group decision-making. *Journal of Political Economy* 56:23–34.

—————.1948b. The decisions of a committee using a special majority. *Econometrica* 16:245–61.

—————.1958. *The theory of committees and elections.* Cambridge: Cambridge University Press. Reprint, 1987, Dordrecht: Kluwer.

Bonneau, Chris W., Saul Brenner, Thomas H. Hammond, Forrest Maltzman, and Paul J. Wahlbeck. 2004. Selecting the majority opinion on the Supreme Court. Paper presented at the annual convention of the Midwest Political Science Association, Chicago, IL.

Boucher, Jr., Robert L., and Jeffrey A. Segal. 1995. Supreme Court justices as strategic decision makers: Aggressive grants and defensive denials on the Vinson Court. *Journal of Politics* 57:824–37.

Brazill, Timothy, and Bernard Grofman. 2002. Factor analysis versus multidimensional scaling: Binary choice roll-call voting and the U.S. Supreme Court. *Social Networks* 24:201–29.

Brenner, Saul. 1982. Strategic choice and opinion assignment on the U.S. Supreme Court: A reexamination. *Western Political Quarterly* 35:204–11.

Brenner, Saul, and John F. Krol. 1989. Strategies in certiorari voting on the United States Supreme Court. *Journal of Politics* 51:828–40.

Brown, Theodore L. 2003. *Making truth: Metaphor in science.* Urbana: University of Illinois Press.

Caldeira, Gregory A., John R. Wright, and Christopher J. W. Zorn. 1999. Sophisticated voting and gate-keeping in the Supreme Court. *Journal of Law, Economics, and Organization* 15:549–72.

Clayton, Cornell W. 1999. Strategy and judicial choice: New institutionalist approaches to Supreme Court decision-making. In *Supreme Court decision-making: New institutionalist approaches,* edited by Cornell W. Clayton and Howard Gillman, 43–63. Chicago: University of Chicago Press.

Coombs, Clyde H. 1964. *A theory of data.* New York: Wiley.

Darwin, Charles. 1859. *The Origin of Species.* London: John Murray.

Dawes, Robyn. 1998. Behavioral decision making, judgment, and inference. In *The handbook of social psychology,* edited by Daniel T. Gilbert, Susan T. Fiske, and Gardner Lindzey, 1:589–97. Boston: McGraw-Hill.

Dorff, Robert H., and Saul Brenner. 1992. Conformity voting on the United States Supreme Court. *Journal of Politics* 54:762–75.

Downs, Anthony. 1957. *An economic theory of democracy.* New York: Harper and Row.

Edelman, Paul H., and Jim Chen. 1996. The most dangerous justice: The Supreme Court at the bar of mathematics. *Southern California Law Review* 70:63–101.

Epstein, Lee, Valerie Hoekstra, Jeffrey A. Segal, and Harold J. Spaeth. 1998. Do political preferences change? A longitudinal study of U.S. Supreme Court justices. *Journal of Politics* 60:801–18.

Epstein, Lee, and Jack Knight. 1998. *The choices justices make.* Washington, DC: Congressional Quarterly Press.

Gely, Rafael, and Pablo T. Spiller. 1990. A rational choice theory of Supreme Court decision making with applications to the *State Farm* and *Grove City* cases. *Journal of Law, Economics, and Organization* 6:263–301.

Gibson, James L. 1981. The role concept in judicial research. *Law and Policy Quarterly* 3:291–311.

Green, Donald P., and Ian Shapiro. 1994. *Pathologies of rational choice theory: A critique of applications in political science.* New Haven: Yale University Press.

Grofman, Bernard, and Timothy J. Brazill. 2002. Identifying the median justice on the Supreme Court through multidimensional scaling: Analysis of the 'natural courts' 1953–1991. *Public Choice* 112:55–79.

Hammond, Thomas H. 1996. Formal theory and the institutions of governance. *Governance* 9:107–85.

Hammond, Thomas H., Chris W. Bonneau, and Reginald S. Sheehan. 1999. Toward a rational choice spatial model of Supreme Court decision-making: Making sense of certiorari, the original vote on the merits, opinion assignment, coalition formation and maintenance, and the final vote on the choice of legal doctrine. Paper presented at the annual convention of the American Political Science Association, Atlanta, Ga.

————. Forthcoming. A court of appeals in a rational-choice model of Supreme Court decision-making. In *Institutional Games and the U.S. Supreme Court*, edited by Jon R. Bond, Roy Flemming, and James R. Rogers. Charlottesville, VA: University of Virginia Press.

Hammond, Thomas H., and Brian D. Humes. 1993. "'What this campaign is all about is . . .': A rational choice alternative to the Downsian spatial model of elections." In *Information, participation, and choice: An economic theory of democracy in perspective*, edited by Bernard Grofman, 141–59. Ann Arbor: University of Michigan Press.

Hammond, Thomas. H., and Brandon C. Prins. 1999. The impact of domestic institutions on international negotiations: A taxonomy of results from a complete information spatial model. Paper presented at the annual convention of the American Political Science Association, Atlanta, GA.

Hogarth, Robin M., and Melvin W. Reder. 1987. *Rational choice: The contrast between economics and psychology*. Chicago: University of Chicago Press.

Horn, Robert A. 1957. A quantitative study of judicial review. *Political Research: Organization and Design* 1:27–30.

Kort, Fred. 1957. Predicting Supreme Court decisions mathematically: A quantitative analysis of the "right to counsel" cases. *American Political Science Review* 51:1–12.

Krol, John F., and Saul Brenner. 1990. Strategies in certiorari voting on the United States Supreme Court: A reevaluation. *Western Political Quarterly* 43:335–42.

Landau, Martin. 1972. On the use of metaphor in political analysis. In *Political theory and political science: Studies in the methodology of political inquiry*. New York: Macmillan.

Lax, Jeffrey R., and Charles M. Cameron. 2001. Opinion assignment in the Supreme Court: theory and evidence. Paper presented at the annual convention of the American Political Science Association, San Francisco, CA.

Luce, R. Duncan, and Howard Raiffa. 1957. *Games and decisions: Introduction and critical survey*. New York: Wiley.

Maltzman, Forrest, and Paul J. Wahlbeck. 1996a. Strategic policy considerations and voting fluidity on the Burger Court. *American Political Science Review* 90:581–92.

————.1996b. May it please the Chief? Opinion assignments in the Rehnquist Court. *American Journal of Political Science* 40:421–43.

Maltzman, Forrest, James F. Spriggs II, and Paul J. Wahlbeck. 2000. *Crafting law on the Supreme Court: The collegial game*. New York: Cambridge University Press.

Marks, Brian A. 1988. A model of judicial influence on congressional policymaking: *Grove City College v. Bell*. Working Papers in Political Science, P-88-7, Hoover Institution, Stanford University.

Martin, Andrew D., and Kevin M. Quinn. 2002. Dynamic ideal point estimation via Markov chain Monte Carlo for the U.S. Supreme Court, 1953–1999. *Political Analysis* 10:134–53.

McGuire, Kevin T., and Barbara Palmer. 1995. Issue fluidity on the U.S. Supreme Court. *American Political Science Review* 89:691–702.

Morton, Rebecca B. 1999. *Methods and models: A guide to the empirical analysis of formal models in political science*. New York: Cambridge University Press.

Mueller, Dennis C. 1989. *Public choice II*. New York: Cambridge University Press.

Murphy, Walter F. 1964. *Elements of judicial strategy*. Chicago: University of Chicago Press.

Perry, H. W. 1991. *Deciding to decide: Agenda setting in the United States Supreme Court*. Cambridge: Harvard University Press.

Poole, Keith T., and Howard Rosenthal. 1997. *Congress: A political-economic history of roll call voting*. New York: Oxford University Press.

Pritchett, C. Herman. 1948. *The Roosevelt Court: A study in judicial politics and values, 1937–1947*. New York: Macmillan.

Rathjen, Gregory James. 1974. Policy goals, strategic choice, and majority opinion assignments in the U.S. Supreme Court: A replication. *American Journal of Political Science* 18:713–24.

Rehnquist, William H. 1987. *The Supreme Court: How it was, how it is*. New York: William Morrow.

Riker, William H. 1962. *The theory of political coalitions*. New Haven: Yale University Press.

———.1982. *Liberalism against populism: A confrontation between the theory of democracy and the theory of social choice*. San Francisco: W. H. Freeman.

———.1986. *The art of political manipulation*. New Haven: Yale University Press.

Rohde, David W. 1972a. Policy goals and opinion coalitions in the Supreme Court. *Midwest Journal of Political Science* 16:208–24.

———.1972b. Policy goals, strategic choice, and majority opinion assignments in the U.S. Supreme Court. *Midwest Journal of Political Science* 16:652–82.

Rohde, David W., and Harold J. Spaeth. 1976. *Supreme Court decision making*. San Francisco: W. H. Freeman.

Rogers, James R. 2001. Information and judicial review: A signaling game of legislative-judicial interaction. *American Journal of Political Science* 45:84–99.

Rokeach, Milton. 1968. The nature of attitudes. In *International encyclopedia of the social sciences*, edited by David L. Sills, 1:449–57. New York: Macmillan.

Rosen, Jeffrey. 2001. A majority of one. *New York Times Sunday Magazine*. June 3. Electronic archive version.

Schmidhauser, John, and David Gold. 1958. Scaling Supreme Court decisions in relation to social background. *Political Research: Organization and Design* 1:6–7.

Schubert, Glendon A. 1958. The study of judicial decision-making as an aspect of political behavior. *American Political Science Review* 52:1007–25.

———.1959. *Quantitative analysis of judicial behavior*. New York: Free Press.

———.1965. *The judicial mind: The attitudes and ideologies of Supreme Court justices, 1946–1963*. Evanston, IL: Northwestern University Press.

———.1974. *The judicial mind revisited: Psychometric analysis of Supreme Court ideology*. New York: Oxford University Press.

Segal, Jeffrey A. 1997. Separation-of-powers games in the positive theory of Congress and courts. *American Political Science Review* 91:28–44.

Segal, Jeffrey A., and Harold J. Spaeth. 1993. *The Supreme Court and the attitudinal model.* New York: Cambridge University Press.

―――.1994. Symposium: The Supreme Court and the attitudinal model. *Law and Courts* 4:10–12.

―――. 2002. *The Supreme Court and the attitudinal model revisited.* New York: Cambridge University Press.

Signorino, Curtis S. 1999. Strategic interaction and the statistical analysis of international conflict. *American Political Science Review* 93:279–97.

Smith, Alastair. 1999. Testing theories of strategic choice: The example of crisis escalation. *American Journal of Political Science* 43:1254–83.

Snyder, James M., Jr. 1992. Committee power, structure-induced equilibria, and roll call votes. *American Journal of Political Science* 36:1–30.

Spaeth, Harold J. 1979. *Supreme Court policy making.* San Francisco: W. H. Freeman.

Spaeth, Harold J., and David J. Peterson. 1971. The analysis and interpretation of dimensionality: The case of civil liberties decision making. *Midwest Journal of Political Science* 15:415–41.

Spiller, Pablo T., and Rafael Gely. 1992. Congressional control or judicial independence: The determinants of U.S. Supreme Court labor-relations decisions, 1949–1988. *RAND Journal of Economics* 23:463–92.

Thurstone, Louis L., and James W. Degan. 1951. A factorial study of the Supreme Court. University of Chicago, Psychometric Laboratory, Report No. 64.

Ulmer, S. Sidney. 1958. Label thinking and the Supreme Court: A methodological note. *Political Research: Organization and Design* 2:25–26.

Wahlbeck, Paul J., James F. Spriggs II, and Forrest Maltzman. 1998. Marshalling the Court: Bargaining and accommodation on the United States Supreme Court. *American Journal of Political Science* 42:294–315.

Westerland, Chad. 2001. Attitudes and institutions: Understanding opinion writing behavior on the U.S. Supreme Court. Unpublished paper, Department of Political Science, State University of New York at Stony Brook.

Index

Agenda, 31, 58, 111, 135

Agenda-control model, 96, 108, 109, 110–125, 129, 130, 133, 134, 135, 137, 138, 139, 140, 142, 161, 162, 165, 222, 223, 224, 231, 236, 237, 238, 244, 264, 266, 267, 268, 282n9, 286n4 (chap. 10), 286n5

Agenda-setting, 18, 19, 47, 48, 266, 267, 287n11

Aggressive granting, 216, 226, 227, 228, 233, 234, 252, 286n1

Arrow, Kenneth J., 54, 75

Attitudes, xv, 1, 9, 11, 12, 18, 22, 26, 29, 30, 31, 32, 33, 40, 42, 43, 44, 45, 279n8

Attitude-activation, 11, 12, 13, 16, 23, 29, 32, 33, 41, 42, 43, 45, 46, 48, 53, 54, 56, 57, 67, 279n7, 279n8, 279n9, 279n10

Attitudinal model, xv, xvi, xvii, 16, 26, 39, 40, 41, 42, 43, 44, 45, 46, 47, 48, 49, 50, 51, 52, 53, 54, 60, 61, 246, 250, 274, 279n8

Axelrod, Robert M., 55, 259

Bailey, Michael, 247

Bargaining, 127, 128, 135, 239, 240, 264, 282n10

Baron, David P., 266

Baum, Lawrence, xxiii, 8, 49, 277n2 (chap. 2), 279n5

Bergara, Mario, 277n2 (chap. 1)

Biskupic, Joan, 215

Black, Duncan, 54, 75, 99

Bonneau, Chris W., 246, 263, 271, 280n12, 286n4, 286n5, 287n12

Boucher, Jr., Robert L., 24, 57, 226

Brazill, Timothy, 247, 280n2 (chap. 5)

Brenner, Saul, 24, 57, 245

Brown, Theodore L., 9

Burger Court, 40

Burger, Chief Justice Warren, 82, 234, 251, 263, 286n2 (chap. 10), 286n4 (chap. 10)

Caldeira, Gregory A., 277n2 (chap. 1)

Cameron, Charles M., 268, 277n2 (chap. 1)

Certiorari, xvi, 2, 7, 18, 23, 24, 29, 47, 52, 57, 63, 89, 90, 92, 95, 136, 215–228, 233, 234, 238, 241, 243, 251, 252, 269, 273, 278n6, 281n3, 283n14, 285n1, 286n1 (chap. 9), 286n2 (chap. 9), 286n3 (chap. 9), 286n4 (chap. 9), 286n10, 287n9, 286n10, 286n12

Chang, Kelly H., 247

Chen, Jim, 286n3 (chap. 10)

Chief Justice, 2, 23, 59, 82, 93, 95, 97, 163–214

Choice, theories of, 14

Clayton, Cornell W., 1

Coalitions, minimum winning, 51, 55, 56, 113, 119, 120, 121, 123, 128, 133, 138, 232, 239, 240

Coalition formation, xvi, 6, 39, 47, 50, 52, 55, 59, 61, 63, 91, 95, 96–138, 140, 164, 232, 233, 237, 239, 242

Commitment, 165, 210–212, 236

Concurrence: regular, 92, 93, 95, 96, 250, 259, 260, 261, 262; special, 50, 92, 96, 250, 259, 260, 261, 262, 282n11

Concurring opinion, 61, 92, 261

Conference vote, xvi, 2, 6, 18, 28, 47, 52, 63, 91, 92, 93, 94, 95, 96, 118, 141, 153, 154, 156, 157, 158, 164–214

Convergence conditions, 196, 200, 201, 206, 207, 208, 211, 212, 213, 214

Coombs, Clyde H., 32, 33, 44

Darwin, Charles, 71, 280n3 (chap. 4)

Dawes, Robyn, 45

Defensive denial, 226, 227, 228, 233, 234, 252

Deference, 264; norm of, 239, 266, 267

Delay, 234, 251; costs of, 266

Degan, James W., 27

Dickerson v. United States, 256, 287n1

Dimension, 33, 34, 40, 57, 80, 81, 90, 232, 247, 262, 264, 265, 268, 272, 280n1 (chap. 5), 288n4; affirm/reverse, 263, 265; attitudinal, 30; issue, 33, 56, 57, 202; liberal vs. conservative, 80, 246, 263, 273; multiple dimensions, 246, 247, 263, 264, 265, 266, 268, 269, 280; single dimension, 80, 83, 99, 232, 239,

246, 247, 250, 262, 280n2 (chap. 5)

Discuss list, 215, 269

Dissent, 2, 93, 96, 97, 125, 127, 128, 260, 262, 282, 287n1

Dissenting opinion, 22, 50, 53, 61, 92, 95, 96, 259, 261, 284n6

Dissenting justices, 30

Dorff, Robert H., 245

Downs, Anthony, 54, 99

Edelman, Paul H., 286n3 (chap. 10)

Epstein, Lee, 4, 10, 18, 19, 20, 23, 47, 48, 49, 50, 57, 58, 59, 60, 79, 91, 136, 226, 234, 235, 238, 254, 263, 286n3 (chap. 10)

Equilibrium, 58, 109, 132, 206; analysis, 58; majority rule, 266; multidimensional, 264; opinion, 128, 244; outcome, 58, 201, 264; policy, 131, 197, 200, 264, 265; strategy, 137

Ferejohn, John A., 266

Final vote, xvi, 6, 13, 15, 16, 17, 18, 19, 20, 21, 22, 23, 24, 28, 29, 31, 39, 46, 47, 48, 49, 50, 51, 52, 55, 57, 59, 61, 63, 91, 92, 95–138

Formal: analysis, 6, 58, 59, 250; approach, 60, 92; decisions, 26; equilibrium analysis, 58; literature, 277n2 (chap. 1); mathematical studies, 21; model, xvi, 3, 4, 5, 6, 19, 28, 58, 59, 60, 61, 63, 66–78, 79, 80, 82, 86, 90, 229, 231, 238, 250, 268, 270, 272, 273, 274, 277n2 (chap. 1), 280n2 (chap. 4), 280n3 (chap. 4), 280n4 (chap. 4); perspective, 77; rational-choice model, 4; results, 82, 177; techniques, 60; theorists (modelers), 5, 75, 76, 264, 270; theory, 2, 5, 7, 275, 280n5 (chap. 4)

Gely, Rafael, 42, 277

Gibson, James L., 9

Gold, David, 27
Green, Donald P., 280
Grofman, Bernard, 247, 280n2
    (chap. 5)
Grutter v. Bollinger, 270, 281

Hammond, Thomas H., 246, 263,
    271, 280, 288
Hogarth, Robin M., 45
*Hopwood v. University of Texas Law
    School*, 270, 281n4 (chap. 5)
Horn, Robert A., 27
Humes, Brian D., 288

Ideal point: definition of, 80–83;
    estimating location of, 254; in
    attitudinal theory, 33, 34, 35,
    36, 38, 43
Independence of cases, 92,
    254–258
Information: perfect, 90, 127, 135,
    249, 250, 251, 252, 253, 286n1
    (chap. 10), 286n2 (chap. 10);
    imperfect, 282n10, 283n13
Indifference points, 43

Knight, Jack, 4, 10, 18, 19, 20, 23,
    47, 48, 49, 50, 57, 58, 59, 60, 79,
    91, 136, 226, 234, 235, 254, 238,
    263, 286n3 (chap. 10)
Kort, Fred, 27
Krol, John F., 24, 57

Landau, Martin, 9
Lax, Jeffrey R., 268, 277n2 (chap.
    1)
Legal model, 44, 273
Legal Realists, 1, 44
Luce, R. Duncan, 55

Maltzman, Forrest, xvii, 4, 13, 18,
    50, 57, 59, 60, 240, 251, 252,
    280n11
Majority coalition, 96, 101, 102,
    103, 107, 108, 111, 120, 128, 131,
    133, 134, 162, 239, 243, 245, 263
Marks, Brian A., 42

Marshall, Chief Justice John, 23
Marshall, Justice Thurgood, 40
Martin, Andrew D., 247
McGuire, Kevin T., 17
Measurement, theories of, 14
Median-holdout model, 96, 109,
    129–134, 135, 136, 137, 138, 139,
    162, 212, 222, 223, 231, 236,
    238, 245, 259, 267, 268, 283,
    286n5; strategy, 268, 269
Mendeleev, Dmitri, 71
Metaphor, 8, 9, 10, 11, 31, 42, 43,
    46, 54, 55, 57; metaphorical
    reasoning, 9; psychological, 8,
    9, 10, 42, 45; rational choice, 8,
    10, 11, 42, 45, 79, 249
Michigan State University, xv
Minority side: definition of,
    88–89
Miranda v. Arizona, 256, 257,
    287n1
Morton, Rebecca B., 76
Mueller, Dennis C., 264, 265
Murphy, Walter F., 4, 11, 18, 26,
    29, 30, 50, 55, 57, 79

Negotiations, 132, 135, 251, 252,
    264, 266
New Jersey v. New York, 253, 270
Nonconvergence conditions, 196,
    201, 207, 208, 209, 212, 213, 214

Occam's Razor, 70
O'Connor, Sandra Day, 82,
    283n12
Open-bidding model, 96, 109,
    125–129, 130, 134, 135, 136, 137,
    138, 139, 162, 164, 212, 222,
    223, 231, 236, 238, 244, 245,
    246, 259, 267, 268, 269, 282n9,
    283n13, 286n4 (chap. 10),
    286n5 (chap. 10)
Opinion assignment, xvi, 6, 47,
    48, 52, 55, 56, 61, 63, 70, 91, 92,
    95, 136, 137, 139–162, 164, 165,
    166, 168, 169, 172, 180, 181,
    182, 183, 184, 186, 187, 188,

189, 191, 192, 193, 194, 195,
196, 202, 206, 207, 209, 210,
211, 212, 213, 214, 233, 234,
235, 236, 237, 242, 243, 251,
258, 259, 262, 267, 283n1,
283n2, 285n16
Opinion assignor, 223
Opinion writing, xvi, 61, 109,
115, 161, 165, 179, 200, 202,
242, 250; costless, 94; costly,
268, 269–270, 282n9; sophisticated, 58
Opportunity cost, 73, 266, 281n3
Original intent, 1, 10, 271, 273
Original vote on the merits,
284n1

Palmer, Barbara, 17
Perry, H. W., 251
PGA Tour v. Martin, 255, 256
Plain meaning, 1, 10, 49, 273
Plurality, 167; opinion, 21, 96,
242, 260, 269, 282n11, 283n16
Policy goals, 10, 11, 12, 29, 42, 43,
44, 54, 56, 57, 70, 78, 94, 96,
165, 207, 231, 236, 271, 277n2
(chap. 2), 278n3 (chap. 2),
285n16
Poole, Keith T., 278n7
Precedent, 1, 46, 49, 51, 160, 242,
271, 273; precedential power,
282n11; precedential value,
262, 269
Preferences, xv, xvi, xvii, xviii, 1,
4, 6, 11, 18, 19, 22, 24, 26, 27,
28, 29, 30, 31, 40, 43, 46, 48, 49,
50, 51, 54, 55, 59, 61, 79, 80,
125, 129, 235, 249, 250, 251,
252, 253, 254, 263, 265, 266,
267, 271, 272, 273, 279n8; clear
and fixed, 253–254; exogenous,
271–272; sincere, 234
Preferred-to set: definition of,
85–89
Prins, Brandon C., 280n4 (chap.
4)

Pritchett, C. Herman,1, 3, 4, 8,
11, 26, 27, 30, 42
Psychological perspective, xv, xvi,
45,
Public law, 1, 10, 15, 17, 28, 61,
273, 277n3 (chap. 2),

Quinn, Kevin M., 247

Raiffa, Howard, 55
Rathjen, Gregory James, 57
Rational-choice, 10, 11, 15, 33, 45,
55, 56, 279n8, 286n6; assumptions, 56; definition of, 91–92;
literature, 80, 91; perspective
(approach, interpretation), xv,
xvi, xvii, 28, 43, 45, 48, 54, 55,
60, 274, 279n8, 279n9, 279n10;
research, 54; sincere, 19; strategic, 19, 57; theory (model), xvi,
xvii, 4, 6, 10, 13, 22, 23, 41, 42,
45, 47, 53, 60, 79, 80, 239, 274,
277n2 (chap. 2), 279n8, 279n9
Reder, Melvin W., 45
Rehnquist, William H., 40, 82,
215, 281n1, 284n1, 284n2
Rehnquist Court, 283n12
Reputation, 29, 51, 165, 211,
258–259
Research agenda, 273
Richman, Barak, 277
Riker, William H., 54, 55, 278n9,
288n4
Rogers, James R., 277n2 (chap. 1)
Rohde, David W., 39, 40, 41, 43,
44, 45, 51, 55, 56, 57, 59, 79,
119, 239, 240, 241, 279n8,
279n9, 279n10, 280n11
Rokeach, Milton, 43, 44, 45,
279n8
Roles, social, 9
Rosen, Jeffrey, 283n12
Rosenthal, Howard, 278n7
Rule of four, 90, 215

Scalia, Antonin, 287n1

Scaling, multidimensional, 31, 32,
    34, 36, 40, 46
Schmidhauser, John, 27
Schubert, Glendon A., 11, 15, 16,
    23, 26, 27–39, 42, 43, 44, 45,
    53, 55, 56, 79, 278n2, 278n3,
    279n4, 279n5, 279n6, 279n7,
    279n8
Segal, Jeffrey A., xv, 4, 9, 10, 18,
    19, 20, 24, 39–57, 79, 226, 260,
    262, 277n2 (chap. 1), 277n3,
    279n5, 279n8, 281n1, 288n3
Self-assignment, 139, 140–142,
    144, 146, 147, 151, 152, 153, 156,
    157, 158, 162, 183, 208, 209,
    213, 242
Shapiro, Ian, 280n6
Sheehan, Reginald S., 246, 263,
    271
Signorino, Curtis S., 278
Sincere behavior, 92, 163, 169,
    170, 172, 177, 180, 181, 185,
    186, 189, 190, 196, 216, 220,
    227, 241, 242, 243, 278n10,
    281n8, 285n12
Single-peaked, 272; preferences,
    273; utility function, 81
Smith, Alastair, 278
Snyder, James M., Jr., 278
Spaeth, Harold J., xv, 4, 9, 10, 18,
    19, 20, 39–57, 79, 260, 262,
    277n2 (chap. 1), 277n3, 279n5,
    279n8, 281n1, 288n3
Spatial model, 80, 280n1 (chap. 5)
Spiller, Pablo T., 42, 277n2 (chap.
    1)
Spriggs, James F., II, xvii, 4, 13,
    18, 50, 57, 59, 60, 240, 251,
    280n11
Stare decisis, 1, 10, 277n3
State supreme courts, 84, 270, 272
Status quo, xvii, 21, 23–24, 38, 39,
    56, 59, 83–85, 86, 88, 96, 97,
    108, 138, 167, 216, 220, 222,
    231, 232, 233, 234, 237, 239,
    240, 241, 245, 246, 247, 260,

261, 262, 269, 270, 272, 280n4
    (chap. 5), 281n4 (chap. 5),
    281n3, 283n16, 287n12, 287n13
Stimulus, 33, 34, 35, 36, 37, 38, 44,
    56, 279
Stimulus-response model, 11, 12,
    33, 57
Strategic behavior, 6, 19–23, 29,
    49–52, 55–60, 91, 137, 163, 165,
    166, 168, 169, 172, 173, 182,
    183, 188, 189, 192, 195, 196,
    201, 211, 212, 213, 220, 221,
    227, 232, 235, 236, 238, 241,
    243, 244, 252, 278n10, 281n8,
    283n15, 284n2 (chap. 7),
    285n13, 276n7, 287n12
Rationality: nonstrategic (sin-
    cere), 19–23, 22, 49, 241, 242;
    strategic, 19–23, 49, 55, 63, 238,
    242, 243, 254

Thurstone, Louis L., 27
Trust (trustworthiness), 165, 166,
    209–212, 235–236, 244, 245,
    255, 258–259, 286n7

Ulmer, S. Sidney, 27
U.S. Courts of Appeals, 84, 91,
    250, 270, 272, 273, 280n3
    (chap. 5), 280n4 (chap. 5)
Utility function, 80–82, 159, 160,
    161
Utility maximization, 10

Vote switching, 232, 243–246,
    254, 287n8

Wahlbeck, Paul J., xvii, 4, 13, 18,
    50, 57, 59, 60, 240, 251, 280n11
Warren Court, 40, 55
Westerland, Chad, 288n3
Win-set, definition of, 86

Zorn, Christopher J.W., 277n2
    (chap. 1)

3